T0393656

Animated Parables

Theology, Religion, and Pop Culture

***Series Editor*:** Matthew Brake

The *Theology, Religion, and Pop Culture* series examines the intersection of theology, religion, and popular culture, including, but not limited to television, movies, sequential art, and genre fiction. In a world plagued by rampant polarization of every kind and the decline of religious literacy in the public square, *Theology, Religion, and Pop Culture* is uniquely poised to educate and entertain a diverse audience utilizing one of the few things society at large still holds in common: love for popular culture.

Titles in the Series

Animated Parables: A Pedagogy of Seven Deadly Sins and a Few Virtues, by Terry Lindvall
Theology and Batman: Examining the Religious World of the Dark Knight, edited by Matthew Brake and C. K. Robertson
Theology, Religion, and Dystopia, edited by Scott Donahue-Martens and Brandon Simonson
Theology and H. P. Lovecraft, edited by Austin M. Freeman
Theology and Breaking Bad, edited by David K. Goodin and George Tsakiridis
Theology and the Star Wars Universe, edited by Benjamin D. Espinoza
Theology and Black Mirror, edited by Amber Bowen and John Anthony Dunne
Dread and Hope: Christian Eschatology and Pop Culture, by Joshua Wise
Theology and the Game of Thrones, edited by Matthew Brake
Theology and Spider-Man, edited by George Tsakiridis
René Girard, Theology, and Pop Culture, edited by Ryan G. Duns and T. Derrick Witherington
Theology and Horror: Explorations of the Dark Religious Imagination, edited by Brandon R. Grafius and John W. Morehead
Sports and Play in Christian Theology, edited by Philip Halstead and John Tucker
Theology and Westworld, edited by Juli Gittinger and Shayna Sheinfeld
Theology and Prince, edited by Jonathan H. Harwell and Rev. Katrina E. Jenkins
Theology and the Marvel Universe, edited by Gregory Stevenson

Animated Parables

A Pedagogy of Seven Deadly Sins and a Few Virtues

Terry Lindvall

LEXINGTON BOOKS/FORTRESS ACADEMIC
Lanham • Boulder • New York • London

Published by Lexington Books/Fortress Academic

Lexington Books is an imprint of The Rowman & Littlefield Publishing Group, Inc.
4501 Forbes Boulevard, Suite 200, Lanham, Maryland 20706
www.rowman.com

86-90 Paul Street, London EC2A 4NE, United Kingdom

British Library Cataloguing in Publication Information Available

Library of Congress Cataloging-in-Publication Data Available

ISBN 9781978715035 (cloth ; alk. paper) | ISBN 9781978715042 (electronic)

∞™ The paper used in this publication meets the minimum requirements of American National Standard for Information Sciences—Permanence of Paper for Printed Library Materials, ANSI/NISO Z39.48-1992.

Figure 0.1 ***Chevauchée des péchés capitaux, in Miroir Historial, Ride of the Deadly Sins.*** *Source*: Vincent of Beauvais (de Vincent de Beauvais), 1463.

Dedication

I owe almost every idea in this book to my longtime friend and co-conspirator, cartoonist John Lawing, with whom I first taught an animation course in 1978. John instructed me on how to throw snowballs and break a dean's window when we were grown-up faculty members and interviewed and counseled my dates when I was a bachelor professor. We would travel four hours to meet and hear Bob Clampett, Chuck Jones, Friz Freleng, and Don Bluth or spend hours howling over Bruno Bozzetto's Allegro non Troppo. *And John made me think about cartoons, not only what made them funny, but what made them important. Thank you, John!*

Contents

Preface xi

Acknowledgments xxiii

Introduction: A Brief Pedagogy of Parables 1

PART I: AESTHETIC ROOTS: PARABLES, ICONS, AND MOVING IMAGES 11

1 Parables and Fables 13

2 Emergence of the Visual Parable 37

PART II: DEAD BRANCHES: THE SEVEN DEADLY SINS 69

3 Sin, Judgment, and Blindness 71

4 Pride (*Superbia* of the Peacock) 89

5 Envy (*Invidia* or the Wolf) 105

6 Anger (*Ira* or the Lion) 117

7 Sloth (*Acedia* or the Ass) 131

8 Avarice (*Avaricia* or the Camel) 149

9 Gluttony (*Gula* or the Swine) 165

10 Lust (*Luxuria* or the Goat) 193

Conclusion: Virtues and Redemption 213

Bibliography 243

Index 255

About the Author 259

Preface

In 1941, Walt Disney produced a short moral tale entitled *Lend a Paw* (Clyde Geronimi) (figure 0.2). When Mickey Mouse adopts an orphaned kitten, his dog Pluto grows jealous and schemes to get rid of it. A shoulder angel and devil vie for his conscience when the kitten falls into a well. The angel urges him to save the poor critter, while the devil goads Pluto to let the kitten drown. As his better nature prevails, he saves the kitten and Mickey rewards him with a warm bath. His angel adds a didactic moral: "Kindness to animals, my friend, will be rewarded in the end." Four years later, Disney promoted the pedagogical potential of his global celebrity, Mickey, in an article entitled "Mickey as Professor." Through his cartoons, the plucky animated personality taught the world to learn. Disney credited the small rodent for his ability to instruct on topics from health, mechanics, and geology to infant feeding and nutrition. He prophesied that short cartoons had the potential for "speeding up learning, increasing retention, and compelling interest."[1]

Critics Henry Giroux and Grace Pollock interpret the Disney educational structure more ominously. They argue that learning through Disney cartoons leads to the end of innocence and corporate domination and consumerism.[2] Watching Disney cartoons is like having "honey rammed" down one's throat.[3] Where these two contrasting opinions agree, however, is that the short cartoon teaches. Simply put, the short animated film follows a long tradition of indirect moral exhortation through cartoon images. The best contemporary parables of the last century are animated films that offer a hortatory pedagogy of vice and virtue.

During the fall of 1971, I sat in a class on Theology and Film at Fuller Theological Seminary, when the professor lectured on how religious

Figure 0.2 In Walt Disney's Moralistic *Lend a Paw* (1941), a Devil and an Angel vie for the Conscience of Mickey's Dog, Pluto. *Source*: Screenshot taken by the author.

Figure 0.3 Milan Blazekovic's Hapless Zagreb Chap Wanders through Life as *The Man Who Had to Sing* (1971). *Source*: Screenshot taken by the author.

messages hide incognito in many mediated forms.[4] He then shared a short film from Zagreb entitled *The Man Who Had to Sing* (Milan Blazekovic, 1971), in which a hapless little character repeatedly sang "yeah-yeah; yeah-yeah-yeah-yeah-yeah" throughout his sad, little life (figure 0.3). Rejected by parents, bullied by classmates, dismissed by psychologists who found him hopeless, and abandoned by his wife, he wandered from his cradle to his grave singing his jolly, but irritating, little song. It appeared he did not even leave a tiny footprint to mark his existence. However, as society buried him, and thinking it had silenced him, one heard his indestructible refrain of "yeah-yeah; yeah-yeah-yeah-yeah-yeah," bursting out of the tomb.

The film came from the creative explosion of the 1960s Zagreb School of Animation and offered a fable for both resistance to political oppression and a hint of a life beyond death.[5] One could discern a song of Easter about to erupt out of the tomb for those rejected by the world, a psalm of a divine "yes" given to a seemingly insignificant life. This animated film enchanted my limited imagination to probe how lessons and themes I had learned in Sunday school now existed even in cartoons.[6] In one sense, I asked the question, "Did someone smuggle ethics and theology into cartoons?" With that question percolating in my imagination, I left the seminary and headed to the University of Southern California to study communication. Eventually, the substantial historical work of another Trojan, Maureen Furniss, inspired this foray into animated parables.[7]

The short animated film pops up as something more than a mere cartoon or commercial product. Too frequently, relegated as an extraneous gargoyle on cinematic cathedrals, a recognition of the rhetorical force of animation has been slow to arrive. Beyond the commercialization of a variety of lucrative TV cartoon series and the Hollywood blockbusters of feature-animated films, a third, and to me the most fascinating category of animation pokes out at us around Academy Award seasons and during international festivals at Zagreb, Ottawa, Hiroshima, and Annecy: the short, mostly independent, animated film parable. Overlooking its potential for communicating diverse content, on race, gender, morality, and other salient issues robs education of a fertile and provocative medium. While animated feature films like *WALL-E* (Andrew Stanton, 2008) offer illuminating parabolic moments on gluttony and sloth, my focus here is on those shorter cartoon parables that reflect the *brevity* of the parabolic form.

In his medieval novel, *The Name of the Rose*, semiotician Umberto Eco answered the objection of seeing the Divine in such a vulgar experience as laughter. His Franciscan monk, William of Baskerville, exhorted his solemn brethren by arguing that "divine things should be expounded more properly in figures of vile bodies than of noble bodies." Eco continues,

> First, because the human spirit is more easily freed from error; it is obvious, in fact, that certain properties cannot be attributed to divine things and become uncertain if portrayed by noble corporeal things. In the second place, because this humbler depiction is more suited to the knowledge that we have of God on this earth: He shows himself more in that which is not than in that which is, and therefore the similitudes of those things furthest from God lead us to a more exact notion of Him, for thus we know that He is above what we say and think.[8]

Corresponding with Baskerville's defense of laughter, the unseemly member of the short animated cartoon also offers a lively pedagogical tool for ethics and religion. In his quest to understand the moral and spiritual lives of children, Harvard professor Robert Coles taught a course on "The Literature of Social Reflection" at Harvard University, using paintings, poems, short stories, and the drawings of children to awaken classical virtues of wisdom and justice, of teaching students how to live prudently and courageously. Like these discrete and singular works of art, animated films possess the potential to awaken and rouse. Neglected cartoons are beguiling and provocative buried treasures, *les oeuvres d'art minatures*. Decades before Pixar produced its award-winning short cartoons, a storehouse of international and independent animated films captivated my curiosity as modes for reflection. I wanted to explore how and why they stayed in my imagination longer than lectures or sermons.[9]

In the autumn of 1947, the *Hollywood Quarterly* published an article by Screenwriter Charles Palmer extolling the opportunities of using the "Cartoon in the Classroom."[10] His panegyric for the educational use of animated films delineated a fundamental difference between the live-action film's appeal to the physical eye and the animated cartoon that "represents the mind's eye, anything that can be imagined." Using Disney's propaganda cartoon, *Reason and Emotion* (the forerunner to Pixar's *Inside/Out*), Palmer explores how the animated film can teach through "fantastic analogy." In this "fantastic analogy," "the powers of animation find their most effective expression." He argues that Disney was able to take a "picture of a thought" as he moved his camera "right inside a character's brain to play spectacled Reason against caveman Emotion in a vivid conflict."[11]

British animation scholar Paul Wells points out a remarkably compelling example of this pedagogical potential of an animated cartoon, which—in this case—appeared in a classic Hollywood feature film, eight years after Palmer's article appeared. In *The Blackboard Jungle* (Richard Brooks, 1955), an inner-city high school teacher Richard Dadier (Glenn Ford) shows his delinquent students (including a young Sidney Poitier) a *Jack and the Beanstalk* cartoon to awake their slumbering apathy. Wells emphasizes that the "language of the cartoon, with its use of comedy, lack of obvious didacticism, and assumed ideological innocence, presents no threat to the class, and gives them amusement and diversion from the formality of normal classroom practice." In the film, the class learns to interrogate the cartoon, its narrative, its characters, and the moral and ethical issues raised. Even more significant is how the boys interpret the cartoon, tasting the "visceral pleasures of enjoying the film and laughing at its jokes." They "start to locate the questions raised by the cartoon within their own experience." Such pleasures of the text augur how a cartoon can extend beyond its own construction to address social and religious issues and "address the human condition with as much authority and insight as any live-action film."[12] Augustine, who enjoyed puns, saw the value in such comic bits: "Jokes should not be accounted lies," he wrote, "seeing they bear with them in the tone of the voice, and in the very mood of the joker a most evident indication that he means no deceit. A person should not be thought to lie, who lieth not."[13] In the fabricated story (Latin *geste*) of the cartoon, one finds a jest that opens up indirect communication of truths that are not lies. The cartoon, even the funny ones, can function as a parable.

Likewise, in writer/director Preston Sturges' *Sullivan's Travels* (1942), chain gang prisoners rediscover laughter, watching a Disney cartoon in a black church. A Pluto cartoon jolts the Hollywood director Sullivan (Joel McCrea), incarcerated with the other convicts and despairing of hope, to realize how a simple animated comedy can usher a viewer into an unexpected epiphany.[14] It awakens the imagination to see light in darkness, *post tenebras lux*. And, wonder of wonders, the film is shown in a church of the oppressed. The preacher instructs his devout parishioners about their responses to the chain gang, "For we is all equal in the sight of God, and He said, 'and the chains shall be struck from them, and the lame shall leap, and the blind shall see and glory in the coming of the Lord.'" They join in singing, "Let my people go," as prisoners and parishioners share enslavement. Animation historian Donald Crafton points to this specific cartoon, *Playful Pluto*, at which they all laugh, as "a parable that teaches the virtues of civility and cooperation."[15] It employs infectious "instrumental laughter" to catch the viewer unaware of its power to unveil hidden agendas.

Such concise animated pearls work as parables. Do not suppose the method has no precedent here, or that the parable itself is specific to oral retellings or literary prose. The emergence of parables in artwork cut a centuries-old path; animators only continued that walk into modern times.[16] Two pertinent precursors of the animated parable come to mind for this study. First, we recognize a historical tradition of the practice of oral and literary parables. Second, we discover the evolution of select religious and moral art as indirect communication of vices and virtues. The form of parables and narrative art construct a backdrop of how the animated film fulfills the trajectory of both traditions. What both contribute is a revival of the faculty of imagination in religious and moral teaching, challenging the Benjaminic notion that art exists primarily as mechanical reproduction or a shadow in Plato's allegorical cave. Something more happens with the parable.[17] Its aura, its aesthetic authority, eludes rational structures of thought to reveal vivacious truths that transcend logic without denying it.

The art of the parable starts with the imagination, which psychologist Sandra Levy proposed plays a key role in faith and moral development. Expanding on this idea, Emmanuel Magro argued that this human faculty "facilitates the transformative process of instruction in the faith, telling Jesus' stories to appropriate the faith, accepting and making one's own the Kingdom of God as envisaged and taught by Jesus through his stories and parables."[18] He argues, quite convincingly, that creative storytelling appeals to "serving the process of personal imagination," so that it promotes a vibrant faith formation. The way that the scriptures promote an active imagination is through the parables. In fact, Magro asserts, a title that one should add to the person of Jesus should be one of Storyteller.[19]

According to educator Kiernan Scott, in spite of what seems a dominant modernist scholastic tradition, religious education does not necessarily lead to a "restrictive and petrified imagination."[20] The formation of faith and an ethical system requires both didactic instruction and creative engagement. In the first function, one finds the conscience figure of Jiminy Cricket from *Pinocchio* (Disney, 1939), who guides his charge with direct moral advice (e.g., "Let your conscience be your guide"). Wells argued, however, that certain cartoons are more successful when "children can see the consequences of dangerous situations, and the harm they may do, but in a self-evidently artificial way."[21] The aim to carry a message, to preach a sermon, and to instruct a child in the way he or she should go remains a didactic chore, but one that can be approached through more indirect narrative strategies.

Faith formation requires what Oxford don and Narnian storyteller C. S. Lewis called two ways of knowing, characterized by two French verbs, *savoir* and *connaitre*, meaning knowing about something and knowing experientially.[22] Lewis famously argued that modern educators do not need to cut down jungles (i.e., analyze and deconstruct) as much as irrigate the deserts of the imaginations of students.[23] According to Levy, the religious imagination enables humans to perceive the Kingdom of God and to "receive and respond to God's revelation in [their] everyday lives."[24] One learns what it means to be uniquely created in the image of God and to live up to that image. This imaginative world offers novel, fresh, and alternative modes of understanding and engagement. Animation historian David McGowan cleverly floated the argument that an animated personality such as Mickey Mouse works as such a global educator of the imagination. Not only has an animated character like Bugs Bunny been a spokesperson for selling war bonds, but a cartoon character like *Gerald McBoing-Boing* (Robert Cannon, 1950), can teach how one can achieve "acceptance . . . *because* of his uniqueness" (figure 0.4).[25]

One of the most perceptive theorists of public pedagogy, Henry Giroux, reflected on the accessibility of new media technology that enables repeated viewings. Building on the notion that no education is "ideologically neutral," he explored the assumption that "animated films stimulate imagination and fantasy, reproduce an aura of innocence and wholesome adventure, and, in general, are good for kids . . . . One of the most persuasive [functions] is the role they play as the new 'teaching machines.' These films inspire at least as much cultural authority and legitimacy for teaching specific roles, values and ideals [as] more traditional sites of learning such as public schools, religious institutions, and the family."[26] Giroux argues convincingly for the production of "agency" among students, of the opportunity and challenge to interpret for

Figure 0.4 In Robert Cannon's Academy Award–winning *Gerald McBoing-Boing* (1950), the Unique Child Endures Rejection, until He Finds His Peculiar Purpose. *Source*: Screenshot taken by the author.

themselves. Animated morality plays provide that kind of narrative that does enlarge their perspective to the world, to others, and to themselves.[27]

Jesus brought together in a playful, inventive, and disruptive way his understanding of the Kingdom of God through elements from everyday life, making his hearers agents of a deeper understanding. The parables of Jesus mediate and evoke a realm not transferred through mere rationality, the *savoir* of comprehension. They invite hearers and spectators into placing themselves within the parable and identifying with its characters, be they publicans and Pharisees or lost coins, sheep, sons, or foolish virgins.[28] "They are to become part of the story and dwell in the envisioned realm to tease out its meaning and relevance for them. This approach challenges them to decide whether to take some type of action or not."[29]

However, Matthew Rindge warns us that "in our own contemporary context" such imaginative engagement is "unfortunately in short supply" and has become a lost art. He adds that "developing such skills is a fundamental spiritual need" if one hopes to understand the parables of Jesus and allow them to permeate our lives.[30] Magro echoes that this sentiment "highlights, in one regard, the importance and significance of imagination in religious education and, in another regard, the necessity of training and tutoring the imagination: Jesus' stories and parables are at the core of Christian religious education."[31]

In *Teaching and the Religious Imagination*, author Maria Harris investigates ways to evoke the religious imagination and asks the question about what kinds of method might "*seduce*" an audience to "rapt attention?" She suggests a creative range of activities such as "masks, incognito, irony, humor, asides, and digressions," to which her colleague at Union Theological Seminary, Sara Little, adds parables, drama, and film.[32] Echoing their insights, philosopher and educator Maxine Greene writes in her *Releasing the Imagination* that "the role of imagination is not to resolve, not to point the way, not to improve. It is to awaken, to disclose the ordinarily unseen, unheard, and unexpected."[33] Imaginative works add other unexpected perspectives, providing vantage points that stir the conscience, reveal truth, and inculcate empathy. It is the parable that best fulfills this task for faith formation. As Eugene Peterson observed, "parables trust our imagination, which is to say, our faith."[34]

How does one awaken the imagination? Parables assume the function of a riddle. They stump and tease the mind. They whisper softly so that one has to listen hard. In doing so, they pose a wide assortment of paradox, incongruities and ordinary humor. They play and open up alternative ways of thinking and imagining. In the religious sphere, the parable confronts the audience with a mystery about fundamental realities and eternal truths. Parables come to confound a stiff-necked or hard-hearted audience, to disturb their universe of ease and complacency, and to challenge them with hard or important questions. Emily Dickinson once wrote that one should tell one's stories "slant," a little off-kilter, a bit oblique: "Tell all the truth but tell it slant/Success in circuit lies."[35] To communicate concepts as dense as grace, sin, redemption, and sanctification, one must find alternative, and even "slant," ways of expressing them, without being burdened by the baggage of theological language. Once one has tasted the biblical experience, the religious language can follow, if that is important.

I have divided this book into three major sections. First, in an era in which fewer people read sacred texts, I highlight the role of the imagination in faith and moral formation. In a syllabus for a creative engagement of moral philosophy, I explore the ancient forms of the parable and the fable and their place in hortatory religious communication. Herein, I argue that parables are fruitful modes of both direct and indirect communication and teaching and that their modern costume are international animated cartoons. Second, I highlight how fabulous, comic, and vivid images in both Christian iconography and secular art have historically embraced the nature and functions of parables. As cathedrals are sermons in stone, so visual parables decorate the margins of sacred places, even when they are grotesques and teach through opposite examples, *via negativa*. I follow the trajectory of the static icon into the emergence of the moving image of the film itself as an amalgam of the parable and visual communication, in conveying religious and moral truth, culminating in the short cartoon.[36] Third, the major part of this work then looks at how animated films function as exemplary (ethical) and revelatory (theological) parables, focusing on depictions of the Seven Deadly Sins, in exposing vice and even in inculcating virtue throughout global communities. I conclude by showing the hortatory importance of parables in espousing transcendent truths of virtue, grace, incarnation, and redemption.

Vice and virtue compete in these films, often tugging the viewer into an either/or combat. In the aforementioned *Lend a Paw*, the shoulder angel cannot outshout the devil, so it triumphs by punching the devil in the face to chase it off. However, such direct admonition to violence is not the way of the best of these animated parables. They will go about their business of teaching in a more indirect, or as Emily Dickinson penned, slanted way to tell the truth.

NOTES

1. Disney, Walt, "Mickey as Professor," *The Public Opinion Quarterly* 9: 2 (Summer 1945), 121; Disney's pedagogical passions culminated into the overtly didactic, anti-Nazi propaganda *Education for Death* (Clyde Geronimi).
2. Giroux, Henry A. and Grace Pollock, *The Mouse that Roared: Disney and the End of Innocence* (Rowman and Littlefield, 1999).
3. Byrne, Eleanor and Martin McQuillan, *Deconstructing Disney* (Pluto Press, 1999), 1.
4. I would see the film again on PBS with Jean Marsh hosting a program entitled "The International Festival of Animation." Mass Media Ministries would pick it up and distribute it. The film led to an odd obsession (at least until I got married) of purchasing 16 mm animated films from around the world.
5. See William Moritz on "Narrative Strategies for resistance and protest in Eastern European animation" in *A Reader in Animation Studies* (ed. Jayne Pilling) (John Libbey, 1997), 39–47 for his keen insights on political parables.
6. One odd little devotional book is Steven L. Case's *Toons that Teach: 75 Cartoon Moments to Get Teenagers Talking* (Zondervan, 2005) in which Case seeks to show that there is "a basic holiness that permeates all things," connecting the animated cartoon with biblical principles.
7. Furniss, Maureen, *A new History of Animation* (Thames and Hudson, 2016).
8. Eco, Umberto, *The Name of the Rose* (trans. William Weaver) (Warner Books, 1984), 91.
9. Okay, I do remember a 1976 sermon by my friend, Dr. Ben Fraser, on "The wages of sin is death." On a chaotic and frustrated Sunday morning in which nothing was going right for his church service (a singing group wouldn't cease; he lost his sermon notes; the temperature in the rented building was hot), he repeated the verse of Romans 6:23 six times and couldn't find his way to his next point. Even after a moment of silent prayer, he began again with "the wages of sin is death," and I laughed out loud (perhaps a bit of *Schadenfreude*) and he concluded the service. But I have never forgotten the very brief sermon. The moment itself was a parable of all our labors.

10. Palmer, Charles, "Cartoon in the Classroom" *Hollywood Quarterly* 3:1 (Fall 1947), 26–48.

11. Ibid. 27, 29.

12. Wells, Paul, *Understanding Animation* (Routledge, 1998) 4; Likewise, he finds corroborating evidence in the cultural (and therapeutic) effect of a *Playful Pluto* cartoon (1943) in Preston Sturges' Hollywood satire, *Sullivan's Travels* (1941). Both films "foreground the animated film as *the vehicle by which significant moments of revelation and understanding take place*." (6) Italics added.

13. Augustine, *On Lying* (ed. Philip Schaff) (Createspace, 2015), 5.

14. Lindvall, Terry, *Divine Film Comedies* (Routledge, 2016).

15. Crafton, Donald, "Infectious Laughter: Cartoons' cure for the Depression" in *Funny Pictures* (eds. Daniel Goldmark and Charlie Keil) (University of California Press, 2011), 74. Crafton links director Preston Sturges to the conceit of infectious laughter from Leo Tolstoy's concept of art as a "medium for the transmission of emotions." For the Russian author, art not only arises from feeling and from joining humanity together, but "good art conveys positive spiritual values." (79) Redemptive cartoons aspire to such ideals.

16. Regarding parables, I am not emphasizing adaptations from the Synoptic Gospels, although they form part of this project, but of those works that follow classic patterns of the parable and the fable, but in a kinetic visual form. In his reception history of the Synoptic parables, David Gowler looks at the reception and interpretation of a variety of parables in the last two thousand years. He examines forms as diverse as Flannery O'Connor, the movie *Godspell*, and the blues. Gowler, David B., *The Parables after Jesus: Their Imaginative Receptions across Two Millennia* (Baker Academic, 2017).

17. I must acknowledge the contributions of Walter Benjamin as storyteller as well in the publication of *The Storyteller, Tales out of Loneliness* (ed. Sam Dolbear) (Verso, 2016) which enhances his theoretical lectures. Technology and war had silenced his generation and he sought a sacred commonality, a shared experience that countered the newsreel information that proliferated in modern society. He lamented that, no longer sharing stories or even listening to others, people received piles of dry facts and useless information. He argued that every story offers an overt or covert lesson, a hint that the aura of the parable was needed. The "tangible motives" of his stories offered lessons to instruct, amuse, or even connect with others. In particular, he celebrated the fairy tale of children because "it was the first tutor of mankind .... Few storytellers have displayed so profound a kinship with the spirit of the fairy tale as did [Nikolai] Leskov. This involves tendencies that were promoted by the dogmas of the Greek Orthodox Church." Such stories are endowed with wisdom, kindness, goodness, and such virtues that enable one to magically escape the boredom of life into a holy delight. Benjamin, Walter "The Storyteller: Reflections on the Works of Nikolai Leskov" https://arl.human.cornell.edu/linked%20docs/Walter%20Benjamin%20Storyteller.pdf (Accessed February 22, 2020), 11.

18. Levy, Sandra M., *Imagination and the journey of faith* (Eerdmans, 2008), 3.

19. Magro, Emanuel P., "Jesus and the Play of Imagination: The Role of His Stories and Parables in Faith Formation" *Journal of Research on Christian Education* (2019), 71–83.

20. Scott, Kieran, "Tradition and imagination in interplay" *Religious Education*, 110(3), (2015), 263, 262–268.

21. Wells, Paul., *Animation: Genre and Authorship* (Wallflower, 2002), 58.

22. Lewis uses two medieval hermeneutical terms, Contemplation (external, abstract and impersonal knowledge) and Enjoyment (engaged, participatory, personal, tasted knowledge), as modes of light or knowing. Lewis. C. S., "Meditation in a Toolshed" *God in the Dock* (Eerdmans, 1970), 212–214.

23. Lewis, C. S., *Abolition of Man* (HarperCollins, 1974).

24. Levy, *op. cit.* 3.

25. McGowan, David, *Animated Personalities* (University of Texas Press, 2019), 174.

26. Giroux, Henry, "Animating Youth: The Disneyfication of Children's Culture" *Socialist Review* 24:3 (1994), 23–25.

27. See Giroux, Henry, *The Mouse that Roared: Disney and the End of Innocence* (Rowman & Littlefield Publishers, 1999).

28. I do remember how we single seminarians heard a chapel sermon about the Wise and Foolish Virgins at the Wedding Feast, with the memorable last line being: "So, would you young men rather be in the wedding feast with the wise virgins or in the dark with the foolish ones?" None of us answered too quickly.

29. Rindge, M. S., "Luke's artistic parables: narratives of subversion, imagination, and transformation" *Interpretation: A Journal of Bible and Theology*, 68(4), (2014), 411.

30. *Ibid.*

31. Magro, E. P., *Imagination's role in religious and spiritual education.* In T. van der Zee & T. J. Lovat (Eds.) *New perspectives on religious and spiritual education* (Waxmann, 2012), 165–177.

32. Harris, Maria, *Teaching and the Religious Imagination* (HarperSanFrancisco, 1987), 70; Little, Sara *To Set One's Heart* (John Knox, 1983), 61.

33. Greene, Maxine, *Releasing the Imagination: Essays on Education, the Arts, and Social Change* (Jossey-Bass, 2000), 28.

34. Peterson, Eugene H., *Living the Message* (Zondervan, 1996), 204.

35. Dickinson, Emily, *Complete Poems* No. 1129 (Back Bay Books, 1976), 758. Tinsley, John "Communication or 'Tell it Slant'" *Theology Today* (January 1979), 163–170.

36. I have dealt with this at length in my *Sanctuary Cinema: The Origins of the Christian Film Industry* (NYU Press, 2011).

Acknowledgments

I am humbled by the support of the Lexington editors, Neil Elliott (who, just before his retirement, approved this foolhardy project), and three Virgil guides, Gayla Freeman, Matthew Brake and Arun Rajakumar. For encouraging fellow pilgrims like Maureen Furniss and Christopher Lehman, I remain full of gratitude. Key to this project, however, were two readers and incisive critics: my friend of over forty years, Steve Sylvester, for his acute insights on structure, organization, purging critiques, and all-round good wit, and my daily friend, Craig Wansink, for his gentle wisdom, guidance, and pastoral mashing of my style. I deeply thank such patrons of the art as Barbara Newington, Dolly Rasines, Tony Speiser, and Frank and Aimee Batten Jr. Other people, quite unaware, contributed greatly to my descent into the Seven Deadly Sins, such as the Spenser reading group of Kellie Holzer, Michael Hall, and the formerly Stroyeck sisters, Lauren, Katie, and Morgan; my unofficial tutor of art, Joyce Howell; my former Fuller Seminary cronies, Lyle Story, a parable scholar, and Ben Fraser, an indirect communicator. I borrowed freely, okay stole, from our rector, the Reverend Andy Buchanan. The writings of fellow scholars in animation studies, Donald Crafton, David McGowan, Paul Wells, Chris Pallant, Jayne Pilling, and the wonderful Giannalberto Bendazzi, stimulated me more than they realize, A special thanks goes to animation colleague Kathy (and her Joe) Merlock-Jackson. So, too, I thank our special student, Alisa Crider, who received a grant to visit and interview Canadian animator, Richard Condie. Finally, I thank those cartoon characters who make up my family, my beatific wife, Karen; my funny comic writer son, Christopher, and Caroline and Cary, my merry daughter and son-in-law who teach English to animated Middle School pupils. Lastly, to the One Who seeks to remove the seven (and probably more) Peccata from my forehead, *ad Dei gloriam.*

Introduction

A Brief Pedagogy of Parables

If you want an audience to listen, tell a story, preferably a brief one. Out of a rich Hebrew tradition, parables appear, ushering in one of the most democratic of the concise teaching formats. We read the works of philosophers with the mind; we hear parables with the imagination. "God tells the truth in parables," wrote Lincoln, "because they are easier for the common folk to understand and recollect." No doubt, telling a farmer or a grocer that one harvests what one plants communicates more clearly than discussing a law of reciprocity. This parable, however, often stymies the understanding, as impenetrable and enigmatic to the professional as to the layperson, to the priest as to the fisherman. The democracy of the parable is that all are equal in deciphering its meaning. Logic or wit gives no advantage. Neither does good practical common sense. We need only the willingness to listen and ponder.

For fantasy writer C. S. Lewis, the task was to speak in the vernacular of culture, to talk the argot of the people. By doing so, he sneaked past watchful dragons of political/spiritual/cultural correctness to communicate truth and wisdom. Monty Python animator, Terry Gilliam, pointed out how he could perform "wonderful acts of smuggling" viewpoints through his cartoons.[1] One still remembers his cutout cartoon god, the hirsute old man wearing a crown, surrounded by clouds in a golden hue, as the modern caricature of God who tells His followers to "stop groveling" (figure I.1). When the Supreme Being smites someone with his giant thumb, it cements a fantastic and vivid image of an arbitrary divinity in one's head.[2] Significantly, Gilliam's mischievous and irreverent art borrows directly from fourteenth-century illuminated manuscripts, with such sketches as a cock on top of a windmill or a giant bellicose snail attacking a knight. Like Gilliam's marginal decorations (even with *obscena* like bare-bottomed nuns), such icons communicated in the vernacular, often smuggling in anti-clericalism.[3]

Figure I.1 The Cartoon Divinity of Terry Gilliam Is Not Amused (*Monty Python and the Holy Grail,* 1975). *Source*: Screenshot taken by the author.

The primary form of speaking in the vernacular is the short parable, an earthly story with an unexpected meaning. Ordinary anecdotes often camouflage significant lessons on life. In his article on "Speaking in Parables," New Testament Professor Scott Spencer argues that these seemingly simple, pedestrian stories of everyday life are "often teasers." The "punch line at the end more often than not leaves us a bit punch-drunk and off-balance, wondering what just hit us and what does it all mean."[4] They confound many with hidden messages.

Jesus did not teach without parables. He dropped observations about neighbors, state dinners, and wedding feasts, as if they were bits of juicy gossip. He drew pictures of goats and sheep, crooked judges, sleepy friends, runaway children, and even taxes that astounded and amused his listeners. Although Jesus employed this peculiar form of parabolic teaching, much preaching and teaching today remains direct and didactic.[5] Thus, it is worth reviving this more subtle and engaging strategy of indirect communication, employing persuasive word-pictures that sneak into the imagination through the back door.

In particular, it is worth seeing the contemporary parable in its most neglected and most compelling form: the animated cartoon.

The word "parable" derives from the Greek παρα (which means "beside," as in a term like "paranormal") and βαλλω (meaning, "to throw," and related to the English word "ballistics"). Combined, these two Greek elements mean to "throw beside." Thus, a parable is a form of teaching that uses comparison: one thing thrown beside another. In his first parable, Jesus explained how people received his teaching by casting it in the familiar agrarian imagery of a Sower and his seed. Even as the Sower flung seed beside the road, on rocky places, among thorns, and into good soil, so the parable is a throwing beside, a comparison that catches the intellect off guard and baffles it. Its oblique, unpretentious nature is received by unsuspecting sorts of audiences who overlook its mysteries.

Over one-third of Jesus' teaching in the Synoptic Gospels fits into the category of a parable. The genre presents itself so unobtrusively and humbly that one does not immediately realize that teaching is occurring. Rather parables arouse curiosity. Theologian Karl Barth aptly illustrated the process of reading biblical stories as looking out of a window and seeing people in the street gazing up over the roof above your head, pointing excitedly at something that has happened. You cannot really stretch out your neck and see what is there, but you surely wonder what is over and above one's vision. What are other people seeing? Barth's description points to something over our heads that we strain to apprehend and comprehend. Jesus seemed to want the inside of people's heads decorated with curious pictures that make them muse their meaning.

Historically, parables follow the structure of Hebrew comparison, of the parallel poetry of the *mashalim*. Etymologically, a parable is a *mashal* (its Hebrew root signifying "to be like") that employs a short narrative fiction to reference a spiritual symbol or transcendent truth. Often distinguished from other types of *meshalim*—like proverbs, riddles, or words of the wise—they share the characteristics of being primarily oral and short. Like dark sayings (σκοτεινον) or enigmas (αινιγματα as in Proverbs 1:5–6), *meshalim* invite the wise person to consider a proverb, to probe the riddle. John Meier illustrates such instructive forms that quicken a moral principle or shock its audience with a hidden truth, as in Nathan's parable of the ewe-lamb (2 Samuel 12:1–9). As the prophet pranks King David into judging himself, we realize that something subversive is going on here, even tricky.

For here, as the Psalm announces, is the utterance of things hidden since the foundation of the world. Some *marshal*, mystery, or riddle has arrived and now compels and dares its hearer to open it, to try to figure it out. What do these short stories of sheep, thieves, sleepy neighbors, virgins, and wine have to do with truth, religion, or God? Parables stymie the legal and religious leaders of our world. They silence logicians with ambiguity. In the Gospel of Luke (11:37), Jesus addressed Pharisees and lawyers, weaving stories that began amusingly enough, but then slammed them upside the head. He did not employ gentle persuasion, but mocked them and called them names. "You look like the gunk in a month-old cup of coffee." "You got a huge tree in your eye, buddy." These succinct narratives disorient and subvert expectations. Those who say long prayers in the marketplace and seek seats of honor are not of God's house. To stiff-necked people, the best way to invade their minds is through a massage. Parables tend to begin like an easy massage. The religious parable, wrote P. G. Wodehouse is one of those stories "which sounds at first like a pleasant yarn, but keeps something up its sleeve which suddenly pops up and knocks you flat." It may be playing, he noted, but it is a "fairly rough contact sport."

Episcopal theologian Robert Farrar Capon described three divisions of biblical parables: parables of the kingdom of God, parables of grace, and parables of judgment. They address themes of the coming of God into a broken world, an appeal to the least, the last, and the lost, and a foretelling of his own death and the coming Day of the Lord. What is most important about Capon's dialogue with the parables erupts out of his recognition that they are not so much "word-pictures about assorted external subjects as they are *icons* of himself. Like good poems, they not only *mean*, but *be*: they have a *sacramental* effectiveness."[6]

A sampling of religious scholarship provides a technical definition to parable. Sallie McFague sees the parable as "an extended metaphor, that is, as a story of ordinary people and events which is the context for envisaging and understanding the strange and extraordinary."[7] The classic work of C. H. Dodd on parables explains that such literary expressions "are the natural expression of a mind that sees truth in concrete pictures . . . drawn from nature or common life, arresting the hearer by its vividness or strangeness, and leaving the mind in sufficient doubt about its precise application to tease it into active thought."[8] It works by *disorienting*.

More compelling, poet Marianne Moore envisioned parables as "imaginary gardens with real toads in them."[9] While the scholar explains, the artist captures the living nature of the parable that teaches in short, pithy, and pungent ways.

For example, take *The Frog's Day Out* (Arena Dilsukhnagar, 2012) in which an army of desert frogs go merrily hopping along until two fall into a pit. In this graveyard of amphibians, they see dozens of skeletons of comrades who have not made it out (figure I.2). A multicolored group of frogs looks down helplessly at the duo, as the light-yellow frog panics. Out of the shadows emerges a fat, bespeckled green frog mocking their imminent demise. With a gesture of slitting his throat, the resident frog then laughs uproariously at the two. The blue frog encourages his friend to try to climb up and then out. They slowly scale the side of the abyss, as the pompous crater-dweller mocks them. Suddenly, a slimy, grinning turquoise snake appears from behind a rock, tongue flitting as it salivates watching the two slip and scramble on their ascent. At the last moment, the leader of the colony catches the four-fingered grasp of her desperate cronies as they clamber up the crevices. The scoffing frog eerily feels the forked tongue of the reptile behind him. Animator Dilsuknagar suggests that those who believe can find a way out of the grave, with a little help from their friends. Those that have no faith and seek no help shall be swallowed up in darkness and death. The

Figure I.2 In *The Frog's Day Out* (Arena Dilsukhnagar, 2012), Carefree Frogs Are about to Meet Their Destiny. *Source*: Screenshot taken by the author.

narrative of an ordinary frog in a pit disorients at first. Then tale teaches a need for others.

A story told in such a concise form demands attention, but it also enables us to remember and repeat it. One key for Klyne Snodgrass zeroes in on its strategy of "indirect communication. Parables are expanded analogies, referring outside themselves and compelling interest by the power of their stories, thereby attending to meaning in a new way. The goal of a parable is not to convey information, but to *invite* meaning."[10] In subverting the notion that parables simply supply knowledge, Soren Kierkegaard wrote a quirky little parable in which a man stuffs his mouth so full of food (i.e., information) that he could not chew or swallow and so starves to death. One must be able to chew and digest the story to live.

Parables are not merely stories, but particular kinds of stories, expanded analogies used to convince and persuade. They offer lenses that correct myopia. For Snodgrass, they "allow us to see what we would not otherwise see, and they presume we *should* look at and see a *specific* reality. They are not Rorschach tests; they are analogies through which one is enable to see truth." A good parable creates a liminal moment; it allows one to sit back and engage the story's provocations. One receives space to try to figure out what the speaker is communicating. Harvard University professor Amos Wilder sharply focused on these snapshots of life as stories that demanded a decision. The parable aims to arouse sluggish awareness and dormant conscience. Jesus did not use the story merely as a springboard to a moral life, but as a shining light into the drama of one's destiny, a "prophetic unveiling of the secrets of the future."[11] What happens when Jesus looks at his audience and asks, "If salt has lost its taste, how can its saltiness be restored?" The metaphor stuns the listener. Questions abound.

Building upon Wilder's insights on metaphor, William Kirkwood highlights two rhetorical functions of parables and ultimately, the animated cartoon: the exemplary and the metaphorical. Kirkwood defines them as brief narratives "told primarily to instruct, guide, or influence listeners."[12] The exemplary offer moral constructs intended to teach, by comparison, to show the way to live and conduct one's life. The exemplary or "illustrative" usually reinforces pre-knowledge, is much more expandable, and reveals key tenets of faith or principles of conduct. In the sense that they tell one a moral, like many fables, and show explicitly what one is to do, they are examples for virtuous behavior.

Exemplary parables end with an application that advises one to follow. Obey this moral admonition or spiritual advice. In the parables of the Good Samaritan or the Rich Fool (go and sell everything) or the wise and foolish virgins (be ready), the point is "Go and do likewise." Or "Do not go and do likewise. See this as a warning." Many of Aesop and Fontaine's fables serve as this kind of parable. "Don't go into the woods alone." "Don't talk to strangers." Or, paradoxically, "be kind to strangers." Parables are concerned not primarily with knowing but with doing, to believe and to act, even more than to get it. They offer examples showing us how to live. Yet, the exemplary parable may also propagandize. The poet W. H. Auden warned that the Gospel parables cannot be thrown at people like a stone. Conscious of a didactic moral inclination of exemplary instruction, Auden himself preached, "You cannot tell people what to do. You can only tell them parables, and that is what art really is, particular stories of particular people and experiences, from which each according to his immediate and peculiar needs may draw his conclusion."[13] His poetic teaching sought to "surprise, shock or woo the reader in to serious self-examination," leading to the second category of parable.[14]

While examples recommend conducting oneself in ethical ways and are less confrontational, metaphors demand participation and personal decisions from their listeners. The metaphoric, also known as revelatory or theological, parables are stubbornly irreducible and tend to call attention to unsuspected truths. Revelatory parables offer quick snapshots of the Kingdom of Heaven or some transcendent truth. For example, the parable of the Prodigal Son is not a recommendation to spend all the family inheritance, live wildly, and then go home sheepishly and enjoy a party. The parable reveals the remarkable grace of a father in welcoming his wayward son back into the family and his invitation of the elder lost son to the banquet. The revelatory parable opens up alternative visions of life. It makes one reconsider what one normally accepts as the way things are. Religious parables in the Jewish and Christian traditions range from the provocative political story of the trees who wanted a king (Judges 9:7–15) to these canonical Gospel tales of the Good

Samaritan and the Prodigal Son.[15] Such parables extend throughout history, teaching by analogy, as did the writings of Danish philosopher Kierkegaard.[16]

For Kierkegaard, men and women exist under illusions. Only indirect surgery can correct such a condition. Kierkegaard suggests a strategy he provocatively calls "deceit."

What then does it mean, "to deceive?" It means that one does not begin directly with the matter one wants to communicate, but begins by accepting the other man's illusion as good money. So one does not begin thus: "I am a Christian; you are not a Christian. Nor does one begin thus: It is Christianity I am proclaiming; and you are living in purely aesthetic categories. No. One begins thus: let us talk about aesthetics."[17]

Kierkegaard's deceit underlies what he saw as an indissoluble aspect of the Gospel's tactical device of communicating its message indirectly.[18] In his study on the Kierkegaard's parables, Thomas Oden characterized the category of indirect communication as usually having a condensed plot, and being short and succinct, which made it easy to memorize for oral transmission, or retelling. Generally, the story would catch the hearer off guard with an unexpected reversal that made the listener reevaluate all that he or she had heard. Such is the formula for the pedagogy of the animated film.

The old scholar Vilna Gaon met with the remarkable Preacher of Dubno and asked if he would help him to understand why the parable is so influential. "If I recite Torah, there's a small audience, but let me tell a parable and the synagogue is full. Why is that?" The *dubner maged* answered, "I'll explain it to you by means of a parable." Once upon a time Truth went about the streets as naked as the day he was born. As a result, no one would let him into their homes. Whenever people caught sight of him, they turned away or fled. One day when Truth was sadly wandering about, he came upon Parable. Now, Parable was dressed in splendid clothes of beautiful colors. And Parable, seeing Truth, said, "Tell me, neighbor, what makes you look so sad?" Truth replied bitterly, "Ah, brother, things are bad. Very bad. I'm old, very old, and no one wants to acknowledge me. No one wants anything to do with me."

Hearing that, Parable said, "People don't run away from you because you're old. I too am old. Very old. But the older I get; the better people like me. I'll tell you a secret: Everyone likes things to be disguised and prettied up a bit. Let me lend you some splendid clothes like mine, and you'll see that the very people who pushed you aside will invite you into their homes and be glad of your company." Truth took Parable's advice and put on the borrowed clothes. And from that time on, Truth and Parable have gone hand in hand together and everyone loves them. They make a happy pair.[19]

Marked by simplicity and symmetry, these brief narrative forms characterize many animated cartoons. Cartoons borrow the clothing of entertainment and disguise themselves in playful costumes, even a bit of motley. Animated cartoons are short and succinct, and eagerly retold by their viewers. These parables do surprise, amuse, and disturb their viewers. Short cartoons also share similarities with the fable and fairy tales as well as the parable, but all of these are designed as concise, entertaining, instructive, and confrontational stories that interrupt expectations with surprise, disrupt ordinary ways of thinking, and construct fresh avenues of imagining. What makes them remarkably useful, however, is that they exist in available, convenient, economical, and entertaining formats for teaching, persuasion, and edifying discourse, just like those parables of a lost coin, lost sheep, or lost sons.

Animated parables may contain masked elements of reversal, humor, or shock, in order to arrest the attention and thought of the viewer. Lessons on death, resurrection, and even the incarnation inhabit animated films with an inspired purpose. Animated parables are "word-pictures" that invite one's curiosity and subvert one's normal modes of thinking. And these remarkable and clever artistic constructions fit quite snugly in a tradition of veiled parable-making.

Two caveats are worth mentioning. First, I confess that my interpretative judgments on such diverse delights are recognizably subjective. Analyzing cartoons with wholehearted solemnity runs the risk of belying their frisky, unpredictable, and maverick nature. With this first qualification and a healthy sense of chutzpah, I attempt to connect the dots with reasonable interpretations. Second, I describe many of the films as accurately as possible, but, respecting their free-spirited independence as lively and independent texts—I will show more frequently than tell. I suspect the creative hermeneutic of the reader will see even more than I do and view their kinetic images in more wildly imaginative ways. Of course, as the host, I may pull out my Procrustean bed to make an animated film fit comfortably in my inn.

NOTES

1. Cited in Paul Wells' *Animation and America* (Rutgers University Press, 2002), 5. In animating sequences for the Holy Grail, Gilliam confessed he goes to libraries like the Bodleian, looking for "free things." "There's a lot of dead painters and a lot of dead engravers, so we could use that stuff, start playing with it." McCabe, Bob *Dark Knights and Holy Fools: The Art and Films of Terry Gilliam* (Orion, 1999), 24, 34.

2. In an interview, Gilliam quipped, "making films is just a cheap version of being God," possibly in reaction to the idea of control in his Presbyterian upbringing. His *Deus ex machine* Supreme Being is as much a medieval image of all powerful deity, but of course he is the one who inscrutably gave nipples to man. Derbyshire, Jonathan "Interview: Terry Gilliam" (October 15, 2009) https://www.newstatesman

.com/film/2009/10/interview-films-world-god (Accessed June 8, 2020) See also Gilliam, Terry *Animations of Mortality* (Methuen, 1978).

3. Meuwese, Martine "The Animation of Marginal Decorations in *Monty Python and the Holy Grail,*" *Arthuriana* 14: 4 (Winter 2004), 45–58; One primary source was Lilian, M. G. Randall's *Images of Gothic Manuscripts* (University of California Press, 1966).

4. Spencer, F. Scott "Speaking in Parables: Methods, Meanings, and Media" *Review and Expositor* 109 (Spring 2012), 161.

5. In his six categories of animated films, Richard Taylor's third category is the "didactic," whose messages are their motives. *The Encyclopedia of Animation Techniques* (Focal Press, 1996), 126.

6. Capon, Robert Farrar, *The Parables of Grace* (Eerdmans, 1988), 2, 8–9.

7. TeSelle, Sallie *Speaking in Parables: A Study in Metaphor and Theology* (Fortress Press, 1975).

8. Dodd, C. H., *The Parables of the Kingdom* (Scribner's, 1958).

9. Ricoeur, Paul, "Love and Justice," in *Figuring the Sacred: Religion, Narrative, and Imagination* (Minneapolis: Fortress, 1995), 329; Moore, Marianne, "Poetry," in *Twentieth Century American Poetry* (ed. Conrad Aiken) (Random House, 1944), 177.

10. Snodgrass, Klyne, *Stories with Intent: A Comprehensive Guide to the Parables of Jesus* (Grand Rapids: Eerdmans, 2008), 9.

11. Wilder, Amos, *Early Christian Rhetoric: The Language of the Gospel* (Harvard University Press, 1964), 76.

12. Kirkwood, William G., "Parables as Metaphors and Examples," *Quarterly Journal of Speech* 71 (1985), 422–440.

13. Auden, W. H., "Psychology and Art," in *The Arts To-day*, ed. Geoffrey Grigson (John Lane, 1935), 18–19.

14. Tinsley, *op, cit.* 166.

15. Allusions to the parable of the Prodigal Son appear in diverse places, such as *King Lear*, where his faithful, but contrary daughter asked him: "And wast thou fain, poor father/To Hovel thee with swine and rogues forlorn/In short and musty straw?"

16. Oden, T. C. (ed.), *Parables of Kierkegaard* (Princeton University Press, 1978).

17. Kierkegaard, Soren, *Point of View* (trans. Walter Lowrie) (Oxford University Press, 1939), 40–41.

18. See Benson Fraser's *Hide and Seek: The Sacred Art of Indirect Communication* (Wipf & Stock, 2020).

19. Weinreich, Beatrice, *Yiddish Folktales* (Schocken, 1997), 7. I am indebted to Professor Ben Fraser's *Hide and Seek: The Sacred Art of Indirect Communication* (Wipf and Stock, 2020) for pointing me to this tale.

Part I

AESTHETIC ROOTS

PARABLES, ICONS, AND MOVING IMAGES

Chapter 1

Parables and Fables

Three stories set the stage for understanding the background of the parable: one involving Gideon, second, a rooster, and third, treasure. Refusing the power and prestige offered by the elders of Israel, the Hebrew judge Gideon stands as a noble character, asserting that only God should rule over His people. However, one of the children of a Shechemite concubine, the ruthless Abimelech, declares his authority over the seventy sons of Gideon. He murders all but one of them on the rock of Ophrah. The only survivor is the youngest, Jotham, who cleverly and courageously calls Abimelech and his people to account with a parable in the Hebrew book of *Judges* (9:8–15). He tells a nature fable, slowly spinning a tale that will expose his adversary's motives.

> Once the trees went forth to anoint a king over them, and they said to the olive tree, "Reign over us!"
>
> But the olive tree said to them, "Shall I leave my fatness with which God and men are honored, and go to wave over the trees?"
>
> Then the trees said to the fig tree, "You come, reign over us!"
>
> But the fig tree said to them, "Shall I leave my sweetness and my good fruit, and go to wave over the trees?"
>
> Then the trees said to the vine, "You come, reign over us!"
>
> But the vine said to them, "Shall I leave my new wine, which cheers God and men, and go to wave over the trees?"
>
> Finally all the trees said to the bramble, "You come, reign over us!"
>
> The bramble said to the trees, "If in truth you are anointing me as king over you, come and take refuge in my shade; but if not, may fire come out from the bramble and consume the cedars of Lebanon." (Judges 9:8–15, NASB)

The parable eerily serves as a raw prophetic piece for every age, but it plays here specifically as an indirect confrontation with the powerful Abimelech.[1] It also suggests a similarity of the parable to the fable through non-human agents, anthropomorphizing vegetation, which we will address soon.

Near the end of the eighteenth and the beginning of the nineteenth centuries, Rabbi Nachman of Breslov founded the Breslov form of Hasidic Judaism, in which he sought intimacy with God, through spontaneous and informal ways of talking with Him.[2] He modeled how one could engage God in ordinary conversation, the way one would speak with a best friend. Like a psalmist, he secluded himself in meadows or woods to hear and respond, often at night, practicing what he called *hitbodedut*. One could talk to God about anything and everything (e.g., how not to eat raw onions), and even share stories or scream silently. In doing so, he collected Jewish parables, or *mashal*, from the oral tradition to enliven up the interaction. Why not tell God a story? Why not translate God's Torah and Tanakh in the form of stories? Perhaps his pupils might not study as diligently as they should, but they would listen to his tales. He answered,

> It is very good to pour out your thoughts before God like a child pleading before his father. God calls us His children, as it is written (Deuteronomy 14:1), "You are children to God." Therefore, it is good to express your thoughts and troubles to God like a child complaining and pestering his father.[3]

As Rabbi Nachman would begin: "Now I am going to tell you a story." In one memorable folktale, the Rooster Prince, a royal son goes mad, thinking he is a rooster. Stripping naked and sitting under a table, he pecks at his food like any chicken. His parents are appalled, calling forth doctors and sages to heal him. None can. Finally, one wise man arrives. He takes off his clothes and sits naked under the table with the prince, claiming to be a rooster. As they converse, the prince comes to trust the sage as a fellow fowl and friend. The wise man teaches the prince that a rooster can wear clothes, sit normally at the table, and eat with normal manners. Slowly, but surely, the prince accepts the idea and begins to practice a normal life until he is fully cured.[4] The parable quietly suggests both the importance of becoming all things to all people, and the necessity of *kenosis*, of emptying oneself of power and authority in order to communicate fully. One must become a naked rooster to engage other roosters.

The third tale called "The Treasure" presages Russel Conwell's "Field of Diamonds" sermon, in which a man hears of a treasure under a bridge in Vienna. He travels and waits upon the bridge, only to discover that the treasure is actually back in his house. In the pouch of tales that the Rebbe told are disguised truths of God, hidden and revealed in "wondrous awesome ways." One learns to speak of God's hidden mysteries in allegory and parable. As these stories contain "wondrous, highly motivating moral lessons (*mussar*)," they are as sweet as honey in our mouths.[5] The parable offers a unique form for play.

Throughout the last century, critics contested the nature of religious parables, from allegorical interpretations to existential applications. In interpreting Homer's *allegoria*. Heraclitus found the poet to be speaking one thing but signifying something beyond its literal meaning.[6] That a reader may read multiple meanings into such texts, most of which are not there, is a creative pleasure of eisegesis. The most recognizable examples of the allegorical reside in Edmund Spenser's *Faerie Queene* and John Bunyan's *Pilgrim's Progress*. In the latter, the character Christian must steer his way through the pond of Despond, the Dungeon of Doubt, and such unequivocally allegorical sites. The metaphor communicates to a "person what he already knows, although it communicates it in symbolic and altered fashion."[7] These little allegories fit comfortably within the parables' cousin of fables.

Earlier than the Rabbinic stories, the Greeks employed talking animals to teach moral lessons, most vividly practiced around the fifth-century BC, when the slave Aesop told stories. The collection of oral fables attributed to him includes a fox that thinks unattainable grapes are sour, a tortoise that beats a hare in a race, ants that watch a grasshopper freeze, a mouse that helps a lion, to the classic contrast of a town mouse and a country mouse that must learn to appreciate their own locales. Aesop would make his way into early Christian communities. Around 220 CE, Philostratus wrote out the imaginary journeys of the first-century Greek philosopher and holy man Apollonius. While accused by historians like Eusebius as a charlatan, he championed the teaching of virtues through tales such as those of Aesop. One of Philostratus' key contributions communicated Apollonius' understanding of Aesop's strategic writing:

> like those who dine well off the plainest dishes, [Aesop] made use of humble incidents to teach great truths, and after serving up a story he adds to it the advice to do a thing or not to do it. Then, too, he was really more attached to truth than the poets are; for the latter do violence to their own stories in order to make them probable; but he by announcing a story which everyone knows not to be true, told the truth by the very fact that he did not claim to be relating real events.[8]

Traditional parables and classic fables blend into each other. Theologian Klyne Snodgrass, argues that the parable belongs to the narrative genre of the fable, "a fictitious saying picturing truth."[9] Aesop's collection of fables set human follies and foibles onto a public stage, scripting a two-part structure. First, it tells an anecdote regarding animals, usually unfortunate, and then as an appendage, attaches a pithy moral injunction. The twelfth-century French poet and theologian Alan of Lille described the book of nature (*liber naturae*) as being composed of these talking animals and explained that "every creature in the world is like a book, a picture, and mirror of ourselves." He recognized a book of beasts that functioned as a sort of didactic "encyclopedia of animals" (figure 0.1).[10] In his *Imitation of Christ*, the humble Thomas à Kempis echoed this truth: "If your heart is upright, then every creature [and object] is like the mirror of life, and it serves you as a book of holy doctrine."[11] Key to all is the revelatory power of the story to provide both a window and a mirror to one's own soul.

Although the Latin word for fable (*fabula*) derives from an imaginary story or myth, both parables and fables function as invented short stories containing moral or spiritual lessons. Like fables, parables are not historical moral tales or even saints' legends (which are frequently as fictitious as a fable). Parables mostly contain human characters only, while fables depict talking animals or natural elements, as in the vines and brambles of the biblical story. Parables mostly inhabit real-world contexts with spiritual truths. Fables remain in the province of morality as in the beast fable of Chaucer's *Nun's Priest's Tale* of the vain rooster Chanticleer or Emerson's fable of the mountain and the squirrel. The brief fable or allegorical animal story frequently includes an apologue (derived from the Greek ἀπόλογος, a "statement" or "account") that explains its moral so that even the densest student can understand. Using exaggerated details and rhetorical purposes, the fable conveys a clear and pointed moral instruction. Examples like the trickster Br'er Rabbit or Anansi spider stories function as pleasant metaphorical vehicles to persuade children to attend to the moral lessons.

One of the most influential didactic bestiaries was *The Owl and the Nightingale* (c 1216), which merrily satirized the church and the wrangling between law and grace.[12] Two contentious female birds debate and trade insults (a bit of avian mudslinging, or flyting) over who was the better bird. They poetically debated whether weeping and repentance should characterize religious practice or joyous celebration should shape worship. After several sneering personal abuses, the Owl retorts that Nightingales only have one talent, to sing in summer, a season of lechery, in which its gay melodies tempt women to act promiscuously. The Owl boasts that it aids churches by ridding them of rats. Ah, no, responds the Nightingale defending herself, she reminds the congregation of the glories of Heaven. The Owl scowls that people must first repent of their sins. Mournful music reminds them of this duty. So she screeches:

And by my song I teach all men
They'd better turn their backs on sin,
And warn them against evil ways

Lest they be fooled for all their days;
Far better weep a while before
Than burn in hell forevermore!

The nightingale responds that she offers more positive helps to religious congregations than such penitent practices.

And helped by me, however meagerly,
They sing out all their hymns more eagerly.
Thus I warn them, for their good,
to contemplate in a joyful mood,
and bid them to seek earnestly
the hymn that rings eternally.

Regarding the use of natural creatures for sermons, Alan of Lille opined that in such natural picture books, "our life, our death, our present condition and our passing are faithfully signified."[13] The universe is quite loquacious, at least regarding the mortal life. (Resurrection is harder for nature to preach on; although St. Julian of Norwich's story of the significance of the little hazelnut celebrates the love of God toward everything). Yet a different lesson comes through in this bestiary fable, namely the compelling rhetorical force of good comedy, demonstrating that sometimes wit is more highly valued than moral instruction, as it will be for many animated films.[14]

The animated film does differ from the parable in some fundamental ways. For one, its use of cartoon animal figures is nearer to the fabulous form. However, we find a fluid comic inversion of anthropomorphic critters and the creatures made a little lower than the angels throughout literature. George Orwell's pigs becoming men in *Animal Farm* and Franz Kafka's man degenerating into a cockroach in *Metamorphosis* are teeter-totter versions of each other. Satirist Jonathan Swift captured these topsy-turvy transformations in his "The Beast's Confession":

When beasts could speak (the learned say,
They still can do so ev'ry day),
It seems, they had religion then,
As much as now we find in men.[15]

Swift's sinful beasts panic when a plague breaks out and rush to confess to the priest. The pious wolf repents of breaking his Friday night fast while the ass allows that he loves jests so much that he cannot leave dunces alone, even if they were his friends. There follows an *auto-da-fé* of a swine proud of his shape and beauty, a mimicking ape, and a goat who had made a pious resolution to keep chastity as much as monks do. They form an interspecies confessional line with a lawyer, doctor, politician, and knave. Seeing such a motley crew of two-legged sinners without feathers, the poet would accuse Aesop (to his face) for "libeling the four-foot race . . . . For here he owns, that now and then, Beasts may degenerate into men." Aesop's fabulous animals serve as hieroglyphs in unveiling human nature, that is, they work in parabolic ways. As C. S. Lewis observed in his poem "Impenitence":

Why! [the animals] all cry out to be used as symbols,
Masks for man, cartoons, parodies by Nature
Formed to reveal us
Each to each, not fiercely but in her gentlest
Vein of household laughter . . .[16]

Even anthropomorphic cartoon figures can carry spiritual significance as they expose or confess their sins. Animal caricatures of silly rabbits and wily coyotes perform as cryptographs in unveiling human nature, its virtues as well as its vices. Animator Chuck Jones explained that his signature character of the stubbornly inept Wile E. Coyote (*Carnivarous vulgaris*) reflected a "history of my own frustration and war with all tools."[17] Asking, "Who is the enemy of the Coyote?" Jones responded, "Why the Coyote." Of course, just as Pogo recognized, "we have met the enemy and he is us." The sin in these fabulous characters is our own, masks for humans that reveal our condition through a gentle vein of household laughter. In contrast, Mickey Mouse stood as an exemplary model of pluck, fortitude, and determination during the Depression years, Disney's social model of a Horatio Alger with a rodent's tail and large ears. Mickey was Disney's "Professor," with his cartoons functioning not as substitutes for lectures or laboratories, but as "supplements."[18] The parable and fable were taught without one realizing one was learning.

In his commentary on Cicero's *Dream of Scipio*, Macrobius Ambrosius Theodosius points out that "Fables serve two purposes: either merely to gratify the ear or to encourage the reader to good works, [drawing] the reader's attention to certain kinds of virtue."[19] So too did Mickey and some porcine friends aspire to do both, as the most popular song of the early 1930s came from a country's fears of a ravenous big bad wolf of hunger, vanquished by *Three Little Pigs*.

Visually, such animal stories dress in the form of a fable, a moral narrative in which animals speak and act like human beings (even though in real life we probably find more examples of the reverse). In the history of the United States, animation has had fewer human figures than mice and rabbits. Many cartoon characters (e.g., Tom the Cat and Jerry the Mouse or Sylvester the Cat and Tweetie Bird) star as mere slapstick figures, but also signify comic versions of the inexhaustible David and Goliath motif.

Mary Ann Beavis likens the parable proper (i.e., narrative or story parable) to the Greek fable. The latter is "limited to narratives with animals or plants as characters and have prudential lesson, while the former has human characters, a religious or moral lesson, and are typically Semitic."[20] Significantly, the *Oxford Classical Dictionary* defines a fable as "typically an anecdote of animal life with a moralizing application; it may, however, be drawn from inanimate nature or directly from human experience." Ben Edwin Perry echoes the point, showing that the designation of fable encompasses several kinds of brief narratives:

> A fairy tale (*Maerchen*), an aetiological nature-myth, an animal story exhibiting the cleverness or stupidity of this or that animal, or a series of amusing actions, a novella, like the story of the widow in Phaedrus . . . a myth about the gods, a debate between two rivals, or an exposition of the circumstances in which a sententious or witty remark was made.[21]

By focusing upon the complex Hebrew term *mashal* as the source of the Greek term for parable, Beavis points out how "parable" refers to "a wide range of literary forms that utilize figurative language" that include any hidden or allusive truth in proverbs, riddles, and dark sayings. She does make a distinction by claiming that the *mashal* requires that readers and hearers respond by seeking personal meaning. She points out that the Hebrew Bible does contain some fables, such as Jotham's aforementioned *mashal* of the Trees (Judges 9:7–15) and Ezekiel's *mashal* of the Vine and the Eagles (Ezekiel 17:3–10). However, she acknowledges the most parabolic short narrative as the prophet Nathan's *mashal* of the Poor Man's only Lamb (2 Samuel 12:1–4), exposing King David's adulterous affair with Bathsheba. One hears a parable and discovers a mirror.

Later Rabbinic literature employs parables for interpreting scripture, teaching, and offering guidance for living. Citing David Stern's definition of the rabbinic parable as "an allusive narrative told for an ulterior purpose," Beavis underlines the parallel lines between the story and the "actual situation" to which the parable points. She concludes that "the parable is neither a simple tale with a transparent lesson nor an opaque story with a secret message; it is a narrative that actively elicits from its audience the interpretation and application of its message."[22] One can conflate these two traditions of fable and parable into short dramatic tales that reveal, recommend, warn, and entertain.

Many religious traditions utilize such short narratives as the ones found in Aesop's Greek fables, the kōans and anecdotes of Zen Buddhism, and the teaching stories of the Hasidim. One parable attributed to Gautama, the Buddha tells how "a man was chased by a tiger to a precipice. Catching hold of a wild vine, he swung himself over the ridge. However, down below another tiger awaited him. Two mice, one white and one black, started to nibble on the vine. Hanging precariously, the man saw a luscious strawberry near him. Grasping the vine with one hand, he plucked the strawberry with the other. How sweet it tasted." The simple instructive lesson conveyed that one should "enjoy life while one can."[23] Such a moral maxim, attached to the end of the tale, is as old as Aesop.

Specialists may distinguish fine points between fables and parables. As literary forms, the two differ in several ways. Unlike fables that deal with talking animals and "fabulous" episodes, parables generally deal with the ordinary. These mini-stories frequently include unexpected reversals. Both, however, are brief fictional works constructed to provide moral instruction or indirect revelation. With a parable of sheep and goats making decisions, are we not closer to a fable? Do not the olive tree, the fig tree, and the happy vine behave in both fabulous and parabolic ways? The overlap becomes obvious with a sense of the rhetorical functions of the two forms. According to Perry, both are connected as one finds the rhetorician Aelius Theon's definition of fable as a "fictitious story picturing a truth," a rendering that is complete, tidy, and accurate.[24]

We conclude that parables and fables are not that different. The realistic portrayals of human vices and motives in Aesop's fables approximate the transcending parables of Jesus. Finding these literary and historical origins in the Semitic East, Perry connects the Greek fable to the Hebrew *mashalim* of Judges 9:7–10 and 2 Kings 14:9–10, both of which offer a compelling "precursor of the Aesopic fable."[25] Beavis agrees, averring that Aesopic fables are much more than animal tales teaching prudential lessons.[26] Zoltan Varga echoes her perspective on cartoons themselves. Varga finds levels of constructing meaning through ambiguous and cryptic images of what he called the "Aesopic" language within Hungarian animated films during the decades of Communism. For example, in one Hungarian film nominated for an Academy Award, Geza Toth's *Maestro* (A. Kedd Bemutatja, 2005), a mechanical arm mixes and pours a drink in a dark room, and then turns on dressing-room lights for a tuxedoed, bug-eyed, bird preparing for some kind of musical performance. The arm twirls him about, gives him a straw to drink, dusts him off, tidies and powders him up a bit, and does voice scale exercises; all to be showcased as an opera singer rehearsing his aria. Having brushed his top hat, the mechanical arm lays out his purple tie, smacks his lips, burps, and pushes him out onto what seems to be a stage. However, the bird abruptly jerked from his dressing room and now appears only coming out of an opening to blurt "cuckoo."[27] The significance of imprisonment in a cuckoo clock, in a communist-controlled country, suggests that its fabliaux form carries various hidden meanings for knowing spectators. The text of the fable, like that of the parable, carries unique interpretations. Like the language of poetry, the animated film offers a *sensus plenoir*, a fuller or double sense that frequently circumvents the vigilant eye of the official cultural ideology. For sermonic purposes, the cuckoo is a human.

Hungarian Ferenc Rofusz "was not allowed to make *Gravity* unless he was willing to change the naturally red (i.e. Communist) colors of the apples [in his film] to . . . blue." Graphic artist and animator István Orosz's *Mind the Steps!* (1989) employs the black and white illusions of M. C. Escher to express this "Aesopic" language to sneak in his message. He embeds hidden meanings in his dizzying visual images, throwing paradoxes and ambiguities at the spectators (figure 1.1). Orosz noticed that certain phrases in the late 1970s and early 1980s, such as "Read between the lines," and "Look behind the pictures," were very popular.[28] He built a very ordinary setting, a shabby staircase in a Central European apartment building, to construct a parable of human life where people doing normal activities (e.g., a boy plays with a soccer ball; two men carry a wardrobe) are warped in a spatial Kafkaesque manner.[29] A prostitute, an old flasher, and a body in the shadows quietly juxtapose a Soviet tank in the public square. The Escher-like fluidity of the stairways, of rising and falling, disorients the viewer as if in a psychic labyrinth of Communist confusion, and all of the time, the football unceasingly rolls up and down the stairs.[30] *Mind the Steps!* works as both political fable and existential parable.

In her work, Beavis demonstrates the variety and flexibility of contemporary parable, emphasizing that "fables also include a surprising or ironic element of reversal that is reminiscent of Jesus' parables." They function in a similar rhetorical manner. While we usually think of fables as fantasy stories of talking animals with a straightforward moral, as in Aesop, classic fables encompass various kinds of short narratives. Beavis also points out that both

Figure 1.1 István Orosz's *Mind the Steps!* Satirizes the Confused Chaos of a Communist Regime. *Source*: Screenshot taken by the author.

are brief narratives that shed light on aspects of human experience and behavior, that usually involve ordinary human characters and situations—like quarreling siblings who are corrected by a loving father—and that, despite their realism, often contain an element of extravagance or surprise. Most fables, like the parables of Jesus, illustrate religious and ethical themes but do not have miraculous interventions or fairy-tale magic.[31]

As part of their *gymnasma*, Roman schoolchildren paraphrased Aesop as an elementary exercise to learn grammar and simplicity of style. By hearing, reciting, and writing, they learned how to write and memorize moral tales.[32] The great Latin orator Quintilian held that, in rhetoric, fables were "especially attractive to rude and uneducated minds, which are less suspicious than others in their reception of fictions and, when pleased, readily agree with the arguments from which their pleasure is derived."[33] Roman pedagogy extended into the middle ages, even to the time of the plague, where fable tellers and parable makers would provide hidden fruit.

Around the third or fourth century AD, an odd didactic text appeared around Alexandria, with a host of allegorical tales about real and fabulous animals. The anonymous *Physiologus* catalogued and described a zoo of natural and exotic animals (e.g., owl, donkey, viper) and fantastic beasts (e.g., unicorn, centaur, phoenix). St. Clement of Rome employed the phoenix as a creative symbol of the Resurrection, in which the mythological bird builds itself a nest of frankincense and myrrh and other spices. It dies and comes back to life. Such zoomorphic iconography is aimed at showing "metaphysically, morally, and, finally, mystically, the transcendent significance of the natural world."[34] Its theological source stemmed from the Apostle Paul's idea that "the invisible attributes of God can be seen through the visible."

As an example, *Physiologus* cites David's cry that "I am like the pelican in loneliness" (Psalm 102:7) and promotes the notion that the loving pelican mother kills her chicks for their violence, but laments over them with compassion. However, on "the third day, their mother strikes her side and spills her own blood over their dead bodies (that is, of the chicks) and the blood it-self awakens them from death. *Physiologus*, therefore, spoke well of the pelican." Likewise, its portrayal of the viper connects to where Jesus likened the Pharisees to a brood of vipers (Matthew 3:7). The *Physiologus* teaches that "Just as the viper's brood kills its father and mother, so this people, which is without God, kills its father, Jesus Christ, and its earthly mother, Jerusalem."[35]

One finds the relevance of such animal tales in their later functioning as allegorical and moral ways for medieval readers. As a precursor to the bestiaries of the medieval era, these stories shaped the imagination of the devout. A monastic guide for thirteenth-century sisters who withdrew themselves in holy vocation, *Ancrene Wisse*, appropriated the allegorical trope of

Figure 1.2 A Bonnacon Wards off Its Attackers with a Strategic Spray in the *Physiologus*. *Source*: Screenshot taken by the author.

the pelican nourishing her young with her own blood.[36] She compared the bird to a passionate anchoress that draws blood from its breast to revive its young chicks. Such stories offered both theological and moral instruction told through the types of beasts.

The *Physiologus* reigned as one of the most popular vernacular books in the Middle Ages, populated with stories of the regal lion and eagle, or imaginary beasts like the bonnacon (who defended itself by "spraying fiery dung" at its predators, quite a comic legend ready to script an animated film) (figure 1.2). Elizabeth Morrison, the senior curator of manuscripts at the Getty Museum, quipped that, "One can only imagine that medieval audiences found the story as funny as modern ones (think of Pumbaa in *The Lion King* as a contemporary *bonnacon*!)."[37]

Not intended as a "natural history" along the lines of the writings of Aristotle and Pliny, the work stands as a compendium of moral and religious parables one learned by observing the animals. It communicates theological doctrines and moral instruction through the characteristics, habits, and legends of familiar and fantastic beasts. For example, the Hebrew book of *Proverbs* (6:6) orders the slothful to "go *watch* the ant, you lazy person" (italics added) and Jesus in the Sermon on the Mount directs his hearers to "*look* at the birds of the air." What is significant in the *Physiologus* is this inclusion of illustrative visual material to *show* as much as tell. Medieval bestiaries would spring from this ancient Christian source. Paul Wells pointed out that such texts preached a "moral ecology" that assumed that "wild animals inhabit a moral universe and that people would do well to emulate the innate morality—the natural law—of the wild."[38]

The transition to the visual parable appears unobtrusively. Inspired by Greek and Roman sources like Aesop's Fables and Plutarch's Lives, medieval emblem books, engraved as woodcuts, offered allegorical illustrations with pithy explanatory moral texts. These "mute images" were illustrated proverbs, often ridiculous, but offering wisdom. They encouraged the "reading of both picture and text together. The picture was subject to numerous interpretations: only by reading the text could a reader be certain which meaning was intended by the author."[39]

Around the time of the great plague of 1348, Giovanni Boccaccio, the prolific Florentine writer of naughty and nice stories, praised poetry for its ability to whet the appetite and challenge the mind in deciphering a fable.

> It is obvious that everything that is acquired with toil has more sweetness in it than that which comes without trouble. The plain truth, because it is so quickly understood with little effort, delights us, and is forgotten. So, in order that truth acquired by toil should be more pleasing and that it should be better preserved, the poets concealed it under matters that appear to be wholly contrary to it. They chose fables, rather than any other form of concealment, because their beauty attracts those whom neither philosophic demonstrations nor persuasions could have touched.[40]

Beavis reiterates these shared similarities between fables and parables. Both are concise narrative structures. They are short, pithy, and engaging. They share common content, with moral or religious themes. They employ elements of surprise or irony, often in playful ways. Finally, at the end of their utterance, they attach secondary morals and applications called *epimythia*, which confront the listener with a demand for action. To know is not enough. One must also act.[41]

The seventeenth-century heir to Aesop was fabulist Jean de la Fontaine (1621–1695) who wryly noted, "I use animals to teach men." He set forth his fresh collection of humorous moral tales, which he called a "basket of strawberries." Familiar tales like "The Ant and the Grasshopper" offer admonitions on industry and sloth, a lively education in morality. Walt Disney emulated such instruction for the screen in his Silly Symphonies like *The Grasshopper and the Ants* (Wilfred Jackson, 1934). The same lesson of diligent work appeared as well in Disney's classic *The Three Little Pigs*. Anecdotal tales, even though told through ants or pigs, speak sharply to human concerns.

Addressing the Dauphin of France, La Fontaine presented 250 fables in twelve books. He opened his literary treasure by honoring his source:

I sing those heroes whose father is Aesop,
Whose tales, fictitious though indeed they be,
Contain much truth.
Here, endowed with speech—
Even the fish—will all my creatures teach
With human voice; for animals I choose
To proffer lessons that we all might use.[42]

Like those children in the Roman gymnasia, French schoolchildren read, recited, and memorized these fables. Often published on trade cards, with images (and even with a chocolate inside), they made the schoolwork more alluring. Familiar fables (e.g., *The Tortoise and the Hare* (*Le lièvre et la tortue*); *The Fox and the Grapes* (*Le renard et les raisins*); and the parallel story to the Hebrew trees and brambles, *The Frogs Who Desired a King* (*Les grenouilles qui demandent un roi*)) conveyed moral lessons to unsuspecting pupils.

Filmmaker Frank Tashlin directed a typical example of the Aesopian form in his Color Rhapsodies Screen Gem version of *The Fox and the Grapes* (1941) (figure 1.3). The fable on greed and gluttony featured the gullible and frustrated Fauntleroy Fox and the wily and canny Crawford Crow. The derby-wearing bird offers to swap some tantalizing grapes for the fox's picnic lunch, but a whistling fox wants it all. With numerous blackout gags (those rapid-fire slapstick bits that ended in the lights going out, which would inspire Chuck Jones' Road Runner/Coyote cartoons), crow espies the fox and his meal. He tempts him to stop at his perfect picnic grounds, the "Garden of Eat In," punningly reserved for "the Little Foxes." Persuaded, the fox sets up lunch, only to find the sneaky crow grabbing his sausages. The fox retaliates by giving the bird a hot foot. However, crow does his research in *Aesop's Fables* to find that "foxes are suckers for grapes" and discovers a postscript that adds "especially in Glorious Technicolor." Seeing the hanging (vividly purple) grapes (tacked onto the tree), the fox repeatedly attempts, futilely, to reach them, falling to earth (even with prayer) and crashing repeatedly. Crow marks the myriad times the fox vainly tries; when the fox trades in all his food, the crow reneges and offers nothing. Frustrated and vexed, the fox ties himself to a Roman candle, lights it, and smashes into the tree, finally capturing the grapes, only to find them sour. Where the unfulfilled craving leads to a devaluing of the object of desire, here, the coveting of the grape leads to a frustrated and embittered recognition that such longings are futile. One not only undervalues and thus disparages what one cannot have, but one discovers in such obsessive hungering, that the yearning is not satisfied. Envy is self-poisoning and the wanting endures. The typical Tashlin twist of classic literary material still captures the moralistic *epimythium* of Aesop.

Figure 1.3 In *The Fox and the Grapes* (Frank Taslin, 1941), the Crow Tempts with Glorious Technicolor Fruit. *Source*: Screenshot taken by the author.

Religious irony resides in "Le Rat Qui S'est Retire du Monde." La Fontaine relates how a rat grew weary of all the cares of life and withdrew to a novel hermitage in a Holland cheese. He had everything a rat could desire, and "grew fair, fat, and round. 'God's blessings thus redound to those who in His vows retire.'" When some desperate and poor delegates came from "Rat-United-States," for some aid in their great cat-war, this devout rodent excuses himself as a poor recluse who can only pray. The author writes that the sanctimonious rat shuts the door in their faces, and then asks,

What think you, reader, is the service
For which I use this niggard rat?
To paint a monk? No, but a device.
A monk, I think, however fat,
Must be more bountiful than that.

La Fontaine's witty parable satirized a wealthy, secluded religious establishment, indicting such quarantined selfishness. The amiable but sometimes obstinate fabulist could take an everyday anecdote and make it into an ironic religious fable. In one actual incident, a priest accompanied a dead man in the funeral car, the car upset, and the coffin broke the neck of the poor cleric. La Fontaine embellished the tale in *Le curé et le mort*, where a priest chants the usual psalms and litanies over the dead, even while calculating how much his fees will amount to on this lucrative occasion, thinking of wine and hard cash. He eyes the corpse as jealously as though someone might steal it from him; when suddenly, the car crashes and his most generous parishioner crushes him to death. Echoing Jesus' parable of the rich man who builds bigger barns (Luke 12: 16–21), the grisly end of avarice is death.

A preface to La Fontaine's free verse tales, put to eighteenth-century Parisian vaudeville tunes, points out that their purpose was to "give them an attraction to useful lessons which are suited to their age [and] an aversion to the profane songs which are often put into their mouths and which only serve to corrupt their innocence."[43] His literary tales remain remarkably fresh, tickling the imagination with vivid images. It is no wonder that publishers produced many of them as portrait postcards, combining verse and apt illustrations.

The charming animal fables of Jean de la Fontaine, written with a natural free verse, depicted a menagerie of creatures, sly foxes, vain dogs, scheming cats, lazy grasshoppers, envious frogs, and the proverbial ass in the lion's skin and allowed for a bemused raised eyebrow or shared mischievous wink. This "basket of strawberries" taught and delighted simultaneously, as one would nibble one tale and keep on eating.

Before the Puritan's educational program and John Newberry's *A Little Pretty Pocket-Book* (1744), medieval literature aimed to teach children with books that did more than giving spontaneous pleasure or making them "*profitably* quiet." Historian Daniel Kline points to a mix of those works that were *earnest and game*:

> What we find in many medieval works, whether sermons, school texts, saints' lives, romances, fabulae, lyrics, or plays, is a mixture of morality and mirth, teaching and delight—something, I dare say, we still value in present-day Newberry or Caldecott Award winners.[44]

What such works did overtly was combine dogma with delight, or as Horace would have it, *utile et dolce*.[45] Such works, sweeter than honey, including bestiaries or saints' lives, taught and gave pleasure. In some texts, piety and playfulness met, with a work like *Ypotis* utilizing the *peur senex* (wise child) trope "to startling effect in its communication of Christian doctrine."[46] A medieval work like the *Ecolgues of Theodulus* stood as a mainstay of high Medieval Latin education, integrating two traditions of Greco-Roman mythology and Old Testament narratives.[47] In discussing medieval literature for children, Brian Lee focused upon the staple entertainment of a "direct and delightful account of a schoolboy's temptation and eventual redemption."[48] However, Mark Twain mercilessly parodied such moral didacticism in his upside-down stories of good and bad little boys.

A century later, a Polish poet and Bishop of Warmia, Ignacy Krasicki, touted as the Prince of Poets, scribbled forth *Fables and Parables* (1779). In his explanatory work *On Versification and Versifiers*, he instructed that "a fable should be *brief*, clear and, so far as possible, preserve the truth."[49] His mock-epic poems and satirical verses called for reform of abuses of contemporary religious orders. The graphic imagination of Krasicki's work invited visual interpretation, which came through the prolific art of French illustrator and engraver Gustave Doré, who illustrated everything from the Bible to Rabelais's *Gargantua et Pantagruel*, as well as nineteenth-century comic strips in the modern style of Rodolphe Töpffer.

In the same treatise, Krasicki explains that a fable "is a story commonly ascribed to animals, that people who read it might take instruction from [the animals'] example or speech . . . ; it originated in eastern lands where supreme governance reposed in the hands of autocrats. Thus, when it was feared to proclaim the truth openly, simulacra were employed in fables so that—if only in this way—the truth might be agreeable alike to the ruled and to the rulers."[50] He could sugarcoat a bitter truth (such as how the strong exploit the weak) in such an oblique way that the pill could be swallowed without giving too much indigestion, but still invade the system.

A somewhat Horatian satirist, gentle, grinning and skeptical, Krasicki celebrated the Aristotelean golden mean, more akin to being a disciple of Horace and Erasmus. Writing poetry was for him a calling, to "intervene as a moralist in human affairs," but his intervention was more like play than scolding.[51] Polish king Stanislaw August Poniatowski and King Frederick the Great honored him, which may have given rise to this self-reflective fable of the Two Dogs as an explanation as to his favored status:

"Why do I freeze out of doors while you sleep on a rug?"
Inquired the bobtail mongrel of the fat, sleek pug.
"I have run of the house, and you the run of a chain,"
The pug replied, "Because you serve, while I entertain."

Krasicki wrote a fine sarcastic preface in "To the Children." It was addressed to those who have "cast aside every good grace, chasing a toy at a tremendous pace, chasing a toy flying too high in the air, Listen my children to the fables I bear." One finds the targeted audience not to be children, but to the congregation of the village community, communicating enlightened ideas to the illiterate in comic ways. Scholar Gerard T. Kapokla points out that his fables became "one of the best means for making society conscious of its weaknesses. Behind the humor, the animal characters, and even behind the moral lessons, there lurks a bitter realism."[52]

For example, in a succinct and very dark political commentary entitled "Compassion," he wrote

The sheep was praising the wolf for all his compassion;
Hearing it, fox asked her: "How is that? In what fashion?"

"Very much so!" says the sheep, "I owe him what I am.
He's mild! He could've eaten me, but just ate my lamb."[53]

A less cynical and more comic Christian view of the world spun out of the wit of eccentric Danish author Soren Kierkegaard (1813–1855), who would compose some of the best parables of the nineteenth century, taking on the spiritual emptiness of Christendom. He was a character 'twixt Hamlet and The Happy Prince. He believed the church has so compromised itself in Denmark that there existed a basic equivalence and similarity between the church and the state. The crowd was identical with the congregation. Christianity was coterminous with the world. The church was so formal, civilized, and polite, that a christening and a cocktail party went hand in hand. The Danish clergy seemed as substantial as a cheese Danish. These clerics were worldly religious leaders who championed lives of aesthetics and political concerns.

While his fellow Dane, Hans Christian Andersen, painted sentimental fairy tales in "The Little Mermaid" and "The Happy Prince," espousing personal sacrifice for the happiness of others, Kierkegaard stripped the pretensions of a hypocritical culture, blending the fable and parable into one comic image. For example, he cleverly answers the classic palindrome of "do geese see god?" by describing a congregation of such feathery fowl who gather every Sunday to hear a gowned goose preach.

> The gist of the sermon was as follows: What a high destiny geese have to what a high goal the creator—and every time this word was mentioned, the geese curtsied and the ganders bowed their heads—had appointed geese.
>
> It was this way every Sunday. Afterwards, the assembly dispersed and each one waddled home to his family. And so to church again next Sunday, and then home again—and that was the end of it. They flourished and grew fat, became plump and delicate, were eaten on St. Martin's Eve—and that was the end of it.[54]

Like his mentor Socrates, Kierkegaard was both a gadfly and a midwife in illuminating truth indirectly. He masked his parables in both metaphor and simile. A metaphor like the geese would be matched with a comparison of those who understand life like lazy schoolboys: "They cheat their master by copying the answer out of a book without having worked out the sum for themselves." For Kierkegaard, faith must be lived: it must be subjective about its object. His autobiographical confessions revealed the mysterious ways of God in his own life. "If Christ is to come and take up his abode in me," reflected Kierkegaard, "Christ came in through locked doors." What he sought to do was to educate in its etymological roots: to "educe" or draw out a discovery of the self before God. He recognized the limits to traditional forms of discourse. A direct communication usually assaults the hearer and arouses her defensive reactions, often only strengthening the other's will against persuasion. The task of his parables is not to gain mere intellectual assent, but to confront his audience with the ultimate questions of life. The "maieutic" approach of indirect communication invites the readers to ask questions of himself or herself. As Pascal observed, "We are more generally persuaded by the reasons we discover for ourselves." Thus, the modes of discourse that prove most effective and edifying are those oblique and indirect ones, those that create an environment for lingering (through ambiguity), employing puzzles, riddles, jests, humor, parables, testimonies, fables, and all manner of stories that evoke a response.

Kierkegaard's parables are weapons in his religious and ethical arsenal. They are improvised tools in conflict of ideas. However, they are more like scalpels than battleaxes; designed for surgical, rather than bludgeoning, uses. As such, they challenge corrupt powers (whether political or one's own soul) as in the following tale.

In the days of Jewish persecution, an old rabbinic parable subverted the powers of economic exchange. An old Jewish rabbi owed a greedy and lascivious usurer a large sum. The loan shark threatened to throw him into prison unless his beautiful young daughter would consent to be his consort. Her appeals landed on deaf ears. Ever the gambler, the usurer assented to a play of chance. Among the many stones laid about the ground, he would choose a white one and a black one, and if the daughter picked the white one out of his bag, she and her father would go free. However, if she selected the black one, she would become his concubine.

The young woman watched as the usurer picked up two black stones. With no voice to protest, she reached into the bag and chose one of the stones. The usurer grinned with smug malevolence.

Just then, the daughter dropped her stone among the many on the ground. No one saw which stone she dropped. "Oh," she exclaimed, "no need to worry. We can just look in the bag and see what color is left. I would have chosen the opposite."

Not only would such a story surprise the hearer, but it would also frustrate the venal ambition of one's enemies. Yet as a sharp weapon in the philosophical arsenal of the oppressed, the parable was also infused with an element of play; however, not the play of nursing homes, kindergartens, and parlor games, but a fairly rough contact sport, more rugby than tennis. Parable and storytelling function as means of delight. Their ludic element subverts the solemnity of analytic academic debates. They disarm and delight the hearer or reader, putting him/her in a more open, less definitive position. One does not know what to expect, as if one is on a roller coaster in the dark.

Yet, Kierkegaard's parables do not merely "a-muse," negating inspiration, but confront, edify, heal, or build up.[55] This requires of the parable, unlike the fable, an active participation by the subject. Kierkegaard would tie the narrative knot, and "if anyone were to profit by this sort of communication, he must himself undo the knot for himself." The old classic technique of the enthymeme was to offer a syllogism with one part missing: "All short cartoons in this book are parables. *One Froggy Evening* is a cartoon in this book." The author does not need to add a conclusion. The reader discerns it intuitively.

Parables thus function to involve the hearer, the listener, to provoke her to listen more carefully and ponder. It requires a "double reflection," demanding the active participation of the listener. Each person must undo the knot for himself/herself, figure out the riddle, and get the joke. They confront hearers with a choice; they aim at changing not just the mind, but also the will. Enticing, and demanding this act of the will, Kierkegaard's parables would jolt the self and bring about a tiny new birth, a radical re-understanding. For Kierkegaard, the parable functions as indirect communication, enticing and causing people to examine themselves. It seduces first; then it jolts them powerfully, challenging a person's view of self, world, and God.

Finally, for Kierkegaard, one must remember and repeat the parable. The parable serves tradition, extending the wisdom of the past. Of all kinds of communication, parables lend themselves most easily to memory and repetition. One last apt example from Kierkegaard illustrates these principles, being

> It happened that a fire broke out backstage in a theatre. The clown came out to inform the public. They thought it was just a jest and applauded. He repeated is warning; they shouted even louder. So I think the world will come to an end amid general applause from all the wits, who believe that it is a joke.[56]

For Kierkegaard, his "whole life is an epigram to make people aware" and he made them aware through his word pictures, the inward images of the self, or what he would call Shadowgraphs:

> I call these sketches Shadowgraphs, partly by the designation to remind you at once that they derive from the darker side of life, partly because, like other shadowgraphs, they are not directly visible. When I take a shadowgraph in my hand, it makes no impression on me, and gives me no clear conception of it. Only when I hold it up opposite the wall, and now look not directly at it, but at that which appears on the wall, am I able to see it. So also with the picture I wish to show here, an inward picture that does not become perceptive until I see it through the eternal. This external is perhaps not quite unobtrusive, but, not until I look through it, do I discover that inner picture that I desire to show you, an inner picture too delicately drawn to be outwardly visible, woven as it is of the tenderest moods of the soul.[57]

By the late nineteenth century, Victorian literature commandeered children's books, fables, and parables to become vehicles for more didactic "edifying" causes. Victorian fables mixed playful wit and moral tradition to unleash something akin to Kierkegaard's edifying discourse.[58] In her *Inside Picture Books,* Ellen Handler Spitz opens up the impact of those images from reading to children that linger in the museums of their minds. Conversational reading and looking together boost memories, develop "inner possibilities," and even shape a child's life later into adulthood. As such, she publishes her own discoveries of how classic children's books "transmit psychological wisdom, convey moral lessons, shape tastes, and implant subtle prejudices."[59] Images and stories had consequences. However, by 1900, visual parables had not only supplanted verbal ones, but they were starting to move.

NOTES

1. A second, more famous, Hebrew parable also challenged authority. After King David had appropriated Bathsheba and murdered her husband Uriah, resting in the words of Mel Brooks', "It's good to be king," his bony prophet Nathan approached him about a problem in his kingdom. 2 Samuel 12.

2. Martin Buber would translate many of his tales and bring them to life. A parable is told of Martin Buber himself, who found a fine pearl in a rubbish heap. Many had passed by and trampled it, but Buber bent down and picked it up and "polished it until its brilliant luster shone for all to see. Now that it shone so brilliantly, it was set in crowns of poetry and song. The pearl is Hasidism; the rubbish-heap, its disregard; the trampling, the scorn that was its lot. As for Buber's beautification, that is the form he gave it in German translation." Loar, Dan, "Agnon and Buber: The Story of a Friendship," in *Martin Buber: A Contemporary Perspective*, ed. Paul Mendes-Flohr (Syracuse University Press, 2002), 82.

3. Kaplan, Rabbi Aryeh (trans.), *Rabbi Nachman's Wisdom* (Breslov Research Institute, 1973), Wisdom #7.

4. Kaplan, Aryeh, *Rabbi Nachman's Stories* (Breslov Research Institute, 1983), 479–80.

5. Nachman of Breslov, Rebbe (trans. Rabbi Aryeh Kaplan), *The Seven Beggars and Other Kabbalistic Tales* (Jewish Lights, 2005), 121, xiv, xvii; The tale of "The Seven Beggars," for example, contains numerous references to Talmudic and biblical sources, which he told because God's people had disregarded the Torah. The seventh beggar does not appear with a wondrous gift, suggesting that they still wait for the Messiah.

6. Cited in Grant, R. M., *The Letter and the Spirit* (London, SPCK, 1957), 9–10.

7. Via, Dan O., *The Parables: Their Literary and Existential Dimension* (Wipf & Stock, 1967), 7.

8. Philostratus, *The Life of Apollonius of Tyana* Book V: 14 (trans. Christopher P. Jones) (Harvard University Press, Loeb Library, 2005).

9. Snodgrass, op. cit. 8. Snodgrass also argues for a similarity in that a fable can be seen as a "tactical maneuver to prompt new thinking and that their author engages to manipulate," to which he adds, "That is also the case with parables."

10. De Lille, Alan, "Omnis mundi creature Quasi liber et pictura Nobis est et speculum." (trans. Laura Hobgood-Oster), *Holy Dogs and Asses: Animals in the Christian Tradition* (University of Illinois Press, 2008), 76; Around 77 CE, Pliny the Elder in his *Historia naturalis* argued that by virtue of a divinely bestowed *ratio* (reason), the human is enabled to learn from animals, since "animals were instruments, even mediators, between man and the divinity in nature." See Cynthia White's *From the Ark to the Pulpit* (Louvain-La-Neuve: Publications de L'Institut D'Études Médiévales: 2009), 9.

11. Alciati, Andrea, *A Book of Emblems: The Emblematum Liber* [1531] *in Latin and English: 1492–1550* (trans. and ed. John F. Moffitt) (McFarland, 2004), 6; Alciate's work was considered a Rosetta Stone for interpreting the visual rhetoric of the Renaissance and Baroque eras of art.

12. One interpretation of the debate poem even turns toward their identities as King Henry II as the irreverent and merry nightingale with St. Thomas a Becket as the sagacious and solemn owl.

13. Cited in O'Neil Michael, "A Latin Poem and Natural Theology" in *Theology and Church* (February 25, 2014), https://theologyandchurch.com/2014/02/25/a-latin-poem-natural-theology/ (Accessed June 5, 2020).

14. Paul Wells argues convincingly that the iconography of animals allows artists to comment indirectly on incendiary social, religious, and political issues. In short, he supports (however presciently) my thesis of the parabolic nature of animated cartoons using anthropomorphic animals as moral and religious stories. *An Animated Bestiary: Animals, Cartoons, and Culture* (Rutgers University Press, 2000).

15. Swift, Jonathan, "The Beast's Confession" https://www.poetryfoundation.org/poems/45265/the-beasts-confession (Accessed December 21, 2020).

16. Lewis, "Impenitence" *Poems* (Harvest, 1964), 2.

17. Jones, Chuck, *Chuck Amuck* (Farrar Straus Giroux1989), 219; Once asked with which character he most identified, Jones conceded that "I go to bed every night dreaming that I'm Bugs Bunny, but every morning I wake up and realize I'm Daffy Duck." (*Chuck Jones: Memories of Childhood* Turner Classic Documentary Film).

18. Disney, Walt, "Mickey as Professor," *Public Opinion Quarterly* 9: 2 (Summer 1945), 119–125.

19. Macrobius, Ambrosius, *Dream of Scipio* (trans. William Harris Stahl) (Columbia University, 1952), 1.2: 7 and 9.

20. Beavis, Mary Ann, "Parable and Fable," *The Catholic Biblical Quarterly* 52 (1990), 474; See also Boucher, M., *Mysterious Parable: A Literary Study* (Catholic Biblical Association of America, 1977), 13 and Jeremias, J., *The Parables of Jesus* (Scribner's Sons, 1972).

21. Perry, Ben Edwin in Simon Hornblower (ed.), *Oxford Classical Dictionary,* 4th Edition (Oxford University Press, 2012), 476.

22. Beavis, According to H. J. Rackham in *The Fable as Literature* (Athlone Press, 1985), a fable has an "unmistakable meaning or else it fails miserably" (238).

23. In his semi-autobiographical Zen novel, *The Dharma Burns*, Beat generation novelist and poet Jack Kerouac contrasted the sublime, even transcendental experiences of the Matterhorn and nature with his jazzy and wild San Francisco city life. He inserted spoofs of classic kōans and haikus into his Buddhist search, such as: "'Does a dog have Buddha nature or not?' 'Woof.'" Or his classic *ice cream kōan*. "If you have ice cream I will give you some. If you have no ice cream I will take it away from you." What such riddles of paradox and ambiguity produced were thought experiences that would awake and enlighten one. See "Zen kōans: unsolvable enigma" https://www.youtube.com/watch?v=9p5Oi4wPVVo (Accessed January 28, 2020).

24. Perry, "Introduction," op. cit. Babrius and Phaedrus xxiii and Theon's *Progymnasmata* 3, xix–xx.

25. Ibid., xxviii–xxxix.

26. Beavis. op. cit. 478.

27. Varga, Zoltan, "Look Behind the (Animated) Pictures. Notes of the Aesopic Language in Hungarian Animation," *Acta Universitatis Sapientiae, Film and Media Studies*. 10.10.1515/ausfm-2015-0030 (August 2015), https://www.researchgate.net/publication/300370404_Look_Behind_the_Animated_Pictures_Notes_on_the_Role_of_the_Aesopic_Language_in_Hungarian_Animated_Film/citation/download (Accessed April 25, 2020).

28. M. Tóth, Eva, *Animare necesse est . . .* (Kaposvari Muveszeti Egyetem Muveszeti Foiskolai Kar—Pannoniafilm Kft, 2004), 71; See also William Moritz, "Animation in the Post-Industrial Era," in *The Oxford History of World Cinema*, ed. Geoffrey Nowell-Smith (Oxford University Press, 1996), 551–558.

29. One suspects allusions to both Laurel and Hardy films and to Roman Polanski's early silent comedy short, *Two Men and a Wardrobe* (1958), in its surreal symbolism.

30. Hernández, María Lorenzo, "The Double Sense of the Animated Images. A View on the Paradoxes of Animation as a Visual Language," *Animation Studies* 2. http://journal.animationstudies.org/category/volume-2/maria-lorenzo-hernandez-the-double-sense-of-animated-images/ (2007), 36–44 (Accessed May 12, 2020); See also Kuttna, Mari *Hungarian Animation: A Survey of the Work of the Pannonia Studio* (Budapest, 1970).

31. She points out only two that have miraculous interventions: Luke 12:13–21; 16:19–31.

32. Quintilian *Insitutio Oratoria* I ix.1 (trans Walter Russell) (Harvard University Press, 2012).

33. Ibid., V xi. 19.

34. Curley, Michael J., *Physiologus: A Medieval Book of Nature Lore* (University of Chicago Press, 2009), xv.

35. Ibid. 10.

36. "*Ancrene Wisse*" in Alistar McGrath's *Christian Literature: An Anthology* (Blackwell, 2001), 202. One of the curious rules of the order was it allowed no pets, except cats, creatures who appear often in iconography of Julian of Norwich.

37. Morrison, Elizabeth, "Medieval England and France, 700–1200," *British Library Newsletter,* https://www.bl.uk/medieval-english-french-manuscripts/

articles/beastly-tales-from-the-medieval-bestiary?_ga=2.222092635.2134215847.1558340667-448530374.1523626106 (Accessed September 2, 2020). The site includes animated bestiary films on the crane and the whale.

38. Wells, op. cit. 76.

39. Russell, Daniel, *The Emblem and Device in France* (French Forum, 1985).

40. Boccaccio, Giovanni, *Life of Dante* (trans. J. G. Nichols) (Hesperus Press, 2002), 52.

41. Ibid., 483.

42. Hollander, John, "Introduction"; La Fontaine, Jean, *The Complete Fables of Jean de la Fontaine* (trans. Norman Shapiro) (University of Illinois Press, 2007), xxiii.

43. Metz, John, *The Fables of La Fontaine, a Critical Edition of the 18th Century Settings* (Pendragon Press, 1986), 3–10.

44. Kline, Daniel T. (ed.), *Medieval Literature for Children* (Routledge, 2003), 2.

45. Horace would also be an early physician of the seven deadly sins: *avaritia, laudis amor, ividius, iracundus, iners, vinosus, amator* (covetousness, love of praise—or pride, envy, anger, sloth, gluttony, lust) Cf. Paul Jordan-Smith, "Seven (and More) Deadly Sins," *Parabola* 10:4 (1985), 34–45.

46. Judith Deitch, "Ypotis: A Middle English Dialogue," in *Medieval Literature for Children*, ed. Daniel Kline (Routledge, 2003), 227–248.

47. Cook, Patrick, "The *Ecloga Theoduli*," *Medieval Literature for Children* (2003), 188–203.

48. Lee, Brian S., "Occupation and Idleness," *Medieval Literature for Children* (2003), 249–283.

49. Libera, Zdzislaw, "Introduction"; Krasicki, Ignacy, *Bajki: wybór* (*Fables: a Selection*) (Warsaw: Państwowy Instytut Wydawniczy, 1974), 5.

50. Ibid., 5.

51. Czeslaw, Milosz, *The History of Polish Literature*, 2nd ed. (Berkeley: University of California Press, 1983), 176.

52. Kapolka, Gerard T., "Krasicki's Fables," *The Polish Review* 32: 3 (January 1, 1987), 271.

53. Krasicki, Ignacy, *Fables and Parables* (trans Christopher Kasparek), 1779.

54. Lowrie, Walter, *A Short Life of Kierkegaard* (Princeton University Press, 1970), 235–236; Elsewhere, Kierkegaard satirizes the bourgeois' love of God which "begins when vegetable life is most active, when the hands are comfortably folded on the stomach, and the head sinks back into the cushions of the chair, while the eyes, drunk with sleep, gaze heavily for a moment towards the ceiling" (*The Journals*, 9).

55. Postman, Neil *Amusing Ourselves to Death*: Public Discourse in the Age of Show Business (Viking Penguin, 1985).

56. Oden, Soren, *Parables of Kierkegaard*, 3. David Wilcox animated this parable in 1987 at Regent University.

57. Kierkegaard, Soren, *Either/Or* Volume 1 (Penguin Classics, 1992).

58. Golden, Catherine, *Victorian Studies of Autumn* (1998–99), https://dspace2.creighton.edu/xmlui/handle/10504/83504 (Accessed June 7, 2020).

59. Spitz, Ellen, *Inside Picture Books* (Yale University Press, 2000).

Chapter 2

Emergence of the Visual Parable

Within DreamWorks' biblical epic, *The Prince of Egypt* (Brenda Chapman, Steve Hickner, Simon Wells, 1998), appears a series of "inserted parts" or εμβλεμα, an inlaid work of hieroglyphic art (literally "secret or sacred writings") (figure 2.1). They tell the backstory of the Pharaoh's infanticide and the rescue of Moses. The embedded mini-story fascinates in its condensed and enigmatic silent form, with a montage of crocodiles, genocide, and thrilling escapes.[1] The visual impact of the pictographs needed no dialogue. The symbols on the walls showed the horrors and hope of the narrative.

Religious storytelling adapts in several ways as it moves from oral and literary traditions into visual modes. The messages remain remarkably consistent. In charting *Storytelling in Christian Art from Giotto to Donatello*, Jules Lubbock notes the narrative cycles of Giotto frescoes in Scrovegni's Temple in Padua. They stitch together a series of illustrations showing the life of Christ, the life of the Virgin, and monochromatic panels contrasting vices and virtues.[2] The iconography stretches from the Annunciation to Mary and the Nativity of Jesus throughout the ministry of Jesus, his Baptism, the Wedding at Cana, the Crucifixion, Resurrection, Ascension, and Pentecost. It illustrates the sacred story of salvation from beginning to end, all in striking visual representations. As Pope Gregory observed, in gazing upon images, the illiterate read; the forgetful remember; the slothful rejuvenated. Art historian Joyce Howell points out, however, that Giotto's personal interpretation of religious narratives is "less important than his finding a visual rhetoric comparable to letters." His significance as an auteur rests in his observation of the perceptual world and the legibility of his art through rhetorical gestures. He communicates faith through images as a miming orator.[3]

Additionally, one finds a similar pattern in the lower nave of the Basilica of St. Francis of Assisi, in which a pictorial sequence of twenty-eight frescoes

Figure 2.1 The Hieroglyphics in *The Prince of Egypt* (1998) Shockingly Expose the Massacre of the Hebrew Boys. *Source*: Screenshot taken by the author.

charts the life of St. Francis. It quite fitly works as a precursor to an animator's storyboard. These examples of visible speech (or images that speak) capture and hold a spectator's attention through variety, novelty, copiousness, and an abundance of things to look at, enjoy, and contemplate.[4] To paraphrase Lubbock, where the image seizes the attention and arouses the senses, the mind then can interrogate the image and appropriate its sermon for oneself.

Roman Catholic media scholar Marshall McLuhan's adage that the "medium is the message" opens up the rhetorical benefits (and liabilities) of visual communication. McLuhan's student, Neil Postman argued: "The medium is the metaphor." As he believed media do not communicate fact-based messages, he opted for metaphor. "The forms of our media . . . are rather like metaphors, working by unobtrusive but powerful implication to enforce their special definitions of reality."[5] Budapest University Professors András Benedek and Kristóf Nyíri point to how the digital age has unleashed an unprecedented barrage of images and animations, arguing that the challenge of the pictorial is explicit and conspicuous.[6] Visual rhetoric brings an immediate response and persuades by suggestion. Like Medusa, the hypnotic stare of a cockatrice, or the cunning Kaa in Walt Disney's adaptation of *The Jungle Book*, the visual petrifies, fascinates, or invites one to believe one's eyes. Like parables, images hold one's attention while they show and hide, reveal, and conceal.

In seeking to assess the use and abuse of images in Christian theology and practice, Anthony Thiselton examines a range of religious visual representations. They exist in Gnostic as well as biblical tropes, in medieval mystics as well as Radical Reformers' metaphors. The symbolic use of plants and animals, rooted in Jesus' vivid visual of fig trees and sheep-and-goats imagery, allows a certain measure of ambiguity. Some acts of interpretation resemble the challenge of making sense of a classic conundrum like the Old Woman/Young Lady, Louis Necker's Cube Glass, or Jastrow's duck-rabbit. Each offers alternative meanings, which leads to the suspicion that all interpretations of visual artifacts are relative. Such a concern for misleading and seductive images led French sociologist Jacques Ellul to articulate arguments against visual images in *The Humiliation of the Word*, as he believed technology downgraded the written word with the hegemony and privileging priority given to the visual. One has only to look at the graphic engravings in John Foxe's *Book of Martyrs* (1563) to recognize the potentially massive influence of the visual as propaganda (especially with Queen Elizabeth calling for the distribution of copies in every cathedral in England along with the *Book of Common Prayer* and *King James Bible*). Thiselton points to how printer John Day's lurid woodcut illustrations of Protestant martyrs being burned at the stake or tortured in cruel ways, under the horrible and bloody reign of Roman Catholic Queen Mary, adversely shaped British attitudes toward the Papacy in enduring ways.[7]

Christians have continually sought to teach, warn, inspire, provoke, and perplex their communicants with visual art. Out of catacomb painting, Christian sarcophagi, and wall mosaics rose a material cultural tradition of Christian iconography, with images of Jonah swallowed by the big fish, praying, cast up, and under the gourd vine; the good Shepherd, the raising of Lazarus, Noah's ark, and the three Hebrew youths in the fiery furnace in Babylon making their debut. Clement of Alexandria suggested which visual representation Christians might blessedly engrave on signet rings or as seals.

> And let our seals be either a dove, or a fish, or a ship scudding before the wind, or a musical lyre, which Polycrates used, or a ship's anchor, which Seleucus got engraved as a device: and if there be one fishing, he will remember the apostle, and the children drawn out of the water. For we are not to delineate the faces of idols, we who are prohibited to cleave to them: not a sword, nor a bow, following as we do, peace; nor drinking-cups, being temperate.

Yet as Robin Jensen points out, "What looks like a Good Shepherd to one set of eyes could be regarded as a representation of Hermes as the ram bearer to another. An image of Sol Invictus, Apollo, or Orpheus could be adapted to a Christian iconographic purpose in order to relay the idea of Christ as the bringer of light into the world or a tamer of souls."[8] However, most of the art was clearly Christian, in panel paintings, illuminated manuscripts, images of Christ's passion and miracles or, later, the ubiquitous hand from heaven on marginalia. The Virgin Mary and Child, stories from the Bible and the legends of the saints would follow. On cathedrals like Strasbourg, the statuary of the parable of wise and foolish virgins would draw much interest.[9]

Long before British academic MacNeille Dixon opined that "the mind of a human being is more like a picture gallery than a debating chamber," an apologist arose to contend against Iconoclasm and become the patron saint of visual communication.[10] When Iconoclasts arose in the Byzantine Empire, St. John of Damascus (676–754) rushed to the defense of employing images to teach and preach through visual imagery, articulating an *Apologetic Treatises against Those Who Revile the Holy Images* that provided a theological foundation for artists working in the visual media.[11]

For the iconophilic monk, the Incarnation marked a dynamic event in the history of Christian communication, moving the people of God from an oral culture to a visual one as well. "In former times, God, being without form or body, could in no way be represented. But today, since God has appeared in the flesh and lived among men, I can represent what is visible in God." St. John sets forth his argument that Christians are not to despise matter, "for it is not despicable. God has made nothing despicable. To think such things is Manichaeism."[12]

He sets forth his argument with succinct power. John holds up the example of Bezalel, the artist, as the first person filled with the Holy Spirit and given "ability and intelligence, knowledge and all craftsmanship to devise artistic designs, to work in gold, silver, and bronze, in cutting stones for setting and in carving wood for work in every craft."[13] Demonstrating that human hands constructed the ark, the staff, and the mercy seat, serving as a copy and shadow of the heavenly sanctuary, he celebrated the handiwork created to the glory of God. Such images are important, for just as words edify the ear, so also the image stimulates the eye. "What the book is to the literate, the image is to the illiterate."[14] Both images and sermons serve the same purpose. One can show the Word of God through both preaching and pictures. Virtue is communicated to those who cannot read by "teaching without use of words those who gaze upon them, and sanctifying the sense of sight." "Both painters of words and painters of pictures illustrate valor in battle; the former by the art of rhetoric; the latter by clever use of the brush, and both encourage everyone to be brave. A spoken account edifies the ear, while a silent picture induces imitation."[15]

St. John argued that "since the creation of the world the invisible things of God are clearly seen by means of images." These images, dim lights, not only reflect the work of God, but also remind us of God. They hint at His mysterious workings through "something hidden in riddles and shadows . . . . The brazen serpent, for example, typifies the cross and Him who healed the evil bite of the serpent by hanging on it."[16]

Pope Gregory III took up his cause, eventually excommunicating the Iconoclasts and pronounced that the image was a vital means of communication for the church, writing that: "pictures are for the illiterates what letters are for those who can read." During the eleventh through the twelfth centuries, Pope Gregory's articulation of a comprehensive apologetic for holy aesthetics, namely that painting can teach as well as illustrate religious ideas, diffused throughout Europe. As art historian E. H. Gombrich pointed out, "Images lived on in the minds of the people even more powerfully than did the words of the preacher's sermon."[17] In the thirteenth century, Saint Bonaventura carried on the legacy of Pope Gregory and the Council and summarized the pontiff's defense of using images in churches. He offered three reasons for the indispensable worth of images:

> They were made for the simplicity of the ignorant, so that the uneducated who are unable to read Scripture can, through statues and paintings of this kind, read about the sacraments of our faith in, as it were, more open Scriptures.
>
> They were introduced because of the sluggishness of the affections, so that men who are not aroused to devotion when they hear with the ear about those things which Christ has done for us will at the least be inspired when they see the same things in figures and pictures, present, as it were, to their bodily eyes. For our emotion is aroused more by what is seen than by what is heard.
>
> They were introduced on account of the transitory nature of memory, because those things which are only heard fall into oblivion more easily than those things which are seen.[18]

This triad of functions served as cures for human weaknesses: for ignorance, sloth, and forgetfulness.[19] Images in the churches were the *libri idiotarum*, the books of the illiterate, a truth repeatedly emphasized by Pope Gregory the Great: "We do no harm in wishing to show the invisible by means of the visible."[20] Around 600 AD, Gregory would extend his argument "for what writing offers to readers, a picture offers to the ignorant who look at it, since in it the ignorant see what they out to follow, in it they read who do not know letters; when for gentiles a picture is a substitute for reading."[21]

From this point on, the church increasingly translated its doctrines and ideas of the transcendent through images: through panel paintings, illuminations, calendar manuscripts, brass fonts, and even candlesticks and misericords (mercy seats). An apologetic for religious imagery slowly but surely developed within the Roman Catholic tradition. The vital distinction made by the Seventh Ecumenical Council ultimately hung on the difference between honoring and worshipping icons.[22] The scandal of the visible was resolved at the Council of Nicaea in 787, which decreed that pictures, the cross, and the Gospels should be given their due salutation and honorable reverence.[23]

Essentially the justification of the icon grew from the fact that Jesus Christ was very man and that the Gospel records were truly historical and actual.

In Padua around 1305, one of the earliest of visual *auteurs*, the painter Giotto, "followed the advice of the friars who exhorted the people in their sermons to visualize in their mind, when reading the Bible and the legends of the Saints, what it must have looked like . . . when the Lord was nailed to the cross." Gombrich also argued that these great, richly painted and adorned cathedrals "gave the faithful a glimpse of a different world; they would have heard in sermons and hymns of the Heavenly Jerusalem with its gates of pearl, its priceless jewels, its streets of pure gold and transparent glass (*Revelation* xxi)."[24] All these vividly served as devotional images, signs, and traces of God's work among His people, leading the faithful into true imitation of Christ and the saints.

Other artists followed to show how to communicate visually. While many re-created biblical scenes and saints legends, others ventured into mystical parables. The heavenly ladder or Ladder of Divine Ascent from the Eastern Orthodox theological teachings of the abbot, St. John Climacus, appeared as a dramatic icon in the late twelfth century at St. Catherine's Monastery at Sinai. It represented the arduous pilgrimage to the heavenly realms, with monastic pilgrims taking thirty steps or rungs, from renunciation of the world, obedience, true repentance, and defeat of such vices as anger, avarice, sloth, and pride, while acquiring virtues like meekness, simplicity, and humility. Monks precariously climb the ladder toward their leader John Climacus, conveniently resting on a top stair as Jesus offers him His helping hand. While angels and praying saints encourage the persevering saints through their ascetic labors, they are equally tempted and accosted by devils that shoot arrows at them or tug them downward with ropes and chains toward the ominous gaping Maw to be consumed in the fires of hell and devoured by the prowling devil.[25] Climacus would marvel at how some monks would so easily eschew virtue and succumb to the temptations of the world, the flesh, and the devil. They followed the witty aphorisms of Oscar Wilde in his *The Picture of Dorian Gray*, namely, "the only way to get rid of temptation is to yield to it." Or "I can resist everything except temptation."[26]

This icon appeared around 600 years after St. John's treatise for Eastern Christian monasticism and communicated his words with vivid pictorial illustration.[27] The icon transcends the limits of language. Whether Greek, Latin, Arabic, Goth or Vandal, a viewer would shake with fear viewing this visual allegory with the lurid horrors of being swallowed up by Hell or the blessed hope of receiving the reward of faithful perseverance and salvation.

An apt template for such iconic communication occurs in an odd little film, *Wildebeest* (Birdbox Studio, 2012), a truly cautionary tale, of wildebeests standing on a water bank and looking at a craggy "thing" in the water (figure

Figure 2.2 ***Wildebeest*** **(Birdbox Studio, 2012) Suggests the Playful Ambiguity of a Visual Parable.** *Source*: Screenshot taken by the author.

2.2). Standing on the shore, studying the rugged floating object, one wildebeest visually suggests to another in a thought bubble that it is a crocodile. No, says the other shaking its head, it is just a log. The debate is conducted totally in thought images, as the two creatures trade picture bubbles to convince the other of their opinions. The first one tosses a pebble at it, pokes it with a stick, and splashes water on it. "Log," asserts the second one, and the two debate repeatedly. However, the first tentatively steps out onto the "log" which quickly swallows him. The other wildebeest concludes in a thought bubble: "crocodile." Another skeptic arrives and argues: "log." The uniqueness of their communication is that it unfolds entirely in visual images, as the characters debate with illustrated emblems.

As the medieval church developed a systematic universe, it added visual aids in teaching its illiterate population (including many clergies). Stories appeared in stone, wood, stained glass, tapestries, frescoes, and canvases, depicting biblical events, the lives of saints, and moments of salvation history. For example, Raphael's extant "Cartoons" (1516) and storytelling tapestries afford a series of seven scenes from the Gospels and the Acts of the Apostles. Commissioned by Pope Leo X for the Sistine Chapel, one salient parable stands out in particular as a pedagogical treasure in an era of simony, in teaching the cautionary story of Ananias, whose greedy deception over money led to his sudden death.[28] However, with the rise of cathedrals and universities, the publication of manuscripts of scholastics and the mischievous labors of monkish scribes and illuminators, another marginal mode of cartoony communication snuck into human consciousness: drolleries.[29]

Devotional books and illuminated manuscripts emerged out of scriptoria. The Irish were saving civilization in their creative works, such as the *Lindisfarne Gospels* and the *Book of Kells*.[30] The Gospel writers found appropriate emblems of living creatures to mark them from each other. The man of Matthew pointed to the family lineage in that gospel; the lion of Mark alluded to the "voice crying in the wilderness": the bull of Luke referred to the temple sacrifice of the ox; and the eagle of John celebrated the lofty mysteries of the first chapters of his gospel. The artists adapted them from the prophet Ezekiel (1:1–21) and the book of Revelation (4:6–8). The great apologist St. Irenaeus explained the emblems:

> "The first living creature was like a lion," symbolizing His effectual working, his leadership, and royal power. The "second was like a calf," signifying His sacrificial and sacerdotal order; but "the third had, as it were, the face as of a man,"—an evident description of His advent as a human being. The "fourth was like a flying eagle," pointing out the gift of the Spirit hovering with His wings over the Church. And, therefore, the Gospels are in accord with these things.[31]

Some devotionals were lavishly illuminated to the "Glory of God" with many personalized with border decorations and an unstinting use of gold leaf. In one text, a miniature image depicts monks singing in a choir, illustrating Psalm 96: "Sing to the Lord a new song: sing to the Lord, all the earth." Others would illustrate stories such as Lazarus, Abraham, and Dives (the rich man being tortured in hell) or the tale of Theophilus from the *Golden Legend*. They served as aids against illiteracy, forgetful memories, sloth, and all the vices that assaulted the human soul. Apologetics on the importance of visual representation summoned such diverse Christians as Hildegard of Bingen, Thomas Aquinas, Dante, and the mystic Meister Eckhart.

By the mid-seventeenth-century, all such emblems functioned as "instructions which must enter through the eyes in order to pass through them toward the soul. These images are obtained from all perceivable objects, and from these we can represent spiritual things by using human figures, Hence, Nature, the Arts, Fables, Proverbs . . . and the fictions of the Poets are all material proper to emblems; for all these provide images which can instruct us."[32] They fulfilled their primary task of instructing through delight, *docere cum delectation*.

Joining these esteemed symbols of spiritual realities and truths were mischievous bits, less likely to instruct. Artists produced illuminated manuscripts primarily for elite audiences—not to educate the illiterate. Economic concerns took precedence over religious education. Small decorative images added humor in the margins of devotional books like the Book of Hours, psalters, and illuminated manuscripts by cleverly creative, and perhaps bored, monks. Those decorations often became as important as the text, more than

Figure 2.3 Medieval Marginalia Delights with Its Dogs and Rabbits Jousting on *grillo* Snails (Courtesy of Bodleian Library, Oxford). *Source*: Screenshot taken by the author.

mere illustration. Some were intentional symbols, some pious reminders and some were comic doodles, known as drolleries. For example, one might find knights fighting or jousting snails or rabbits (or rabbits riding snails) or monkeys throwing poop (figure 2.3). Cartoon creatures would slip into crawling grotesques called *grillos* with only a head and legs or hands or some other anthropomorphized monstrosity with no trunk, but arms feeding porridge into a bodiless head.[33] The irreverent and ribald marginalia (lowbrow jokes of excrement or of a nun picking penises off a phallus tree in the *Roman de la Rose*, c.1353) previewed a form of wild manga, in which sins could be visualized as beasts to teach and delight those who perused the manuscripts.[34]

Around the thirteenth century, Japan also developed a historic artistic form called the *Choju Giga*, animal scrolls that depicted comic beast sketches, such as frogs and rabbits wrestling or a monkey dressed as a monk worshipping a frog Buddha. By the late eighteenth century, modern-day versions of manga evolved from illustrated yellow jacket books called *Kibyoshi*, which used woodblock printing to tell tales with wit and romance in graphic form.[35] One erstwhile founder of *manga* was the lively and humorous Japanese artist of *Ukiyo-e* (floating world pictures) Katsushika Hokusai. While best known in the West for his *Thirty-six views of Mount Fuji* series. Hokusai also published fifteen volumes of "whimsical sketches" for his students. His *manga*, like the *grillos*, included comic and exaggerated caricatures as in his *Blind Men and Elephant* or *Blind Men Fighting*. His wonderfully vulgar humor appears in his series of facial contortions and farting scrolls. He was a precursor of much contemporary animation.

Beginning around the mid-thirteenth century, these miniature drolleries were hybrid creatures (animals, plants, and human beings—roosters with human heads, birdlike dragons, etc.) that decorated the religious texts with bizarre graffiti-like shapes. They emerged from a tradition of the gloss or explanatory note intended to clarify a difficult passage. They not only pointed to vices of naughty nuns and flatulent monks, but also sought to awaken thoughtful laughter, often at the expense of the religious hierarchy, such as when a monkey in a red cardinal's robe would lead a crowned lion with his foolscap rod. Curiously, some of the illustrations offered ass-themed marginalia that one might find as fodder for Terry Gilliam's Monty Python cutout animations. Along with such eye-popping graphic images were side commentaries, inserted by the scribes copying the sacred texts. One excused himself by scribbling in "Let me not be blamed for the script; for the ink is bad, and the vellum defective, and the day is dark." Another jotted down this colophon bit at the end of his work: "Now I've written the whole thing. For Christ's sake, give me a drink."[36] While some Books of Hours became "breviaries for dummies" for a lazy laity, they still communicated clearly and with good wit.

In describing images on the edge of the texts, historian Michael Camille tells about Marcolf, a trickster figure known in oral and written tradition throughout the Middle Ages, who engages in witty dialogues with King Solomon, Marcolf is forever turning the king's "turgid truths into turds." Solomon speaks that one should "give the wise an opportunity, and wisdom will be added unto him" and Marcolf retorts, "Let the belly be stuffed, and shit will be added unto you." Such a farcical tale delighted readers as the drolleries of these manuscripts would provide fodder for some sixteenth-century Flemish artists.

Many of the woodcuts and engravings of Albrecht Dürer highlight religious themes, offering biblical lessons on *The Last Supper* (1510), *Ecce Homo* (1498), or *The Four Horsemen of the Apocalypse* (1497). At the start of his career, as a young man in his twenties, Dürer created during his journeyman years a series of woodcuts to illustrate Swiss humanist and lawyer Sebastian Brant's best-selling *Das Narrenschiff* (*The Ship of Fools*, 1494). This "Divine Satire" of vernacular verses mocking the corruption and sins of the Roman Catholic Church predates Martin Luther's protests by two decades.[37] As 100 passengers embark for Narragonia, the "land of fools," Brant tweaks Misers, Gluttons, and even churchgoers ("who went to church for respectability's sake, or to show off a gaudy dress, or a fine dog?"). Mischievously, his first target exposes the book fool, seated at his desk laden with tomes and wearing giant comic spectacles. Key to the book's popularity were the clever illustrations making the book quite pleasing to the eye and quite instructive on its own. Due to Gutenberg's invention of the printing press, engravers disseminated images quickly.

For example, Dürer allegedly drew the folly of the preacher who conceals truth; even as he wears the coxcomb, his congregation falls asleep. This collection of moralizing stories ranged from teaching about the Antichrist to prattling in church, all of which artists illustrated in bold, memorable ways.

Northern Renaissance artist and engraver Lucas Cranach the Elder (1472–1553) maintained a close relationship with his neighbor, Reformer Martin Luther, and became the primary purveyor of Protestant visual propaganda for the Protestant Reformation. Although renowned for his numerous portraits of sixteenth-century dignitaries and paintings of religious topics like Law and Grace, Adam and Eve, and the Crucifixion, he also dabbled in the satiric art of crude woodcuts. He blasted the depravity of the Roman Catholic hierarchy for its venal and luxurious lifestyle in a series of thirteen pairs of images for the 1521 pamphlet, *Passional Christi und Antichristi*, contrasting the Passion of Christ with the corrupt Papacy. For example, Cranach juxtaposed an image of Jesus washing the feet of the disciples and of Pope Leo demanding servile followers kiss his feet or contrasting scenes of Jesus chasing the moneychangers out of the Temple and the Pope welcoming them into his throne room.

The savvy Cranach decorated many a treatise for the Wittenberg monk, becoming the most significant propagator of Lutheran reform through his paintings, woodcuts, and leaflets or *Flugschriften*, brazen Protestant broadsheets that combined elements of religious propaganda, political pamphlet, yellow journalism, and early comic book pleasures. His iconic portraits of Luther (and Katie von Bora) made him (and her) the most recognizable celebrity on the continent, a "household face and name throughout the Holy Roman Empire of the German nation."[38]

Art historian Bendor Grosvenor explained how two major innovations emerged from Cranach's workshop: The first was the "transformation of the woodcut from a relatively undervalued medium of artistic expression to a powerful tool of evangelism and propaganda". The second was the development of a "model of cultural industrialization that enabled images to be produced on a sufficiently large scale to serve a movement of ideas growing at a quite remarkable rate between 1517 and 1525."[39]

This set of cultural innovations coming out of German enabled Cranach to disseminate his exquisite and subversive engravings, woodcuts, and cheap pamphlets. They established a visual mass medium to propagate ideas, appealing to more than an educated and clerical elite. Aesthetics combined with Protestant theology and mass technology to woo and provoke a curious public. One of his most famous woodcuts was the *Allegory of Law and Grace* (1529), a powerful example of *Merkbilder*,[40] those didactic illustrations of theological doctrine. Acclaimed as the most "influential image of the Lutheran Reformation," the pictorial rhetoric vividly demonstrates that one receives salvation through faith and God's grace and not through any "good works." Cranach's *Allegory* celebrated the crucifixion of the Lamb of God and His victory over death and sin as a blessing to the faithful.[41] Alternatively, on the left side, a nude sinner, under the law, flees in torment, pursued by demons and tumbling toward the fires of hell.

Luther required that art should clarify ideas so that the illiterate would benefit spiritually. Didactic art was essential to instruct children and others in the Reformation catechism, particularly in the doctrine of salvation by faith. Thus, visual imagery transformed from a seductive, emotionally charged illustration to something clear and compelling. For example, regarding Cranach's depiction of the martyrdom of Saint Andrew in his book *Das symbolum oder gemeine Bekentnis der zwelff Aposteln* (1539), Fiona Neal writes: "In spite of the violent subject matter, the image shows young children in the crowd. The later reproduction of the 1539 edition, with a commentary by Luther, intended to instruct young people in their Protestant faith. Woodcuts were a powerful tool of evangelism, guiding Christians both young and old towards Christ and the biblical messages. Pictures of martyrdom also educated the believers about the violent history of the 'new' Protestant religion."[42] Such visual propaganda as *Foxe's Book of Martyrs* (1563) and the Anabaptist *The Bloody Theater or Martyrs Mirror (1560)* magnified the cruel and grisly excesses.

Cranach's works were as crude as Luther's vituperations, such as in one very popular 1523 pamphlet depiction called *der Papstesel* (aka The Pope as Doctor of Theology and Master of the Faith or the pope-ass). Illustrating one of Luther's more notorious works, *Against the Papacy in Rome, Instituted by the Devil* (1545), Cranach created horrific woodcuts that captured Luther's venting against the Vatican as the house of the Anti-Christ. One of the more notorious woodcut caricatures was "The Kingdom of Satan and the Pope (2 Thessalonians 2)," used as the title page of this *Flugschriften*. The pope, with long donkey ears, sits enthroned in the jaws of hell with various demons attending him.[43]

Before the Dutch artist Hieronymus Bosch (1450–1516) reached the age of forty, he had joined a conservative religious group, one that may have influenced his specialization in apocalyptic parables, with a few little devilish themes thrown in. Echoing the folly and hypocrisy of Brant's *Ship of Fools*, the Flemish painter re-created it around 1500 with prodigal passengers wasting their lives in eating, drinking, flirting, vomiting, and playing cards, rather than doing good. Symbolism abounds, with a Muslim crescent on the yellow banner flying from a mast, an owl in the tree symbolizing heresy, and a monk and nun intimately singing together with the ripe erotic imagery of the lute and bowl of cherries. In his art Bosch communicated as a spiritual teacher, although not always too clearly.[44]

Bosch surfaced as one of the most dazzling, peculiar, and cryptic "animators" of the era. Historian Yona Pinson sees in Bosch's enigmatic *Wayfarer* a parable of *memento mori*, an instructional reminder of sin and its consequence of death. Of particular significance is its emblematic significance of the moral landscape, where the fool-sinner does not realize, even with a mirror, his own folly. Bosch also "employs the mirror imagery ironically by turning it toward the viewer. Thus, the itinerant becomes the beholder's own self, on the road of sin leading toward perdition."[45] Art historian Erwin Panofsky described how the landscapes of such renaissance paintings point toward moral significance, using the term *paysage moralisé*. Its animated legacy endures in a trope used in Canadian animator Richard Condie's *The Apprentice*, where a fool does not realize that a symbolic tree stands as the crux of a *paysage moralisé*; a tree, or "cross," that keeps him from his appointed destruction of the broad way.

Several years ago, journalist Claudia Massie opened an article with the apt question: "Want your children to love art? Start with Hieronymus Bosch." She warned that he would be stimulating, "if they're not prone to nightmares, obviously."[46] Nevertheless, she caught onto something connecting Bosch and cartoons as roads to becoming curious about art. Here are images that we have not seen before. A horrific and malicious SpongeBob may have even appeared in a Bosch painting somewhere. Dutch animation film director Erik van Schaaik explores this "heavy-metal artist" in his *Hieronymous: A Boy and His Monsters* as a "coming of age" story rather than a series of bizarre and disturbing images. Domesticating the medieval prophet, his feature seeks to assist children in enjoying art.[47] On the other hand, animator and filmmaker Terry Gilliam confessed to the darker side of a Bosch imagination: "If I have a visual style it's incredibly eclectic. I've always been obsessed with viscera, guts of things whether they're physical or mechanical; showing the inside of things, not just the surface of things. When it comes to ironic, or disturbing, or surreal images, I rush back to Bruegel, to Bosch, to Magritte, to Max Ernst."[48] With his flying fish, killer rabbits, and odd characters, Gilliam identifies with Bosch's humanistic side as well, seeing his humor, joy, and love of humanity, while still having the audacity to show the bowels of darkness.

Among Bosch's triptychs, *The Garden of Earthly Delights* (1504) amuses, instructs, and even titillates. Its nudes, voluptuous fruit, and amusing animals in paradise and on earth contrast with the horrific depictions of punishments of sinful humanity. Like a flickering nightmare, a wild universe of monsters and chimeras, and its unimaginable fantasies, the work causes one to stop and ponder its fantastic images, discovering how it reflects late medieval didactic sermons. Moral and spiritual truths seem to lurk in between the frames, describing what very speculative critics, Dirk Bax and Peter Glum, have seen as visual translations of verbal metaphors, wordplay, and puns drawn from biblical, folkloric, and theological Tractarian sources.[49] One can at least interpret that the wages of sin end with grisly torment and lurid torture, whatever the arcane emblems may ultimately mean.

The iconography on the left celebrates paradise and its gardens of love contrasted with the disquieting wasteland of hell on the right. In between, the garden of earthly pleasures delights. However, for the viewer, the cruelty of the cosmos crowded with sins and perverse follies, its gothic monsters with morally deformed physiognomies, disturbs the quiet. Tortured hallucinations of a knife blade cutting two gigantic ears, broken eggs and bubbles with amorous couples, a perverse bestiary with dead fish and slithering freaks, show the horrors of hell. One man is hung on a key; another shivers before a ladder in the hollow of a shell tree man (arboreal images to be frightfully described by George MacDonald in his supernatural thriller *Phantastes*), and a sow wearing a nun's veil (not to mention all the enemas and arrows in buttocks). A bird-headed monster swallows a man out of whose buttocks fly crows, while he digests and excretes them into a transparent toilet. The degradation of human nature into bestiality, lasciviousness, avarice, malice, and sloth exhibits a thorough knowledge of sin and its consequences.

Bosch's pictorial story of "The Garden of Earthly Delights" prefigures the gothic and grotesque religious themes in the writings of Flannery O'Connor and the surreal animation of Japanese pioneer, Yoji Kuri. All three have captivated and beguiled readers and spectators with their strange yet compelling works. The opening scene of Kuri's hallucinatory *The Midnight Parasites* (1972) looks like water flowing out of a drain only to pull back and see it is excrement coming out of an odd beast drinking in a lake (the image will also close the film to suggest the eternal recurrence of its horrors) (figure 2.4). A trousered pair of legs with a bird head sticking out of the waist marches by while a smiling shell-like woman with trees growing out of her, carrying the owl and the crescent flag from Bosch's *Ship of Fools*, skates on with tiny people sitting inside her waiting at tables. An acorn creature with a tiny penis and a single eye in his belly saunters about.[50] The film's *paysage moralisé* situates the world of Bosch's *The Garden of Earthly Delights* beside a Dutch windmill on the shore of a lake. The waters spew up large naked women immediately devoured by flying fish. A man battles a pterodactyl that eats him alive while a slimy frog creature swallows humans wholesale. A man, impregnated by a flying female, gives birth to a parasitic offspring that eats him to the bone and then breeds into a flying female. All the skewering and regurgitating activity of these beasts culminate in a mercenary cycle of killing, feeding, and defecating gold coins for others to feast on in an endless circle of digestion, excretion, death, and reproduction. These fabulous and bizarre monsters hint at the deserved punishments of so many self-consumed creatures. Animation critic Chris Robinson suggested that Kuri's biting

Figure 2.4 Yoji Kuri's *The Midnight Parasites* (1972) Conjures up Grotesque Imagery from Bosch. *Source*: Screenshot taken by the author.

satirical cartoons "mock and shock, attacking technology, population expansion, monotony of modern society," and they allude to the "devastation of his country followed by the quick rise of Western inspired materialist culture and rampant consumption."[51]

A parable enables one to understand spiritual truths metaphorically, in comparison with material things, so that even the simple can fathom its mysteries by an exercise of faith and imagination. Bosch's viewers could uncover hidden spiritual truths, some quite lucid and others quite esoteric. A medieval Quadriga supplied four different modes of meaning. First, a text or an image could be interpreted literally or historically to get its plain meaning. Second, it perceives allegorical (or figurative) significance in which an event such as crossing the Red Sea may convey baptism. Third, one can find a moral (or how one ought to behave considering the story) meaning, advising how one ought to behave considering the story. Lastly, anagogical interpretations relate to the meaning of life, one's telos, and the possibility of eternal salvation. For Augustine, what appears in the scriptures may have several interpretations.[52] What appears in images, and animated parables, carries as many possible meanings as viewers, although not always the ones the artist intended.

Bosch mixed Christian allegory, alchemical, fantastic, esoteric symbols of sin, and surreal imagery as themes for reflection. Some of his visual works like *St. Jerome in Prayer* invite introspection and call sinners to meditate upon their lives in light of saints. Such paintings capture the doctrine of the *Imitation of Christ*, illustrating the virtues of a life of self-denial, prayer, and meditation. It functions as an exemplary parable for the ordinary peasant, to consider the righteous life of the saint and to emulate it.[53] Yet one finds some of his more bizarre and enigmatic visual symbols that puzzle the spectator.

The work most relevant to our task deals with Bosch's circular "Lazy Susan-type" tabletop painting of the Seven Deadly Sins. Following Virgil out of the Inferno of the *Divine Comedy* (1320), the pilgrim Dante must now climb the mountain of Purgatory. In the two lower realms, he maps out each of the seven deadly sins, first, escalating in order from the least evil to the worst, and then reversing the hierarchy in Purgatory.[54] The wonderfully weird Hieronymus Bosch would illustrate Dante's list with his "The Seven Deadly Sins" painting. Painted on poplar, King Philip II of Spain acquired it and hung it in a private chamber rather than in a church.

Scenes drawn from ordinary life, more familiar than the allegorical oddities of Bruegel's etchings on sin, Bosch places Christ rising from the concave mirror or tomb in the center, the pupil of the painting. A moral exemplum surrounds the iris with the instructive words "*Cave, cave; Deus videt*" "Careful, careful God is watching" along with the *tondos* of the four last things. Death, the Last Judgment, Hell, and Heaven. Through allusions, innuendoes, and graphic tropes, Bosch communicated his moral and spiritual messages, with the all-seeing eye of God at their center, allowing for a variety of subtle and deliciously wicked interpretations.

Guides for interpretation come from two banderoles below and above the central circle, and set between the *tondos* of the Four Last Things. They cite the Latin texts of *Deuteronomy* warning against unbridled pursuit of the seven deadly sins. "For they are a nation void of counsel, neither is there any understanding in them. O, that they were wise, that they understood this, that they would consider their latter end!" (32:28–29). Below, between Hell and Paradise, the words ring out "*Absconda*: I will hide my face from them; I will see what their end shall be" (32:20). The paths through death and judgment lead either to Heaven or to Hell.

The four corners hold illustrations of the Four Last Things, visual sermons on Death, Judgment, Heaven, and Hell. Death creeps in with an emaciated sinner receiving last rites by several clergies. Death hovers nearby, with its arrow well aimed. An angel drifts over a bedpost while a dark, haunting demon climbs over the headboard, ready to steal the soul. The Last Judgment is marked by heralding angels awakening the dead with the trumpets of the Lord. Some dead rise from the earth looking heavenward, while others put their hands to their ears. Christ awaits all.

Those in the Abyss of Hell already know torments, where visual parables abound. Almost like a film trailer, the painting previews each of the seven deadly sins in bizarre ways, with wailing and gnashing of teeth off in the distance. Anger holds a naked man down on a slab of wood tormented by a lizard-like dragon while a devil with a sword prepares to castrate him.

Avarice boils others in oil in pots of gold, or flays one over the fires, with leering creatures watching. In lust, a shadowy demon and a platypus interrupt coitus between a man and woman on a giant bed. Wild dogs and beasts devour men stuck in envy. A gluttonous man gasps at a frog and snake on a table before him, while a creature in a habit pounds a naked slothful sinner's bottom with a hammer. A bronze pig with wings holds him down. Finally, in pride, a sack-hatted demon holds up a mirror to a woman, a frog covering her pudenda.

In Heaven, or Gloria, St. Peter welcomes the naked redeemed (even as one little froglike devil tries to kidnap a blonde woman). However, a huge angel protects her with his sharp staff. A trio of angels play praises with harp, dulcimer, and horn as the rest of the saints await the arrival of these new blessed ones.[55] Circling the center eye of God are seven equal sections (seven being the perfect number), with each showing one of the deadly sins in everyday actions. God watches all of them.

In preparation for our exploration of the seven deadly sins in animated parables, we look at how Bosch structures his lessons. The first segment is Wrath (*Ira*), where outside a tavern a toppled table signifies an untamed temper. A woman tries to stop a drunken man brandishing his sword from brawling with a cloaked man, whose nose seems to be bleeding and wears a piece of furniture on his head for protection. As one moves clockwise, one espies within Envy (*Invidia*), a peasant couple look covetously at a wealthier man holding a falcon, even as the husband holds a dog bone that his dogs, with their own bones, crave. A suitor holds a flower out for their daughter, tempting her desire to have more. In Greed (*Avarice*), a judge sitting on a bench takes a bribe while hearing the case of two men; other wise men see the vice and do nothing.

Gluttony (*Gula*), containing the most obvious symbols, situates a hefty father gorging himself as his wife serves him an entire chicken, and his little fat son following his father's example reaching for his mead. Another skinny man gulps a swig of ale. Both have given themselves over to bodily appetites of consuming food and drink, with a symbol of evil, an owl, overlooking the sinners from a niche. Sloth (*Acedia*), asleep with his cat by the fire, ignores a charitable nun offering prayer beads and a Bible. Amid the folly of Lust (*Luxuria*), seductions, dalliances, and a gathering/plucking of a red rose arise in a red tent. A jester typifies their folly of indulgence, recognizing that both men and women can incite lust in the other and receive their just desert. (In the circle of hell, the lesson warns of sleeping with the wrong person, which will end up sleeping in hell with demons.) In the worst of the sins, Pride (*Superbia*), a woman preens herself in front of a devil's mirror. Usually pride symbolized male leadership, but here, the vain woman succumbs to the image of herself. The mirror in Bosch is slyly self-reflective. Acclaimed art history

Joseph Koerner insightfully shows that while Bosch indicts prideful image-making, he calls attention to himself at the same time. His punning and self-deprecating self-portraits are embedded everywhere in his artwork, especially in drawings such as *The Field Has Eyes* and *The Owl's Nest* (1510).

Inheriting the fabulous imagery of Bosch, Pieter Bruegel the Elder (1525–1569) created his own parables, products of a vibrant Dutch visual culture. The artist marshalled various bits from fables and popular stories of folklore that reaffirmed an "ideal of a stable, hierarchical society."[56] Bruegel played with the quiddity of life in the Netherlands, using moments of everyday life to create visual proverbs that entertained and instructed. Generally, Bosch's more theological work pointed to Christian doctrine, while Bruegel focused on human culture and daily life.[57] Even with his religious themes, Bosch triumphed with phantasmagorical paintings, playing with the bizarre, the diabolic, and the surreal, while Bruegel showed a greater integration of genre (i.e., images of people in everyday life) and the landscape. In the midst of the political and religious turmoil of the Spanish Inquisition and the Dutch Revolt, Bruegel would emulate Bosch's macabre artistic endeavors with a more comic and mundane lens. Under clouds of war, the economic prosperity of Antwerp enabled the artists to find markets for their sermons; Bruegel joined with a print publisher aptly named Hieronymus Cock, in remembrance of Bosch, of course, at his shop of the Four Winds.

Among his landscape paintings, Bosch treats Jesus' *Parable of the Sower* (1557) in contemporary images, with a church tower, thatched Flemish huts, and horses capturing the authenticity of the story. A sower casts his seeds upon the four types of ground. Even more compelling is Bruegel's depiction of *The Parable of the Blind* (1568), diagonally showing the trajectory of the blind leading the blind. Ophthalmologists like Dr. Steve Scoper can diagnose various disorders of the eye within the painting, as two men on the left suffer from leucoma of the cornea and amaurosis, and a third has his eyes gouged out. What is most dramatic is the direction of their hopeless situation: they fall into the ditch. Each follows the leader, already fully prostrate on the ground, unable to fathom what is to befall them. As viewers tilt their heads back to study the painting, one realizes that one imitates the posture of the pathetic blind men themselves, and that we too are fated to share their destiny. Bruegel invites us not only to recognize the parable but also to enter it as well.

Art critic Kavaler points to the "riddle-like" quality of Bruegel's robust iconography, along with his use of ambiguity and irony, all of which reside in the nuances of the artist's "visual rhetoric." Bruegel wants us to resolve the meanings for ourselves, poking us to decipher their significance in our lives.[58] Borrowing the theme of the *Seven Deadly Sins*, Bruegel offered ludicrous images of the vices that invited a dialogue with his engravings. His scenes of daily life, or genre, established the dominant pictorial modes of the vices. Each sin would not only depict a female personification, but also a symbolic animal, all surrounded by surreal characters, landscapes, and monsters.

Like Bosch, Bruegel morally instructed his viewers by depicting human nature's tendency toward sin. Their surreal landscapes, their distorted creatures, and hybrid images work as visual strategies to perplex their viewers and tease them into thinking about what they are seeing and what it all means. Looking at motifs such as broken eggshells, amorous couples in bubbles, hooded monks, and odd beasts like rats, a platypus, or an odd owl, one recognizes similarities between the two artists. Both terrify and amuse simultaneously with their parabolic incongruities.[59]

The parabolic laughter of many animated films finds root in this era. Gibson points to two strains of laughter that marked this era, the carnival tradition as seen in Rabelais and the humanist wit of Erasmus, and he sees them being wed in Bruegel's Flemish proverbs. The two authors reflect two competing views of laughter, with robust and bawdy laughter being "proper to man" in Rabelais and polite laughter being more decorous in the Dutch humanist. Erasmus insisted that "loud laughter and the immoderate mirth that shakes the whole body . . . are unbecoming to any age but much more so to youth . . . and the person who opens his mouth wide in a rictus, with wrinkled cheeks and exposed teeth, is also impolite."[60] However, the epoch saw both forms of laughter in a more positive light. In a work intended to describe the ideal courtier or court lady, the *Book of the Courtier* (1588), Count Baldassare Castiglione has one of his main characters, Cardinal Bibbiena, state that laughter "restores the spirit, gives pleasure, and for the moment keeps one from remembering those vexing troubles of which our life is full."[61] In the tradition of Cicero, laughter contributed a significant commodity offered by the Netherlandish *rederijkers*, or rhetoricians, who shared a fondness for proverbs and puns, especially as relief from present troubles and tensions. Bruegel would imitate them with delight. As well as culling from biblical, classical, and folklore sources, Bruegel enjoyed "jokes, pun, and riddles."[62] For example, Bruegel comically portrays a *Misanthrope Robbed by the World* (1568) in his Twelve Flemish proverbs. A little man in a bubble cuts a moneybag from under the misanthrope's hooded robe. What he does not see will not hurt him; he will not miss his purse, as he is so preoccupied with a perfidious world and his own vain mourning. One laughs at the contrast between the deceiver and the deceived in *The Misanthrope*. At any rate, his biographer, Karel van Mander comments that Bruegel painted many "humorous scenes" and that this led to his being nicked "Pieter the Droll" by a considerable number of people because he could incite laughter. Bruegel's works, employing digestion, vomiting, pissing, and the recurring figure of a *kakker* (shitter), imply more than they depict.[63]

Parables thrive under Bruegel's genius. He contrasts industry on the one hand and idleness and frivolity on the other in *The Parable of the Wise and Foolish Virgins* (1563). The former maidens who kept extra oil and showed preparedness were welcomed into the wedding feast, while the other virgins are locked out (stumping the seminarian's answer to whether he would prefer to be with the wise virgins at the wedding feast or with the foolish virgins in the dark). A more secular parable (and Flemish proverb) underlies *The Ass at School* (1557). "Though a donkey go to school in order to learn, he'll be a donkey, not a horse, when he does return."

A precursor of children's cartoons is Bruegel's *Netherlandish Proverbs* (1559) in a topsy-turvy world, as well as his *Children's Games* (1560) as they tease the viewer playfully, but also point to proverbial wisdom, not giving a "folkloristic inventory, but as a warning to adults not to fritter their life away as if it were a childlike game."[64] Warnings against over a hundred immoral and stupid, foolish and sinful, behaviors (e.g., leading each other by the nose; pissing against the moon, or shitting on the world; pounding one's head against a stone wall; casting roses before swine; and the ubiquitous blind leading the blind, etc.) mock the foibles of various communities of fools that inhabited the era.

Happily, such works of Bruegel have been adapted to animation. Martin Missfeldt put Bruegel's 1559 wood-panel oil painting, *The Netherlandish Proverbs* (1998), into amusing motion in which a character persistently knocks his head against brick walls or a woman cloaks a cuckolded husband, all to the lively "Scheming Weasel" composition by Kevin MacLeod.[65] Scoring the iconography of Bosch and Bruegel with the music of Metallica ("The Call of Ktulu"), Russian artist Andrey Zakirzyanov worked with the National Gallery of Denmark on bringing *Christ Driving the Traders from the Temple*. Scenes as diverse as Jesus whipping the moneychangers (with one man quickly scurrying away with his rooster, only to stumble and lose it) to crawling and crippled beggars, a zoo of donkeys, sheep, and pigs, a baby's bottom being spanked, and a woman having her tooth extracted are brought to kinetic life in a grand illumination.[66]

Even more impressive is Professor Carolina Loyola-Garcia's limited animation of *The Garden of Earthly Delights* (2016), produced at Robert Morris University in which the triptych comes quietly alive with a bird gliding into the Edenic panel on the left, unicorns at a pool, and a monkey riding an elephant. One slips into the central panel where stranger practices are unveiled, a man hangs on a limb and another rides a horse and lifts his head for the delectable pleasure of blueberries. In a bower of adultery, a man offers a woman a giant strawberry and she whispers to him as he nods; while another plucks fresh fruit from an apple tree, tossing it up and down until it bops him on the head. A man with a blueberry head woos a supine woman, his legs kicking back in delight. Blackberries fall on heads and a woman sticks flowers into the rear of a bending fellow. As moments of erotic play become more bizarre, the bluebird of happiness flies across the landscape into the third, far right, panel of hell. Animals evolving out of the sea, triple-headed or encased in an eggshell, crawl upon the land where strange, diabolical creatures roam. Giant serrated knives cut giant human ears; a sword impales a man; dragon monsters eat a knight alive; others flounder in a sea of darkness. A huge bird devours a man while another vomits in the pit. Finally, the camera pulls out to scan the triune landscape.[67] The doodles and drolleries of the margins of medieval manuscripts come to life, mostly as grotesqueries, inviting spectators into a game of riddles to interpret, many seemingly as cautionary tales against perverse sexuality. In his critical studies, Stefan Fischer sees many of Bosch's characters whipped up in lust, with the healthy fecundity of cherries, strawberries, raspberries, and grapes. In contrast, one sees a catalogue of deviant sins performed by lewd grillos and depraved hybrid creatures heading toward the consequences of hell.

Most notably, Antoine Roegiers' impressive exhibition of his series of seven ink-on-paper animated films of *Les Sept péchés capitaux* (*The Seven Deadly Sins*, 2011) begins with a crawling creature, then an army of grillos, with horns and shields (an amphibious two-legged man with a knife inserted in his hat) run along. A hybrid animal donning a mitre rides a snail.[68] The brightly colored peacock of Pride/*Superbia* flashes purple, blue, and yellow; while hair washing and face massaging expose the vanity of human flesh.[69] One man begs for objects and then takes them to a house of money. People smash at shells to gather small pieces, while a big fish eats a little fish, subsequently killed in turn. Clerics and wanton women cavort while a purple-cloaked man with a bagpipe leads a religious man riding a skeletal horse. A couple hump in an adultery tree. An art-video presentation installs each sin, exposing the general folly of the human being. Roegiers' multi-paneled animation of the *Temptation of St. Anthony* follows suit with the saint sitting in the desert writing, while devils appear tempting him with women and mocking him with flagellating brush. Fish-head and chicken-legged creatures assault him, even as a *Géant* peasant destroys a ship of passengers and fornicates with an empty house. Yet, his disciples carry the praying saint to safety with a curtain drawn across the Flemish landscape to restore the hope of normalcy and sanity.[70]

Various cartoons footnote the fantastical work of both Bosch and Bruegel on the *Seven Deadly Sins* (1558), displaying uncanny and bizarre creatures. They appear, along with Salvador Dali–inspired images, in Bob Clampett's *Porky in Wackyland* (1938). ("It can happen here."). Dissimilar parts combine in crazy and seemingly nonsensical metaphors. They also exist in more terrifying forms in animated films like Paul Berry's *Sandman* (1991), Disney's

Night on Bald Mountain (1941), and Ladislav Starewicz's comically horrific devil's party in *The Mascot* (1933). Bruegel's *The Fall of the Devil Angels* (1562) offers a prologue for how these grotesque creatures metamorphosed and emerged out of the shadows of art.

In a Russian animated film by Valeriy Ugarov, *The Caliph Stork* (1981), images of Bosch and Bruegel populate a classic Arabian fairy tale (figure 2.5). The powder of an evil magician's snuffbox enables a person to utter the word "Mutador," and change into any animal and understand its language. However, the subject must understand when in such a metamorphosis, if one laughs, he would forget the magic word and remain the animal forever. The young noble looks out at storks, watching how they dance, swallow frogs, and laugh. He envies them. Yet he imagines becoming a fish or a spider, interacting with various creatures. So tricked by the magician in disguise, the wealthy young Caliph chooses to become a stork. However, he meets a playful and lighthearted Lady Stork, who charms him so much that he laughs with her and finds himself cursed. Having laughed, he forgets the magic word and is condemned to this bewitched state. He comes upon an enchanted salamander who has also been cursed by an evil magician named Miszra. They travel together to the conjurer's place in the desert, a dead tree, passing creatures out of Bosch or Bruegel's weird worlds. A giant sinkhole swallows them down into the sands, past rock-like corpses, into the darkness. They find the palace of the evil vivisectionist conjurer, who like a stunted Dr. Moreau, experimented on animals and humans to create monsters. However, the salamander, who is revealed as a fairy princess, enables the young Caliph to hear the word and be rescued by speaking it. The disobedience of one action, the laugh, with its dire consequences, finds forgiveness in the confession of the word.

The Dutch painted parables and fables of laughter in their golden age. Hendrick Goltzius' mischievously painted *Unequal Couple* (1614) presents an ugly wrinkled old crone, holding a bag of gold in her lap. She cradles a young semi-nude man who rejects her. Lust knows no age limit. One typical image based on the comic work of Cornelis Saftleven (1768) appears in *Who Sues for a Cow*, showing that while "two farmers fight over a cow, the animal is being milked by a laughing lawyer in his robes, sitting on his law books."[71]

Two closing artists deserve mention in charting a trail toward the animated film parable: the British William Hogarth mapped out cautionary comic-strip sets of "modern moral subjects" notably in *A Rake's Progress* (1735), *Industry and Idleness* (1747), *Marriage A-la-Mode* (1753), and *The Four Stages of Cruelty* (1751). *The New York Times* likened his satirical visual literature as more akin to soap operas than parables, but they function as the latter, inviting one to follow the trajectory of vices.[72] A consuming public would purchase these commercialized engravings.[73]

Figure 2.5 In Valeriy Ugarov's *The Caliph Stork* (1981), a Curse Awaits Those Who Laugh. *Source*: Screenshot taken by the author.

Actor David Garrick's inscription for Hogarth's tombstone aptly captured his gift to the animated film parable. Saying farewell to this great painter, Garrick eulogized that Hogarth "reach'd the noblest point of Art / Whose pictur'd Morals charm the Mind / And through the Eye correct the Heart." Hogarth gave us moral etchings, prints, and lithographs that brought forth narratives of the bad life: *The Rake's Progress* or a *Harlot's Progress* (1731) advance moral tales and clever parables that literally show more than some verbal admonitions to be good. A logical extension of these scenes of moral parable, of a modern method of sequencing his art, prepared the template of storyboards for the animated film, with visual images appearing twenty-four times a second.

Both the telling of oral parables and the seeing of visual parables come together with technology at the end of the nineteenth century. Moving pictures did not begin as stories, but as actualities and spectacles showing the marvels of movement and showmanship. The Lumière brothers documented ordinary events from workers leaving a factory to the feeding of a baby. Georges Méliès would perform his wondrous and comic theatrical magic acts for a film. A precursor to these moving visual shows occurred back in 1646, when Jesuit Father Athanasius Kircher developed his magic lantern. His experiments with projecting phantoms and fleeting images not only sparked the curiosity and admiration of his fellow monks, but his conjuring up images of ghosts and devils also brought down the wrath and displeasure of his superiors. Like any astute academic, threatened with ex-communication, exorcism, loss of tenure, or worse, he quickly realized the dilemma of all academics that he must publish or perish. He explained his work in *Ars magna lucis et umbrae*, *The Great Art of Light and Shadow*, lest some inquisitor takes too robust a curiosity in his life and writings.[74] His influential work sought to explain the marvels of the natural sciences, of light, mirrors, and sundials, and to demonstrate how God's designs enabled him to trick the eye and play with vision through the *camera obscura* and magic lantern.

After the Episcopal priest and amateur chemist, the Reverend Hannibal Goodwin, developed flexible, transparent celluloid in 1885, the move to incorporate magic lanterns and stereopticons for church worship burgeoned. By the end of the century, churches and theaters exhibited numerous photoplays on Passion Plays of the life of Jesus, shot everywhere from the Holy Land and Oberammergau, Austria, to rooftops in New Jersey. By 1898 a traveling evangelist and journalist, Colonel Henry Hadley prophesied that movies were soon to be "the best teachers and preachers in the history of the world."[75] A preaching cinema would move toward telling parables, especially as moving pictures were originally only one reel long. However, the early cinema is what film historian Tom Gunning called a "cinema of attractions," directly "solicit[ing] spectator attention, inciting visual curiosity, and supplying pleasure through an exciting spectacle."[76] By the turn of the first decade, true narratives emerged, taming the attractions for a more sensational cinema in fantastic crime thrillers and ancient-world spectacles like Bible stories.[77]

While some saw the stories told in this modern medium as "a school of vice and crime, offering trips to hell for a nickel," others saw the potential for parables of virtue.[78] As early as 1911, the Reverend Herbert Jump justified the use of film in the church as a religious tool by appealing to Jesus' use of parables. He lambasted the tendency of sermons and religious discourse to be "dull" and thus recommended the use of moving pictures. In particular, he featured the dramatic story of the Good Samaritan (Luke 10:30–37), arguing that it had much in common with movies of the day and could easily be adapted as a thrilling moving picture. First, both the parable and contemporary films were taken from contemporary culture and, like the movies, the parable was not explicitly religious in its telling. Second, both parables and moving pictures excited their audiences, and thus, became remarkably interesting, "even to the morally sluggish."[79] Third, both had realistic and morally negative features in them, portraying religious leaders as villains and letting the bandits get away free at the end of the story. Finally, Jump argued, the silent moving pictures were true to life and could both exhibit the heart of the Gospel and, like the parable, could confront and challenge their spectators.

Many scholars see feature films as parables. Robert Palma exegeted theological parables within director Paul Schrader's various films such as *Taxi Driver*, revealing how Schrader wrestled with identifying elements of human mystery through the everyday, disparity, and a bit of stasis.[80] Film critic Christopher Deacy insightfully probed how other contemporary films function religious parables in exploring the moral values of Western culture. He argued that such films are "capable of engulfing and overwhelming—even transforming the audience." He differentiated the parable from myth, in that the former aims "to provoke us, challenge us, and transform us, reminding us of our limits and limitations, and laying the groundwork for the possibility of transcendence." For Deacy, film parables are "human renderings and allegories of stories that encapsulate, stimulate, and pave the way for transcendental insight."[81]

However, while feature films offer insights into the human heart, they fall short of being cinematic parables. Feature films, so astutely analyzed, lack one thing to be exemplars of a parable: *brevity*. As features, they are not concise.[82] Even the excellent scholarly works of Annalee Ward and Christopher Heard's focus on animated *feature* films (e.g., *The Lion King*, *Prince of Egypt*).[83] Hope for finding the authentic cinematic parable arrives in the enduring and succinct category of the short animated film.[84] Parables are by nature brief narratives, metaphors, relating in as short a space as possible, a story with a double meaning, teasing viewers into figuring out the fiddles. Films in the garb of a parable will follow four rules. They will be brief. They will be compelling (exciting), inviting a fresh angle. They will hint at some spiritual truth indirectly, breaking through defenses and skepticism. Finally, working subversively, these stories will make a difference, undermining dull attitudes, disorienting, and provoking (reorienting) fresh meanings.[85] As such, parables challenge and perhaps even transform their audience. It is not their content, but their effect that matters most.

As a way of explaining how the short animated film works more like a parable, experimental filmmaker Stan Brakhage articulates how such visual arts enable one "to *see differently*. An implicit proposal is made that seeing within a ritualized setting allows for a transformation of personal identity and that type of seeing is endemic to religious practice itself."[86] The animated religious parable enables one to *see differently*, even as one watches cartoons about the seven deadly sins and finds them more like mirrors than windows.

From St. John of Damascus through Bosch and Bruegel, the visual arts effectively wedded moral and religious purposes with the saucy entertainment of parables and fables, and often with humor.[87] Then it was time to make those cartoon images move.

NOTES

1. One of the professional pleasures of my academic life was to be invited twice to meet with Jeffrey Katzenberg during the production stages of *The Prince of Egypt*. Whether my comments altered the process ["Religion: Mixed Reviews" *Los Angeles*

Times (February 6, 1999), B2-B9], the opportunity to share in the film's development was a sheer delight.

2. Lubbock, John, *Storytelling in Christian Art from Giotto to Donatello* (Yale University Press, 2006), 39–84.

3. Correspondence with Professor Joyce Howell (July 29, 2020). See also Baxandall, Michael, *Giotto and the Orators* (Oxford University Press, 1986).

4. Ibid., 270.

5. Postman, Neil, *Amusing Ourselves to Death* (Viking, 1985), 15.

6. Zoltan Kovecses, "Metaphor and Parable" 35–46 and Stoellger, Philipp, "Living Images and Images We Live By: What Does It Mean to Become a Living Image?" in *Beyond Words: Pictures, Parables, Paradoxes*, eds. András Benedek and Kristóf Nyíri (Peter Lang, 2015), 17–34.

7. Thiselton, Anthony C., *The Power of Pictures in Christian Thought: The Use and Abuse of Images in the Bible and Theology* (SPCK, 2018).

8. Jensen, Robin M. and Mark D. Ellison, *The Routledge Handbook of Early Christian Art* (Routledge, 2018), 3.

9. Ibid.

10. Along with John of Damascus, Leslie Brubaker points to a Cappadocian father ally, Gregory of Naziansus, *Vision and Meaning in Ninth-Century Byzantium: Image as Exegesis in the Homilies of Gregory of Nazianzus* (Cambridge University Press, 1999). It illustrates such ninth-century miniature images as Job on his dung heap, "Besellel (*sic*) and the sanctuary" and "Ezekiel in the valley of the dry bones." Brubaker points out how pictures might serve as scripture as with the Orthodox tradition of Nikephoros averring that anyone "who accepts the written account will necessarily accept the pictures as well." (48)

11. The blessing of the Orthodox aesthetics could be found in how The *Book of Common Prayer* celebrates January 29 as the lesser feast day of the monk and icon writer Andrei Rublev, who, "inspired by the Holy Spirit, provided a window into heaven for generations to come, revealing the majesty and mystery of the holy and blessed Trinity." Influenced by the mystical and iconic tradition of Rublev and the Russian Orthodox Church, the father of Russian animation, Alexander Krolikov, created his *Slivnoy Bachok Isportilsa* (1912) as a "moving spiritual essay on forgiveness in which primitive anaglyphs fall to earth from the night sky." In his *Zakat* (1922), Krolikov conflated the suffering and joy of an infant brother's death with reference to Schiller's "kurz ist der Schmerz, und ewig ist die Freude." The pain is short and the joy is eternal. See Pluie-Toile, P., "The Influence of Religion on Early European Animation," *Animation World* (April 1977), 42–43.

12. St. John of Damascus, *On the Divine Images* (trans. David Anderson) (St. Vladimir's Seminary Press, 1994), 24; John of Damascus quoted St. Basil in pointing out that "both painters of words and painters of pictures illustrate valor in battle; the former by the art of rhetoric; the latter by clever use of the brush, and both encourage everyone to be brave. A spoken account edifies the ear, while a silent picture induces imitation" (68–69).

13. *Exodus* 31: 2–5.

14. St. John, op. cit. 25; However, their loathsome idolatry does not make the Christian veneration of images wrong. "Just because the pagans used them in a foul way is no reason to object to our pious practice." (32) One must give unto Caesar what is Caesar's and to God what is God's, namely the image of God, oneself.

15. Ibid., 39.

16. Ibid., 21.

17. Gombrich, E. H., *The Story of Art* (Phaidon Press Ltd., 1972), 130.

18. Saint Bonaventura. Liber III, *Sententiarum*: Dist. IX, Art. I, Quaestio II, *Opera Theologica Selecta* (Florence, 1941), 194; While uneducated people could not read books, they could read images on a wall. Poet Francois Villon rhapsodized on this experience in verses written for his mother in the mid-fifteenth century: "I am a woman, poor and old,/Quite ignorant, I cannot read./They showed me in my village church/A painted Paradise with harps,/And Hell where the damned souls are boiled./One gives me joy, the other frightens me." Gombrich, 130.

19. St. Thomas Aquinas echoed Bonaventura: "The instruction of the unlettered, who might learn from them as if from books; second, so that the mystery of the Incarnation and the examples of the saints might remain more firmly in our memory by being daily represented to our eyes; and third, to excite the emotions which are more effectively aroused by things seen than by things heard." *Commentarium super libros sententiarum: Commentum in librum* III dist. 9, art. 2. qu. 2. See also Michael Baxandall's *Painting and Experience in Fifteenth-Century Italy: A Primer in the Social History of Pictorial Style* (Oxford University Press, 1972), 41 and *Presence: The Inherence of the Prototype within Images and Other Objects* (ed. Robert Maniura) (Ashgate Publishing, 2006), 59fn10.

20. Gregory the Great *Lib. IX, Epistola LII Ad Secundinum* in PL 77, cols. 990–91. Cited in David Freedberg's *The Power of Images: Studies in the History and Theory of Response* (University of Chicago Press, 1989), 470 fn9. Dionysius Areopagaticus also emphasized how the cult of images enabled meditation: "We are led up, as far as possible, through visible images to a contemplation of the divine." *De ecclesia hierarchia*, 1.2 (trans. by Ernst Kitzinger) (1952), 137–138.

21. See Chazelle, Celia, "Pictures, Books, and the Illiterate: Pope Gregory I's Letters to Serenus of Marseilles," *Word and Image* 6:2 (April–June 1990), 138–153.

22. As the scriptures (2 *Corinthians* 4:4) indicated, Jesus Christ was the image of the Father. Thus, the Council declared that one could "render icons the veneration of honor (*proskune-sis*), not true worship (*latreia*) of our faith which is due to the divine nature." Such an honor shown to the icon is conveyed to its prototype, passing to the One depicted. So Christ could be worshipped as God, just as Mary and the saints could receive their own due veneration.

23. See Pelikan, Jaroslav, *Imago Dei* (Princeton University Press, 1990) and Ousepensky, Leonid *Theology of the Icon: Volumes I and II* (trans. Anthony Gythiel) (St. Vladimir's Seminary Press, 1992).

24. Gombrich, op. cit. (1972), 152; See also Lindvall, Terry, "Images Have Consequences," in *Critical Thinking and the Bible in the New Age of Media*, ed. Charles Ess (University Press, 2004), 216.

25. Exploring the communication of faith through Christian Art, Eileen M. Daily contrasts the rational and linear mode of reading literature as opposed to the reading of painterly images. Daily, Eileen M., *Beyond the Written Word: Exploring Faith through Christian Art* (St. Mary's Press, 2005).

26. Of course, we also have Mae West's aphorisms on temptation: "Between two evils, I always pick the one I never tried before." And "When women go wrong, men go right after them." But I digress.

27. Nelson, Robert, S. and Kristen, M. Collins, *Holy Image and Hallowed Ground: Icons from Sinai* (J. Paul Getty Museum, 2006).

28. In terms of a strategic rhetorical design, the tapestry of Jesus giving Peter the keys to the Kingdom was assuredly a salient document during the early days of the Protestant Reformation.

29. Williams, Anne L., *Satire, Veneration, and St. Joseph in Art, c. 1300–1550* (Amsterdam University Press, 2019) argues, quite convincingly, that humor and satire around the character of St. Joseph played a significant role in sacred art. Laughter was not only a means of devotion and teaching, but offered a recreational sense of holy play.

30. Beautifully adapted into the feature film, *Secret of Kells* (Tomm Moore, Nora Twomey, 2009).

31. Irenaeus, *Adversus Haereses (Against Heresies XI)* Other saints were awarded apt emblems as well, with iconic images being the sword of St. Paul, the anchor of St. Clement, the lion of St. Jerome, and the golf clubs of St. Andrew.

32. Menestrier, Claude-Francois, *L'art des emblemes* (1662) cited in Alciati, (8): "Natural figures are the images of things with which we are familiar, such as an eagle, a lion, a rock, a river. Symbolic figures are the symbols or hieroglyphs denoting certain things, such as the Caduceus of Mercury, the Horns of Plenty, etc. Poetic figures are images belonging to virtues, vices, passions and other moral, civic and spiritual things which do not submit to the senses" (basically representing moral or spiritual states such as virtue, the soul, life, honor, glory, etc.).

33. Mori, Yoko, "The World of Bruegel in Black and White," http://www.yoko-mori-bruegel.jp/resources/pdf/black&white_01.pdf (Accessed February 3, 2020), 10–11.

34. Camille, Michael, *Image on the Edge: The Margins of Medieval Art* (Harvard University Press, 1992); Randall, Lillian, "Exempla and Their Influence," *Images in the Margins of Gothic Manuscripts* (Berkeley, 1966).

35. See Adam Kern's *Manga from the Floating World* (Harvard UP, 2006).

36. Lord, Victoria, "The Medieval Scribe and the Art of Writing," *Ultimate History Project*, http://ultimatehistoryproject.com/the-medieval-scribe.html (Accessed January 11, 2020).

37. Gaier, Ulrich, "Sebastian Brant's 'Narrenschiff' and the Humanists," *PMLA* 83:2 (May, 1968), 266.

38. Ozment, Steven, *The Serpent and the Lamb: Cranach, Luther, and the Making of the* Reformation (Yale University Press, 2011), 18, 122.

39. Grosvenor, Bendor, "Cranach's role in the Reformation," *Art History News* (October 31, 2016), https://www.arthistorynews.com/articles/4226_Cranachs_role_in

_the_Reformation (Accessed January 9, 2020); Cranach's tombstone in Weimar reads "*pictor celerimus*" (i.e., the swiftest painter).

40. Ehrstine, Glenn, "Theater, Culture, and Community in Reformation Bern: 1523–1555," *Studies in Medieval and Reformation Thought* 85 (Brill, 2002).

41. Noble, Dr. Bonnie, "Lucas Cranach the Elder, *Law and Gospel (Law and Grace)*," in *Smarthistory*, August 9, 2015, https://smarthistory.org/cranach-law-and-gospel-law-and-grace/ (Accessed March 1, 2021).

42. Neale, Fiona, "Lucas Cranach the Elder and Reformation Illustrations," in *Seeing the Reformation: Religion and the Printed Image in Early Modern Europe* (University of Glascow Library, April 30, 2018), https://universityofglasgowlibrary.wordpress.com/2018/04/30/lucas-cranach-the-elder-and-reformation-illustrations/#_ftn2 (Accessed January 9, 2020), 1; See also Frances Carey, ed., *The Apocalypse and the Shape of Things To Come* (University of Toronto Press, 1999), 102.

43. Lehmann, Helmut T. and Eric W. Gritsch (eds.), *Luther's Works* (Fortress Press, 1966), 41:257; See also "Luther Visualized" https://redbrickparsonage.wordpress.com/tag/lucas-cranach/ (Accessed January 9, 2020).

44. One could look at Bosch's *Prodigal Son* and recognize the crisis in the son's temptation to dissolute and desperate living, with an amorous couple, a man urinating, and seven pigs. Yet, one sees on the right side, an invitation to return to the Father, with the wise owl beckoning him to enter the narrow gate, beyond which an oblivious cow waits for the feast to begin. Parable scholars were asked to reflect on how parables might be interpreted in other media. David Gowler pointed to the "deceptively enigmatic *meshalim*" of the parable of the rich young fool in Luke's gospel as seen through Rembrandt's painting of the scenario, showing how the artist's manipulation of light and shadow create a sense of mystery and an invitation to consider how both Jesus and Rembrandt illuminate some things clearly, while other aspects remain obscure, placed (deliberately) in the shadows. Gowler, David B., "The Enthymematic Nature of Parables: A Dialogic Reading of the Parable of the Rich Fool (Luke 12:16–20)," *Review and Expositor* 109:2 (2012), 199–217; I owe all insight of Freudian imagery to my friend and colleague Michael Hall.

45. Pinson, Yona, "Hieronymus Bosch: *Homo viator* at a Crossroads: A New Reading of the Rotterdam tondo," *Artibus et Historiae*, 26:52 (2005), 57–84.

46. Massie, Claudia, "Want your children to love art? Start with Hieronymus Bosch," *The Spectator* (April 23, 2016), https://www.spectator.co.uk/2016/04/want-your-children-to-love-art-start-with-hieronymus-bosch/ (Accessed January 10, 2020).

47. Studio Smack explored such religious themes as sin, temptation, and debauchery in a fallen work in their experiment with Bosch's remarkably brightly colored *Paradise*.

48. https://arthive.com/publications/1816~Bosch_is_on_their_side_10_filmmakers_who_inherited_the_helm_of_Hieronymus_Bosch (Accessed June 9, 2020).

49. Bax, Dirk, *Hieronymus Bosch: His Picture-Writing Deciphered* (CRC Press, 1978); Glum Peter, *The Key to Bosch's "Garden of earthly delights" Found in Allegorical Bible Interpretation* (Chuo-koron Bijutsu Shuppan, 2007). Adam McLean's

website on Bosch has been most illuminating on these texts, https://www.alchemy-website.com/bosch/Index.html (Accessed January 5, 2020).

50. Two other sections of the panel point to Greed in "Death and the Miser" and an "Allegory of Gluttony."

51. Quoted at http://www.openculture.com/2018/11/watch-midnight-parasites-surreal-japanese-animation-set-within-world-hieronymus-boschs-garden-earthly-delights-1972.html (Accessed June 9, 2020).

52. Augustine, *On Christian Doctrine* (Beloved Publishing 2014), 97.

53. He also taught *via negativa*, with an image like his *Death and the Miser*. Based on the 1465 edifying text of *Ars moriendi*, it offers a cautionary tale, where a man dying is attended to by a guardian angel pointing to the crucifix; however, death has already entered and his work is made easy by the help of a lot of little demons hiding about the frame. All the dying man sees is a money bag offered by a devil. Zeri argues that his framing demonstrates a "modernity which we could almost call cinematic." Zeri, Federico *Bosch: The Garden of Earthly Delights* (Bologna: Poligrafici Calderara, 2000), 16, 32.

54. While the uneven *Dante's Inferno: An Animated Epic* looks more like a crude video game of slashing and maiming, with Dante as an erstwhile violent crusader rather than a humble pilgrim, and Beatrice oddly becoming a damsel in distress who has born Dante's stillborn, unbaptized baby, the distorted adaptation of the great literary classic still takes one through the levels of the Inferno to discuss the seven deadly sins and their punishments.

55. Fisher, Stefan, *Hieronymus Bosch: The Complete Works* (Cologne, 2013).

56. Kavaler, Ethan Matt, *Parables of Order and Enterprise* (Cambridge UP, 1999).

57. See Koerner, Joseph Leo, *Bosch & Bruegel: From Enemy Painting to Everyday Life* (Princeton UP, 2016).

58. Ibid., 257.

59. See Kritsky, Gene and Daniel Mader, "The Insects of Pieter Bruegel the Elder," *American Entomologist* 57: 4 (Winter 2011), 245–251; Hagen, R., *Pieter Bruegel the Elder c. 1525–1569: Peasants, Fools and Demons* (Taschen, 2007); Sullivan, M., "Bruegel's proverbs: art and audience in the northern Renaissance," *Art Bulletin* 73 (1991), 431–466; Sybesma, J., "The reception of Bruegel's Beekeepers: a matter of choice," *Art Bulletin* 73 (1991), 467–478.

60. Gibson, 38.

61. Ibid., 39.

62. Sybesma (1991) cited in Kritsky, Gene and Daniel Mader, "The Insects of Pieter Bruegel the Elder," *American Entomologist* 57: 4 (Winter 2011), 245–251; See also Ortiz, Lucia, "Vices of Life: A Survey of Genre in Bruegel's Seven Deadly Sins" (May 2015). https://static1.squarespace.com/static/57148b46b6aa60f0aa704823/t/589e321b59cc684e62ff2a21/1486762641536/Ortiz-Luci%CC%81a-ARTH496D-Bruegel-SevenDeadlySins.pdf (Accessed January 6, 2020).

63. Cited in Gibson, 35; English critic Roger Fry would stigmatize Bruegel as "essentially an illustrator rather than an artist. He is the counterpart in his day of a great *cartoonist*." (Italics added), 6.

64. Hagen, Rose-Marie and Rainer, *Bruegel: The Complete Paintings* (Taschen, 2000), 32.

65. https://www.youtube.com/watch?v=2droERRboso (Accessed February 3, 2020).

66. https://www.youtube.com/watch?v=wQTBaVHEdf4 (Accessed February 4, 2020).

67. https://www.youtube.com/watch?v=ruOhtCZyX7A (Accessed February 3, 2020).

68. https://www.youtube.com/watch?v=scNxBy5cZ98 (Accessed February 3, 2020).

69. The Bible Project animated the vanity, futility, vapor, or *hevel* of human existence in its edifying and intriguing summary of *The Book of Ecclesiastes* and the meaning of theodicy in *The book of Job* (Jon Collins and Tim Mackie, 2016) at https://www.youtube.com/watch?v=VeUiuSK81-0 and https://www.youtube.com/watch?v=GswSg2ohqmA (Accessed September 6, 2020).

70. Roegiers, *Temptation of St. Anthony* (2008), https://vimeo.com/9465677 (Accessed February 3, 2020).

71. Tummers, Anna, Elmer Kolfin and Jasper Hillegers, *The Art of Laughter: Humour in Dutch Painting of the Golden Age* (Frans Hals Museum, 2018), 123, 141.

72. Hoge, Warren, "18th-Century Bad Boy Who Fathered English Art," *The New York Times* (June 14, 1997).

73. Krysmanski, Bernd W., *Hogarth's Hidden Parts: Satiric Allusion, Erotic Wit, Blasphemous Bawdiness and Dark Humour in Eighteenth-Century English Art* (Georg Olms, 2010).

74. See Godwin, Joscelyn, *Athanasius Kircher: A Renaissance Man and the Quest for Knowledge* (Thames and Hudson, 1979).

75. Ramsaye, Terry, *A Million and One Nights* (Simon and Schuster, 1926), 375.

76. Gunning, Tom, "The Cinema of Attractions: Early Film, Its Spectator, and the Avant-garde." *Wide Angle* 8: 3/4 (Fall 1986), in *Early Cinema: Space, Frame Narrative,* eds. Thomas Elsaesser and Adam Barker (British Film Institute, 1990), 58.

77. Christie, Ian, "The Visible and the Invisible: From 'Tricks' to 'Effects,'" *Early Popular Visual Culture* 13:2 (2015), 106–112.

78. Crafts, Wilbur F., *National Perils and Hopes* (O. F. M. Barton, 1910), 39.

79. Jump, Herbert, *The Religious Possibilities of the Motion Picture* in Terry Lindvall's *The Silents of God* (Scarecrow Press, 2001), 54–78.

80. Palma, Robert, "Theological Parables in Paul Schrader's Films," *Perspectives* (August/September 2001), 13–15, 18.

81. Deacy, Christopher, "Integration and Rebirth through Confrontation: *Fight Club* and *American Beauty* as Contemporary Religious Parables," *Journal of Contemporary Religion* 17: 1 (2002), 67 (61–73); Pastor Edward N. McNulty viewed feature films as *Visual Parables*, in his monthly on-line publication dedicated to exploring "Film & Faith in Dialogue." https://readthespirit.com/visual-parables/ (Accessed January 19, 2020).

82. A host of works exploits the idea of feature films as parable. See Kahle, Roger, *Popcorn and Parable* (Augsburg, 1971); Meyer, Janet L., *Visual Parables:*

Engaging the Spiritual Elements of Film (Institute of Southwest Publishing Division, 1997); Hogan, James, *Reel Parables: Life Lessons from Popular Films* (Paulist Press, 2007) and *Reel Parables Revisited: Catholic Truths from Films* (CreateSpace, 2018); Rindge, Matthew S., *Profane Parables: Film and the American Dream* (Baylor University Press, 2017).

83. Ward, Annalee, *Mouse Morality: The Rhetoric of Disney Animated Films* (University of Texas Press, 2002); Heard, Christopher, "Animated Films," in Eric Mazur's *Encyclopedia of Religion and Film* (ABC-CLIO, 2011), 26–31; "Drawing [on] the Text: Biblical Reception in Animated Films," in Rhonda Burnette-Bletsch's *The Bible in Motion: A Handbook of the Bible and Its Reception in Film* Part I (De Gruyter, 2016), 267–283.

84. However, before proceeding one final concern announces itself. British author C. S. Lewis, whose classic children's fantasy, *The Lion, the Witch and the Wardrobe*, was adapted into a mediocre animated feature film (Bill Melendez, 1979), warned that there was "death in the camera." What he meant was that characters and events one meets in reading texts are frozen when they appear in film. The imagination of the spectator dies with this embalmed set of images. See Terry Lindvall and Fraser, Benson "Embalmed Images: C. S. Lewis and the Art of Film" *Inklings* (Spring 2015).

85. Johnston, Robert K., "Film as Parable: What Might This Mean?" in *Doing Theology for the Church: Essays in Honor of Klyne Snodgrass*, eds. Rebekah A. Eklund and John E. Phelan Jr. (Eugene, OR: Wipf & Stock, 2014).

86. Brakhage, Stan, "Metaphors of Vision," *Film Culture* 30 (1963) cited in Brent Plate, S., *Religion, Art, & Visual Culture: A Cross Cultural Reader* (New York: Palgrave, 2002), 13.

87. Klein, Sheri R., "Art and Visual Humor"; Attardo, Salvatore, *Encyclopedia of Humor Studies* (Sage, 2014), 63–68.

Part II

DEAD BRANCHES

THE SEVEN DEADLY SINS

Chapter 3

Sin, Judgment, and Blindness

The Greek word for sin (ἁμαρτία hamartia) means literally to "miss the mark," fatally falling short of or not measuring up to an ideal standard of what God expects of His people. Yet, we don't have to sit in the presence of God to acknowledge sin. All of us know two things. First, we know we should live in a certain way. Secondly, we don't actually live that way. Sin, persistently practiced, wilts into a habit of vice. Yet every vice is born of a virtue. Evil does not exist without a foundation in the good, but as it grows, it distorts, twists, warps, spoils, and ruins the good.

Vice frequently appears with a mask, with a bit of ambiguity. As each has a root in virtue, it can appear as morally camouflaged. A branch of vice attaches itself to a vine of virtue, such as pride pretending to be charitable and making a public show of generosity. The fruit of such an act looks good. However, when the vice disconnects itself from the vine, it becomes a dead branch, only good for fire kindling. Vices may morph into false virtues, as when greed moves into its costume of thrift or unrestrained capitalism. The erosion of virtue can also produce a bad thing that is so insidious, latent, and deceptive that one may even think one is doing good for another. A mother smothering a child with obsessive love and control may well rear a beast. One libertine wag could even twist the scriptures into "*eros* covers a multitude of sins."

If everything created was good, then all manifestations of evil grow out of a good creation. The explanation is that through free will, virtues perverted or practiced to excess can spoil into deadly vices. The varieties of love themselves can be distorted, as C. S. Lewis points out in *The Four Loves*, where the unchecked love of a nation becomes jingoistic and xenophobic. Thus, the art of finding the heart of goodness in the vices is a worthy and laudatory venture; however, to identify the vice as the virtue is not only naïve, but dangerous.

Both Plato and Dante warned about the dangers of reading stories about vice and absorbing their messages uncritically.[1] For those who read of Zeus seducing a young woman, the temptation to lust may be inflamed. Even as Francesca confesses to Dante that when she and her illicit lover, Paolo, read the erotic episodes of Lancelot and Guinevere with "delight," they succumbed and did not refrain from imitating their adultery. There are dangers in reading, hearing, and seeing wicked tales and ribald images, but there are also good lessons to learn.

Historian Walter Gibson points out that "Preachers had long employed exempla, or little exemplary stories, some of them comic, not only to illustrate a point but also to keep their listeners awake."[2] Indeed, Boccaccio justified (however mischievously, we do not know) the often bawdy tales his characters told one another in the *Decameron*. He rationalized that since "the preachments made of friars, to rebuke men of their sins, are nowadays for the most part seen full of quips and cranks and gibes, I conceived that these latter would not sit amiss in my stories written to ease women of melancholy."[3] Yet, his stories faithfully featured sin. To paraphrase him, "if preachers can make tales of sin, so can I." In fact, looking at animated characters as real personalities, scholar David McGowan identifies what he calls the "star disobedience" of a cartoon celebrity. Even Disney's Mickey could be elusive and obstinate and could "sometimes muff a role or a dramatic moment."[4] To put it simply, cartoon stars sin.

Oxford University Press and the New York Public Library joined to produce a very uneven, but illuminating, lecture series on the Seven Deadly Sins. Public intellectual Eric Dyson stressed what St. Augustine saw as the worst sin in *Pride*, tracing how a sense of self-worth or a delight in one's country can become a deadly sin. The practice of hubris leads one to the presumption that one's particular way of thinking or living is fully superior to others and destroys both the individual and every relationship. As Dante dramatized in Purgatory, the proud carry heavy boulders on their backs and walk with their heads to the ground, purged of their own conceit or narcissism.[5]

Sins tend to lead one into blindness. In Jesus' admonition to his disciples, who were often so obtuse they could not understand the simplest of his parables, he acknowledges, even highlights, the obscurity of his teachings. In the gospel of Matthew they ask him why he spoke in parables, he responds enigmatically:

> To you it has been given to know the secrets of the kingdom of heaven, but to them it has not been given. For to those who have, more will be given, and they will have an abundance; but from those who have nothing, even what they

> have will be taken away. The reason I speak to them inparables is that "seeing they do not perceive, and hearing they do not listen, nor do they understand." With them indeed is fulfilled the prophecy of Isaiah that says: "You will indeed listen, but never understand, and you will indeed look, but never perceive. For this people's heart has grown dull, and their ears are hard of hearing, and they have shut their eyes; so that they might not look with their eyes, and listen with their ears, and understand with their heart and turn—and I would heal them. But blessed are your eyes, for they see, and your ears, for they hear."[6]

The focus is upon the ensuing blindness of not only their eyes (and the deafness of their ears), but upon that stubborn resistance to see or hear with their hearts.

A key theological theme in parables is the parting of the broad and narrow roads and their relation to the religious journey, an idea of which Bruegel was well aware. His publisher, Cock, issued a print by Marten van Heemskerck entitled *The Narrow Way to Salvation* (based on Matthew 7:13–14, "Enter by the narrow gate; for the gate is wide and easy that leads to destruction").[7] Likewise, the charge against being spiritually blind fit a corrupt church, with priests who kept concubines and hoarded money and wine, neglecting to feed the poor. Likely to be displayed publically, Bruegel's work on *The Blind Leading the Blind* offered an indictment on all those sects who twisted scripture to fit their self-serving agendas. Yet the care that Bruegel devoted to their faces "emphasizes their humanity and invites pity as they grope their way forward with faces uplifted toward a light they cannot see." Few recognize when they are on the wide way to destruction or blindly heading down into a ditch. One of the most intriguing aspects of Bruegel's art is its ability to arrest one's attention, involve the viewer, and raise questions. He not only creates a satisfying aesthetic experience but also playfully provokes his viewers to think and argue. As art historian Joseph Leo Koerner writes, while every painting by Bruegel can sustain a lifetime of learning, Bruegel "realizes the old saying so concretely that it vanishes into a portrait of life."[8] His image of a roving band of beggars and jongleurs marching toward their destruction becomes a lived parable.

Perhaps no parable is as universally recognized and as potentially both comic and tragic as the aphoristic "the blind leading the blind." Out of the Hindi *Upanishad*, the Buddhist way of knowing of the *Canki Sutta*, the writings of that happy Roman satirist Horace, and the Gospels erupted this enduring metaphor of morality, a parallel epigram and moral palindrome warning about the blind leading the blind. In addition to Bruegel (1568), such artists as Bosch (1516) David Teniers the Younger (1655), Jacopo Tintoretto (1767), and too many moderns to list have visually interpreted this ancient proverb. Even the ancient Mick Jagger composed lyrics for a song on blindness for the film, *Alfie* (2004) and Mumford and Sons released the song, "Blind

Leading the Blind" (2019). As an intercultural and trans-historical metaphor, the disability refers more to spiritual negligence than physical affliction. One stupidly follows his or her own way, or one obeys without thinking, leading to the ditches of life. While semioticians are more interested in interpreting signs and symbols (i.e., the blindness and the ditch), the rhetorician studies how an artist or musician manipulates those elements to persuade an audience.

The parable and the fable come together with variations on this theme. A sixteenth-century poem by Johann Theodor de Bry extends this into "The Blind Man and the Lame."

A blind man was carrying a lame man on his back,
And everything was going well, everything's on track,
When the blind man decides to take it into his head
That he needn't listen to all that the lame man said.
"This stick I have will guide the two of us safe," said he,
And though warned by the lame man, he plowed into a tree.
On they proceeded; the lame man now warned of a brook.
The two survived, but their possessions a soaking took.
At last the blind man ignored the warning of a drop,
And that was to turn out their final and fatal stop.
Which of the two travelers, you may ask, was to blame?
Why, 'twas both the heedless blind man and the trusting lame.[9]

Similarly, Krasicki's parable "The Blind Man and the Lame" does not employ the typical anthropomorphism that characterizes his fables. Nevertheless, according to Czelaw Milosz, while his parables "are drawn from more quotidian human life" than his fables, both "point to elegant moral lessons" for his readers.[10] Blindness stands as a metaphor for obtuseness. The Buddha employed the simile of blind men to suggest those led astray by their own desires.[11] He paints the drama of a king bringing in an elephant for several blind men to describe. Holding on to different aspects of the beast, they dispute and begin to fight with each other (perversely entertaining the king). Buddha explains his tale by exposing the bias of various teachers and preachers who remain ignorant, and therefore blind. "Just so are these preachers and scholars holding various views blind and unable to see. In their ignorance they are by nature quarrelsome, wrangling, and disputatious, each maintaining reality is thus and thus." The quarreling monks cling to their "perception" and wrangle with each other, even though they only see one side of the elephant. One imagines a herd of surly Mr. Magoos bickering with each other.

Whazzat? (1975), Arthur P. Pierson's clay-animated parable of the six blind men and an elephant, revived the ancient Indian and Arabic folk tale. Six men stumble upon an elephant with each interpreting a different aspect of the strange creature (i.e., its tail, ears, tusks, trunk, etc.). Dealing with adapting literature into short films for children, Maureen Gaffney argues that such a film communicates "our inability to understand the nature of reality since each person experiences only a part of it."[12] After working together to cross a chasm, the blind men cooperate (although one slowpoke almost endangers them all) as they negotiate their way around this large unknown creature. Each uses their limited perception, but remain blind to the larger meaning. Isaac Bashevis Singer once warned against didacticism in storytelling as "once a [folk] story is made to teach, one can foresee what it is going to say."[13] But parables have a way of exploding our perceptions (even the didactic ones). Nineteenth-century American satirist and poet, John Godfrey Saxe, adapted this tale as "The Six Men of Indostan" to identify the elephant as a metaphor for God, with the company of blind men representing various religious traditions. Their loud disputations averred that each was in the right ("and all were in the wrong!"). The moral concluded that as often in theological wars, the disputant "rail on in utter ignorance/of what each other man,/ And prate about an Elephant/Not one of them has seen!"

The animated film sparks discussion and debate, but it is still about the elephant in the room. Like the blind men, various cartoon characters remain oblivious to their own predicaments and the jams into which they wander. Characters blind to experience, logic, and wisdom, such as the proud Wiley Coyote and sadistic Tom the Cat, relentlessly and foolishly follow their own ways into the ditches they dig for themselves. One pithy short by Gaëtan Borde, *Dinosaure d"Aveugle* (2014), plays with the notion of a pet dinosaur of a blind man, who takes his creature out for a walk. However, the dinosaur turns out to be blind as well, and echoing the hilarious ending of Marv Newland's classic *Bambi Meets Godzilla* (1969), inadvertently crushes the blind man. The state of blindness equates to a spiritual obliviousness to all the elephants and dinosaurs of our lives.

The challenges of *Blind Vaysha* (Theodore Ushev, 2016) are time-oriented. Out of her left blue eye and right brown eye, she sees only the past and the future, respectively. She remains unfortunately blind to her present reality, with regrets about the past and anxieties about the future. The film raised the dilemma of whether we look at the world with either eye of Vaysha the Blind or with a sense of realism. With such revelatory or "poetic metaphors," animated parables provoke thought and decision more than they illustrate beliefs. While the illustrative parable shows general moral principles, the metaphoric parable transcends typical argumentative analysis and confronts the listener with a less obvious strategy. It involves that direct personal appeal and challenge. Although seemingly amusing, the parables are, at their cores, quite disturbing. They offer a topsy-turvy view of the world, inviting the listener to stand upon his or her head, open one's eyes, or turn around one's way of thinking, literally, to repent. Questions raised by Ushev's film challenge one's obsession with the past or worry about the future rather than cultivating an appreciation for living fully in the present.

Marek Skrobecki's ambiguous *Danny Boy* (2010) can be read both as a tribute to the idea that love is (or must become) blind or to the stupidity of conformity (figure 3.1). Reminiscent of Saramago's novel *Blindness*, where sightlessness strikes everyone but one woman, this town teems with headless people, except for one curly, black-haired boy who possesses a head and eyes. He watches a bank robber indiscriminately shoot down innocent citizens and a woman orders an ice cream cone only to splat it on her ample bosom. The dark comic absurdity unravels with people continually bumping into light poles, hit by cars, which careen into each other and then crash, all of which recount the proverbial ditch of the blind men. Most village idiots stagger about like the Minister of Silly Walks, John Cleese. With a slapstick touch of naiveté, the boy meets a headless woman who reaches out to him. He takes her to a silent movie theater where an animated cartoon about a headless chicken projects upside down. Another woman stuffs popcorn into her empty neck.

When the boy gives his woman a bouquet of flowers, she discovers that he has a head and flees in horror. He returns home to construct a guillotine and proceeds to chop his own head off, at which point the funereal song "Danny Boy" appears. Blood splatters and his detached head rolls into a corner with his eyes slowly shutting. He stumbles through the foggy streets, picking up a cane from a dead cripple, and finds his beloved. With his Chaplinesque twirl of the cane, they walk off into the sunset, as a plane ominously hits a twin tower in the background. Whether one loses one's head over romantic

Figure 3.1 Marek Skrobecki's Darkly Ambiguous *Danny Boy* (2010) Invites Variable Interpretations. *Source*: Screenshot taken by the author.

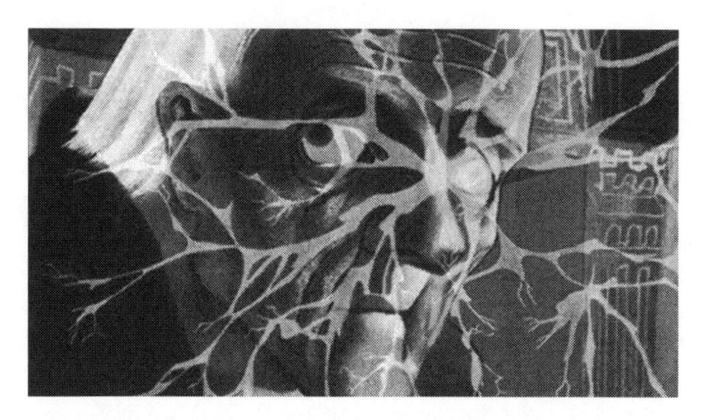

Figure 3.2 Edgar Allen Poe's Classic *The Tell-Tale Heart* (Ted Parmelee, 1953) Inflames the Haunting Guilt of Sin. *Source*: Screenshot taken by the author.

attachments or that love requires one to give up one's reason, the cartoon suggests that the blind will find and follow each other. However, the tasty obscurity of the narrative requires a moral engagement to interpret the actions of a character facing a romantic and moral dilemma. His decision will have both intended and unintended consequences, in that he wins the woman, but he loses his head. Blindly, however, he leads her toward the crash site where nothing good awaits them.

Shades of sin and its surreal consequences haunt UPA's stylish adaptation of Edgar Allen Poe's *The Tell-Tale Heart* (Ted Parmelee, 1953) (figure 3.2). The Academy Award–nominated cartoon plunges a deranged murderer into the guilty aftermath of his actions of killing his landlord because of his "evil vulture eye." Receiving an X-rating from the British Board of Film Censors at the time, the short cartoon, narrated by the menacing voice of actor James Mason, marks a man's descent into madness as he hears the incessant heartbeat of his victim whom he buried under his floorboards. With the foreboding feeling of Dostoyevsky's *Crime and Punishment*, the film warns of the reverberation of willing to harm another human being and of a descent into madness. The wondrously stylized parable that *Life* magazine opined as "movie landmark" diagnoses the vexing horrors of a guilty conscience.[14] What makes it particularly salient and mesmerizing is the focus on the eye of the old man, as in the oracular center of Bosch's tabletop. At the center is the eye that one cannot escape.[15]

In his apologetic work *Orthodoxy*, G. K. Chesterton observed that the idea of original sin is the "only empirically verifiable" theological doctrine of the church. The proof is in every human heart, that each one sins and cannot fully conquer sin. The image of one's vices running out of control mushrooms in Ian Eames' *The Beard* (1978). Sin corrupts, ruins, and perverts the natural body as much as the soul. Unbridled, natural inclinations, desires, and the flesh can transport one to heights of ecstasy, but then they begin to demand one's full attention, turning increasingly nightmarish. In traditional catechism, the stomach was made for the pleasures of food and the sexual organs for the rapture of marital intercourse; however, both can slide into immorality. Both can go twisted or tyrannical.

The Beard, like Bill Plympton's sillier *Nosehair* (1994), depicts a man's metaphorical struggle against his own nature. In Plympton's cartoon, the man tries to shake a thick follicle from his nose, plucking at it, pulling it, as it refuses to go. That thin line dangling from his nostril, attached like an umbilical cord to his brain, still sprouts with unrestrained abandon. He bites it off only to see it seek restitution by invading his life in numerous ways and designs, like a Steinberg doodle, as a woman's body, a fire hose, a tongue, steps, a fish line and hook, an obese trapeze artist, and copulating lines. The preening man attempting to control his nature and groom it for respectable presentation does not realize that he himself is "ungroomable." Sin has distorted even nasal hairs that go their own way.

Likewise, in Eames' existential parable of *The Beard*, a man stands in front of a run-down bathroom, a dozen razors at his feet, as he hums and shaves. A razor blade repeatedly shaves his neck as a faucet incessantly drops and plops in the sink (figure 3.3). The tedious process continues until suddenly, a red beard sprouts and encircles the man. A man should be able to control his own facial hair, but this long scratchy, serpentine beard takes on a life of its own, knocking him in the stomach and bopping him on his head. It soon encompasses him as in a cocoon. The beard takes on an unrelieved anger and its line finally cuts the man in two halves. The hair dangles the man like a puppet on a string kicking himself in the face, and twisting him up, casting him aside. How can one control the rampant power of one's depraved hairs? What can save the self from natural instincts gone feral? The ink-on-paper animated film cautions against letting the shaggy parasite take over its host; yet it shows that one cannot simply save oneself from such inner hirsute demons. Like any vice, its twisted natural power wreaks vengeance upon its victim; it destroys its host. Eames explained that "the Beard is my life. The tap keeps dripping; the sun keeps setting. The Beard keeps growing. I use an electric shaver so I'm one step ahead, for now . . ."

Cartoon Brew's Amid Amidi insightfully connects an artist wrestling with his work with the animated man's battling his own intransigent beard.[16] From his innovative airbrushed work with Pink Floyd, Emes now offers a scratchy and gritty parable, almost tactile, in illumining not only the artist with his art, but of a man "kicking against the pricks" of his soul. If one cannot tame one's own hair, what can one control in life?

After escaping temptation with a married woman in Constantinople, Evagrius of Pontus (345–399), called a group of monks to live in harmony

Figure 3.3 In Ian Eames' *The Beard* (1978), Fallen Human Nature Goes Ballistic with Hair Follicles. *Source*: Screenshot taken by the author.

and holiness in the Egyptian desert. Writing a collection of guiding rules in his *Prakitos*, Evagrius challenged this community to seek a "purity of heart" so that they might "see God." One did so by chasing out passions or shaving away eight phantasms (or just evil thoughts, *logismoi*, or perhaps eight proliferating hairs of the beard) that would cloud the mind and lead monks astray. This master of monastic pedagogy, Evagrius, and later his disciple John Cassian (360–434), identified eight main obstacles swirling out of self-love: gluttony, pride (*hubris*), apathy and sloth (*acedia*), sadness (*tristitia*), anger (wrath), greed (avarice), lust (fornication), vainglory (boasting). Envy would later supplant sadness and vainglory.[17] The hope that seclusion would rid them of demons and magnify their intimacy with God was naïve. The darkness of their own contentious hearts grew as rampantly as their beards. (Curiously, he named the two greatest temptations as bishops and women, and for what it is worth, he was right about one of them.)[18]

Cassian bequeathed the schemata to Pope Gregory the Great, who with his fascination with sevens (Will Willimon calls it his *Hebdomania*) reduced the list of (*septem principalia vitia*) principle or cardinal vices to the seven that dominate medieval stories and art.[19] They are interconnected and generative, giving birth to one another. For example, "the devil, through envy, inflicted the wound of pride on healthful man in Paradise." On his commentary on the *Moralia of Job*, Gregory sticks it to the proud person with a simple riddle: "Will the rhinoceros be willing to serve thee?" Like the hairs of the beard, sins combine, intertwine, and compound one another in creating a mess.

The inspiration (if one can call it that) behind all these vices, however, saunters in with the devil, who alternatively disguises and advertises himself throughout history. Yet he incites spiritual battles for the common pilgrim and the ordinary settler. In the fifth century, Prudentius personified virtues as champion women and vices as demonic monsters in his gruesome allegorical poem, *Psychomachia* ("war of the soul"). Expanding upon St. Paul's admonition to put on the whole armor of God, Prudentius fleshes out *Psychomachia* as seven intense battles of the soul over these sins. In this instructional graphic comic book, Lowliness beheads Pride (who falls into a ditch dug by Deceit); Chastity spears Lust (in an apt Freudian trope). On the battlefield, a monstrous Greed stuffs money and plundered booty under her robe and then must fight Reason, Good Works, and Thrift. Patience waits out a foaming Wrath until it commits suicide. Greed cunningly follows the brutal battles of other souls that have been defeated, and then scavenges all the abandoned weapons, garments, and jewels, stealing from the dead and the debris of war. "Her young, like ravenous wolves, prowl across the field."[20] She deviously disguises herself as Thrift, changing her name to hoodwink good men as she pretends that she is providing for her children while merely hoarding as a miserable miser. Prudentius combines the gladiatorial excesses of his day with Christian virtue, visualizing the slaughter and the waste of this context as a public display.[21]

Such battles with evil are precursors to their animated adaptations. Edmund Spenser's *Faerie Queen* assembles all the vices together at Lucifera's House of Pride. The devil's six counselors accompany her carriage, such as Gluttony as a loathsome, deformed creature riding on a filthy swine, sweating and carrying a boozing can, "whose mind in meat and drinke was drowned on" not actual hunger, but a craving for food to fill a void. Spenser caricatured each vice as a motif of disease or sickness: for example, "Sloth, sleepy and sluggish, shakes with a raging fever. Gluttony, deformed, overweight, and sick with dropsy, brutishly spews up his gorge. Lechery, concealing his filthiness with fine clothes, suffers from rotting marrow and brain (the syphilitic consequences of his sins). Avarice is tormented by gout; Envy spews leprous poison from his mouth; and Wrath trembles, swelled with choler."[22] What is remarkable about Spenser's poetry is that it portends the visual arts and animated films. Augustan poet Alexander Pope commented that "After reading a canto of Spenser two or three days ago to an old lady, between seventy and eighty years of age, she said that I had been showing her a gallery of pictures. I do not know how it is, but she said very right." The images of the vices are miniature paintings that quicken one's imagination and wit.[23]

George Ungar's moody adaptation of Michel Tremblay's short story "The Devil and the Mushroom" turns into a darker, eschatological parable in *L'Étranger* or *The Wanderer* (1988). The devil comes quietly into a bucolic village, bearing gifts. People are planting, buying and selling, children playing catch, when a Wanderer passes by a crucifix on the outside of town. The Hispanic milieu enhances the sense of mystery, as the cloaked stranger turns suddenly into a devil and a wolf, before returning to his original appearance.

He steps into a merry inn, and generously buys drinks for all, passing them around to grotesque faces. He offers food, roasted pig, fish and fowl, and then music and flowery delights. A woman gladly takes the gift of a hat, as it blossoms and she seems to turn beautiful. The dilated gaze of the men awakens appetites. He transforms a broom with which a child sweeps the floor into a rifle. He distributes magic balls, cages of birds, mirrors, and gold.

For all this spurious beneficence, the people begin to dance and swirl as music crescendos. Men drink and do cartwheels. Then, at midnight, clouds pass over the sleeping and snoring gluttons and drunkards, as the sun rises on the town. Grinning with malicious glee, the Wanderer turns into a raven and flies away. The devil has sowed his seed. Carnival begins with costumed people, masks, and an excess of goods leads to licking one's lips, staring vainly into a mirror, when the scene escalates menacingly. Suddenly, the community turns into a mob of misers, thieves, murderers, and hoarders of jewels. A woman with a chicken is attacked and her food stolen by others, with men tearing at her coat. Pinscreen images of a scythe, a pitchfork, a spider web, and gnarled trees seem to stop the chaos. Suddenly, the excessive drinking in the inn turns violent, with skull masks masquerading lust and anger. Lechery is unleashed with desire and rape, as their eyes widen even more. Eating a pig head on a stick twists a healthy appetite into a grotesque act. Amid the bestial and demonic faces, the young boy is seduced and joins the nightmare of pleasure, killing discriminately and brutally with his rifle. While the deadly vices play out their consequences, the Wanderer watches from a hill, metamorphosing into his demonic zoomorphic disguises of bearded horned goat and scavenging crow. The church remains empty and still, as the sinister stranger has twisted a mundane world into a warped and phantasmagoric nest of vices.

Along with the devil and his judgment comes the medieval theme of *memento mori*, the admonition to "remember that you must die." Everything from rotting fruit and flowers to skulls symbolize the inevitability of your demise. Hourglasses and waning wax candles warned of the inescapable fate of all fallen humanity. Peter Bruegel the Elder's iconic *The Triumph of Death* (1562) looks like a zombie apocalypse with an army of skeletons wreaking havoc on all classes of society, suggesting for a secular society that this is all there is to be. *Memento mori*. The desolate landscape exposes the fragility of human life, with corpses strewn about, an emaciated dog chewing a child's face, a skeleton sardonically wearing a slumping cardinal's red hat, and another throwing a wayward teacher with a millstone hung around his neck into water. Death rides over the barren *paysage moralisé* with a scorched earth policy sparing no one. Judgment comes to all.

One of the most direct confrontations with death comes in the legendary manuscript illustration from the fourteenth-century De Lisle Psalter of the

"Three Living and the Three Dead." As three gentlemen ride on a hunt, they stumble across three corpses, who warn them "*Quod fuimus, estis; quod sumus, vos eritis*" ("What we were, you are; what we are, you will be"). Such a shocking encounter previews many animated films that bring the dead and living into disquieting meetings.[24] However, rather than intending to foment fear or cynically mock in a morbid manner, the classic art of "Three Living" seeks to inspire, prompting one to amend one's life with a celebration of carpe-diem.

In the great birthplace of humorists, Basel, Switzerland, Hans Holbein published his wonderfully grim *Dance of Death* series (1526), a stunning triumph of Renaissance woodblock printing and Reformist satire. In 1522, just before he began *The Dance*, Holbein had illustrated Martin Luther's influential translation of the New Testament into German, but here he enlivened the biblical passage of the wages of sin is death. His mini visual parables showed how death interrupted all the estates. For example, Death seizes a Mendicant friar just as his begging box overflows. While a young nun kneels at the altar, a troubadour lover playing his lute distracts her as Death, meantime, arrives as a hideous old hag, to tidy up and extinguish these altar candles. Death stands in the pulpit behind the loquacious Preacher, and prepares to strike him down with a jawbone, I suspect from preaching a bit too long. His time is up.

Holbein's heir is the self-proclaimed misanthrope and animator, Polish Kajetan Obarski. His ironic and surreal Kiszkiloszki Death Fairy Tales follow the theme of *Danse Macabre* with his skeletal fairy wearing pink wings and a purple skirt. His perversely sanguine character dances macabrely through life destroying whatever is in his path, although he does waver a bit considering what to do with a little girl and her balloon. The cheery bony creature prances about with his lethal wand, striking anyone and everyone with what seems like arbitrary destruction. Creating dark animation riffing on classic artworks became what Obarski called his "main indoctrination tool."[25]

Like Holbein's Skeletons, his harbingers of Death show no favorites. In particular, one senses the grim dread of losing a child to death as Holbein engraved a mother cooking dinner, looking forlornly as Death abducts her young son. Obarski redirects this profound grief to a droll juxtaposition of the Death Fairy being in a quandary about what to do when confronted with a little girl and her red balloon. Death simply wants the red balloon (figure 3.4). In one brief episode in a forest, the Death Fairy merely looks quizzically at the girl holding her balloon. Distracting her, he is able to strike quickly. In a subsequent scene, we see the red balloon silently floating above the trees.

Such diverse forms as Francisco Goya's Black paintings, a slice of Kafka, several dollops of Greek mythology, and a slew of Slavic folk tales twisted his unique imagination. As he conceded, "When you connect dying with Chaplin's slapstick vanity with Frank Zappa's music and misanthropy with

Figure 3.4 The Hilariously Morbid Kajetan Obarski Gifs His *Kiszkiloszki Death Fairy Tales* with Medieval Abandon. *Source*: Screenshot taken by the author.

Lechosław Marszałek. Reksio you get Kiszkiloszki." It is a deliciously lethal and bubbly stew. Obarski also follows the literary tradition of the poet William Dunbar as well. The Scottish makar's work attained a quality best described as "eldritch." Dunbar combines the weird, sinister, and exuberant in his *Dance of the Seven Deadly Sins*, where writhing vices frolic with spooky abandon. Their riotous dance mixes horror with sheer dark comedy, where fiends make lurid gestures and laugh so hard that hearts would burst. With Obarski, one gets that frisky, grisly sense of the uncanny that Dunbar captures so well.

Yet, in these tiny gifs Obarski is quick to point out that his key interest is narration, even in 10 seconds of animation.[26] Here is the genre of the revelatory parable of the rich man trying to go through the eye of a needle, only to be stricken with the rod of destruction. He asserts, "I'm more of a story teller than a visual artist." Pictures are there to stimulate the imagination, and like Holbein's own darkly humorous reminders of *memento mori*, Obarski follows suit, in spades. His loopy images linger too long into the nighttime, evoking both fantasies of fear and prayers of laughter. What Obarski does with silly brilliance is condense his narratives into moments. A simple gif of Death riding a cloud or skipping through urban streets works as effectively as Holbein's woodcuts in telling a parable with economy and wit. Short animations can work fantastic wonders.

Death has a hard time collecting its due in various comic renditions. In *Dji Death Fails* (Dmitri Voloshin, 2012), the hooded Grim Reaper arrives in a hospital room with his scythe and hourglass, only to lose his victim, with a power outage. In several short cartoons, he has even more trouble securing elderly women for the afterlife. *The Lady and the Reaper* (*La dama y la muerte*, Javier Gracia, 2009) pits Death against modern medicine in a struggle over one widow's life. The most spectacular battle, however, occurs in *How to Cope with Death* (Ignacio Ferreras, 2006). An old woman quietly sits in her rocking chair, sleeping in front of a television. The specter of Death hovers over her, sweeping its wings and caressing her face. Its grinning skull comes close to her closed eyes and entwines itself around her with barbed spine. Unperturbed, the woman does not move, until the skeletal Death raises its scythe. Unexpectedly, the little old lady ducks her head, springs up into action, discards her old robe, transforms into a master of Kung Fu, and ferociously fends off Death. She pummels him like Muhammad Ali. With sharp teeth snarling, he rushes to catch her, but the woman is simply too agile and evasive. With one fatal blow of her rocking chair, she slays Death. She squashes him like a bug, pounding him a dozen times just to be safe. The woman then goes about her business, tidying up and restoring her simple pattern of life, securely and serenely falling asleep in front of the television. *Carpe-diem* with panache.

Fallen Art (2006), directed by Polish Tomek Beginski, shocks with his aesthetic take on death (figure 3.5). On a high tower in barbed-wired prison hovers an oppressive-looking sergeant, with thorny stubble on his square-jawed chin. He stands with a puny soldier on a plank and jabbers forth "blob, blob,

Figure 3.5 ***Fallen Art*** **(Tomek Beginski, 2006) Challenges a Cavalier and Artistic Treatment of War and Death.** *Source*: Screenshot taken by the author.

blab, blob," pins a medal on his chest, pats him on the back, and kicks him over to plummet to the ground. A cadaverous-looking man peers out of his tiny glasses at the fallen and bloody body and then photographs the corpse. The photo transfers immediately to a large, lumbering animator who places it on an Animation Light Box to create a film from hundreds of similar images of dead men. He projects images of broken bodies and splattered blood with accompanying music. The desensitized artist smiles and dances alongside his grisly work. His choreography matches the leaping and cavorting positions of the corpses, enacting a human *Danse Macabre*. His machine stops and he gasps for breath, standing in front of an auditorium of empty chairs. Exhausted, the animator looks around and realizes he is not done, signaling to his photographer and the sergeant that it is time for another framed bit of "fallen art." Another body falls and a resident frog croaks. Beginski symbolically captures the cruelty of war, especially done for patriotic, entertainment, and aesthetic purposes.

However, two final films play with Death. In a mischievous take-off of the *Danse Macabre*, Stan Prokopenko's wonderfully concise *Unbalanced* (2013) one discovers one cannot defeat death, even in playing Jenga. Stan the Man (live action) continually loses to Skelly, the skeletal death trope. Skelly mocks, teases, and does not even play fairly, but neither does Death. In contrast, Bruno Bozzetto's *Dancing* (1991), a large-nosed man wearing a motley fool's cap stands stranded on a green deserted island (figure 3.6). Suddenly he starts dancing like a holy fool to Carnivalesque music, but just as suddenly,

Figure 3.6 In Bruno Bozzetto's *Dancing* (1991), Death Itself Discovers the Life-Giving Festival of Carnival. *Source*: Screenshot taken by the author.

it turns ominously dark. A boat shuttles up carrying a skeletal Death and his scythe, ordering the fool into his boat. He complies and offers his brightly colored headgear to Death, who tosses it away. Creaking his neck, he reconsiders. After blindfolding his passenger, he puts the hat on and hops about the island. Stripping down to bare bones, he stomps his feet and begins the dance macabre like Walt Disney's early Silly Symphonies, *The Skeleton Dance* (1929). Peeking out of his blindfold, the fool feels the rhythms and dances with his Grim Reaper, only to unintentionally toss him into the ocean, where he drowns. The happy hat surfaces and the happy fool puts it on and continues his dance of life. Joy has defeated Death, with a sort of *Risus paschalis*.

Artists such as Bosch and Brueghel and authors from Dante to Spenser personified the seven deadly sins, all performing the work of the Evil One, and ending with the fatal forfeit of life itself, the wages of sin. The artists caricatured them as types, turning them into people and animals that seem quite familiar. The proud woman is a peacock; the gluttonous man a pig; envy, a sickly woman with yellow and green skin. These artists made images that told stories that not only resonate, but also prepare the way of a cartoon parable, a gallery of pictures that the old woman saw in Spenser. It is to those seven vices that we now turn, finding them showcased in short animated films that unmask their presence and warn of their consequences.

NOTES

1. Plato, in particular, wanted to exclude amusing poets and clowns from his *Republic*; Dante was kinder to comedy as Andrew Moran capably shows through Canto 21. https://www.youtube.com/watch?v=7oWt9IDpjls (Accessed December 24, 2021).

2. Gibson, Walter S. *Pieter Bruegel and the Art of Laughter* (University of California Press, 2006), 37. See also "Jocular Preachers," in *God Mocks,* op. cit. 49–53.

3. Boccaccio, Giovanni, *Decameron* (trans. John Payne) (Independent, 2020), 497.

4. McGowan, op. cit. 189–190. Pixar's *A Bug's Life* (John Lasseter, Andrew Stanton, 1998) rocked audiences with hilarious laughter with its outtakes and bloopers where one sees how the bugs muffed their lines or pranked each other. For example, when the frightful grasshopper, Hopper, threatens Atta, the Princess of the Ants, he asks, "Are you saying I'm stupid? Do I look stupid to you?" Unable to answer "no," she suddenly explodes in laughter. After several takes, a demoralized Hopper needs to go back to his dressing room.

5. In his collection of studies in the *Dubliners,* James Joyce sought to write a "chapter of the moral history of Ireland." He connected a motif of darkness and a habit of hats with the Seven Deadly Sins, the practice of which in Ireland is as common as wearing hats. As a modern-day, anti-Roman Catholic version of *Piers*

Plowman, the work catalogues the "seven deadly sins and incarnations of saints and sinners." French, Marilyn, "Missing Pieces in Joyce's Dubliners," *Twentieth Century Literature* 24: 4 (Winter 1978), 443; See also M. W. Murphy who points out how the "seven deadly sins form a sort of moral frame" for the action of the stories. "Darkness in 'Dubliners,'" *Modern Fiction Studies* 15:1 (Spring 1969), 97–104; A father in "Counterparts" commits the sin of wrath. While angry at his employer, he bullies his son (and wears a hat whenever he is going to sin). In the novella, "The Dead," Joyce invites a table of pitiful sinners (a drunk, a pompous and conceited professor, his melancholic wife, and others) for an annual Epiphany dinner and dance hosted by the elderly Morkan aunts. Duke University Chaplain Will Willimon describes the scene as purgatorial, where the consequences of sin join the living and the dead. Near the end of "The Dead," Joyce wrote, "One by one they were all becoming shades," a harbinger of the heartless and sightless souls crossing the River Styx. Joyce, James "The Dead," in *Dubliners*, ed. Margot Norris (Norton, 2006), 151–194; As professor Michael Hall showed me, the maid encapsulates the selfishness in the best line in the story: "The men that is now is only all palaver and what they can get out of you."

6. Matthew 10: 13–16.

7. Sullivan, Margaret A., *Bruegel's Peasants: Art and Audience in the Northern Renaissance and Bruegel and the Creative Process, 1559–1563* (Cambridge University Press, 1994).

8. Koerner, *Bosch and Bruegel*, 30.

9. de Bry, Johann Theodor "The Blind Man and the Lame," *Emblematta saecularia* (Oppenheim, 1596), n.p.

10. Czesław Miłosz, *The History of Polish Literature* (University of California Press, 1983), 178.

11. Buddha Udana, 6:4, 68, 69; *Canki Sutta* Mallisena, *Syādvādamanjari*, 19:75–77. Dhruva, A.B. (1933), 23–25.

12. Gaffney, Maureen, "Evaluating Attitude: Analyzing Point of View and Tone in Film Adaptations of Literature," *Children's Literature and the Media* 3 (1981), 118–120.

13. "Isaac Bashevis Singer on Writing for Children," *Children's Literature* 6 (Johns Hopkins University Press, 1977), 9.

14. Cited in Adam Abraham's *When Magoo Flew: The Rise and Fall of Animation Studio* (Wesleyan University Press, 2012), 171.

15. In his thorough work on the UPA studio, Abraham tells a wonderfully creepy story of a visit by Aldous Huxley during the shooting. The author of *Brave New World* had "deteriorating eyesight" and designer Paul Julian noticed how it eerily looked like the old man's "damned decrepit-looking eye." (105)

16. "Interview with Ian Eames," https://www.cartoonbrew.com/cartoon-brew-pick/short-pick-of-the-day-the-beard-by-ian-emes-181688.html (Accessed July 23, 2020).

17. Cassian, John, *The Institutes of the Coenobia* (trans. Boniface Ramsey) (Newman Press, 2000).

18. In his *Institutes,* Cassian collated the wisdom of the Desert Fathers in a more communal, or coenobitic, Latin form of monasticism that would influence St.

Benedict of Nursia (480–547) and the development of his Benedictine Rule. Cassian emphasized the role of the will (although ultimately insufficient in itself in producing spiritual health) in addressing the vices of the Christian life. Everyone was called to work and worship in community and in community these faults could be seen and too easily practiced., In Books 5–12 of his *Institutions*, John Cassian preaches on rules of morality, focusing upon what he saw as eight vices and their matching virtues on controlling them. The principal vices included gluttony, lust, greed, hubris, wrath, listlessness, boasting, with envy merging *acedia* and *tristitia*, spiritual lethargy and sadness; at which point we lost one of the best complementary virtues, namely *hilaritas*.

19. Gregory the Great, *Morals on the Book of Job* (trans. John Henry Parker and J. Rivington) (Patristic Publishing, 2018) Volume I Book 7: 34, https://litpress.org/Products/GetSample/CS249H/9780879071493 (Accessed February 7, 2020).

20. Prudentius, Aurelius Clemens, *Prudentius* (ed. and trans. H. J. Thomson) (Loeb Classical Library, 1961) lines 467–469.

21. Judgments will be fitting, however: the eyes of envious who looked hatefully upon the good fortune of others are sealed with threads of wire. The proud bear heavy stones to lower their haughty spirit and the gluttonous starve, awaiting the completion of their purification. No wonder the medieval Roman Church could sell indulgences so easily.

22. Schimmel, Solomon, *The Seven Deadly Sins: Jewish, Christian, and Classical Reflections on Human Psychology* (Oxford University Press, 1997), 17.

23. Spencer, Edmund, *Spenser's Faerie Queene* The Project Gutenberg eBook, https://www.gutenberg.org/files/15272/15272-h/15272-h.htm (Accessed April 1, 2020).

24. The poignancy of death taking children is set forth in moving films like *The Little Match Girl* (Don Hahn, 2006) and *Death and the Mother* (Ruth Lingford, 1988).

25. https://culture.pl/en/artist/kajetan-obarski (June 11, 2020).

26. I must also celebrate the truly comic gifs of French blogger and artist Boulet (aka Gilles Roussel), with his sinful "Calvinist" facsimile character (akin to cartoonist Bill Watterson's famous strip *Calvin and Hobbes*, but hitting middle age). His quick witty sketches of the Seven Deadly Sins captures the desire of each vice and an apt *contrapasso*. See Amid Amidi's *Cartoon Brew*: https://www.cartoonbrew.com/internet-blogs/the-seven-deadly-sins-in-animated-gif-form-66992.html (Accessed December 21, 2021). See Boulet's site: http://english.bouletcorp.com/2012/07/22/ordinary-day/.

Chapter 4

Pride (*Superbia* of the Peacock)

Pride is first. Of course, it is. No other vice could dethrone it. Most deadly of the deadly sins is Pride, the capital (*capa* or head) sin that rules and ruins all the others. In Edmund Spencer's *Faerie Queen*, the Knight Redcross comes to Lucifera's House of Pride, whose ostentatious carriage is drawn by her six other "counselors." These six other vices, each with an animal symbolizing it, are mere lackeys to this high and mighty, almost almighty, vice. Its appearances in animated films run from the motley costume of mere vainglory to the full stature of a Miltonic rebellion against a cartoon character's creator. An anthropomorphized Pride (*huperēphania*) struts like a peacock, spreading out her splendiferous and mesmerizing feathers, but, alas, ends up a pajock.

Bruegel paints a flashy, fashionably dressed woman springing from the Latin root *Superbia*. She sits bestride her haughty peacock (whose feathers protrude from the tails of other monsters), gazing at her reflection in a hand glass. Behind her skirt, a grinning frog-faced demon mocks her vanity. Beauty parlors/barbershops abound, with one woman injected with something akin to Botox and another having her hair washed with urine that drips down a roof. Demons (one wears a papal tiara) stare narcissistically into mirrors (or another just looks at its ass), no doubt serving as satirical reflections of the woman.

Pride arrogates to the self the glory of God, claiming authority and commanding the universe to fall at one's feet. It approximates the grand Ouroboros serpent of pride that turns in or curves in on itself, *curvatus in se*—as Augustine puts it, in so much as it practices a centripetal life, perpetually consuming itself. The self ends up swallowing its own tail, which rather than a symbol of infinity, turns into an idol of self-absorption. It not only looks at its own ass, it devours it. The silent deadly sin of pride hides behind such masks of self-exaltation, self-promotion, self-justification, and smug self-preoccupation. In fact, any centripetal action of the soul exposes that smudge of pride, even as the vanity of a magnifying mirror reveals not the natural beauty of the face, but the greasy pores and wicked wrinkles in its reflection. Bill Plympton's *the trouble with facelifts* (1990), for example, shows the artificial beauty of a female face melting into a pool of fleshy goo.

The Hebrew prophet Isaiah took time to denounce what he called the silly cows of Bashan, the pampered housewives of Judah for that most superficial variety of pride, vainglory. Csaba Varga's *Augusta Makes Herself Beautiful* (1985), exposes this sweet conceit as an ordinary maid of clay attempts extravagant means to beautify herself, only to realize that a smile and a flower in her hair were sufficient. Seeking to emulate the glamour of Marilyn Monroe, sweet Augusta goes to painful lengths to capture an artificial visage. This inane sin of vanity shoots up from a root of vainglory, that "keen desire for attention and approval," as Rebecca Konyndyk DeYoung displays it in her *Vainglory: The Forgotten Vice*. The prophet Isaiah revealed its ironic consequences,

Because the daughters of Zion are proud
And walk with heads held high and seductive eyes,
And go along with mincing steps
And tinkle the bangles on their feet,
Therefore the Lord will afflict the scalp of the daughters of Zion with scabs,
And the LORD will make their foreheads bare. (Isaiah 3: 16–17)

Singing, "You're so vain, you probably think this song is about you," Carly Simon escalates the irony of this narcissistic peccadillo. DeYoung connects such trifling vices in popular culture from "Dr. Seuss to SpongeBob SquarePants" and points out that the lyrics of "Gaston's Song" in Disney's *Beauty and the Beast* (1991) include "examples of every single form of vainglory identified by Thomas Aquinas in the *Summa theologiae*." She reflects on how Disney borrows "the traditional trope of a person gazing at himself in a mirror" to reveal Gaston's egoism.[1] As Chesterton quipped, the silliest sin in the world appears not a wine glass, but a looking glass. However, this venial sin of the adorable Augusta is slight compared to other more sinister manifestations.

Pope Gregory catapults pride and vainglory, as Latin *superbia* and Greek *hubris* (that overweening, egotistical, haughty, and condescending selfishness that will hoard for itself as many adjectives that it can), into first place among the wannabe vices. Pride poses in a posture of arrogance where one "favors himself in his thought; and . . . walks with himself along the broad spaces of his thought and silently utters his own praises." Augustine lifted it to its top rung. It stands as the first and original sin, the one for which Milton would later cast Satan from heaven. "What is pride but a diverse desire of height?" Such is also the story of Icarus, a Greek myth paralleling a Hebrew proverb: "Pride goes before destruction and a haughty spirit before a fall" (16:18).

This archetypal pattern of the fall of overweening pride inhabits the animated versions of the Greek *Myth of Icarus and Daedalus* (Jeremiah Dickey, 2017). Educator Amy Adkins unpacks this sad story of the conceited master craftsman. Daedalus audaciously helps a cursed Queen Pasipahe circumvent her husband Minos. Impregnated by his prize white bull, she gives birth to the Minotaur. For such a perversion, the king forces Daedalus to design an inescapable labyrinth for the Bull/man creature. Imprisoned in Minos' giant tower, he and his son Icarus plan to escape. Even in the tower, one of the most common metaphors of Pride (think of the ivory tower), the soaring vice of presumption comes as he skillfully weaves together feathers with wax to construct wings for himself and Icarus. As witnesses on the ground look at him, he seems like a god. Warned not to fly too high, the son disobeys, and the sun melts the wax, with Icarus plunging into the sea. Pride goes before a fall is a truism that proves too true.

This didactic parable reappeared as a Saturday morning children's limited animation program, *Icarus and Daedalus* (Peter Bollinger, 1998) by Nelvana studio, based on Laura Geringer's book series of *Myth Men: Guardians of the Legend* and *Sun Flight* (Gerald McDermott, 1966) from the Caldecott Award–winning children's book. The National Film Board of Canada's quietly stylized *Icarus* (Paul Bochner, 1974) connects the anger of the encased Minotaur in its labyrinth, with the curiosity of Icarus studying the flight of birds. From the stationary Cretan prison, he gathers feathers and soars with his father, laughing into the heavens. In his youthful hubris, he does not heed the advice to avoid flying near the sun. The solar fires burn him and he falls like a flaming comet. This delusional desire to be like a god is one that thinks too much of itself. Its cure is humility, not in an abject sense of worthlessness, but in thinking of oneself less. For Aquinas, the root of pride "consists of man not being, in some way, subject to God and His rule." Whether it is self-love in one's mastery of *techne* like Daedalus or in Icarus' youthful aspirational sense of invincibility, one will be broken on a wheel of fortune. In Bruegel's painting of Icarus falling from the sky, the world turns away. No one knows or cares about the disaster. A ploughman keeps plowing; a ship sails on. The fall of pride itself is a mere splash in the water, a forsaken cry. As poet W. H. Auden observed gazing upon Bruegel's painted fable, "everything turns away, quite leisurely from the disaster" of pride.[2]

Dante demonstrates purging cures for each of the sins in the second book of his *Divine Comedy*. Beginning with pride, Dante and his guide Virgil ascend toward Paradise, with an angel removing the 7 "P's" *peccatum* (sins) from his forehead as he traverses each canto. After cleansing each wound with appropriate penance, the pilgrim can plod his or her path to Paradise. However, this first, and worst, sin blocking the path is pride, attested to by Ecclesiastes and numerous church fathers like Augustine. Thirteen exquisitely sculpted carvings decorate the marble floor of Canto 12; each preaching a vivid visual sermon against pride (e.g., Satan falling from heaven, Nimrod ruined by Babel, etc.).

Following a principle of *contrapasso*, sinners suffer a fitting punishment for their sins, sometimes resembling or re-enacting and sometimes contrasting and parodying their vices. In this lowest place on the seven-story mountain of Dante's Purgatory, a crushing boulder is loaded on one's back to push one's face down into humility, into the humus and the earth of reality. One thinks of the myth of *Sisyphus* and the Academy Award–winning film by Marcell Jankovics (1974), underlining the consequences of the King of Corinth's deceitfulness and self-aggrandizement (figure 4.1). Using dynamic line drawings and an intensely breathy soundtrack, Jankovics captured the infernal punishment of pride. As Proverbs 26:27 warns, not only will he who digs a pit will fall into it, but he who rolls a stone, it will come back on him, *curvatus in se*.

Pride literally goes before a fall in Ferenc Rofusz' *Gravitáció / Gravity* (1984) (figure 4.2). Opening a bucolic scene of birds flying about an apple tree of life, Rofusz teases the viewer with his satiric take on the pride of youth. The film employs a cautionary parable on chronological snobbery, on the hubris of a progressive ripe apple over the weary, but enduring tradition (in this case, a reflection on modernity and tradition in Hungary). A male-faced apple emits a restless groan. It looks disdainfully at old fruit faces

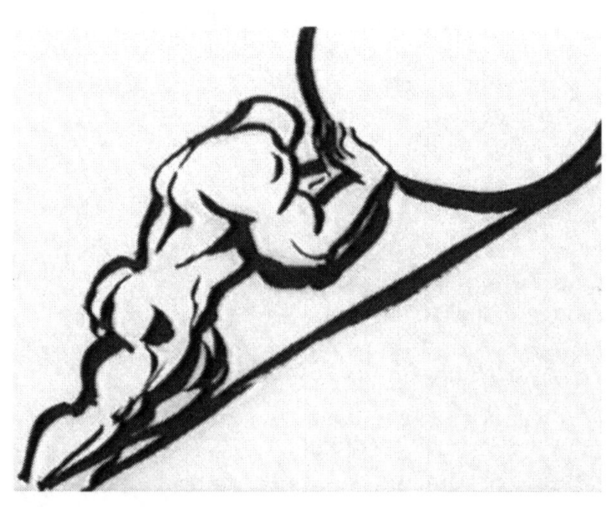

Figure 4.1 Having Cheated Death Twice, Marcell Jankovics's *Sisyphus* (1974) Suffers Zeus' Eternal Punishment of Rolling a Boulder up a Hill, Only to See It Roll Down. *Source*: Screenshot taken by the author.

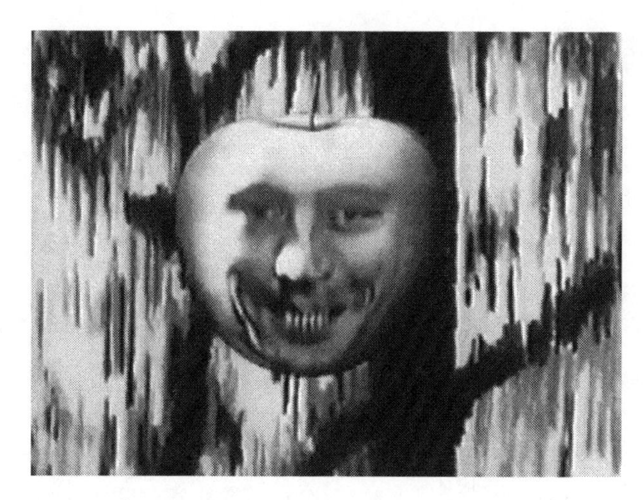

Figure 4.2 Ferenc Rofusz' *Gravity* (1984) Depicts the Fullness and the Heaviness of the Title, Where Pride Must Fall. *Source*: Screenshot taken by the author.

hanging languidly on the tree. Violently shaking itself up and down on its branch, the apple head strains and grunts, strenuously attempting to liberate itself from the source of its life. Finally, after arduous agitation, it succeeds in cutting its stem from its source. Liberated at last, it exhales with relief and then smirks with victorious pride as it soars through space, finally smashing to the ground as the older fruit faces watch in pity. A butterfly comes and goes, and the successful attempt at freedom finishes in a fall to destruction.

A tragic pride in one's inventive talents takes its heartbreaking toll in *The Kinematograph* (Tomasz Bagiński, 2009) (figure 4.3). The camera descends into a quiet Victorian village and zooms into the atelier of an inventor, like Daedalus. He watches a sound movie about his wife, protesting his filming of her. She tries to encourage him through a dry and frustrating period of creativity, as he wants to produce not only a sound film, but also one with color. She quietly advises him to publish what he has produced, but he stubbornly resists as he is "working on the *greatest* invention of the century, not some half-baked idea." He does not spot the severity of her cough, but goes to his shop, kicking a can in the street, a slight symbol of his own self-preoccupation.

He apologizes and she feeds her husband soup; then suggests a solution to his dilemma of combining two strips of red and blue color. He exclaims that she is a genius and runs to his work. In a brilliant montage of his ingenious labors, working day and night, he achieves his dream. His wife privately suffers a discharge of blood. Unaware of her condition, he blithely brings her to his laboratory, and with two gramophones and a stereo sound system, proceeds to film her (in color) explaining how she makes one of her delicious apple pies.

Figure 4.3 ***The Kinematograph*** **(Tomasz Bagiński, 2009), Asks One to Weigh the Value of One's Artistic Work to Actual Life.** *Source*: Screenshot taken by the author.

He examines his work, marveling at the hues of his film more than realizing the subject of his wife detailing her own creative work of baking. He calls for her to see what he has done, but she has collapsed on the kitchen floor. Discovering her, he murmurs, "What's the matter? Say something. Dear God."

At the hospital, a doctor expresses regret that nothing will help. He remembers a colorful spring day long ago in which he was walking in a park with his camera apparatus. He stumbled, dropped everything, and lost his glasses. Finding them and looking up, he saw his wife for the first time, who bent down to pull him up. As a candle extinguishes in her hospital room, the glorious real world fades to sepia in a cemetery. He returns home, lights his incandescent lamp, and projects her in brilliant colors, talking about pies. The camera pulls out of the solitary inventor, back into the street where a newspaper boy proclaims the great cinematic invention of the Lumière brothers, as moving shadows cover the streets. With gentle melancholy, the parable asks what does it profit a man if he gains the whole world yet loses his soul/mate? One's noble obsessions, one's pride and joy, need a sense of value and worth in the hierarchy of one's life. One's spouse, one's children, one's neighbor are the most sacred priorities that pride too easily forgets.

One is sympathetic toward Icarus, the apple, and the Kinematographer. None is an insufferably proud character like Cartman of *South Park*, who manipulates and mocks others, lacks compassion, remains stubbornly selfish, and shows anti-Semitic bigotry. While he is an equal-opportunity jerk, his pride removes him from the gene pool of human humility and compassion. He deserves his comeuppance. However, not just Cartman, but all four stand and fall on their own self-absorption.

Figure 4.4 The *Conceited General* (Te Wei, 1956) Stands as Cipher for All Reigning Authority. *Source*: Screenshot taken by the author.

Just desserts are easier to expect in stubborn and narcissistic cartoon characters. *The Conceited General* (or *The Proud General*, Te Wei, 1956), produced by the Shanghai Animation Film Studio, honors the glorious victory of a formidable military leader (figure 4.4). Yet the celebration of his impressive campaign over the king's enemies puffs up his conceit and weakens his discipline. He grows lax in preparedness, neglecting to sharpen his swords or practice his martial arts. He becomes a spoiled Epicurean. His haughty and egocentric life of eating, drinking, and partying softens him so that when the enemy returns, he lounges unprepared. While invaders overrun the kingdom, he is humiliated. He flees like a fat rooster waddling through a hole in a fence before his capture. From being cock of the walk, the General falls from the top of the roost to being the butt of his own cockiness. As detective novelist Dorothy Sayers observed, the "devilish strategy of Pride is that it attacks us, not I our weakest points, but in our strongest."[3]

Of Holes and Corks (Ante Zaninovic, 1967) presents a typical Zagreb Studio character, an egoist with a long nose and reading a newspaper oblivious of his castle-like surroundings. He is in charge of his universe. Suddenly small fountains in the ground pop up which he promptly plugs. As each little eruption springs up creating a hole, he sticks in a cork to control it all. After a while, as the little things of life disturb his tranquility, he plays a frantic version of "Whack a mole." Finally, he completes his task and laughs to himself thinking he has won; he even plays with his corks, releasing gas and a particular sound from each one so that he makes music and dances. He removes all the corks, throws his hammer away, grins and returns to reading his paper, a king of his own castle. However, suddenly, an earthquake shakes it all up and we realize that he has been sitting on top of a volcano, which erupts, blowing his whole world away.[4]

In what historian Ronald Holloway has called the "message cartoons" of the Zagreb School of reduced animation, one stands out for its vile and pitiless imagery of ruthless totalitarian governments. In *Spring* (or *Fountain*) *of Life* (Borislav Sajtinac and Nikola Majdak, 1969), a little deformed man wanders the countryside, goes to a village and finds a fountain, drinks from it and is restored to normalcy. A king sitting in his tower window switches to a second head that can spy on the man. He sends down his brutal guard with a giant knife, who hangs the man, cuts him up into various pieces, and throws him against a wall. However, the hanged man revives and meets a community of lame, crippled, and deformed people, telling them about the fountain. Following the king's orders, the guard maims and cuts all these people in half in an act of outlandish genocide. He hangs them all on scaffolds, cutting their heads and limbs in a brutal bloody massacre. Hanging on the gallows against an orange/brown landscape, the bodies look like a Bosch hell. When the guard decides to drink from the fountain himself, the king tosses him in, and he explodes. When the king brings his royal goblet to drink the life and freedom of the fountain, the waters twist him into a deformed, crippled creature.[5]

No salvation exists in or through art, as a little Chaplinesque man in Nedelijko Dragic's *Diogenes, Perhaps* (1967) stumbles into a copy of Da Vinci's Last Supper, with all the disciples sitting on one side of the table. He glides up beside Jesus and tries to tell stories, eat and drink with the disciples, taking out his own lunch. In his small vanity, he toasts the meal with his thermos bottle. However, trying vainly to chat and interact with them remains a futile activity, as they are static simulacra. Art cannot save. He forlornly belches and leaves the great work of art in his sad journey through life.

In his Oxford book on *Pride*, Michael Eric Dyson identifies virtuous foundations of identity, self-respect, and dignity below the vice, while still recognizing the sin of pride in modern practices of racial bigotry.[6] What orthodox theology has always recognized is that every vice is rooted in a good. Sin is only virtue twisted or bent. To celebrate one's identity as *imago Dei*, of being the image of God, is a good thing. To extol that image above its Object is to corrupt it into something graven. As such, pride is the confidence that believes too much in itself, finding a mask in either untamed arrogance or selfish indulgence. A sense of supremacy, of privilege, over another made in the image of God, is to try to lift oneself by one's ass into a higher, and falser, status.

Beyond the Chinese parable of an individual corrupt General, we find stories of arrogant and oppressive social structures. In his *Moral Man and*

Immoral Society, theologian Reinhold Niebuhr argues that individuals are more likely to sin when in groups so that institutionalized structures abet sin. (After observing the corruption of individuals, Niebuhr reconsidered altering his title to *Immoral Man and More Immoral Society*.) One of the most provocative moral parables to deal with the hubris of society and racial injustice is Robert Mitchell and John Kimball's *Free* (Haboush Company, 1972). A small black boy plays with his ball in a park, when it rolls into a bush. A fat, overweight cop (think of the early 1970s designation of "pig") with a baseball bat bullies the kid, while the music of Jess Fuller adapts (and alters) the bluegrass song, "99 Years and one dark day," that carries the film's narrative.

Arresting the boy for not obeying a "keep off the grass sign," the cop takes him before a corrupt judge with a jury of pumpkins. The prosecution connects racist images of Africa, jail, chickens, watermelons, and demeaning stereotypes to convict the kid and send him to jail with a ball and chain. As the kid stands atop a giant rock, he pounds away bits of gravel over his century-long sentence. As he whacks away at his rock, a group of convicts march around him. The music relates that he was "getting mighty old and turning grey; Lordy, Lord, one dark day . . ." and hopes for the light. He ages, becoming a bald, white-bearded, old man, as the convicts slowly turn into skeletons, into dust, and die. Seeing that his life-long prisoner has finished his labors, the brutal cop kicks him back to the park, where he tries to arrest him again. Unexpectedly, the little man's apotheosis transforms him into an angel. He flies away, giving one last Bronx cheer to the despicable official. Then, to top it off, a large devil cop comes to take his human counterpart to the burning fires of hell. Justice is done, at least in the afterlife.[7]

From the *New Yorker* magazine, James Thurber's ironic reversal of a nagged and beleaguered husband slyly upending his overbearing wife's authority plays out with panache in UPA's film version of *A Unicorn in the Garden* (William T. Hurtz, 1953). The superior and condescending wife calls the police to report that her husband has seen a unicorn in the garden. Arrogantly asserting that her husband has seen such a fancy, the harridan orders the men in the little white coats to come and haul him away. Ironically, it is she they take away in the strait jacket. The Hebrew sage recognized that "pride does go before destruction, and a haughty spirit before a fall. It is better to be of a lowly spirit among the poor than to divide the spoil with the proud" (Proverbs 16: 18–19). Who could have guessed one would find a biblical warning against pride in the *New Yorker*?

Dutch animator Paul Driessen's *The Killing of an Egg* (1977) offers a wry and clever parable that requires keen attention (figure 4.5). A man sits in a large white room, with yolk-yellow walls, before his breakfast table. About to crack open a hard-boiled egg placed in front of him, he taps on the egg and hears a voice that says, "Hello. Whosa there?" in a marked Italian accent. The

Figure 4.5 Paul Driessen's *The Killing of an Egg* (1977) Visualizes the Ironic Consequences of Ignoring the Golden Rule of Matthew 7:12: "do to others what you would have them do to you." *Source*: Screenshot taken by the author.

voice continues, "Who is it? What do you want? Just a second." He taps a little harder and the voice pleads, "Stopa that! What are you doing?" The man then viciously smashes the egg with glee with the egg screams in agony. He then hears a knock. "Hello," he answers, "Whosa there?" He hears another knock and says, "Who is it? Just a second," and walks to open a door. No one is out there. Another knock and he sees a crack in his yellow ceiling. "Ah, stopa that!" he yells! And the whole white background overwhelms the yolk-yellow walls and our poor egg-man. What you give shall be given back to you in larger measure. The parable, once it is seen as a just dessert or *karma*, makes complete sense. Students often need to see it twice to recognize the physical and spiritual universes conflating. What you do to others will be done to you.

The proud and premature judgment of others also appears as David Lisbe skewers religious pride and hypocrisy in his *Heavenly Appeals* (2009), with fresh comic aplomb (figure 4.6). Raymond K. Hessle, a sad, little sinner, twisted and weak, seeks to appeal a judgment that sent him to hell. Wearing a ball and chain, he pops up before the heavenly golden gates to find a fat, smug, bureaucratic angel floating on a tiny lounge cloud and eating a pink, sprinkled donut. The obese cherubic guard takes the nervous defendant's file, puts him in the dock, scanning for evidence of a good and worthy life. The man's file shows that he has demonstrated exceptional qualities since he arrived in purgatory, even taking the place of torture for an old woman. His dossier reads, "He continues to take on the torture of others whenever eligible, always greeting his abusers with a smile." He even sabotages pain-tormenting equipment, eliminating torture for a week. The official seraph

Figure 4.6 David Lisbe Skewers Religious Pride and Hypocrisy in His *Heavenly Appeals* (2009) with Panache. *Source*: Screenshot taken by the author.

flips through the chart in a disinterested manner. When it appears that he may be accepted, the heavenly oaf stamps denied on his request and then gleefully afflicts the poor man with mistreatment, stuffing another pink donut in his mouth. The little man endures the persecution, crossing himself and silently suffering. When his gonads suffer a blow, the guffawing angel bellows in *Schadenfreude*. Yet, his ridiculing causes him to lose his balance and fall off his cloud vehicle. His tiny wings cannot keep his corpulent body flying.

About to fall, he asks the little man whom he abused to help him. He extends his thin arm to grab the stout judge, and pulls him up to safety. Catching his breath, the stout gatekeeper looks at his wide-eyed and guileless rescuer, raises an eyebrow, and tips the iron fetter ball off the platform, sending the vulnerable sinner south. Smug and pleased with himself, he looks around and suddenly, the man has sprouted wings and a halo and rises from his hell and the gates of heaven open joyously to him. The peeved angel mouths "What the hell?" He immediately grows his own horns, sees his wings shrink, and desperately folds his hands in prayer. Too late, as his seat cracks and he falls to hell himself. The revelatory parable parallels Gospel accounts of religious leaders, suggesting that they were twice as fit for hell over other sinners.

Religious hypocrisy conflates with other sins of gluttony, greed, anger, adultery, and envy that culminates in thievery and murder in Mark Baker's *The Village* (1993), a misanthropic microcosm of fallen humanity snooping and spying on each other in their castle compound. Showing the darker side of an isolated, rural community, Baker exposes the sins of each villager. The pride of the village priest, who hides his stash of sacramental wine for self-indulgent purposes, shows through in his cruelty to a prisoner in his cell, spitting on him with disdain. When one brute envies a neighbor with glowing gold pieces, he breaks in to steal them and kill the owner. The guilty man schemes to make his wife's lover the scapegoat for his crimes. In a rush to judgment, an enraged community falls for the husband's ruse and thinks that the adulterer has killed the victim. They chop down the sinner's apple trees to make gallows. His lover, the wife of the brute, rescues him just as her husband is about to throw him off the roof; however, the cuckolded husband slips and falls to his own death, the consequence of his previous murder and evil designs. Ants come during the night and devour his body, providing a cover-up for the lovers' getaway from all the sinners of the parish. Love, even illicit love, covers a multitude of sins. Baker's underlying message suggests that while ants cooperate in maintaining a productive community, humans bicker, deceive, steal, judge, and hate.

More pointed and germane to the early 1970s with the rise of televangelists, John Taylor defiantly opposed the use of "totally verbal forms of expression on a visual medium." He thus conceived and produced a satirical short Tricken Film entitled *The Preacher* (Pavel and Stania Prochazka, 1970), sponsored by the World Council of Churches.[8] His minute-long cartoon opens with a close-up of a judgmental man with a lean face garbling words. His large forefinger protrudes menacingly, and seems intent on sending sinners to hell. He folds his hands in a sanctimonious posture and continues to burble. The camera pulls back and we see the preacher is a television evangelist. A bald, overweight laborer in shirtsleeves sits with his feet in a tub, drinking beer, as the preacher drones on and on. After a large gulp, with the preacher haranguing him, the viewer lets out a long belch, his apt amen to the sermon.

Religious pride also slips into *A Note from Above* (Anonymous, 1972) in which a cloud in a stained-glass window sends down floating notes from "above." The first one announces "I am the Lord thy God; Thou shalt have no other gods before me" and the people below throw idols away. Several other commandments follow such as "Thou shalt not steal" and hands appear that return a watch, sheep, a naked wife. Finally, drifting down comes the message: "Thou shalt kill." People begin massacring and killing one another until another note floats down from above, explaining, "Last note should be 'Thou shalt *not* kill.' Sorry, my mistake."

The United States Catholic Conference produced several ecumenical shorts. In one untitled cartoon, a Zagreb-like character builds a wall that blocks the sunshine from another man. He retaliates, shutting out the sun from his neighbor. As a cloud then covers both, they take the wall, make a seesaw, and lift themselves to chase the cloud away. The Catholic Conference adds its *epimythia* moral: "If we all just work together . . . " A second mini-cartoon by US Catholic Campaign for Human Development shows two boats of men meeting each other in the wide-open sea. As they argue, the second boat cracks and begins to sink. The survivors jump in the first boat, which then encounters another alien group of boaters with whom they fight. Their boat follows suit in coming apart. The scene continues through several boat encounters until a large group sits in one boat. Suddenly, it begins to break apart and the men are desperate. One character realizes he has a hammer; then they all receive hammers and fix the boat. The parable of overcoming differences and being in the same boat also concludes with "If we all work together to save . . . " Its didacticism neutralizes its impact. It preaches rather than suggests.[9]

Celebrated in the Screening Room of the *New Yorker* magazine, *If I Was God: a true story* (Cordell Barker. 2015) combines the memory of a documentary with the splashy cartoon styles of a hilarious filmmaker (figure 4.7). When animator Cordell was twelve years old, he confessed to "feeling God-like" when he attended middle school and learned to doodle. He learned how to dissect *Rana pipiens* and how to design a seating chart to get near certain people (Lily) and avoid possible angles of attacks by others (namely a bothersome spitfire girl named Augie) using Euclidian geometry and a "hypotanoose." Once, when using electrodes to spark a response from his frog, Cordell experimented by putting an electrode on his own tongue. He then brings his frog back to life and keeps that frog, like a Frankenstein monster, jumping and dancing. He had the power of life and death over the amphibian. As the redheaded monster Augie starts attacking his secret

Figure 4.7 ***If I Was God: a true story*** **(Cordell Barker. 2015) Allows Each of us to Remember Our Youthful Divine Fantasies of Controlling our Universe.** *Screenshot taken by the author.*

girlfriend Lily with spit wads, he imagines Augie as an annoying fly and he becomes a pig-bird type monster to deal with her peskiness. When a storm arises outside the classroom, and the teacher (who passively/aggressively chalked the phrase "4783 days until retirement" on the blackboard) vainly tries to close the window.

Cordell imagines seeing a mobile of planets over Lily's head. Thinking that if he were a god, he would not just use his power to punish others, but also to get what he wanted, which would be a perfect day with Lily, running across the blackboard and the planets (and yet continually chased and bothered by Augie). As a god, he imagines he could change the whole planet. He walks and rolls on his planet, getting closer to the sun, until he is abruptly brought out of his reverie by the dangling over-stimulated, fried frog intestines on his desk and a tiny fire. As the teacher pulls the fire alarm, he realizes he was not a god; he was not even in grade 8. As the kids leave the classroom, he and Lily wave to each other. Then shoved into each other by Augie, they go skipping out of the doors. With a bit of looming melancholy, he realizes that "at that moment, the world seemed perfect, just the way it was." To recognize that one is not God may be that step toward humility and contentment.

The Oscar-nominated short, *A Single Life* (Job, Joris, & Marieke, 2014) spoofs the illusion that one can control one's whole life (figure 4.8). When a single woman sitting in her room eating pizza gets a knock on the door, she goes to answer and finds a 45 record on the doorstep. She puts the music on and when it skips, she notices that part of the pizza disappears, as if eaten.

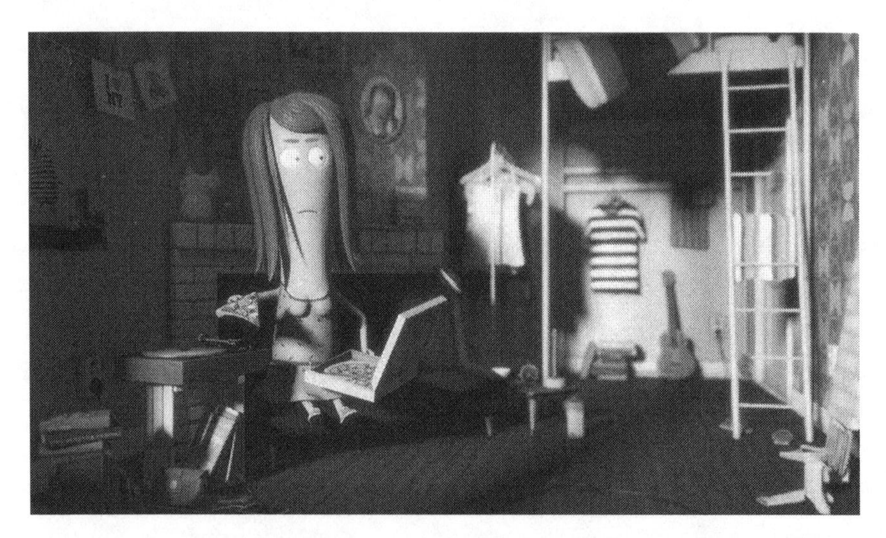

Figure 4.8 ***A Single Life*** **(Job, Joris, & Marieke, 2014) Reminds us That Even with the Sham Sense of Controlling our Lives, We Do Not Control Time.** *Source*: Screenshot taken by the author.

She tinkers with the record player and finds that she can make time go forward and backward, controlling when she wants to exist. She finds her future herself pregnant; then with a baby, and tries to reverse that moment quickly. She finds herself as a little girl and then in a wheelchair wearing a leg cast. Unable to get to the record player, it skips ahead many grooves and she finds herself as a senior citizen on a walker. She cannot move fast enough to get to the record player. Like the Furies cutting the strings of one's time on earth, her cord is snapped. Just as she gets to the player, it ends, and the needle lifts up and returns to its holder. All we see is an urn of ashes.

The tiny bit of pride that one can control one's life finds its ironic end, even as the other parables of pride show the fall that inevitably follows the vice. In Dante's first terrace of Purgatory, the proud souls purge their sins, carrying huge stones on their backs, forced to look at the ground. In a literary precursor to the animated parable, Dante displays an "art of visible speech." First, the Pilgrim marvels at white marble images of the virtue of humility on ledges such as King David dancing before the Ark of the Covenant. One of the penitents is Oderisi of Gubbio, a renowned artist of illuminated manuscripts, who today would have been an animator. His hope lies in iconic statues celebrating the virtue of humility, such as the Virgin Mary receiving the Annunciation as she responds "*Ecce ancilla Dei*" ("Behold the handmaid of the Lord") and Emperor Trajan dismounting from his horse to render justice to a widow whose enemies murdered her sons.[10] These whips of love offer marble examples of humility to those who see.

Two cantos later, Virgil shows Dante a series of bas-reliefs on a bed of rock beneath the feet of the penitents, "as tombs set in a church floor." Bowed and shrunken to humility, Dante's own thoughts reflect on animated images of those who held their haughty heads high, "living carvings" of Satan, King Saul, and Nimrod of the Tower of Babel vividly preached the consequences of their vice. With candid confession, Dante recognizes his place among these sinners: "my soul is anxious, in suspense; already I feel the heavy weights of the first terrace." What also strikes Dante is the consummate art of these illuminated stories.

What master artist with his brush or pen
Could reproduce these shapes and shadings her/
Such art must overwhelm the subtlest mind!
The dead seemed dead, the living seemed alive.[11]

These statuary parables of God's "visible speech" called sinners to repentance, harbingers of these haunting animated films of this chapter. To raise one's head up and gaze upon such narrative images purges one of pride, or, at least, warns penitents of its penalties.

NOTES

1. DeYoung, Rebecca Konyndyk, *Vainglory: the forgotten vice* (Eerdmans, 2014), 3–4.

2. Waxing eloquently on Breughel's Icarus, W. H. Auden penned his "Musee des Beaux Arts" suggesting a parable in how the ploughman "may have heard the splash, the forsaken cry," but turns away as "for him, it was not an important failure; as a boy falling out of the sky had somewhere to get to."

3. Sayers, Dorothy, "The Other Six Deadly Sins" (Methuen, 1943).

4. Holloway, Ronald, *Z is for Zagreb* (Tantivy Press, 1972), 91.

5. Pavao Statler and Zlatko Grgic captured the end of Socialist tyranny with rich irony in *Scabies* (1969) as a dire end comes to those who oppress others. An enormous creature begins to itch (with scabies) and he finds that what is causing him to be irritated are little men moving about his body. He scratches out the first one and squashes it. The itching escalates and soon he is crushing and stomping on all sorts of little men. Finally, all the little men begin to pour out of his pants and sleeves and the giant Big Brother dissolves. Without the consent of the little people, the powers of the state cannot control its own body. At the end of his film about a sad, little, big-nosed man drafted into service, and enlists with his magical frog *Krek* (1968), Borivoj Dovnikovic-Bordo added a credit in thanking "all the sergeants in the world for helping us to make this film."

6. Dyson, Michael Eric, *Pride* (Oxford University Press, 2006).

7. A more subtle and indicting parable on racial privilege is the often misunderstood *Sunbeam* (1980) by Paul Vester, that shows black note females singing "What's at the top of a Sunbeam" along with a Bing Crosby crooner; yet as some characters make their way up the golden stairway to success, they arrive at the end only to find the gates locked to them.

8. Taylor was the subject of a one-hour color TV special prepared by CBS News and transmitted as "World communication Day" that dealt with the possibilities of animated films and other methods of cross-cultural, nonverbal education and communication. Religious News Service (November 22, 1971).

9. Presbyterians deals with racism through animated cartoons, in which a couple finds a new house and finds it just to their keeping, with lots of closet space, but they are rejected. As they leave, a black couple walks up and the original couples says, "If you folks are Irish, forget it!"

10. Vickers, Nancy J., "Seeing is Believing: Gregory, Trajan, and Dante's Art," *Dante Studies* 101 (1983), 67.

11. Dante, *Purgatory*, 130.

Chapter 5

Envy (*Invidia* or the Wolf)

Invidia (Envy) wanted to be first, but got shoved down to the second place and she will not let you forget it. In Bruegel's 1558 woodcut, Dame Envy shows an unhappy woman eating her heart out, contrasting with the virtue of Love where a Christ-like pelican pierces itself to feed its young with its own body and blood. Her emblem of an ugly turkey, in contrast, portrays the realization that she is decidedly not a peacock of Pride.[1] A demon mocks her own toxic vanity (with peacock feathers attached to a hollow tree behind her) by holding up a cheap halo above her head. The facial façades of the buildings behind her reveal a superficial veneer of her resentment. In the far right bottom corner, a cobbler busily mass-produces shoes for potential customers, suggesting a trendy capitalist desire for more and more material possessions.

Shoes are everywhere. A winged fish monster in the lower corner stuffs a shoe into his mouth. A forlorn old woman sitting in a basket endures a shoe on her head, even as she displays shoes she tries futilely to sell. Two women vainly try to fit in the right shoe (previewing the later Grimm brothers' stories of the two stepsisters of Cinderella).[2] Naked sinners await their turn to have shoes all the same size and shape forced on them. Envy longs to be in someone else's shoes or social standing. A corrosive spite desires *Schadenfreude*, encouraging creatures to backstab each other as demons shoot arrows. One creature even piggybacks a conquered soul up a ladder into a burning house, carrying his sinner to a punishment of fire. Such malicious glee over the suffering of others shows as a ship capsizes against a mountain. One thinks of Sebastian Brandt's *Ship of Fools*, but then Dame Envy "only laughs when she/ Has sunk a foes' ship out at sea."[3]

One finds the familiar trope of envy in two dogs fighting over a bone. A funeral procession highlights the Flemish proverb, *invidia horrendum monstrum, saevissima pestis*, namely, "Envy, endless death, and cruel sickness is a self-devouring beast." Looking at dry branches sticking out of a gaping hole, one sees hollow men without eyes in a dead land.[4] So too, a consumptive man with a swollen torso sinks in the back of a boat, with his skeletal leg slung over the side.

Joseph Epstein cleverly points out that envy is the only one of the seven deadly sins that "is no fun at all."[5] Frederick Buechner sees it as "the consuming desire to have everybody else as unsuccessful as you are."[6] Dante seems to concur, as the envious are placed in freezing water. Aquinas explains that demons are frozen in pride and envy. Ironically, the two sins stand at opposite ends of a continuum, with pride boasting its superiority over others and envy resenting that others are superior to it (which is why Aquinas suggests that demons are not a happy tribe). There is no respite for those cold-blooded sinners who begrudge others. Epstein lays out how such spite, with a bit of snobbery, "clobbers generosity, precludes any hope of serenity, and ends in shriveling the heart." Here resides the Grinch who stole Christmas with his malice and hidden rancor.[7] Here stands the Queen before her magic mirror, asking if she is the fairest in all the land. The toxic state of the heart wants what others have or wants to make sure that they do not have it. Based on a competitive spirit, Envy craves what another possesses or desires to deny them what they have. Ironically, we do not easily recognize this hidden sin when it rears its green head, as we bury it deeply in the sands of our subconscious.

Redcross Knight in *The Faerie Queen* stumbles into the House of Pride, where he meets the proud Lucifera and her six dwarfish slaves. Among them creeps a grotesque Envy riding on a ravenous wolf. His cankered teeth drip with poison, due mostly to his habit of chewing on a venomous toad. He grieves at the happiness of others and rejoices at their misfortune, and inwardly chews his own entrails.[8] When he hears of harm happening to others, he waxes wondrously glad. Wearing a many-colored tunic, painted full of eyes, he holds a hateful snake in his bosom, with a mortal sting in its tail. He gnashes his teeth with a greedy covetousness, begrudging the felicity of proud Lucifera. He hates all the good works and virtuous deeds of others, such as feeding the hungry. He sees behind every good, a latent evil motive, as he backbites and spews poisonous spit from his leprous mouth. Envy seems to be a small-town vice, where one measures status quite easily. She is the twisted sister of pride. Pride may puff up, but envy makes the bones rot (Proverbs 14:30).

William Langland's Envy hates a neighbor whom he seeks to annoy at every opportunity. Even "in church he turns from prayer to envy 'Heyne' his new coat." Asked if he pities poor men, he says as much as a peddler pities cats, who "will kill them because he covets their coats." One can easily see how the antidote to envy is admiration, a virtue so far from one who craves what another is or has. In Dante, the apt judgment, the *contrapasso*, occurs as the pilgrim sees threads of iron wire sewing eyelids shut, ostensibly so the envious cannot see and compare their lives with others.

Mixing avarice with envy, the magnificent stop-motion puppetry of *Balance* (Wolfgang and Christoph Lauenstein, 1989) suspends five archetypal men in long dark coats on a floating rectangular platform in space, fishing for items off the edges (figure 5.1). The platform is level and all men are equal. A number marks the back of each man's coat, suggesting a lack of individuality. They are clones and prisoners of a dark gray world. They maintain an equilibrium, a balance among each other that keeps them from falling to their deaths. However, they retrieve a mysterious music box, playing tinny jazz tunes, a symbol of universal desire like the fruit of the knowledge of good and evil. Seeking to examine it, each person movies toward it; yet the box continuously moves and shifts around. As one man moves to the right, the others must compensate by going left, each trying to maneuver the box into his domain. The slightest movement of each person affects the balance of their universe. Eventually, they begin to shove and push each other off the platform, each one desiring to own the box and not allow others to enjoy it. Because of each man's unhappiness, his neighbor cannot bear what seems to be another's happiness. This unbridled selfishness pits each featureless man against his neighbor, resulting in four of the men falling overboard into the void. The final survivor has obtained the box for himself, ridding himself of the competition. Ironically, however, the

Figure 5.1 ***Balance*** **(Wolfgang and Christoph Lauenstein, 1989) Brilliantly Sets Humanity against One Another, Often for No More Than Some Tinny Music.** *Source*: Screenshot taken by the author.

box sits on the opposite side of the platform and every step he would take toward it, would send it over the side of his world. This brilliantly sparse and minimalist film achieves what interviewer Olivier Cotte saw as a "film with a message: you come away from it a little shaken up." The brothers Lauenstein explained that they aimed at creating a "universal picture of human behavior; it a way that everyone would understand. Interdependence is the keyword of this film."[9]

While many may seek to emulate those above them, Epstein identifies the smug and comic German practice of *Schadenfreude*, "a hardy perennial in the weedy garden of sour emotions," akin to envy. Curiously, he finds sophisticated envy in the worlds of the arts and the academy.[10] C. S. Lewis describes hell as a place where everyone has a grievance and lives the deadly sin of resentment, where Screwtape-like devils want to destroy the happiness of their patients, and even, insidiously, devour them.[11] Kierkegaard addresses this existential quality of *ressentiment*, a frustrated sense of one's own inferiority or failure, as he looked at his present age:

> It is a fundamental truth of human nature that man is incapable of remaining permanently on the heights, of continuing to admire anything. Human nature needs variety. Even in the most enthusiastic ages, people have always liked to joke enviously about their superiors. That is perfectly in order and is entirely justifiable so long as after having laughed at the great they can once more look upon them with admiration; otherwise, the game is not worth the candle. . . . The *ressentiment* which is *establishing itself* is the process of leveling, and while a passionate age storms ahead setting up new things and tearing down old, raising and demolishing as it goes, a reflective and passionless age does exactly the contrary; it *hinders and stifles* all action; it levels.[12]

Kierkegaard sees that the mass of people camouflage their envy by making the independent individual an object of ridicule, and often a scapegoat, in order to maintain the illusion of their own specious sense of superiority. Such *ressentiment* (philosopher Max Scheler's special "form of human hate") exposes a self-defeating experience, which exposes how a twisted itch for something ultimately wastes one's time and energy.[13] Sustained envy and misplaced desires ravage the envious much more than the envied. Spite scathingly seethes in one's soul while the envied rarely realize the pain they cause. The Crow enjoys the picnic while the Fox beats himself for his unfulfilled longing. The grapes are sour.

Reflecting the Fox's venal hankering for the grapes is a specialized German term known as *Futterneid*, which combines envy, gluttony, and animal food. What cartoon character wants the bigger bone, the carrot, the cake, or the grapes? *Futterneid* (with *Futter* meaning fodder and *Neid* denoting envy) is when someone else's food looks better and smells better than your own

Figure 5.2 ***Show Biz Bugs*** **(Friz Freleng, 1957) Captures the Classic Professional Envy of Actors.** *Source*: Screenshot taken by the author.

food, his or her piece of cake looks larger, and you want it. One stares at another's feast in hope that he will get some of it.

An even more theatrical evidence of a revelatory parable, *Show Biz Bugs* (Friz Freleng, 1957), serves as a pattern of envy for all Daffy Duck versus Bugs Bunny films (figure 5.2).[14] Employing *Webster*'s definition that envy is a "painful or resentful awareness of the advantage enjoyed by another joined with a desire to possess the same advantage," Daffy will fit the bill, with a bit of malicious mischief thrown in. Arguing that his music hall performances will prove that he is a star, Daffy huffs around to find that his dressing room is a men's toilet ("there can only be one explanation for white tile in a dressing room.") He orders Bugs not to try to trip him up with his big feet. Bugs remain deferential and humble. As two vaudevillians, Daffy and Bugs perform their soft shoe dance wearing tuxedo jackets, top hats, and canes. As they exit the stage, the number elicits rave applause, which Daffy attributes to his own star power. "Hey, listen to that! They love me!" and rushes back on stage and bows, to absolute silence. When Bugs peeks out of the wings, the clapping resumes. Daffy confronts him "I'm sick of people taking credit for my talent." Essentially, Daffy protests throughout, "What about me?"

Trying to compete with Bugs, Daffy promises to kill the audience with his real dancing talents. After a slam-bam routine, Daffy slides to the stage lights and hears nothing, only the sounds of crickets. He exits, and mutters

"Ingrates!" Challenging Bugs to a dance-off, Daffy exhausts himself with rapid-fire hoofing maneuvers, all to nil effect: silence.

Author Gore Vidal's famous quip strikes at the heart of Daffy's envy: "It is not enough to succeed. Others must fail." Thus, Daffy tries futilely to thwart Bug's routines. Even after his trained pigeons all fly away, he skips off, only to get pummeled with a rotten tomato. He sets Bugs up for a fatal fall, confiding with his audience that following his song, "Endearing Young Charms," Daffy will play the xylophone rigged to explode with TNT. "Now's my chance, hmmm, I can get rid of the rabbit; it'll look like an accident when he strikes this note." Instead of the xylophone, Bugs will play the harp. He emits an evil laugh, "nya ha ha." When Bugs misses the key explosive note, Daffy yells, "That's wrong, ya dumb bunny." After a second time, "No, you stupid rabbit! Like this!" He blows himself up as his beak falls off along with xylophone keys.

Bugs juggles successfully and bows, as Daffy fumes: "I hate you!" His vitriolic outburst parallels the complaint of a penitent in Dante's second terrace: "My blood was so afire with envy that, when I had seen a man becoming happy, the lividness in me was plain to see." Daffy's *ressentiment* escalates the stakes. "Now, you forced me to use the act I held back for a special occasion. Try to top this one. I now present an act that no actor has dared to perform. In fairness, I must warn those with weak constitutions to leave the theatre. Lights." He comes out wearing a devil costume, red horns, and a little red spiked tail, calling again for "Lights! Thank you! Some appropriate music maestro."

"First, I drink a generous portion of gasoline. Then some nitroglycerin; a goodly amount of gunpowder; some uranium 238. Shake well. Strike an ordinary match. Girls, you better hold on to your boyfriends." He swallows the match and the whole stage explodes.

Bugs appears out of the wings and exclaims, "That's terrific, Daffy. They loved it. They want more."

"I know, I know," he ruefully concedes, "but I can only do it once." His ghost floats upward.

Theological writing and creative invention join Daffy's grudge against Bugs to describe envy, with Thomas Aquinas noting that this spiteful vice stands in contrast to charity, "whence the soul derives its spiritual life. Charity rejoices in our neighbor's good, while envy grieves over it."[15] Giving generously to others rebukes our greed and envy. Dante echoes the spirit by categorizing envy as that overblown "love of one's own good, perverted to a desire to deprive other men of theirs." One coldly hates other people for what they have and, if their joy cannot be hijacked, one wishes it destroyed altogether. The malicious Iago ironically warned Othello of jealousy, that "green-eyed monster which doth mock the meat it feeds upon."[16] Some thought that

Figure 5.3 Envy Becomes Its Own Prison in Ishu Patel's Glittering *Paradise* (1984).
Source: Screenshot taken by the author.

an overproduction of bile, or gall, that dark-green-to-yellowish-brown acidic fluid produced by the liver, could turn human skin green. A bile reflux, causing frequent heartburn, scalds and eats away from within. It plants a grudge that singes everything it can, even Daffy. Perhaps immersion in freezing water is a most fitting judgment.

The didactic moral narrative of *The Uses of Envy* (Lara Lee and Hannah Jacobs in *The School of Life*, 2019) tries to justify envy and lift it out of its status as a vice, seeking to show something about what is good about envy. "Envy is there," argues the film, "to let us know what we want." The humiliating experiences of envy offer clues as to what we might do to achieve what we want to be. Study the people who make us envious and record an envy diary that will show a future self, trying to break through. The film, unfortunately, does not make a distinction between the begrudging nature of the vice and the virtue of admiration. It advises that one should become a student of one's envious feelings and be realistic, accepting a lesser form of success than what others achieve. Where it conveys wisdom is in listening to those feelings of coveting and trying to understand them, turning them into something better. Such a process shines through Ishu Patel's glittering *Paradise* (1984) (figure 5.3).

In brilliant hues, Patel's parable of envy begins in a lush tropical garden, with purple flowers in a bucolic landscape. An ordinary black crow sits contentedly on a rock, stretching its neck as it hears the alluring song of another bird. Seeing the dazzling lights of a grand vizier's castle, it sneaks to discover the source of the music. The vizier watches his imprisoned beautiful, white cockatoo bird, as she spread her wings, transforming into a multicolored, golden-plumed bird of paradise. She rests upon her master's turban, from which he feeds her, and she continually metamorphoses into luminous gold and pink colors. The crow watches from a distance, as the creature flies, breathes out golden irises, and spreads beauty throughout the castle. Normand Roger's sound design and James Last's score of "The Lonely Shepherd" create a melancholy strain of *Sehnsucht*, of yearning and desire for something beyond our reach.

Looking at itself in a ditch of dull water, the crow comes to covet the beautiful plumage of the other birds. It dreams of possessing rainbow colors that radiate from its ordinary feathers. It begins to gather numerous flowers and feathers from other birds and flowers, stealing and even tossing their young out of their nests. With all its gaudy paraphernalia, peacock feathers, blueberries, it tries to cosmetically alter his look, with a large fake beak, and then sneak into the palace. As the crow poses and pretends to be such a bird of paradise, strutting around more like a clown with its tail feathers falling off, it falls flat in its aspirations. Its artificiality is obvious as it comes before the king. Doing its awkward dance and trying to impress, its antics attract the royal attention, until its beak falls off.

Yet, it receives royal applause and then, suddenly, a golden cage falls upon it. Imprisoned on a tree, it endures a storm, until lightning breaks the cage, and amid the rain, the crow gives up its delusions of grandeur. Crestfallen, and realizing that its freedom had been lost for the sake of artificial beauty, it now rejoices in its liberty. Discovering the grandeur and loveliness of all nature, it dances for joy to be what it is. With all the birds joining in all the colors of the earth dancing in Busby Berkley-like choreography, it realizes the futility of his jealous desire and the wonders of its own freedom. Herein one finds *The Uses of Envy* in that one discovers one's true desires are not in coveting what others have.

Animator Dan Stevers embellishes a biblical narrative from Luke's *Acts of the Apostles* to create a remarkably scary Gothic version of *The Grim Tale of Ananias and Sapphira* (2015). In the creative tradition of Michelangelo's dramatic cartoon of the tragic couple in the Sistine Chapel and director Tim Burton's grotesque animated films, Stevers adapts the cautionary episode regarding religious hypocrisy and lying to the Holy Spirit with the added theme of envy. A proud married couple watch an apocryphal fellow named Joseph selflessly give all that he has to the early church. As they see what praise he receives for his generosity (the fellowship throws him in the air amid acclamation and shouts of joy), they conspire to sell a plot of land and give part of the proceeds to the apostles. They think, "Who is Joseph that he should receive such commendation?" They feel that they deserve such acclaim. They sell the land, pocket most of the profits, and pretend to give it all to the church that they might receive glory. When the disciple Peter questions Ananias about their gift, Ananias boasts and lies to the community. Immediately he falls dead. As they wrap him up and carry him off for burial, Sapphira appears and fibs as well. She falls as quickly as her husband fell.

The consequence of their desire for glory and a desire to receive attention over others leads clearly to the wages of all sin, death.

For Bruno Bettelheim, such grim stories and fairy tales provide vivid and engaging examples of how children resolve conflicts related to such sins of vanity, greed, and envy. One such work holding political as well as moral implications comes from former entomologist Ladislaw Starewicz. After fleeing the revolutionary Soviet Union, Starewicz produced the Aesop tale of the *The Frogs Who Wanted a King* or *Frogland* (1922). In the old fable, "The Frogs prayed to Jove for a King. Not a log, but a livelier thing. Jove sent them a Stork, Who did royal work; for he gobbled them up, did their king" (with the moral: "Don't have kings"). In a similar vein to "The Trees Who Wanted a King" from the Hebrew Scriptures, the clever work of lifelike, taxidermies' animated amphibian figures (executed by the Russian Art Society of Paris) exposes the vice of communal envy, of those trying to imitate what they see as their neighbors' prosperity.

A head frog calls upon his fellow croakers and toadstool pigeons, complaining that their "democratic form of government is all wet." It was time to beseech Jupiter to send them a king as their present "authorities are full of hops!" The stop-action frogs clamor, plead, and entreat on bended knees, until the white-bearded god sitting on the clouds decide to send them a log with a face. Offering tributes to the stump, nothing happens. They catch on that the presidential timber is only a blockhead. Interrupted again, Jupiter decides that, "these frogs know not when they are well off. They're almost human." He sends a sharp-beaked stork. "Long Live King Stork!" the frogs cheer, wearing top hats, waving umbrella parasols (as in Eisenstein's famous Potemkin Steps sequence), with a froggy band. They crown the crane, even with a man with a movie camera recording the *cinéma vérité* event.

The stork then reaches down to pick up the chief frog in his beak, who feeds the royal bird, that immediately swallows the frog, legs and all, as dessert. The congregation panics. One besotted frog drinking throughout the festivities tries to hide in a bucket, but the big bird snatches him up for a snack. As news of the king's appetite "spreadeth throughout the kingdom," the frogs become, excuse Starewicz' pun, "fed up." They petition Jupiter all over again, but he has had enough: "Fickle fools, you're never content. Here's where I give them thunder!" He casts judgment upon them for their foolish ambition to be like others. One last frog speaks his farewell: "Dear Friends, before I make my slide/Into this greedy stork's inside,/Give ear unto my parting moan—Moral: Let well enough alone." He throws a kiss and waves goodbye, and is gulped by the stork. Jupiter goes back to sleep on his cloud. Perhaps as a cautionary tale to the French communists, the Russian émigré sought to wean them off their ambition to become like their Soviet compatriots.[17]

While greed may be the sin of capitalist societies, envy often insinuates itself as a vice of communist countries. Epstein argues that envy fuels much of class conflict from a Marxist perspective, hovering as an act of "implacable collective envy and vengeance" of the dispossessed against the more affluent and privileged class.[18] However, another, and darker, mode of envy occurs beyond the political sphere, percolating within every human soul. *Schadenfreude*, that peculiar pleasure or delight one finds in seeing one's neighbor suffer, inhabits the hearts of humanity. Greeks called it *epichairekakia*, an amalgam meaning the rejoicing over the disgrace of another. "How sweet it is!" Ralph Kramden (Jackie Gleason) of *The Honeymooners* used to say as disaster hit someone else. When Homer Simpson discovered its meaning, he wallowed in its sentiment, wishing misfortune upon his guileless neighbor Ned Flanders when he opens a shop for left-handers, the Leftorium.[19] It is the cartoon caption of two dogs conferring: "It is not enough that dogs succeed. Cats must also fail."

The Pixar director of *Inside Out* (2015), Pete Docter, wished he had included one other emotion in the head of his protagonist Riley. The one that did not make the cut with Joy, Anger, Fear, Sadness, and Disgust was *Schadenfreude*.[20] Feelings of envy, intense envy, invite a desire to see our neighbors suffer, even to participate in their misfortune. Resentment and jealousy can rationalize and justify the crimes of our imagination. Indirectly, one brilliant Pixar cartoon taps into the mischief and just desserts of *Schadenfreude*, the Academy Award–winning *For the Birds* (Ralph Eggleston, 2000). Justice occurs in a form of *karma*, which appears to be a proper consequence of some person's uncivil behavior (figure 5.4). In one sense, the spiritual principle suggests that there is a deserved consequence for individual actions, where the end rewards or punishes the intent of a person. She deserved what

Figure 5.4 Avian Jealousy over Place Marks *For the Birds* (Ralph Eggleston, 2000) with One of the Most Hilarious Finales of Comeuppance. *Source*: Screenshot taken by the author.

she got, is the ordinary way of expressing it. In a comic vein, *For the Birds* exemplifies one of the most delightful extensions of this justified law of cause and effect. A flock of little, spiteful, egg-shaped birds (with apt names like Chipper, Snob, Bully, and Neurotic) perches on a telephone wire, snipping and sniping at each other. When a large gangly and awkward-looking bird squeezes in on the middle of the wire, the others grow irritated, and quite nasty. Territorially jealous of their phone line, the fat aviary congregation feels miffed when the goofy and gawky invader sits happily in the middle of the wire, honking away. Irritated with his presence, the gossipy tribe of tweets imitate and mock the invader's stupidity, Disdain for one's neighbor simmers as one sees the arrogant little fowls showcase both their pride and envy. Taking Dante's definition of pride as "love of self, perverted to hatred and contempt for one's neighbor," they assert their right to the thin line, envious of the space the outsider has taken.

As the weight of the big bird pulls the wire close to the ground, the squashed feathered clique conspires to push him off the wire, by pecking at his toes. The rest titter with devious delight, thinking of how they are going to dump, quite unceremoniously, the big bird. However, one prescient bird realizes the physics of their situation, panics, and tries to get the pecking to stop. As the last toe is unfurled from the wire, the big bird falls off and the wire snaps sharply, thrusting the rest of the birds into the air. As the dumped bird looks around him, he begins to see a shower of feathers fall about him. Then the birds fall: chubby, naked, and desperate to hide. The original victim now laughs at the folly of the envious conspirators, offering a leaf for their nakedness. Wishing to rejoice in their neighbor's fall, they instead become the objects of an unexpected humiliation. The unintended consequences of snooty pride and petty envy culminate in a harmless and hilarious upheaval. Appropriately, "The End" credit closes with a splattering of white guano on the screen. Dante, who makes the sin itself the punishment in the *Inferno*, could not have devised a more appropriate judgment.

NOTES

1. Birds that soar into the heavens often symbolize the heights of pride, as in Tim Fernee's *Animals* (*The Wren, King of the Birds*, 1997), in which the smaller bird outwits an arrogant Golden Eagle in a contest to fly high. The Wren strategically rides the Eagle's back until the larger bird is exhausted, at which point the Wren then springs even higher.

2. See the exquisite work on imagining Envy by artist Adrien Broom "Envy, One Sin, Seven Stories" at https://www.nytimes.com/2015/08/02/nyregion/imagining

-envy-one-of-the-seven-deadly-sins.html (Accessed September 6, 2020), especially as it alludes to a non-Disney version of *Cinderella*.

3. Brandt, Sebastian, *Ship of Fools* (trans Alexander Barkley) (Project Guttenberg, 2006).

4. Eliot, T. S., "The Hollow Men," in *T. S. Eliot: Collected Poems, 1909–1962* (Harcourt Brace Jovanovich, 1991), 77.

5. Epstein, Joseph, *Envy* (Oxford University Press, 2003), 1.

6. Buechner, Frederick, *Wishful Thinking* (Harper and Row, 1973), 20.

7. Seuss, Dr., *How the Grinch Stole Christmas!* (Random House, 1957).

8. Edmund, Spenser, *Faerie Queen Book I Canto IV* (ed. Carol Kaske) (Hackett, 2006), 53.

9. Cotte, Olivier, *Secrets of Oscar-Winning Animation* (Focal Press, 2013), 130.

10. Epstein, *Envy,* 70.

11. Lewis, C. S., *The Screwtape Letters* (Macmillan, 1961).

12. Kierkegaard, Soren, *The Present Age and of the Difference between a Genius and an Apostle* (trans. Alexander Dru) (Harper Torchbooks, 1962), 49–52; Epstein points out that most writers on envy were bachelors, citing Nietzsche's observation that "a married philosopher was a joke." (xix)

13. For Scheler what was once valued as the good is now devalued as "sour grapes" as one cannot receive or achieve it. He sees this spiritual venom as *Ressentiment*, "a self-poisoning of the mind which has quite definite causes and consequences. It is a lasting mental attitude, caused by the systematic repression of certain emotions and affects which as such are normal components of human nature. Their repression leads to the constant tendency to indulge in certain kinds of value delusions and corresponding value judgments. The emotions and affects primarily concerned are revenge, hatred, malice, *envy*, the impulse to detract, and spite." (italics added) *Ressentiment* (1913) (trans. William W. Holdheim) (Schocken, 1972), 45–46.

14. The theme is wildly extended in Chuck Jones' hilarious *The Rabbit Season* trilogy, with a little bit of pronoun trouble and untold number of creative twisting, tweaking, and distortions of Daffy's beak.

15. Aquinas, Thomas, *Summa Theologiae* (Coyote Canyon, 2018), 2. 36, ad. 3.

16. Shakespeare, William, *Othello* (Act 3, Scene 3); Portia in *The Merchant of Venice* also speaks of the green-eyed jealousy (Act 3, Scene 2).

17. The envy of Antonio Salieri toward Mozart is Milos Forman's *Amadeus* (1984) parallels the frogs' pleadings with God for change.

18. Epstein, *Envy*, 52.

19. *The Simpsons* Season 3; episode 3 "When Flanders Failed" https://www.youtube.com/watch?v=B01e7n4RzZc (Accessed March 17, 2020).

20. Wang, Shensheng, "Why Does It Feel Good to See Someone Fail?" *The Conversation* (January 4, 2019), http://theconversation.com/why-does-it-feel-good-to-see-someone-fail-107349 (Accessed March 17, 2020).

Chapter 6

Anger (*Ira* or the Lion)

In his usual sardonic manner, satirist Ambrose Bierce advises his readers to "Speak when you are angry and you will make the best speech you will ever regret." Few of the vices have been as descriptively anthropomorphized as Anger (*orgē*), who stands out as one of the five main characters in Pixar's *Inside/Out*, a squat, molten, red man. Anger is red, in the flag before the bull and in the fire of felt injustice burning in one's eyes. Whether simmering tantrums or blazing rage, the hot vice of wrath smolders in the Devil's Furnace. But anger, or ire or wrath, is also "possibly the most fun sin," according to Frederick Buechner. He describes it vividly:

> To lick your wounds, to smack your lips over grievances long past, to roll over your tongue the prospect of bitter confrontations still to come, to savor to the last toothsome morsel both the pain you are given and the pain you are giving back—in some many ways it is a feast fit for a king. The chief drawback is that what you are wolfing down is yourself. The skeleton at the feast is you.[1]

For *Ira* (Anger), Bruegel alludes to the ultimate expression of wrath, war, and draws an old shrewish woman with a broken arm, cloaked and dressed in armor, knife between her teeth, hovering over a barrel of soldiers, stabbing each other. Another aggressive battle-axe, with an upraised sword and flaming torch, leads a band of soldiers out to mutilate and crush naked victims, with several carrying a large carving knife that cleaves its victims; while her pet, the symbolic bear, gnaws the leg off a slaughtered quarry. Her rallying emblem is a Muslim crescent moon while all about people suffer under instruments of torture (grilling a skewered man upon a spit) in this dog-eat-dog world. Anger not only culminates in murder; it also leads to madness and everyone touched by it becomes its prey and fatality.[2]

The fiercest beast of Spenser's ungodly procession is wrath, personified as a lion, brandishing a burning sword about his head, eyes sternly staring and hurling fiery red sparkles. Wrath holds on to his dagger, trembling with hasty rage and swelling choler. Blood stains his raiment, as he cannot control his hands when a furious fit is upon him. He is marked with cruel bloodshed and tumultuous strife, "swelling Spleen, widespread Frenzy," shaking palsy and the Saint Frances fire of erysipelas. One does not wish to even converse with him.

Cartoon children of this murderous beast flaunting hot and volatile tempers include Warner Bros.' ill-tempered Tasmanian Devil (Taz), whose short-fused anger often spins out of control into a destructive force of nature. So, too, explodes the hotheaded Yosemite Sam, screaming "Ooooooooooooo! Why I hate that rabbit!" at Bugs Bunny. He thirsts for vengeance while blowing smoke out of his ears. Evagirus describes the irascible monk as a solitary wild boar, who sees others and gnashes his teeth. Yet, no other character in animation history personifies anger, as well as Walt Disney's irascible Donald Duck. His life in cartoons is a veritable textbook of the vice of wrath and its consequences. In *Donald's Double Trouble* (Jack King, 1946), for example, the irascible fowl turns a volcanic red with angry eyes over his nemesis' taking Daisy into a Tunnel of Love. He gives the slicing of the throat sign with paper burning on top of his head.[3] Psychologist and author of *The Anger Workbook for Teens*, Raychelle Cassada Lohmann offered anger management therapy for such animated characters, trying to find out what triggered their rage and to redirect it all in socially acceptable ways. One of her chief patients was the easily frazzled Donald Duck, whose nephews, Huey, Dewey, and Louie, would cause him to fly into a fit of uncontrollable rage. She recommended that he work through his negative emotions of frustration and annoyance and find healthy outlets to cool his feathers, maybe even practicing mindfulness.[4] Donald seems to have greater problems, however, as the source of one instance of his fury is frustrated lust. In *A Good Time for a Dime* (Dick Lundy, 1941), a curious Donald wanders into an amusement park and peeks inside an Edison-style kinetoscope (the kind that Disneyland used to feature as a Main Street attraction). He inserts a dime into a machine that offers to show him "Dance of the Seven Veils." Titillated by Daisy gyrating in a harem outfit, the machine breaks obstructing Donald's pornographic voyeurism. His lust stymied, and he blows up in a rage.[5] Disney animators dared to show the devil in the duck over sexual exasperation. Laura Mulvey's "Male Gaze" rarely exposes itself this graphically.

A carefree Donald Duck, smoking his cigar, walks leisurely down a sidewalk in *Cured Duck* (Jack King, 1945), going to meet his paramour, a well-perfumed Daisy (figure 6.1). Electricity sparks between them. To accommodate his girlfriend, he tries to open a window, but it will not budge.

Figure 6.1 Anger Management Does Not Work in *Cured Duck* (Jack King, 1945).
Source: Screenshot taken by the author.

This simple frustration escalates to where he pulls down curtains, breaks dishes, a phone, and a cabinet, until Daisy has had enough. He apologizes but she demands that he go deal with his anger. Forlornly, he reads in a paper "Have you a Temper? If so . . . take the cure by mail. From the Tootsberry Institute of Temperism." Donald submits to a behavior modification program delivered through a record on a phonograph, which teaches him to relax (in an early version of mindfulness), count to ten, and even pray for strength. The program promises that it will give Donald a nice surprise, which turns out to be a brick on his foot, at which the machine cackles with *Schadenfreude* gusto. The technology squirts Donald, beats him up, and pulverizes, but the Duck endures and gets his diploma for completing the program.

When Donald returns to Daisy, he announces, "It's the new me." She asks him to open the window, but it slams on his fingers. He tries to get it up again, but fails; yet he laughs with self-effacing humor as the window falls on him. Through various mishaps of futilely trying to open the window, he consistently laughs. Even when it falls out of its frame and crashes on his head, he grins and bears it. Daisy laughs with him. To celebrate she puts on an outlandish hat with cherries on top. However, when Donald roars with laughter at her headgear, Daisy loses her temper, turning red and enraged herself, pounding him with her broom. The unexpected outburst from Daisy highlights the different ways in which anger manifests itself in the human psyche. One can easily envision Tex Avery's visualized cliché in his *Symphony in Slang* (1951) in which the narrator says, "I was beside myself with anger" and the cartoon shows two identical versions of the person sitting next to an enraged red figure (figure 6.2).[6]

Figure 6.2 Tex Avery's *Symphony in Slang* (1951) Depicts a Man beside Himself with Anger. *Source*: Screenshot taken by the author.

Bugs Bunny's usually placid and cool demeanor endures throughout his films until he announces, "Of course you realize this means war!" (*Porky's Hare Hunt*, Ben "Bugs" Hardaway, 1938). The reality is that the Bunny usually provokes anger in others. When Bugs argues with Yosemite Sam, he suddenly switches to take Sam's position. Sam, however, continues to disagree out of ignorance, anger, and spite. When Marvin the Martian tries to abduct Bugs to go back to Mars with him in *The Hasty Hare* (Chuck Jones, 1952), the Rabbit tricks him by pretending to be a train conductor, who calls for everyone to board the spaceship: "Flying saucer, for Saturn, Neptune, Jupiter, Venus, the Dog Star and Mars now leaving on track five! All aboard!" Marvin obeys and then realizing his mistake, returns and confronts his nemesis: "Oh! That wasn't a bit nice! [huff, puff] You have made me very angry, [huff, puff] very angry indeed!" This classic line parallels the archetypal emotion and psychological makeup of the god of war's red planet, Mars.

Just identifying the cause of anger is not sufficient in dealing with escalating anger. *The Cat Came Back* (Cordell Barker, 1988) seethes with mounting anger (figure 6.3). What begins as a gentle breeze of affection toward an orphaned kitty escalates into a mounting hurricane of frustrated wrath toward all creatures great and small. Based on the catchy Tin Pan Alley tune published by Henry S, Miller in 1893, the folk song shows how anger can spiral out of control, even rocketing a person to the ultimate stage of anger: murder and death.

The old folk song cartoon begins benignly enough with crickets chirping away and stars twinkling until a tuba announces the title with Old Mr. Johnson blaring out the tune. Inauspiciously, a teacup rattles. Pictures of his beloved Mom decorate his homey place. Then an unrelenting knock on the

Figure 6.3 ***The Cat Came Back*** **(Cordell Barker, 1988) Escalates into Full-Fledged Fury.**
Source: Screenshot taken by the author.

door interrupts his musical solo, provoking him to open his one good eye and stop his music. However, the first sign of anger finds Old Mr. Johnson howling in frustration at the disruption. He is not a patient man.

He opens the door dramatically and shouts "Whaaat?!"

Looking about, with a protruding under-bite, he lowers his gaze and sees a bright yellow cat (with a magenta bow tie) in a purple basket. He grabs his giant chin and "ooohs and aaahs" at its apparent cuteness. He claps his hands in glee, grins warmly, and makes silly faces and giggles, reaching down to pick up the adorable feline. He sets it on his table and it purrs. What he has forgotten is that Egyptians once regarded cats as gods. The cats haven't forgotten.

He looks aside at his own 1903 diapered baby photo, holding a pink rattle with a cyan-green bow in his hair. He shakes the rattle before the kitten and then hugs and kisses the memory. The cat gestures toward the rattle, which Mr. Johnson dangles before it. Not a good idea to play with the kitten, almost taunting it with baby noises and rubbery faces. Sticking his tongue out, he teases the pet that throws out a little paw, making him drop it on the floor, where it breaks, much to his dismay.

He looks dismissingly at the cat and tosses him out of the house, slamming the door, and swiftly removing the welcome mat. Then the song begins:

> Old Mr. Johnson makes increasingly manic attempts to rid himself of a little yellow cat that just won't stay away.
>
> Now, old Mr. Johnson had troubles of his own. [The cat sneaks back into the house through the mail slot.]

He had a yellow cat that wouldn't leave his home! [The cat jumps on his bed, dives into pillows, with feathers billowing out. Grabbing it by the neck, he takes it outside.]
A special plan with deception as the key.
One little cat—how hard could it be?

The song continues to prophesy his doom, even as he took steps to remove the little curse. This amusing children's song has been used to teach children tempo, rhythm, and beat patterns, but now it functions as *via negativa* parable on how to handle that little temper. The challenge of controlling one's tantrums recalls John and Faith Hubley's *Cockaboody* (1974), where they animated their children's actual conversations, and showed the rising rage of their daughter Georgia erupting as a sharp-toothed cat monster out of her inner being to scream at her sister.

Mr. Johnson drives the kitten into the woods, but it jumps back in his car quickly. He takes it deeper into the forest, until he is frustratingly lost among the many trees. He makes his way home covered with leaves, and prickly gumballs. "One little cat—how hard could it be?" The cat proceeds to tear down the curtains, the springs of the sofa. Mr. Johnson distracts it with a tiny trophy fish from the wall and catches it in a bag. A victorious yelp of triumph and sea shanty tune starts up as he transports the cat out to sea. However, trying to attach the cat to an anchor, Mr. Johnson becomes tangled. He sinks with the anchor to the bottom of the sea, grimacing. Little green fish nibble at him, snapping at his one floating hair strand. One fish holds on and rides home on the top of his head. Returning home late, he slogs up his path to his door, shakes water from his pants' leg, and enters with eyes wearily at half-mast. "What the . . . ?" as he sees how the golden feline has stripped the sofa down to its springs, and is jumping among the foam. Once again, he snatches the cat and cycles it to a hot air balloon; unfortunately, he gets tangled in the ropes of the ascending balloon and soars off into the Netherlands. His small moments of desperation swell.

Staggering home, one eye bruised, he falls on his face, with teeth falling out. He takes the lucky cat on a railroad track, running over damsels tied to the tracks. He rides over a cow tied to the track (muttering "What the f . . . "), but it is a little thing, a green ladybug cut in half that derails him. He falls into a dark mine shaft and stares about with wiggly eyes. Other eyes appear. He lights a match and sees a rat, then hundreds of rats and snakes. One blows out his match, ominously. Bruised and beaten, his tongue hanging out, he returns home, chased by a bat that suffers its own indignity, smashing flat into a window. He finds the cat has reduced his fish to a skeleton, has drawn a funny face in red crayon over his mother's image, with a target on her nose, an arrow through her head, and paw prints all over. The cat replaces the mother's face with his own; then she tears the photograph in two.

Finally, Mr. Johnson brings in buckets of dynamite sticks; he piles them up to blow up the cat. He lights a fuse, and laughs to himself. However, the fuse turns out to be the one hair on his head. With his head on fire, he panics. Like the man who digs a pit and falls into it, he stumbles to his own destruction in the ensuing explosion. Yet, as his spirit departs from his body, Old Mr. Johnson feels triumph in being able to haunt and taunt the cat that is still alive. "Hello, putty cat" he mocks, dancing around in his white heavenly garb with pink dotted boxer shorts, tiny pink wings, and white socks. His anger issues abated, he celebrates prancing about with superior laughter over the living. He blows a Bronx cheer in the cat's face and cackles uproariously.

However, he did not count on the descent of his body from the explosion, which lands on the cat, crushes and kills it. The chorus repeats, "The cat came back." Then, in a coup de grace, the spiritual lives of the cat begin to appear, one, two, three, up to nine cat ghosts, which, of course, drive Old Mr. Johnson bonkers. He soars away, insanely running into the sun, followed by the nine cats. After the credits, one hears a quiet meow.

The significant parable of *The Cat Came Back* harkens to the insight into how the little things can exacerbate the vice. *The Song of Solomon* cautions against the "little foxes that ruin the vineyards," and Shakespeare in *The Taming of the Shrew* (4:1) warns against those small people who are reputed to be more easily angered than others, akin to "a little pot [that is] soon hot." In Luis Usón and Andrés Aguilar's photorealistic 3D film, *Afterwork.* (2017), that little pot that boils over is a small vegetable. An orange carrot inflames the wrath of a cartoon madness, in both senses of the term.

In an interview with *Cartoon Brew*, Luis Usón explains that one inspiration for their film came from the observation that "the world of cartoons (especially the classic ones) is much nicer and more tolerable than our reality, where problems, pain, disappointments are the norm." As a fan of Chuck Jones' Wile E. Coyote, Usón pointed out how he hoped that the poor sucker would one day catch the "unbearable Road Runner."[7] Here the cartoon within the cartoon is entitled "Falling Down," starring Groompy and Yummy.

Protagonist, Groompy, a wolf, relentlessly chases Yummy, the carrot, an obvious metaphor for trying to find that in life that satisfies. Cartoony Groompy sits watching TV when his stomach starts to gurgle. He slouches out to the kitchen to discover one special carrot in the refrigerator. Grabbing it and about to bite it, the orange vegetable grows legs and arms and takes off running like the Road Runner, jumping out a window. Groompy follows, only to discover, like the Coyote, that he is now plummeting several stories and gravity will have its way with his body. The carrot and the wolf fall together, but Yummy has a parachute. The cartoon ends as our hero hits the pavement. In Prudentius' *Psychomachia*, a puffed-up Pride on her spirited Charger rushes at its humble enemy, Lowliness, only to fall headlong into a pit and, like an overweening Goliath, have her head severed by Virtue. How the mighty have fallen.

The film switches to a photorealistic Groompy, the actor, who drives home, weary and stuck in traffic, after work. He is restless and bored, consumed with tedious habits of watching TV, slopping beans into his face, popping pills, and living a quiet life of desperation, sloth, and emptiness. Every day he returns to the rut of being a foil for Yummy, idling in traffic, and dulling his senses with the electronic wasteland. Turning off the TV late one night, the photorealistic Groompy opens the fridge to find the cartoony Yummy there. The carrot taunts him to chase him. This stultified life begins to simmer with anger. He falls over furniture as he growls, grabs a baseball bat and goes ferociously after the goading carrot. His anger knows no bounds, as he destroys table, clock, and even the reflection of himself in the mirror, pulling a piece of real glass from his fist. He leaps out a window after him, only to land on top of a parked car, dead, but holding the carrot.

In the credits, a person files his death certificate away in a filing cabinet of "EXPIRED" characters: Elmer Fudd, Wile E. Coyote, Sylvester the Cat, Avery's Wolfie, and Tom the Cat, a tribute to all those characters who could not control their appetites, passions, or anger. As Dante saw the consequence of anger ripping people apart, so all these angry hunters found themselves expired in shattered pieces.

Anger can be good. The righteous indignation against injustice marks many a prophet. Jesus demonstrated his anger at the sin of the money changers and hypocritical religious leaders. However, St. Paul advised that one should not let the sun go down on one's anger; in other words, do not let it control you. (Ephesians 4:26). Beginning in Genesis (4:6–7), the Lord warns Cain "Why are you angry, and why has your face fallen? If you do well, will you not be accepted? And if you do not do well, sin is crouching at the door. Its desire is for you, but you must rule over it." A voice of envy in Purgatory is that of Cain's, punished not for his fratricide, but for the jealousy over his younger brother's sacrifice. For Aquinas, the passion of anger was "good, in so far as it is regulated by reason; whereas it is evil if it set the order of reason aside."[8] One of the three root poisons identified in Buddhism, along with greed and delusion, is anger (*dvesha*), which as an addiction leads to a life of suffering, both for others and oneself. That person, observed Evagrius, will see disturbing nightmares and imagine the attack of wild beasts.

One of its chief dangers is not only that wrath can control us, but that it can also swell into an institutionalized deadly sin. Anger can magnify and channel energy into war, even as war is "organized anger."[9] With an individual, it may harm, kill, and murder; as a corporate body, it can promote torturous regimes, racism, and even genocide. It is the most dangerous and deadly of the deadly sins.

One of the most ill-timed cartoon productions was MGM Studio's animated short, *Peace on Earth* (Hugh Harman), ironically released in 1939. The imminent world war with Germany and its Axis powers simmered in Europe with doves of peace shot down indiscriminately. Various animals sing the lyrics of the carol "peace on earth, good will to men" during the Christmas holidays and two young squirrels ask their grandfather what are "men." The grandfather explains that "men" disappeared many years ago from fighting with each other. The animals find a Bible in a church, seeking to inaugurate a new society based on the nonviolent and peaceful ideals shown in the Gospels. The era of war was not conducive to appeals to peace and loving one's neighbor, with the revelatory parables falling on rocky ground.

The quintessential animated parable on anger remains Norman McLaren's Oscar-winning short, *Neighbours* (1952) (figure 6.4). Produced during the 1950s Korean conflict, the pixilated film shows two next-door property owners who move from being friends to becoming lethal enemies that begins with a squabble over one small flower that borders their lots. The tiny act of possessiveness escalates to the annihilation of houses, families, and lives. The word "mine"

Figure 6.4 Total War in Norman McLaren's Oscar-Winning Short, *Neighbours* (1952) begins with the desire for one small flower. *Source*: Screenshot taken by the author.

destroys all that is good between neighbors. As animation historian Maureen Furniss pointed out, the film turned from lighthearted to brutal and gruesome, ending with the explicit biblical admonition to "love your neighbor."[10]

In Fyodor Khitruk's classic political parable, *The Lion and the Bull* (1983), a yoked bull suffers a whip of injustice, collapses, and is abandoned as dead. It survives and grows in strength. It comes to a plain, ruled over by a lion, and peacefully chews its grass. When the lion wakes and roars, all the antelope and other creatures head for safety. It surveys the fields, followed by a cowardly jackal, a scavenger, and pursues a gazelle until it comes upon the sharp-horned bull, that does not flinch or budge. A standoff leaves both creatures in mutual respect and harmony, even as they learn to drink from the same pool of water and walk side-by-side.

The jackal schemes, whispering to the lion about the fierceness of the bull and the power of its mighty horns. The scavenger then spreads lies about the lion's red rage to the peaceful bull, sowing seeds of discord between the two giants. Like Iago to Othello, the jackal propagates distrust, suspicion, and enmity until finally the two titans rise up and attack each other in a fierce assault. Overcoming the bull, the lion realizes the deception that caused him to kill his friend and starts toward the trickster. Yet bloodied and weakened by the battle, the lion also collapses and dies. Only the devious villain remains. As Proverbs 30:33 cautioned, just as pressing the nose produces blood, so pressing strife produces anger, the two grand beasts escalate into enemies.

Such animated films chronicle the history of violence and its escalation, often sparked by mere competition or nationalism. In the Prague studio production of *Players* (John Halas, 1982), two tennis finalists enter the arena to prepare for their athletic competition. They put on their game faces, fix their hair, warm up, and prepare for their match. With heads of the stadium spectators turning back and forth, the tennis ball suddenly goes wacky, transforming into a hammer, an iron fist, a gun, or brass knuckles, anything that increases the hostility between the players. A knife sticks to the ground, cutting it open, and then a bomb blows up in one player's face. The crowd laughs as the two confront each other in this surreal satire on aggression.

The first player sends a screaming eagle. A lion counters it. A return volley throws out a shark that relentlessly pursues his opponent. Soon the Loch Ness Monster battles an octopus, each metamorphosing into Viking ships, Naval cannon ships sinking each other, submarines then soaring as dive bomber planes, then strafing each other in dog fights, until both players parachute to the court for a break. With dizzying speed, the competitors escalate their game into surreal violence.

The headband curly-haired McEnroe-type and the blond-bearded Björn Borg facsimile change sides. In the next serve, Tarzan hits a superhero; King Kong pulls down the empire state building, and the accelerated battles speed through cavemen, Vikings, Romans, Huns, Crusader Knights, and Muslims. The French Revolution slaughters thousands and then Napoleon leads his troop with his tennis racket through the snow to massacre others. The two players attack each other with giant missiles, until a referee throws out a white flag. It is too late, as the war decimates the court. However, the two players shake hands, surrounded by the dead spectators. The escalation of competition into anger and war kills.

Both *History of the World in 3 Minutes Flat* (Michael Mills, 1980) and *Cavallette* (*Grasshoppers*) (Bruno Bozzetto, 1990) mark out the trajectory of seeds of anger into war. Out of the void, Mills opens his film with a resonant voice, musing that he had seven days to create something, but blew six. God draws a circle, turns on a light, and calls forth a bit of movement; then, from Adam and Eve eating the fruit in the garden, civilization begins to deteriorate, resulting in wars, death, and destruction (the Soviet revolution is cleverly represented by the Potemkin Steps sequence) until everyone yells and blames everyone else. Suddenly hearing a Divine yawn, one attentive man whispers, "hey, he's bored; let's dance." Everyone around the globe does a soft shoe singing, "we all are together, together." Unconvinced, the Voice says, "oh well, better try again."

Bozzetto unleashes the human race's proclivity for violence in resolving its quarrels. The evolution of the earth conflicts arises after one man starts a fire; a larger caveman throws him out, until the little man returns with an axe. Grasshoppers keep eating the grass; religions war over worshiping a calf or moon; two angry armies demolish each other so that only the insects persist. From Athenian democracy through a powerful Roman empire, one watches killing and looting. The Cross of Christ stops the carnage for one brief moment and then the violence resumes as Goths and Vandals appear. Through church wars, state wars, inquisitions, crusades, and various invasions, heads roll and skulls multiply. The French king throws the Jacobins a bone that turns into a guillotine. Angry conflicts between cowboys and natives, the tanks of Germans and Soviets, bombs from Zionists and the PLO, deteriorate into an apocalyptic world of chaos. Finally, everyone is dead and only the grasshoppers continue to hump each other and eat grass. The two short films chronicle the organization of anger into identity wars, with no survivors.

Both religious and secular histories exhibit the acceleration of anger, namely because of the humans who twist both classical and biblical texts. Sinful human beings adjust faith traditions not only to justify their ways to others but also to remake God and His will in their own image. Personal quarrels become national wars; squabbles over land, as in *Neighbors*, explode into indiscriminate killing, and even genocide.

With Ernest Gold's memorable overture and singer Andy Williams crooning the *Exodus* song (1960), Nina Paley opens her devastatingly quick and

Figure 6.5 Nina Paley's Devastatingly Quick and Trenchant Satire, *This Land is Mine* (2012), chronicles the history of hostile conflicts. *Source*: Screenshot taken by the author.

trenchant satire *This Land is Mine* (2012) (figure 6.5). Part of her larger project, *Seder-Masochism*, stands alone as a parable of equal opportunity violence against humanity. Promisingly fruitful scenes of Palestine turn into an unceasingly violent video game. As a bearded man stands with his staff and sings, "God gave this land to me," a warrior suddenly spears him. Another Jewish patriarch picks up the lyrics, but an Egyptian shoots him with his bow. The carnage continues as in a King Feature cartoon. A father sings of a place where his children can run free, and a little flock of them skip across the screen only to be killed with arrows. The cycle builds as Assyrians, Babylonians, Persians, Greeks, Maccabees, Romans, and Jewish zealots continue to bloody the land with those who came before them, slicing off hands and chopping off heads. As Seleucid ruler Antiochus IV threatens a Jewish priest, Judas Maccabee appears with a giant hammer and pulverizes him, with globs of blood splattering everywhere. Battling through Roman atrocities, Christian/Muslim Crusades, and Arab/Israeli wars, heads roll and the song continues. Scimitars, swords, and ultimately British guns mow down the "other" in an unceasing bloodbath (almost like a recycled cartoon scene).

After so much tribal and inter-tribal carnage, the colonial British arrive and give Israel its land, much to the dismay of Palestinians. Her satire on the jingoist song (written by Pat Boone) shows the assertion of every warring tribe of ownership. Weapons escalate and become more sophisticated and modern, with Zionists, the Hezbollah, PLO, the Hamas, and other terrorists and survivors facing off and singing "I'll make this land my own, *until I die*," as planes fly overhead. Finally, the skeletal specter of death with its ironic grinning skull welcomes them all into *his* land, arms outstretched and atomic bombs mushrooming. Amid all the geopolitics, a divine right of peoples, and lust for power, Paley traces the long horrific history of anger and conflict in this visual storytelling cartoon, chronicling the wars in which armies, like Bozzetto's grasshoppers, continually replaced each other. In her biting parable, Paley magnifies strife with sardonic aplomb.

Violent scenes of such animated films (stretching from the excessive brutality and carnage of Famous Studio's Noveltoons where cartoon characters are sliced in two, burned to chars, skinned alive, shredded, and impaled on spears to the Itchy and Scratchy parodies on the *Simpsons* or Paley's savage images), the vice of anger ends with body parts thrown asunder. For Dante exposed anger as the "love of justice perverted to revenge and spite." Its penance requires live dismemberment for an unrepentant practice of wrath against God, one's neighbors, and one's self. Punishment in the fifth circle rips apart the sinners' limbs as they had used their arms and legs in committing violence. Aquinas recognized that the passion for revenge that often feeds anger loses control of its reason. The instrument of much language, the tongue, is like that fire that spreads and consumes. Confined to the Styx are the twin vices of wrath and sullenness, anger that is unleashed too quickly and anger that is repressed. The latter stews beneath the bubbling muddy swamp while the wrathful attack and throttle each other with fury, ripping each other apart without mercy. The wrathful penitents in Purgatory smother in thick smoke, their vision clouded and their speech constrained. Choking on their own rage, they envision examples of meekness that would purge their souls.

One sees in these animated parables the escalation of anger, from the temper tantrums of Donald Duck and his ilk to the mass killings of wrath in Paley's wars. In William Dunbar's *The Dance of the Seven Deadly Sins*, ire enters with trouble and strife, with his hand always on his knife. Swaggering in like a bear, perverse "boasters, braggarts, and wranglers" followed Ire in pairs, harnessed in preparation for war. For Dante, such unforgiving souls wore their weapons, wrapped up in wrath and resentful over injuries received (or just perceived). Their cleansing required that they stumble about blinded by an acrid and stinging smoke. For the fires of their revenge needed cleansing and pardoning so that they might see the harm they have done to others and to themselves.

NOTES

1. Buechner, *Wishful Thinking,* op. cit. 2.
2. See Silver, Larry, *Pieter Bruegel* (Abbeville, 2011).

3. Seeking to justify Donald's anger, Devlin Grimm situates the duck in a Disability Visibility Project, as one of the oppressed because of his speech impediment. Donald could curse incoherently with angry gibberish In *Donald's Dream Voice*, the duck's frustration with communication is seen as the root of his problems. While a legitimate factor, Donald's rage goes deeper than simply being inarticulate. "Ducks Don't Back Down" *animationstudies 2.0* (October 5, 2020), https://blog.animationstudies.org/?p=3905 (Accessed October 10, 2020).

4. Lohmann, Raychelle, "Top Five Angry Cartoon Characters" *Psychology Today* (January 16, 2015), https://www.psychologytoday.com/us/blog/teen-angst/201501/top-five-angry-cartoon-characters (Accessed March 27, 2020).

5. I am indebted to Eric Smoodin's reading in *Animating Culture: Hollywood Cartoons from the Studio Era* (Rutgers University Press, 1993), 24.

6. After drawing Donald Duck thousands of times, animator Bill Peet began to despise him, and when "a great stack of duck drawings arrived to be in-betweened," Pete went berserk and shouted at the top of his voice: "NO MORE DUCKS!! NOT MORE LOUSY DUCKS!" The anger of the fowl was contagious. *Bill Peet: An Autobiography* (Houghlin Mifflin, 1989), 90–91.

7. De Wit, Alex Dudok, "A Carrot Drives a Cartoon Rabbit to Madness In 'Afterwork,'" *Cartoon Brew* (December 19, 2019), https://www.cartoonbrew.com/shorts/a-carrot-drives-a-cartoon-rabbit-to-madness-in-afterwork-exclusive-online-premiere-183978.html (Accessed March 27, 2020). He also "realized that there couldn't be a better metaphor for an alienating repetitive work than a cartoon that has to ceaselessly pursue its nemesis and always ends up failing."

8. Aquinas, *Summa Theologica* (2, 158, ad.2).

9. Thurman, Robert A. F., *Anger* (Oxford University Press, 2005), 12; Author Robert A. F. Thurman gives the vice a Buddhist perspective in his book *Anger.* He acknowledges that it is an "inevitable part of life, an evil to be borne, not overcome." A God of wrath that is roused by injustice, by the heinous treatment of His people, is the Jewish/Christian God. For Eastern philosophy, anger is one of three poisons behind human suffering and one must discipline oneself to be liberated from being its slave; one must find a middle way (even as we think of Aristotle's mean of moderation and temperance) between the Charbydis of employing it for social justice and the Scylla of trying to eradicate its fiery destructive power. He argues that "our goal surely is to conquer anger, but not destroy the fire it has misappropriated. We will wield that fire with wisdom and turn it to creative ends." He not only recognizes that giving free rein to our anger tends to degenerate into wars and violence, but he suggests that our addition to "righteous indignation" is rooted in (and disguised by) our own unsatisfied desires and our fears. (8)

10. Furniss, *New History of Animation*, 180.

Chapter 7

Sloth (*Acedia* or the Ass)

Known in ancient times as the noonday devil, sloth, laziness, or listless depression (*akēdia*) comes in comfortable sleepy pajamas to claim its victims. It appears first in this simple, venial manifestation. *Afternoon Class* (Seoro Oh, 2015) takes sloth at this most basic (and relatable) level, a boredom of the body and soul during one of those late afternoon high school classes. One young man struggles to stay away. His classmates have succumbed to the narcolepsy of the tedium of the noonday devil, as if the river of Lethe flowing languidly through the cave of Hypnos, the god of sleep, washed over every student. His drowsy head metamorphoses into a block of bricks, a hammer, a bowling ball, a barrel of wine, and other heavily weighted objects that suggest the arduous labor of trying to keep one's head erect, eyes open, and consciousness alert. His noble fight is lost, but the teacher, seeing a complete siesta overcoming his students, also surrenders and joins those who could not stay awake for his blackboard lecture. It is not surprising that in medieval times, sloth shows itself as a dissolute priest whose attention to his studies was sorely lacking. He can find a hare in a field more easily than his place in a prayer book. Universities are fertile fields for sloths.

When the monks went out to the desert, or later up to mountaintops of the Meteora in Greece, they realized what arduous labor would be involved in just surviving. Thus, those who did not work did not eat. Evagrius of Pontus described such fellows as characterized by full of disquiet and sorrow.

> The demon of *acedia*, also called the noonday demon (cf. Ps. 90:6), is the most oppressive of all the demons. . . . First of all, he makes it appear that the sun moves slowly or not at all, and that the day seems to be fifty hours long. Then he compels the monk to look constantly toward the windows, to jump out of the cell, to watch the sun to see how far it is from the ninth hour, to look this

> way and that lest one of the brothers . . . And further he instills in him a dislike for the place and for his state of life itself, for manual labor, and also the idea that love has disappeared from among the brothers and there is no one to console him. And should there be someone who has offended the monk, this too the demon uses to add further to his dislike (of the place). He leads him on to the desire for other places where he can easily find the wherewithal to meet his needs and pursue a trade that is easier and more productive; he adds that pleasing the Lord is not a question of being in a particular place . . . and as the saying has it, he deploys every device in order to have the monk leave his cell and flee the stadium.[1]

In his *Eight Thoughts*, Evagrius added, "The spirit of *acedia* drives the monk out of his cell, but the monk who possesses perseverance will ever cultivate stillness." John Cassian depicted the apathetic restlessness of *acedia*, "the noonday demon" that could sap strength and will from an otherwise devoted monk. Thus, he explicitly recommended the crucial importance of manual labor as a remedy for sloth, for those who would shirk manual labor and sink into physical inactivity. The depressed have a tendency to withdraw, to slip into stasis, and to not move, or even care.

For Bruegel, the sins of gluttony and sloth comprised the *Land of Cockaigne* (1567), that mythical country of plenty. His social satire of the spiritual emptiness in such a bountiful land attacked the complacency of wealthy people during times of crisis, where partly eaten cheese and partly consumed bread lay about ready to rot. They are the sins of waste. To join the gluttonous swine, the animal that best personifies *Acedia* (Sloth) is the lazy ass. A drowsy hag naps on the beast, her open mouth almost drooling down her arm. A snail moves languidly beside them, suggesting how slowly time will move when everything seems to decay, literally at a snail's pace. Bruegel, in his *Netherland Proverbs*, illustrates other Flemish sayings, "Sloth is the pillow of the devil" and "No pillow leads to heaven" as shown by a one gleeful demon wearing monkish garb transporting a man in his bed to his final destination.[2]

Every head seems downcast, with sleeping figures too lazy to wake up by a bell ringing just over their heads. A sluggish nude female allows demons to grab and molest her, acquiescing to the horrors of life out of slothfulness. Even casting die demands too much effort, as gambling play suggests too much work. Neither pleasure nor pain can arouse the slothful, as a squatting giant's butt shot with arrows and he does nothing, too lazy even to shit himself. Another idle figure dragged from his bed by a stork-like monster in monkish garb cannot even raise his head to eat with the spoon offered by a demon. Bruegel footnotes two Hebrew Proverbs (26:14–15), "As a door turns on its hinges, so a sluggard turns on his bed. A sluggard buries his hand in the dish; he is too lazy to bring it back to his mouth." Everything seems to slouch toward inertia. The Flemish poem at the bottom reads: "Sloth weakens men, until at length,/Their fibres dried, they lack all strength."

In Spenser, Sloth, described in the poem as sluggish, presents Idleness riding a slow, lazy ass. It wears the priestly vest, thin cape, and hood of a monk's hood and carries a portable breviary, "worn out, but not read" as sleep drowns him in lethargy. As the student in *Afternoon Class*, he cannot even uphold his heavy head to look and see whether it were night of day. He shuns manly exercise, and excuses himself from every work even though he lives in riotous living that gave him a grievous malady, with a shaking fever raging continually. British engraver William Hogarth loved to sketch such Idleness.

The classic image of the sloth, the three-toed mammal, only hints at the vice it allegedly represents.[3] For most of us, sloth is simply laziness, and the *Harper's Magazine* spoof of the deadly sins posted an advertisement for sloth that perpetuates the connection. The caption of the ad read, "If sloth had been the original sin, we'd all still be in paradise." Greek mythology personified sloth as the goddess *Aergia*, or inactivity. However, she works, guarding the Underworld realm of Hypnos, or sleep, a cavern court that encourages idleness, indolence, forgetfulness, and laziness. It is a teenager's room with the door shut tightly.

Sloth is not mere idleness. Satirist Evelyn Waugh mischievously argues that sloth is a "mildly facetious variant of indolence and indolence, surely, so far from being a deadly sin, is one of the world's most amiable of weaknesses." Most of the world's troubles seem to come from people who are too busy. If only politicians and scientists were lazier, how much happier we should all be. The lazy [person] is preserved from the commission of almost all the nastier crimes."[4] Idleness in its season may be a virtue. One may be busy and still be slothful, just as one may be active while lying down on a bed with a long piece of chalk. G. K. Chesterton recommends such an idle Sabbath for one's imagination to lay on your back and doodle on the ceiling. As with all vices, sloth is grounded in virtue, one of rest, the commandment of the Decalogue to "remember the Sabbath" as a day to be re-created through rest.

The couch potato is a dominant trope of a lazy human being and such a stereotype partially fulfills medieval theologian St. Thomas Aquinas' conception of sloth encompassing a "sluggishness of the mind which neglects to begin good . . . [it] is evil in its effect, if it so oppresses man as to draw him away entirely from good deeds."[5] Ivan Goncharov's titular character Ilya Ilyich *Oblomov* (1859) symbolically incarnates the vice. He is a good nobleman, but declines, even seems incapable of, undertaking any meaningful activity or making a worthwhile decision. He barely can leave his bed for a chair in his room throughout the first chapters of the novel. Konyndyk DeYoung states that sloth "can show itself in the total inertia of the couch potato or the restless distractions of endless activity."[6] One thinks of A. A. Milne's wondrously gloomy Eyore as emblematic of the former and the endlessly bouncy Tigger in the latter category.

Human inertia is often measured in physical activity; however, sloth slips into something more comfortably lazy and insidious: it dresses in a costume of apathy. The indolent bliss of the poppy field in *The Wizard of Oz*, the sleepy inhalation of marijuana, the Valley Lethe, a prescription of Ambien, all lead to "Lethargiosis," where energy, zeal, drive, and dreams are put to rest. It offers spiritual atrophy. The soul just does not care. It is too easily distracted. Sloth suffers an oppressive sorrow, a state of dejection that keeps one from exercising virtue. Its nadir sinks into that despair and complacency that speaks, "I couldn't care less" and "I don't give a damn."

In temporal terms, sloth translates into procrastination as in Richard Condie's delightful parable, *Getting Started* (1979) (figure 7.1). A large-nosed, nasally speaking, straw-headed fellow named Eugene has a piano recital for which he must prepare.[7] A clock ticks in the background and our hero peeks in at the piano. As a master of procrastination, he postpones his rehearsal as he goes to get a drink and then an apple. Finally, he sits down, only to disappear and go brush his teeth and gargle. At this point, the title tries to come on, much like the pianist trying to get started: "*Gettin . . . Getting . . . Started.*" Even finishing the spelling of "Gettin . . . " took some time.

Just then, the phone rings and his friend Norbert invites him to his party where they will be showing a bunch of slides. A little bug flips over on its back, a happy emblem of our hero's state of mind. Sitting at the piano, he adjusts his seat, rubs his hands, and hits the first note. He looks up, throws

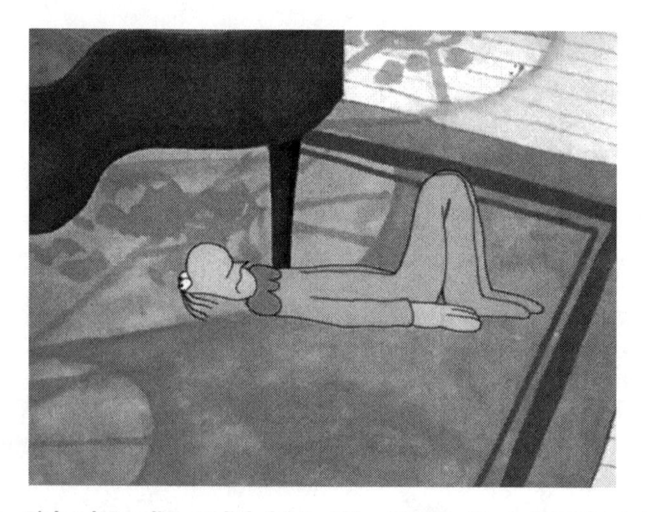

Figure 7.1 Richard Condie's Delightful Parable, *Getting Started* (1979), Brings Sloth Home. *Source*: Screenshot taken by the author.

the apple in the air to catch it in his mouth, but misses. Scratching his eye and ear, he plunks note again and finds it out of tune, opening the piano to find David, his mouse, emerging.

He plays through one refrain and then disappears to look out the window. The clock continues ticking. "Ah, David," he sighs, "tell me to get going. Tell me 'Get Going!' or something like that." Instead, David chases the bug. As the clock strikes the hour, a little man wearing lederhosen gongs a bell by hitting himself on the head with a hammer.

Laying his head on the piano, he gazes off at a photo of his grandmother knitting a sweater for her cat. He slurps his drink, plays with the straw, and blows air in and out. He gets his cup stuck on his nose, but then begins to sing and squawk and talk funny: "Strangers in the night," he croons; then "Here's looking at you, sweetheart." The doorbell rings and a delivery man says, "Hey, here's the cheese you ordered" (as the mouse heads toward the door). "I didn't order any cheese," he says, with the mouse running away. He sits down in front of the TV, changes the three channels from a guy screaming with an arrow through his nose, an opera singer, and some cartoon guy yelling at a bird. He turns the TV off; then on again.

Sitting inertly in a chair, he pulls his knees up, stretches out, and tries different positions, seeing if there is anything on the TV. He sits upside down to look at piano, slithers off a chair to go under the piano, sighs under the piano bench, and daydreams of playing his concert on stage and receiving grand applause. "Thank you, thank you," he says to his imaginary audience. Trying again, but not striking the right notes, he pounds the piano in frustration at not getting it right. He falls on the floor under the piano, turns round and round in a circle, going nowhere, but passing time. His metronome of life has stopped. As the mouse pulls at the cuckoo-clock chains, the little German man strikes again. While he lays down for a nap, the mouse and bug sit in a plant, until the mouse eats the bug. As the clock ticks, he has an inspired idea. He revs himself up and calls Norbert, "Is that party still on? I think I might just come over. Oh, I have lots of time anyway." As the credits roll with Debussy's Children's Corner music playing, we hear him pound his piano once more.

In Ruth Hayes' clever flipbook on *Sloth* (1988), the fourth deadly sin comes "languidly to life" as an artist plays with his jowls and only manages to draw a circle, repeatedly (after all, it is just a flipbook). Such comic idleness and the art of procrastination were anathema to Victorian views (and the Protestant work ethic for Calvinists who sought to demonstrate that they were part of the elect by their labors) which preached the virtue of diligent work to support society and one's family. Through inactivity one invites sin. Idle minds and idle hands are the devil's workshop, or as lyricist, Isaac Watts penned in his essay "Against Idleness and Mischief": "For Satan finds some mischief still for idle hands to do. Satan is the God of sin, the underworld and all things evil."

On the other hand, Ambrose Bierce, thought laziness to be that "unwarranted repose of manner in a person of low degree." It is much better to let sleeping worms lie. Aquinas took sloth into a more profound, and existential, direction, seeing it as "an oppressive sorrow, which so weights upon a man's mind that he wants to do nothing."[8] Here is where acedia turns deadly. It becomes a torpor of the soul, an indifference to God, to others, and even to oneself. One just does not care, culminating in the postmodern mood of "whatever." One of the Screwtape devil's conquests discovers too late that he now sees that "I spent most of my life in doing *neither* what I ought *nor* what I liked."

Sloth or acedia grows more complex and destructive as we watch it bury itself into the soul of its patient. It involves more than just laziness. In fact, for some like detective writer Dorothy Sayers, one is tempted to identify, "that the great, sprawling lethargic sin of Sloth is the oldest and greatest of the sins and the parent of all the rest. It is the sin which believes in nothing, cares for nothing, seeks to know nothing, interferes with nothing, enjoys nothing, loves nothing, hates nothing, finds purpose in nothing, lives for nothing, and only remains alive because there is nothing it would die for."

Dante strategically and conveniently places the slothful in his fifth circle, tossed into a snake pit. The indolent will need to start moving to avoid their fangs; the lazy will need to dance; the morose will need to rejoice. The acedia of the soul dooms one to sullenness, immersed in the bubbling mud of the Inferno, where the gurgling voices complain that they were "gloomy in the sweet air made happy by the sun," and now smothered in slime and darkness. Originally, the allegory of sloth, and its spiritual laziness and lack of caring, stemmed from sadness, apathy, hopelessness, and joylessness, which reflected the sinners' failure to see God's gifts and His goodness. Alas, the punishment seems a just dessert for those who refused to seek God's shining face upon this glorious earth. However, in Purgatory, the slothful demonstrate a fresh zeal, or at least they exercise, showing some vigor in running around a terrace, engaged in ceaseless activity. As they run about, they shout out models of zeal (as the Virgin Mary ran "in haste" to visit her cousin Elizabeth with news of the Annunciation).

Comic writer Wendy Wasserstein sardonically (and somewhat lazily) strips the clothing off sloth, and shows us the naked American body of apathy.[9] Wasserstein's alter ego tells a story of the energetic Eager Beaver and the Sloth. Seeking holiness, the Beaver labors at rebuilding the Chartres Cathedral, but is drowned by a monk; while the Sloth just sucks tree leaves. Her ironic message is that bad things sometimes happen to good busy beavers, so why work? Just suck leaves.

Figure 7.2 ***The Three Little Pigs*** **(Burt Gillett, 1933) Contrasts the Insouciance of Lazy Swine with Their Industrious Brother**. *Source*: Screenshot taken by the author.

Two out of three distinctive characters exhibit habits of sloth in Disney's classic Silly Symphony, *The Three Little Pigs* (Burt Gillett, 1933) (figure 7.2). Produced during the Great Depression of the 1930s, the film championed the work ethic of the little brick pig, a sort of Herbert Hoover-looking porcine, an elder brother who admonished his lazy siblings. However, the little straw and stick pigs play the fiddle, enticing despondent citizens the opportunity to sing the song of the year, namely the trio of Ted Sears, Pinto Colvig, and Frank Churchill's snappy "Who's Afraid of the Big Bad Wolf?" The wolf of hunger and poverty did come knocking as the Dust Bowl chased more people to California in search of grapes and jobs. The ditty put hard times in perspective, or so some would have us believe.

Frivolity offered a fun sort of sloth. The flute-playing pig constructed a cottage of straw while his fiddle-playing brother built his of sticks.[10] They squeal with delight over their quick, shoddy work and dance a jig that mocks the solemnity of their wiser brother. When they refuse access to the wolf ("not by the hair of my chinny-chin-chin"), he threatens "I'll huff and I'll puff and I'll blow your house down." As the indolent and insouciant pigs tremble behind their makeshift walls, they flee to the brick house for safety. Their entrepreneurial elder pig puts on the boiling turpentine cauldron when the menacing wolf climbs down the chimney.

Psychologist Bruno Bettelheim interpreted the tale as cautionary, where the first two little pigs die as they refuse to move out of the stage of the pleasure principle for the more mature status of the reality principle. For the post-Freudian, the earliest stage of child development is Sloth. "The disreputable poor [namely the first two little swine] are those who seem to have elected sloth in favor of work, who choose to live idly and by their wits, who count the indolence of their condition as a morally superior situation to that of the regularly employed worker."[11] Disney does not kill off the lazy child, but he does keep trying to teach them a work ethic, which he followed assiduously.

In his television program, Walt Disney pointed back to the Chinese, Egyptians, and especially to Aesop himself to ground his short Silly Symphonies animated films in a long moral tradition of storytelling. When one elderly lady wrote in recommending that he show the studio's Silly Symphony, *The Grasshopper and the Ants* (Wilfred Jackson, 1934), she opined that "I think the present generation should see it; not only because it is very entertaining, but for the lessons to be learned from it" (figure 7.3).[12] Older generations seem to be perpetually pointing younger people to such lessons. In the cartoon, the Disney Studio preached the importance of working and not loafing, during the heyday of the Depression. Fiddling and spitting tobacco, a grasshopper (again with Pinto Colvig's Goofy voice) dances and prances about. He hops about, sits and eats leaves, and blithely drinks from bluebells. He not only wastes food, but also watches busy ants bringing in beans, saw carrots, pluck corn, and pull cherries and then guffaws a "yuk, yuk, yuk." He laughs at one ant and preaches his own selective sermon: "Listen son, the good Book says, 'the Lord provides.' There is food on

Figure 7.3 ***The Grasshopper and the Ants*** **(Wilfred Jackson, 1934) Reworks the Warning of the Hebrew Proverb into a Happy Disney Fable.** *Source*: Screenshot taken by the author.

every tree. I see no reason to flurry and work, no sire, not me." He then proposes his hedonistic life's motto, "Oh, the world owes me a living; come on, let's play, not like those other foolish ants." The theme of insouciant entitlement invited the impressionable Andy Ant to shirk his community's work ethic.

Andy joins the Grasshopper, but the Queen sees the wayward ant and reproves him. He bows and gets back to carrying his cherries. The Grasshopper chortles, "Ayuk, hiya Queenie." She responds solemnly, "You'll change that tune when winter comes and the ground is covered with snow." He shrugs his shoulders dismissingly, "winter time is a long time off." The scent of Sloth tempts. As the great Livy observed, "prosperity engenders sloth."

As leaves fall, time passes, dandelions blow, and the cold winds come. The colony retreats into their abode as snow falls and covers the ground. The chilled grasshopper wanders about shivering, looking for leaves, checks stomach, tightens belt, and then espies one last leaf. Food, he thinks, but it blows away in the fierce wind. Tightening his belt even more, he picks up his fiddle and faces the wind.

As he turns blue with cold and falls, he sees the ant colony and struggles to get to their colony. He finds they are partying with food and drink. He knocks on the door and then collapses. The gracious ants bring the frozen insect in, warm his legs in buckets of hot water, and cover him with a blanket, turning him back into normal green color. As the Queen approaches him, the grasshopper begs contritely, "O madam Queen, wise as a lion, don't throw me out. Please, give me a chance." She responds in regal fashion: "Just those who work may stay, so take your fiddle. . . . and play!" He changes his tune to "*I owe the world a living*," and adds, "I've been a fool a whole year long and now I'm singing a different song. You were right and I was wrong." The cautionary fable offers hope to those who do learn their lesson.

However, by 1940, enemies worse than hunger had come, so that in Terrytoons' *Harvest Time* (Connie Rasinski, 1940), the ants recruit the fiddling grasshopper to fight a menacing spider. It takes a global war to rouse sloth, or gluttony here. As winter draws nearer, bees gather honey; bugs milk flowers; a ladybug drives caterpillar tread wheels pulling grapes. The oblivious grasshopper plays the fiddle and dances his jig. When a bumblebee squirts him with honey, he licks it and grins. He watches and rubs his belly as the grapes are stomped for wine. He tastes it and drinks it up, and when a bug drops a grape on him, he lands in the vat, fully intoxicated. Tipsy and unable to stand, he imitates a vaudeville routine of a drunken man. Everyone is festive; no one warns of an impending winter or a more sinister danger. A sleeping spider, unshaven and unkempt, wakes and abducts the lovely butterfly lady. However, the grasshopper with his fiddle fights the arachnid, defeating and beheading him. The lovely butterfly kisses the grasshopper, who falls back into the vat of wine and is drunk with love, consummating the romance with a hiccough.

Unlike the Disney and Paul Terry versions, Ladislas Starewicz's stop-action, puppet version of *The Dragonfly and the Ant* (1913) starkly depicts the tragic end of the frisky dragonfly who plays his fiddle while winter approaches. The Russian and European renditions of the fairy tales are predictably grimmer and more realistic, less happy-go-lucky and sanguine, as are the American renderings. An ant loads tiny timbers onto his cart, twenty times his weight, while the dragonfly swigs his beer with a stag beetle. In fact, she finishes a giant bottle and then tries to drink from his fiddle. In her drunken stupor, she uses his bow to torment the ant, who just proceeds to chop down a tree that falls on him. No sympathy comes from the dragonfly, who mocks with his music. When "need and cold" come with the winter, "the dragonfly sang no more." As leaves tumble down around him, she is "cast down by evil grief" and crawls over to the ant, begging for food and warmth until the spring returns. Portrayed as a kind of communist worker, the ant retorts to the royal insect, "Finished crying? Very nice: now you can go out and dance!" Cast out into the drifts of snow, she lays down and dies. The Hebrew proverb (24:33–34) "A little sleep, a little slumber, a little folding of the hands to rest; then your poverty will come as a robber" captures the tenor of Starevich's exquisite work, replacing sleep with debauchery and the robber with winter, but poverty comes to the dragonfly in its final form, death. In assigning virtuous and vicious qualities to animals, the book of Proverbs warns the sluggish creature to "go to the ant. Consider its ways and be wise" as it "stores its provisions in summer and gathers its food at harvest" (Proverbs 6:6).

Certain animated films pose problems of other, more heinous, sins when dealing with our focus on sloth. For example, appalling racism cloaks the dangers of our immediate vice, one that applies to all races. One of the most offensive and racist cartoons of Walter Lantz Studios stereotyped Southern blacks as lazy and oversexed.[13] In adapting Don Raye's nineteenth-century minstrel music of *Scrub Me Mama with a Boogie Beat* (1940), a hard-working laundry woman labors diligently. Under the strains of Stephen Foster's "Sewanee River," the camera pans Lazy Town, a rural Southern locale filled with indolent, sleeping black men. One eats watermelon; another leisurely picks one ball of cotton; a third goes fishing with lines tied to his toes, only to discover all the fish are sleeping as well. Even when a mosquito bites the nose of a dozing man, snoring up a storm, it takes a few moments for him to express languidly an "Owwwch." A cat crawls over a sleeping dog who can barely manage to mutter a "Bow . . . wow . . . " Even a fight between two men offers no more than reciprocal slow motion slaps on the head, Laurel and Hardy's tit-for-tat on extra-strength tranquillizers.

Then a hot young thing from Harlem jumps off the Steamboat to visit Lazy Town. She saunters down the walkway like Lena Horne or one of the Andrew Sisters, waking up all the sleepy bums. Everything speeds up with her sexual energy. She teaches the old Mammy doing laundry how to pick up a beat, infecting her with rhythm. A pack of racist stereotypes pick up steam with "pick ninnies with pigtails," a parade of musicians with trombones, clarinets and saxophones, cue-ball headed babies with well-washed hinnies, Jive dancing couples, lively rooster and hen, and a big-bottomed lady bopping with three thin men. When the boat captain calls her back on board, she leaves, waving her hanky to everyone's clapping and rhythms.[14]

If one could transfer the parable to all races, one might find something about human wastefulness and idleness worthwhile, but unfortunately, it freezes the odious caricature onto one ethnic group. However, according to film scholar Christopher Lehman

> the film does not treat the sloth of Lazytown's residents as a vice or a moral failing. Rather, the film suggests that laziness is a natural condition for a slave or for a rural African American. By the film's release in 1941, so much inaccurate and nostalgic lore had been produced in American literature and film about southern antebellum plantations being a setting of ease for African Americans, who were cared for by landowners or slaveholders. Lantz's film just took that trope and grossly exaggerated it.
>
> Also, as per the Hollywood Production Code of the time, any immoral or evil act by a character in a film would have come with some kind of consequence or comeuppance for that character before the end of the film. However, none of the Lazytown residents are punished for being lazy. None are arrested or hurt in any way or met with any other kind of misfortune. Instead, a light-skinned northerner shows them a more energetic way to perform their labor. The residents stay busy after the northerner leaves Lazytown, and the ending could perhaps suggest a moral that busy-ness is better than sloth. But again, there's no punishment for sloth if you're an African American in Lazytown.[15]

Can one find something humanly recognizable in this reprehensibly offensive cartoon? While the intent was not to showcase sloth, and significantly not to rebuke it, its reprehensible caricatures enable us to reflect on the vice. Of course, Lantz does not present laziness as a sin, but as a natural condition. As such, it fails to awaken any sense of wrong of acedia in either black or white characters. The NAACP rightly castigated the torpidity of the plantation Negro and the exaggerated physiognomy of its vicious caricatures, as "insulting, derogatory and offensive" stereotypes. The film points out how hostile such vituperative images are, much more reprehensible than the vice of sloth itself.[16]

The Academy Award–winning Zagreb film *Ersatz* (Dusan Vukotic, 1961) indicts the ease of technology in a disposable consumerist society. In his

Figure 7.4 Steve Cutts' Jarring Animated Version of Moby and the Void Pacific Choir's *Are You Lost in the World like Me?* (2016) Exposes a Crisis of Contemporary Technology. *Source*: Screenshot taken by the author.

Klee-like imagery with synthetic beach objects, Vukotic makes his own plastic fantasy. The rotund protagonist need not lift a finger to satisfy his needs or desires: beach ball, campsite, fishing pole, and car. He can even blow up a voluptuous siren (who will ironically take up with a more muscular rival) to fit his fantasy. Everything is inflatable and too convenient. Technology seduces one into sloth, but then life deflates it all just as quickly.

The vice of acedia (literally "without care" or having indifference to the work for God or others) not only involves laziness but also encompasses idleness and wastefulness. One wants to maintain equilibrium at all costs, not producing much. One's complacency leads to a lack of imagination and a lack of feeling and imagination. One just does not care. Its nature can be seen in its failure to love God with all one's heart, all one's mind, and all one's soul. Earlier aspects of sloth led to the twin moods of despair and melancholy. This second aspect, sadness, has sadly been lost. Yet its presence, especially in light of digital social media and the onslaught of depression in young people, has proliferated through our culture.

Social loafing is a habitual response of people working on group tasks.[17] One finds a contagious inactivity when people perform in groups, a herd instinct of passivity or sloth. Such a phenomenon occurs in the use of social media as illustrated in Steve Cutts' jarring animated version of Moby and the Void Pacific Choir's *Are You Lost in the World like Me?* (2016) (figure 7.4).

In his incisive satire, Cutts starts with two large eyes. One modest little character dodges about in a swarm of people in a world surrounded by satellites, the systems are failing, and people are hunched over cell phones walking and ignoring reality. When bullies beat up one fellow, everyone records the beating with their phones, but none helps the victim. People eating at a table consult only their phones. While a fire breaks out and fire engines arrive, a woman spends time taking selfies with the flames as background. On the subway, all are addicted to their phones, sleepy eyes, "x" eyes. The little wide-eyed, round-headed protagonist looks up, trying to make some connection. Monstrous bullies shove him around. Another lazy character watches as emoticons show happy faces, LOL, bemused faces, all with more emotion than the owner. A young woman nearby sees laughing emoticons and stars and hearts, but does not recognize another human being. A thug accosts a woman seated on the subway, the little would-be hero imagines himself trying to protect her, but he does nothing.

Apathy and vanity combine to damn a whole culture in the apocalyptic. Its easy indictment of cell phones leading oblivious people nowhere actually goes deeper, into the recognition that our world is lost and does not care. The film exposes the contemporary addiction to smartphones. Even with the Fleischer rubbery style of 1930s animation, in black and white, technology creates a world of unfeeling automatons, of walking zombies, informed by D. H. Lawrence's observation that "People in Los Angeles are content to do nothing and stare at the void pacific."

A sad lonely woman in her unkempt squalid room projects an Instagram image of herself as more attractive and thumbs-up image of herself with a surfboat and pearls. When a dog comes to lick our poor lost boy, someone else kicks it away. People in jail cells, couples in restaurants, looking at their phones while a truck of pigs, sheep and cattle on the way to slaughter, passes by the window. Many people have followed a bright beaming yellow rabbit (think Pokemon hunting) to a trash heap to record it. Behind the blind users, billboards shout out: "These systems are failing."

A couple sits in Moggsy's café; however, the woman seeks Tinder dates. She switches rapidly from one image to another, scanning for her ideal man, strong jaw, wavy hair, and celebrity smile. They drink their wine or Kool-Aid. The lost boy tugs at people, desperately and futilely trying to pull people from their technology. A woman shows off dancing in the midst of a crowd, all of whom recording her ridiculous movements, seeing her simulated image and not her. Other people watch on TellyTube, with the caption OMW, laughing at the gif of "Girl dances badly at party. Fail alert." Realizing that she is an object of ridicule, she walks a road of shame, with crowds of people pointing their mocking fingers at her. Another large woman suffers the results of undergoing lip, breast, and butt Botox. Doctors come up to give her XXXL implants and industrial-strength Butt Filler. Hypodermic needles sticking out of her face.

Even a Disneyfied Cinderella and her prince, start in color, but as they just attend to their phones, their color fades into the black-and-white world of everyone else. A naked baby crawls away from a maternity room where the mother and father are too busy with selfies to notice. Crowds focus their phones on a little girl precariously balanced on a high apartment ledge, about to commit suicide. She plummets to her death and smashes on a sidewalk, abandoned by everyone except the one Charlie Brown boy, who drops a lone tear for her. The rest of the world walks blindly out of the city, continues to a cliff, and watches their phones fanatically. They fall over the cliff, like proverbial lemmings to their own death. All systems are failing. One observer ironically noted, "Guess what you are doing during the video?" By the end, the mass of human lemmings follows the myth of suicidal creatures running over the cliff. The blind continue to follow the blind. While people throw knives at a dying sun, one hapless fellow seeks to "Dream a dream of God-lit air/Just for a minute you'll find me there." One hopes for a source of love in this God-lit air for the sullen characters buried in technological mud.

Showing these people completely oblivious to the reality around them, Cutts added, "For me the video is about our increasing dependence on technology and about human interaction today, or a certain lack of it. It focuses on the way tech is changing us—how we have become desensitized."[18] People are completely oblivious to the vibrant reality around them. One plaintive voice asks, "Are you lost in the world like me? Look harder and you'll find The 40 ways it leaves us blind."

Sloth also involves the failure to do things that one should do, not only out of laziness, but also out of distraction. The needful thing that one must do, to love God with all one's heart, mind, soul, and strength, and to love one's neighbor as oneself, remains the core commandment of Jewish and Christian traditions. If one fails at this, one has failed completely, even if one can fathom all mysteries and knowledge, gives to the poor, and has a faith that can move mountains. A clear understanding of sin in antiquity was that this laziness or lack of work was simply a symptom of the vice of apathy or indifference, particularly an apathy or boredom toward God.

Acedia becomes the sin of indifference in a self-consumed culture, preferring the ease of technology over the labor and responsibility of relationships. Cell phones make men and women into extensions of technology, machine-like robotic behaviors that tend to siphon all humanity and life out of the users. An extension of such oblivious sloth is what Joseph Campbell entitled the "sin of inadvertence, not being alert, not quite awake, the sin of missing the moment of life."[19]

In her personal exploration of *Acedia and Me*, Kathleen Norris discerns a spirit of restlessness in the heart of sloth. One does not live in the present, but in a paralyzing fear of the future. Torpor overwhelms the slothful, as one has no purpose, no hope, and a dread of making a choice. She adds to that inactivity a lack of caring, of deep apathy about one's personal appearance, one's relationships, one's neighbors, even one's diet and hygiene. One just does not care. Such apathy easily metamorphoses into ennui and depression. Aquinas, who replaced the temptation of sadness with sloth, identified this state of listlessness and not caring as the burden of "the sorrow of the world," a "flight from the divine good."[20] Romantic poets taste this *Weltschmerz*, a deep sadness about the condition of the world leading to inertia, self-pity, and a world-weary abandonment of life. Sin quenches desire and prefers to withdraw, and even in a desperate situation, commit suicide.

The apathy of sloth demands that no one disturb this specious tranquility. A barbed wire fence orders that no one is to invade or even to interrupt one's quiet. Garret Keizer puts the point more poetically this way, "Dead men throw no fits, or it seems they wouldn't. . . . Death hates resurrection. No one likes to be woken from a sound sleep. Where those afflicted by sloth . . . can become most angry is when someone or something—like a dissatisfied spouse—disturbs the tranquility of their sarcophagus."[21]

Sloth leads to the refusal to love one's neighbor. That would require work. While it may seem counterintuitive to include busyness within the rubric of sloth, it fits Aquinas and Norris' condition of not responding to God. For example, the excuse of busyness does not fly in Phil Vischer and Mike Nawrocki's wacky adaptation of the parable of the Good Samaritan called, with apologies to Mr. Rogers, *Are You My Neighbor* (1995) (figure 7.5). In the Veggie Tales episode, Bob the Tomato recounts how Larry (the Cucumber), a shoe person, goes out for a walk with this toy lobster, is attacked by bandits, and is left out in the desert. Falling by the side of the road, upside down with his head in the sand, he waits for help, only to have political figures pass him by and excuse their lack of care. As Larry has no arms, he cannot pry himself free; so, he waits. The first person to pass is the Mayor of Filebber-o-loo, the Dr. Seuss-like shoe city, who is too busy to help. A second person, also from Flibber-o-loo, is the doctor, also too busy to help. They sing a wonderfully catchy, irritating little song:

> Mayor (Archibald Asparagus) sings: "I'm busy, busy, dreadfully busy. You've no idea what I have to do. Busy, busy, shockingly busy, much, much too busy for you."
>
> Larry the Cucumber: "Oh, I see."
>
> Archibald and Doctor (Lovely Asparagus): "We're busy, busy, dreadfully busy. You've no idea what we have to do. Busy, busy, shockingly busy, much, much too busy for you. 'Cause we're busy, busy, frightfully busy More than a bumblebee, more than an ant. Busy, busy, horribly busy; We'd love to help, but we can't!"
>
> Mayor: "Ta Ta!"

Figure 7.5 Phil Vischer and Mike Nawrocki Adapts the Parable of the Good Samaritan, with Apologies to Mr. Rogers, as a wacky *Are You My Neighbor* (1995). *Source*: Screenshot taken by the author.

The sequence highlights acedia, the vice of not caring, of being too busy to tend to one's neighbor. Even busy professionals practice this spiritual sloth, this tepid apathy toward others. Finally, a young boy from Jibberty-lot, the pot and pan city does the right thing and helps Larry. His act of kindness impresses everyone so that they all make peace. For those dreadfully busy running around in circles in Dante's Purgatory, his example stands, and the busy sinners become penitents moving toward love.

The animated parables of sloth run from mere procrastination to the suicidal neglect of apathy, of not caring for anything or anyone. A spiritual rigor mortis sets in resulting from a lack of zeal. As the proverb observes, the sluggard says, "There is a lion in the road! A lion is in the open square. Like the door turns on its hinges, so does the sluggard on his bed. The sluggard buries his hand in the dish; he is weary of bringing it to his mouth again." One excuses one's lack of action out of laziness or busyness or even cynicism, only to find that even snakes may not rouse one back to zeal.

NOTES

1. Evagrius of Pontus, *Praktikos* VI.12 (trans. R Sinkewicz) (Oxford Early Christian Studies, 2003).
2. Davis, Howard McParlin, "Fantasy and Irony in Peter Bruegel's Prints," *Metropolitan Museum of Art Bulletin*, 1: 10 (June 1943), 291.
3. The poster child for a sloth is Flash (Raymond Persi), the "fastest" sloth who works, aptly, at the DMV (i.e., Department of Mammal Vehicles) in *Zootopia* (Byron

Howard, Rich Moore, 2016). After being told a joke by Nick Wilde, the sly fox, Flash slowly, frustratingly slowly, hilariously slowly, gets the joke and opens his face to a gigantic laugh.

4. Waugh, Evelyn, *London Sunday Times*, 1962 (reprinted in *The Seven Deadly Sins*) (Pleasantville, NY: Akadine Press, 2002), 57.

5. Aquinas, Thomas, *Summa Theologiae,* op. cit. (2, 35, ad 1).

6. DeYoung, Rebecca Konyndyk, "The Vice of Sloth: Some Historical Reflections on Laziness, Effort, and Resistance to the Demands of Love," *The Other Journal* (November 15, 2007), 95, https://theotherjournal.com/2007/11/15/the-vice-of-sloth-some-historical-reflections-on-laziness-effort-and-resistance-to-the-demands-of-love/ (Accessed February 1, 2020).

7. Gene Walz described Condie as exactly like Eugene with "thin wispy hair," "strange teeth" who "hates work and does anything he can to get around it." "Interview: Masters and Apprentices" *ASIFA Canada* 19:1 (1991), 4; See also Crider, Alisa, "Richard Condie Interview" (November 14, 2009) in her unpublished manuscript *Condie's World* (VWU, 2009).

8. Aquinas, *Summa Theologica.* IIaIIae Q. 35 a. 1 *resp.*

9. Wasserstein, Wendy, *Sloth* (*and How to Get It*) (Oxford University Press, 2005); Wasserstein offers a delightful parody of self-help literature for achieving slothfulness.

10. Credited to James Orchard Halliwell in 1849, *Three Little Pigs* appeared in a book entitled, *Popular Rhymes and Nursery Tales.* The production cast labels the characters as *Fifer Pig*, *Fiddler Pig*, and *Practical Pig*. The first two are depicted as both idly vain and silly.

11. Lyman, Stanford M., *The Seven Deadly Sins: Society and Evil* (Rowman and Littlefield, 1989), 36.

12. Disney Walt, "Walt Disney World of Color," Television introduction of *The Grasshopper and the Ants* (March 2, 1955) which originally appeared in the April 1934 issue of *Good Housekeeping,* https://www.youtube.com/watch?v=dmGk8JAM-hBw (Accessed March 8, 2020).

13. Lehman, Christopher, *The Colored Cartoon: Black Presentation in American* (University of Massachusetts Press, 2007), 48-ff.

14. The hookworm disease was "popularly, if erroneously, dubbed in the jargon of the age of bacteriology" as "the germ of laziness," that occurred mostly in the south during the early twentieth century. Cassedy, James H. "The 'Germ of Laziness' in the South, 1900–1915: Charles Wardell Stiles and the Progressive Paradox," *Bulletin of the History of Medicine* 45: 2 (March/April 1971) https://www.jstor.org/stable/44449996?seq=1 (Accessed March 9, 2020), 159; In his case against colonialism, Alexander Keese pointed out the British and French debated about African laziness in order to require forced labor, perpetuating the racist stereotype. Keese, Alexander, "Slow Abolition within the Colonial Mind: British and French Debates about 'Vagrancy,' 'African Laziness,' and Forced Labour in West Central and South Central Africa, 1945–1965," *International Review of Social History* 59: 3 (December 2014), 377–407, https://www.cambridge.org/core/journals/international-review-of-social-history/article/slow-abolition-within-the-colonial-mind-british-and

-french-debates-about-vagrancy-african-laziness-and-forced-labour-in-west-central-and-south-central-africa-19451965/112A670B2423C4495B9466BD8CF66D80 (Accessed March 9, 2020).

15. Personal Correspondence with Christopher Lehman (March 31, 2020).

16. Sammond, Nicholas, *Birth of an Industry* (Duke University Press, 2015), 252; Cohen, Karl F., *Forbidden Animation* (McFarland, 1997), 151–153.

17. Ying, Xiangyu, Huanhuan Li, Shan Jiang, Fei Peng, and Zhongxin Lin, "Group Laziness: The Effect of Social Loafing on Group Performance," *Social Behavior and Personality: An International Journal,* 42: 3 (2014), 465–471.

18. Kreps, Daniel, "See Moby's Grim New Video About Smartphone Addiction" Rolling Stone (October 17, 2016), https://www.rollingstone.com/music/music-news/see-mobys-grim-new-video-about-smartphone-addiction-109548/ (Accessed March 9, 2020).

19. Campbell, Joseph, *Myths to Live By* (Bantam, 1981), 123.

20. Aquinas, *Summa Theologica* (Q 35).

21. Keizer, Garret, *The Enigma of Anger* (Jossey-Bass, 2002), 50.

Chapter 8

Avarice (*Avaricia* or the Camel)

Unlike Envy, greed or avarice (*philarguria*) simply does not care about anyone else. Envy has its relational problems, comparing herself to others, but greed just *wants* everything, a concupiscent desire for things. When Mick Jagger sings, "I Can't Get no Satisfaction," even with all of his money, fame, and pleasure, he is singing the anthem of fellow addicts.

Tradition holds that Bruegel's initial model for this sequence of *Avaritia* (Greed) reflected the growing affluence of the Netherlands and its dangers to an emerging and successful middle class. Sitting in the center of the engraving is a prosperous woman wearing a horned headdress ("she is hornyd like a kowe . . . for syn" as the *Townley Mysteries* put it in 1460), counting her hoard of coins while a toad crouches at her feet. Various other measuring devices reflect greedy characters, with thieves seeking to rob houses and other duped and naked characters wandering into brambles of craving. Cupidity abounds with bird and frog-faced servants abetting the acquisitive nature of characters who beg and riot for money.

For Spenser, greed's zoomorphic image is a laden/loaded camel. Like the proverbial leech, it wants more, more, more! Greed, in its many guises and under its numerous names (which is just like greed to get as many synonyms as possible), avarice, concupiscence, or covetousness, craves for money, commodities, power, status, or just attention, wanting more than one needs or can use. It is grasping and hoarding, taking and keeping, as misers show their insatiable cupidity. For St. Paul, "the love of money is the root of all evil" (1 Timothy 6:10). It is a desire for good things that spins out of control. In his fourth circle of the Inferno, Dante envisions that those who want so much, too much, will receive an excess of boiling oil. That should lead one to say, "No more, thank you." The judgment and death throes of the greedy are quite ironic and divinely poetic. They wish for more of everything, but end up with more of the hell of their own cravings. ("It you want to know what God thinks of money," Algonquin writer Dorothy Parker quipped, "Just look at the people He gave it to.")

Former *Publishers Weekly* religion editor, Phyllis Tickle identifies greed as "the Matriarch of the Deadly Clan" of sins. She (greed, not Tickle) is the mistress of all vices. Tickle demonstrates greed's contagious spiritual calamity in the paintings of Peter Bruegel and Hieronymus Bosch (as well as films, Eric von Stroheim's 1924 version of *Greed* and Oliver Stone's 1987 *Wall Street*). In particular, she zeroes in on the alluring and tragic paintings of contemporary Italian artist Mario Donizetti. Tickle enhances our work by pointing out that greed "almost always requires an image to serve as its vehicle if it is to be entered into human conversation." So, inspired by Dante, Donizetti's visual representation of *Avarice* (1996) in his *Seven Deadly Sins* series, shows the naked female form of Greed, sitting on a bag of money and grasping other sacks of money. Yet, Avarice's weary and anxious face exposes an impoverished world without love, fecundity, laughter, creativity, or life itself.[1] As Tickle lays out greed as the "mother and matrix, root and consort of all the other sins," the vice withers and wilts like a fading flower.[2] Greed, it seems, knows no shame like other vices, but hoards whatever it can snatch.

Riding next to lechery in *The Faerie Queen*, Avarice sits precariously upon a camel, laden with gold and precious metal, even holding a heap of coins in his lap. He makes his wicked booty his god. He is willing even to sell himself for money to hell. Accursed usury was his trade, with a threadbare coat and cobbled patched shoes, for he had never tasted a good morsel all his life; he had no one to leave his riches to, and feared nightly to lose it all, living a wretched life all to himself. His wealth makes him poor, that even with enough, he yet wished for more. A vile disease (grievous gout) in foot and hand torments him.

If one word were to encapsulate Avarice it would be *more*. In contrast to a simple virtue of contentment, avarice grows restless, even hungry. The root of this greed is that appetite for something that satisfies, but he places his hope in material things. This greed is global, as in the African parable/fable of the monkey and a jar of nuts. In the *Jungle Doctor's Fables*, an assortment of crocodiles, snakes, hyenas, men, and monkeys interact to instill various moral lessons. For one monkey, Toto, his greed for peanuts in a jar overcomes his common sense, as he sticks his paw through a small hole and grabs too many to withdraw through the narrow opening. With a clenched handful of nuts, he is stuck in the jar. Thus, when Perembi, the hunter, comes upon Toto, the monkey chooses to hold on to his nuts and Perembi easily swings his stick, taking a life and delivering a lesson on greed.[3] The simple moral lesson points to how undisciplined craving leads to snares.

Based on an ancient Chinese fable, "The monkeys fish for the moon but do not catch anything," Communist China set out a parabolic warning about greed lest some capitalist spirit infect their nation. In Zhou Keqin's *Monkeys Fish the Moon* (1982), greedy little simian scamps vainly chase and try to catch a full moon. Playing together and eating coconuts, often mischievously stealing from each other, a troop of monkeys scampers after whatever food and nuts it can find. Hanging upside down, one fresh-faced member is puzzled to see a large round shape. He and his barrel of eight buddies pursue the alluring mystery across hills and up vines, pushing each other aside to be first. Agreeing to climb upon each other's backs to reach the treat, they chatter and wrestle until they fall from their lunar tower of Babel.

Suddenly, the chief monkey sees it below in a pool of water. Even while chased by boars and a snake, they do not desist in their desire for this bright coconut-looking delicacy. The chief organizes a monkey chain all the way down to the water. However, every time they grab at it, it disappears in a swirl, trying to use a coconut shell to scoop it up. Once it appears that it is in that bowl, they celebrate their capture of the moon, congratulating themselves, dancing around until they fight over the container. During the struggle, the coconut falls and breaks. They have lost the moon, and then it is still in the sky.[4]

The Bible is full of rich fools who planned for bigger barns, then died; those who consume while the poor go hungry; or those who steal and bury their treasures in the ground. The tenth commandment mandating that one should not covet attaches itself to those who hide their resources as well as pilfer others' goods. In Luke's book of Acts, Ananias and Sapphira conceal their treasures, claiming to have contributed more to the church and duplicitously pretending to give more than they did. Holding back and hoarding are as sinful as taking. Such greed stems from what Evagrius saw as "thinking about what does not yet exist," a principle linking concerns about future needs, desires, and fears.[5]

An enduring emblem of greed sprouts from Charles Dickens' 1843 portrayal of Ebenezer Scrooge in *A Christmas Carol* (1843). Ironically, that literary figure transmogrifies into an avian incarnation, the more easily recognizable animated caricature of an irascible Scottish Pekin duck, Scrooge McDuck from Disney's *Mickey's Christmas Carol* (Burny Mattinson, 1983). Late Victorian industrial tycoon, he almost fits Nietzsche's criteria for his superman, one marked by the unholy trinity of greed, envy, and hatred. He is, at the least, as acknowledged by *Forbes* magazine, the "Richest Duck in the World," "a billionaire duck known for storing a fortune in gold coins inside a massive Duckburg money bin," who turns into a miserly, misanthropic tightwad, a quacking, cantankerous Croesus.[6]

One other duck deserves dishonorable mention in regard to our present vice: Daffy. In *Ali Baba Bunny* (Chuck Jones, 1957), Daffy Duck and Bugs Bunny are trying to burrow down to Pismo Beach but end up in a cave in some Arabian tale (figure 8.1). The cave belongs to a wealthy sheikh who orders his man Hasan to guard the entrance to his treasure or "jackals shall grow fast on your carcass." With that, he utters his command to the mountain: "Close Sesame!" His servant proclaims, "No one shall pass Hasan," even though he cannot remember the magical phrase, stumbling over Sarsaparilla or Saskatchewan.

As the two Warner Bros. stars lift their heads out of the hole, Bugs wonders if he should have turned left at Albuquerque. Daffy sees the cave full of gold, diamonds, pearls, emeralds, bags of treasure, and "all the clams we can eat," and his eyes narrow in crafty avarice, his tongue licking his beak. He shouts the words of possession: "It's mine! You understand? It's all mine! Mine! Mine!" Stomping on Bugs and trying to pound him back underground, Daffy emits his "Hoo, haa, haa" evil laugh. Bugs pops right back up and inquires, "Eh, what's up, Duck?"

Daffy's eyes radiate circles of greed as the Warner Bros. 1930s song "We're in the Money" blasts in the background. "I'm rich!" Daffy bellows, jumping in the air and tossing coins. Diving into the bed of gold, he screeches, "I'm rich! I'm wealthy! Yahoo! . . . I'm comfortably well off."

Outside, the slow-witted sentry keeps trying ("Open Septuagenarian! Open Saddlesoap!"), until he stumbles upon the right catchphrase, "Open Sesame." He finds Daffy singing, "I'm in the money." Seeing Hasan, Daffy asks him to call him a cab, and be quick about it. Attacked by the brute, Daffy panics,

Figure 8.1 ***Ali Baba Bunny*** **(Chuck Jones, 1957) Digs into the Psyche of Daffy's Avaricious Mania for Gold.** *Source*: Screenshot taken by the author.

flees to his pal Bugs, and begs for help, offering him the treasure. Bugs remains unflappably cool, dusting himself off. Daffy's adversary threatens the duck: "Hasan chops!" "Chop the rabbit," Daffy beseeches; "He brought us here."

Sitting in a jar, Bugs claims to be a genie with light-brown hair. He asks Hasan to release him and he will grant him a rich reward. Daffy, from a safe high perch, protests, "He's lying. Chop him! Chop him!" As Hasan releases his new master, Bugs offers him all the treasures. Bugs raises his eyebrows, performs an oriental dance, speaks gobbledygook, and gives it all to Hasan.

Having stolen a giant diamond from Hasan, Daffy is again fleeing and begging Bugs: "Help, help, save me pal, save me." Bugs asks Daffy why he steals. "I can't help it," he explains. "I'm a greedy slob. It's my hobby. Save me." Bugs persuades Hasan to climb a rope into oblivion. Daffy, realizing that he is safe, rushes back to the hoard of money: "Oh boy, I'm rich. I'm wealthy. I'm independent. I'm socially secure. I'm rich! I'm rich!"

When Daffy finds a magic lamp, rubbing it to think it can bring in a few more dollars, a green genie appears offering him a wish; however, Daffy thinks it is after his treasure and pounds him back into his jar. Yelling "Mine!" The genie accuses him of desecrating the spirit of the lamp and warns, "Prepare to take the consequences." Daffy dismisses his threat: "Consequences, Schmonsequences. As long as I'm rich . . . " Lightning strikes the Duck.

In the end, Bugs rests under an umbrella on Pismo Beach, opening a pile of clams. He discovers a pearl and wonders how that crazy duck made out with the genie. Suddenly, out of a sand hole, a miniature Daffy appears, running up Bugs' body to claim the pearl, "Mine, mine, it's all mine," he demands. "I'm rich!"

"Oh brother," sighs Bugs, and then he says, "Open sesame" and as Daffy shouts "I'm rich!" one last time, the clamshell closes on the doomed duck embracing his pearl. Where Buddha identified the third poison of the human soul (after hatred and delusion) as greed, the *Tao Te Ching* extended the warning: "There is no greater calamity than indulging in greed," as it is "the real dirt, not dust." The wise person will shake off this dirt. For Daffy, no such hope, the mirage of wealth in the sands of the Arabian Desert or on Pismo Beach was his hobby, a hobby that became an addiction. But ducks were not the only greedy animal; the greed of cartoon humans (and even eggs) would equal that of McDuck and Daffy.

Hoodwinked by producer Charles Mintz over the copyright to Oswald the Rabbit, Walt Disney was determined to control his own fortune, to keep his own copyrights, and to build his own fortune. (Mintz would be justly caricatured and villainized as Charles Muntz in Pete Docter's Disney/Pixar feature *UP*, 2009.) Disney's freshly motivated possessiveness expressed itself in his most blatant propaganda regarding greed in *The Golden Touch* (Walt Disney,

Figure 8.2 ***The Golden Touch*** **(Walt Disney, 1935) Retells the King Midas Myth as Musical Cartoon.** *Source*: Screenshot taken by the author.

1935) (figure 8.2).[7] In the last Silly Symphony that Walt Disney personally directed, an "In Gold I Trust" sign hangs above King Midas counting his billions of gold coins. (Within two decades, President Eisenhower would ironically engrave "In God We Trust" on the American dollar.) Midas sings the lyrics of Larry Morey's "Counting Song" robustly, "I'm known as rich King Midas, and when you look at me, you see a king who knows a thing about his treasury." Fat, adorned with a thin combed moustache and wearing a tiny gold crown on his round head, he belts out, "I never cared for women. I never cared for wine. Money is divine. Gold! Gold! Gold! I worship it. I love it. I wish I had more of it. I wish that everything I touched would turn to gold, gold, gold!" A mischievous Brownie named Goldie appears and gives him his wish, first turning his hapless cat to 18k gold.

Willing to trade everything for the golden touch, the king ignores warnings that such a choice will prove a golden curse. "Then curse me," he retorts. Cautioned that gold is the snare of the soul and the root of evil, he abandons all wisdom and riotously touches everything he can: a tree with golden apples, red tulips turned to gold, a fountain sprinkling golden coins everywhere. With his statues of satyrs around him, he boasts, "Hail Midas, thou rascal!" for he has created a universe of gold. Applauding himself in the mirror, he vainly gives himself a gold tooth. However, then the wheel of fortune begins to spin downward.

As he hungrily sits down for roasted pig head, fish, fruit, turkey, grapefruit, and banana, suddenly all his banquet converts to metal by his touch (and each one made into a clever gag). Even a drink of wine turns into tinkling coins.

Turning red with rage, he exclaims, "Zounds! All food to gold." Then he laughs, maniacally. However, realizing that the richest king could starve to death, he espies a gold skeleton in the mirror. Death haunts him and slices his neck. Hiding in the counting room, Midas calls for Goldie. The sprite reappears and is entreated to take away "this golden curse. I would trade my whole kingdom for a hamburger sandwich, just plain old hamburger." Frank Thomas and Ollie Johnson remembered that Walt wanted to throw in a comic one-liner, and the elfin trickster quips, "With—or without—onions?"[8] However, the cartoon remains a dark and grim parable. Midas loses everything he possesses, including his crown and robe—and even offers up his underwear, which Goldie allows him to keep lest the censors appear—to get rid of the curse. His Faustian bargain over, he gets his hamburger, with onions, which he eats contentedly.

This last official cartoon directed by Disney bombed; as Disney legend Jack Kinney whispered, "*The Golden Touch* laid a great big golden egg."[9] It seemed that not everything Disney touched turned to gold. Nevertheless, it preached a compelling sermon against anyone hoarding during the Great Depression when something to eat trumped any useless metal. However, unlike most tales of greed, Disney sugarcoated his ending, enabling grace and repentance to soften the consequences in the Greek myth.

As the 1930s Depression waned, Max Fleischer produced his own very didactic moral fable about what had caused the plight of America: greed. *Greedy Humpty Dumpty* (Dave Fleischer, 1936), like a classic Aesop fable, explains its own moral:

Oh, I climbed too high
To build my wall,
But I got too greedy
And I had a great fall.

In the Paramount short, a throng of shoe-house children play in a Bruegel-like scene in Nursery Rhyme Land. High up on a wall, overlooking them, a disturbingly creepy Egg, eating a chicken leg sits on his "throne." He recites his ditty of desire in building a wall of gold as his throne:

This wall is all my own!
The more I have, the more I want;
I love this glistening stuff!
There's power untold in these pieces of gold,
I've never had enough!

Other minor characters, a knitting Little Bo Peep and the little Boy Blue with his horn, sing a reprise of "Look out! Look out! Someday you're going to fall." They prophesize the end of "all you greedy guys."

You've got to stop
While you're on top—
Or you're gonna take the plop!

The old mother of the shoe also scolds the knavish egghead, prophesying "the end of all you greedy guys." With well-timed Fleischer humor, she ends her admonitory solo, then slips and pratfalls herself, awakening both the merry laughter of her children and a miserly laugh of Humpty, as he pours gold pieces into his waist pocket. He descends into his dungeon-like antechamber treasure room, where he stacks gold coins into a column. As he places one last coin on top, his tower topples fatefully. As he laughs over his hoarded spoils, golden sunlight breaks in from a high window and he wildly yells "Gold, gold, gold!" Then angrily he rants, "Why didn't I know there was gold in the sun? I'll get that too before I'm done." He demands the denizens of his kingdom build up his wall to reach the sun's gold. Old Mother Goose repeats the warning to the yolk-filled tyrant, "the higher you go, the harder you'll fall." He threatens and bullwhips them into a frenzy of work, with three men in a tub stirring the mortar. Witches and pelicans deliver bricks and he finally reaches a place with his own bricks piled precariously upon each other, where he declares it "mine, all mine!" As he takes an axe to the sun, it cracks, but spews out fire and lightning, with an electrical man of lightning bending him over his knee and spanking him.

An ensuring storm is such that his tower teeters and totters until the giant edifice cracks and crumbles, sending Humpty down, desperately clutching at a brick of gold, which he belatedly realizes will not save him. He hits the ground with a thud. The people try to patch his shards together again, but only long enough for him to realize the consequences of his greed. And all the king's horses and all the king's men couldn't put Humpty together again.[10]

Humpty's great sin was not to help others. C. S. Lewis's principle of ownership underlies a sense of greedy possessiveness, beginning with the curious assumption "My time is my own."[11] His devil Screwtape tempts with this notion of claims to ownership, thinking that humans "own" their minds, their bodies, their world. Personal pronoun trouble occurs as one claims a right to "my shoes" and "my waffles" to "my dog," "my country," "my rights," up to "my God." The specious assertion of ownership and control leads to greed.

Fyodor Dostoyevsky includes a similar parable of greed in his classic novel, *The Brothers Karamazov*. A miserly old widow consigned to hell for her avariciousness appeals for help. Her guardian angel, seeing the poor soul in such agony, petitions God for mercy, using as justification for her release the fact that, once upon a time, she had given an onion to a poor woman in need. God agrees to her release if the angel would take an onion and hold it above the fires of hell in such a way as to allow the widow to grasp it and thereby pull herself free. The angel accepts God's terms and does as instructed, and the widow successfully grabs the onion. All is about to be resolved fortuitously.

However, the difficulty God had foreseen arises when other souls in hell observe the rescue in progress. They immediately rush to clutch at and claw the widow in attempts to ride her and her onion out of their torment. Because souls weigh very little, the onion holds this additional burden without compromise, right up until the moment that the widow, greedy to the end and wanting to have the onion only for herself, begins to kick and beat her fellow damned off her onion. As she swings, shoves, and flails at the interlopers, the onion first begins to peel its skins. Finally, it breaks beneath her thrashing and the old widow drops forever back into hell, to spend eternity with those to whom she had, in her selfish greed, denied a share in her near-release.

"The root of all evil is greed," warns the Pardoner in the animated *Canterbury Tales* (BBC, 1998), whose own greed in selling pardons and indulgences exacerbates his own avarice. He proceeds to unravel a story of three drunken friends who set out to meet and kill death. However, they arrive at an old oak tree to discover a treasure, which each secretly wishes to possess. Deciding to celebrate, they send the youngest man to the city to buy wine. The other two plan to kill him when he returns. The young man who buys the wine adds rat poison. However, as the tale finishes, greed leads each member of this gang of three to meet Death.[12]

Even hell cannot stomach avarice. One segment of Bruno Bozzetto's hilarious parody of Walt Disney's *Fantasia*, *Allegro non Troppo* (1976), excoriates the sin of greed with its own hyperbolic excess. Timed to *The Infernal Dance of King Katschev* from Stravinsky's *The Firebird*, a cartoony snake in the Garden of Eden approaches Adam and Eve (created from clay and then transformed into cel animation) with the fruit of the knowledge of good and evil, the proverbial, apocryphal apple. After consideration, the pair resist the temptation and reject the fruit. The slithering snake decides to eat it himself. He falls asleep and finds himself tumbling into a nightmare of hellish proportions. Tormented by demons, assaulted by corrupting images of drugs, alcohol, money, materialism, lust, and the rush of mediated progress, he is overwhelmed with the consequences of his actions. Worst of all, he is made into a modern man, having to wear a suit and a fedora. Waking up, he recounts his horrific dream to the original couple and spits out the apple. Hell will leave greed to humans.

In Bosch's *The Haywain* the defining image of Cupidity is that of a fisherman quietly catching a larger fish with a smaller one. In the artist's image of the carcass of a creature's abdominal cavity, we find the giant maw of a fish engulfing and vomiting other fish. Pieter Bruegel the Elder refined this parable into his "Big Fish Eat Little Fish" motif, a theme evident in both

Michael Mill's *Evolution* (1971) and another Bruno Bozzetto's *Bolero* segment of *Allegro non Troppo* (1976). Herein the predatory dog-eat-dog world of preying and consuming unfolds throughout this survival of the fittest as the instinct to devour another fuses greed with gluttony in a truly vicious cycle of natural selection. A rapacious evolutionary process seems quite natural and supportive of avarice. We see; we conquer; we kill; we plunder.

Similarly, Daffy Duck's attitude of "Consequences, Schmonsequences" reveals a deliberate refusal to listen to truth or to consider the Tao, but only wants and devours. In a story excerpted from the writings of Chuang-Tzu, Hu Jinqing's *Mantis Stalks Cicada* (1988) points back to another old Chinese idiom, meaning to covet gains ahead without being aware of the danger behind it. One does not count the cost of a greedy action. A Cicada rests high on a tree, drinking the dew and chirping, oblivious of a mantis appearing behind, rolling out its own plan. Mantis, bending over and arching up its front leg, is going to catch the cicada, as it sneaks up under the cover of a leaf. The mantis does not know that there is a bright yellow oriole observing it. Seeing the antennae under the leaf, the yellow bird hops up behind the mantis and stretches out its neck, ready to peck at the mantis, as it devours the cicada. Similarly, the golden oriole is unaware that it is also under threat, as a weasel pops down upon it.[13] Each fixated desire remains oblivious to its own trajectory of death.

Tracing a 300-year history of the goodness of greed, author John Paul Rollert begins with what he calls the mischievous moralist and physician Bernard Mandeville, who praised greed as a virtue for an increasingly affluent Britain. In scribbling out a funny poem entitled "The Grumbling Hive" (1705), he suggests the infamous equation that "private vices [yield] public benefits." Such a notion would underlie his allegorical poem, *The Fable of the Bees* that "described a thriving beehive where dark intentions keep the wheels of commerce turning." When the gods removed all vice from the political hive, it deteriorates down to two good bees. He sparks expected outrage by asserting that, "*only* by such means could a nation grow wealthy and strong." His *Fable* bluntly concludes,

T' enjoy the World's Conveniences,
Be fam'd in War, yet live in Ease,
Without great Vices, is a vain
EUTOPIA seated in the Brain.[14]

An obsession to make money off an operatic frog and live in such ease characterizes one of the most popular of animated greed parables. Describing the manic moral fables of the Warner Bros. cartoons, Ray Bradbury said it well: "What better way to preach 'the wages of greed are eternal frustration' than

Figure 8.3 In *One Froggy Evening* (1955) Chuck Jones Created the Apotheosis of Avarice in a Parable of a Showbiz Fantasy. *Source*: Screenshot taken by the author.

through *One Froggy Evening* where the opera entrepreneur's frog burps into silence when his profit-making aria looms?" (figure 8.3).[15] A fable, a parable, a story shown in 1955 in which the crass exploitation of "art" was ironically sung in a lowbrow, neglected art form (until the September 1985 exhibition of Warner Bros. cartoons at the MOMA). Author Jerry Beck introduces it among the *50 Greatest Cartoons* as having the "simplicity of a parable."[16] A frog emerges from a cornerstone of an old building's demotion, croaking out a splendid version of "Hello, My Ragtime Gal." Immediately the man dreams of the money he can make off the (cultured tenor's voice) operatic amphibian. However, Michigan J. Frog will only sing for him and becomes completely listless in the company of any other human. He swings from lively and lithe songster belting out such favorites as "I'm just wild about Harry," "Come Back to Erin," and the catchy Maltese/Franklyn composition, "The Michigan Rag," to devolving into a lumpen and limp pile of frog flesh. Chuck Jones' amphibian was perfect in so many ways. Jones explained his memory as a kid. "Any boy that's ever picked up a frog knows how the body sits and the limbs hang down. So we had to be certain, in those first few seconds on the screen, that when [Michigan] appeared he looked like a frog. Even that his eyes blinked upward."[17]

He foils the avarice of his would-be entrepreneur by ribbitting. At a theatrical agency and a rented theater (even with free beer to customers), the frog will not perform, which renders him penniless. Slumped on a park bench in the cold of winter, he loiters until picked up by the police and sent to a psychiatric hospital. Finally released, he puts the hope of his materialistic fantasies back into another building cornerstone, as time passes (April 16, 1892) to AD 2056, where an Acme Building Disintegration Company Employee opens the box, finds the frog, and dreams of his own wealth. Steven Spielberg once honored *One Froggy Evening* as the "*Citizen Kane* of animated shorts." Part of its secret was, as storyman Michael Maltese confessed: "We wrote cartoons for grownups; that was the secret." Jones left the "spiritual" or religious aspects up to Maltese, quipping, "That's his realm," but together they would hatch a rollicking, ebullient, and brilliantly revelatory parable in a 7-minute cartoon.[18]

The unintended and unexpected wages of greed occur in normal ways as well, as one strives to climb the corporate ladder or achieve something. The mere search for pleasure can detour one into collecting those resources for pleasure. Such is Steve Cutts' satire, *Happiness* (2017), in which rodents run a vertiginous rat race, gradually donning bureaucratic white shirts and ties (figure 8.4). Holding their briefcases and iPhones, they rush to the crammed subway, where signs announce that the train going to "nowhere" will arrive in 3 minutes. They ride up escalators to the tunes of Bizet's "Habanera" and Edvard Grieg's "Morning Mood." Public advertisements promise happiness, selling Blah cologne, Crunchy Crunch, Spandex Contraceptives, and bottles of Pure BS (with a shout out to Aldous Huxley' *Brave New World* with a can of Soma, offers of Starbuck-like Happiness drinks with their offensive holiday cup designs, and "Trump, the Musical"). Hordes of mice rush through mazes with happiness commercials around every corner. They bite, claw, and chew each other over sales openings for HD 60-inch Plasma TVs, with legs

Figure 8.4 Steve Cutts' Satire *Happiness* (2017) Charts the Trajectory of a Life of Material Consumption and Greed. *Source*: Screenshot taken by the author.

and arms severed. A red convertible Joy car gives pleasure for a moment, until it hits a traffic jam. Happiness premium lager beer teases with another possibility of pleasure to "Drink. Forget. Smile" or with an invitation to Old Jim's "Creepy as Hell" Quality Whisky to help "drink the blues away." Finally, a drug capsule prescription offers lots of happiness, which ushers the lucky mouse into 15 seconds of Disney world flights of fantasy. However, that reverie crashes to an ignoble end in a desolate street where authorities forbid "eye contact" and "breeding." (A ubiquitous sign of "Missing Big Toe, Last Seen on Foot Sorely Missed" pops up.) Our rodent follows an elusive mouse dollar until it lands on a desk with a computer, revealed as a mousetrap. The camera pulls away to show a scene similar to director King Vidor's *The Crowd*, in which personal identity is lost. The mouse greedily pursues everything that eventually leads to the mousetrap of a cubicle job. The unintended consequences of ambition, of a vocational greed, defeat those tempted by the literal rat race of a dehumanizing consumer culture. Perhaps the etymology of the word "career" is too accurate: a rut that one greedily runs around with no rest.

Greed (Alli Sadegiani, 2011) begins with a quotation from horror author Stephen King: "Monsters are real, and Ghosts are real too. They live inside us, and sometimes, they win." A tattooed, bald man stands anxiously in a bathroom, before a mirror, discovering a red dot on his upper cheek. He pushes it and suddenly stacks of gold coins appear. "Eureka!" The more he touches the red spot, the more money appears. However, when he touches a larger red pockmark above his eye, the money all disappears. Touching a dot on his nose grows a Hitler-like moustache on his face and a strand of black hair on his bald head. When he hits the big buttons, everything disappears. Hiding under the sink, he is tempted to touch the little button. He gives in to his curiosity and greed. As he is about to push the button, the screen goes black and a scream shrieks out. The Dantesque hell will boil you alive in oil. However, although it is no consolation, one luxuriates in the finest, most deluxe boiling oil that money can buy, but it is still boiling.

What is missing in such parables of greed is the vice's impact not only on one's own soul but also on the lives of others.[19] Medieval theologian Thomas Aquinas opined that the sin was "directly against one's neighbor, since one man cannot over-abound in external riches, without another man lacking them. . . . It is a sin against God, just as all mortal sins, inasmuch as man contemns things eternal for the sake of temporal things."[20] Greed, if unleashed and unchecked, can even lead to violence and to the vice of wrath. An exemplary apotheosis of this sin against God occurs in Run Wrake's sensationally droll horror of *Rabbit* (2005) (figure 8.5).

Rabbit begins like the happy Dick and Jane books of the 1950s twists into Wrake's parable of perverted avarice. Incorporating illustrations from Geoffrey Higham's classic images, Wrake quietly twists one's imagination as a

Figure 8.5 Run Wrake's Sensationally Droll Horror of *Rabbit* (2005) Identifies the Demon Vice of Desire in 1950s Iconography. *Source*: Screenshot taken by the author.

seemingly innocent little girl dreams of a muff. Suddenly, a rabbit is trapped and slaughtered. When she and her brother take the animal corpse home, they slice it open to discover a little golden idol with fantastic powers. It can transform houseflies into diamonds.

Wrake recalls coming upon some educational stickers by Higham. Reflecting upon the innocence of the children, he thought, "It would be interesting to present them as they have perhaps grown up, in an age where greed is often regarded as a virtue."[21] When he found the "I is for idol" sticker, a sinister story began to emerge. As the children gather more diamonds, they trade them in for feather quill pens and jam, which they feed to the idol. They kill, or massacre, more animals to attract the flies that will become jewels. They must feed the idol continually. As capitalism run amok, greed spirals into more greed until it all comes horribly crashing down on them. As Aquinas pointed out, greed does violence to one's neighbor, even when that neighbor is a simple rabbit or any creature great and small.

In 1590, in the Mannerist tradition of a florid and asymmetrical style, Jacopo Ligozzi, a draughtsman at the Medici court, painted his Seven Deadly Sins, often with a bizarre distortion of perspective arising from a fascination with *momento mori*. Among his allegorical paintings, *Avarice* shows a pale young woman sitting before a miser holding a bag of money, and a chest of pearls at her feet. Behind her looms a winged skeleton of impending death, who tempts her with a sack of "more" money. In the background, a thief robs and assaults the woman for her wealth. The revelatory parable, like Wrake's example of *Rabbit*, preaches a cautionary sermon that the true "wages" of avarice is death.

NOTES

1. Newhauser, Richard, *The Early History of Greed: The Sin of Avarice in Early Medieval Thought and Literature* (Cambridge University Press, 2000).
2. Tickle, Phyllis A., *Greed* (Oxford University Press, 2004), 15.
3. White, Paul, "Death Trap," in *Jungle Doctor's Fables* (Pasternoster Press, 1955), 17–20.
4. Giesen, Rolf, *Chinese Animation* (McFarland, 2015), 60–61.
5. Smith, Jordan, op. cit. 41–42.
6. Noer, Michael and David Ewalt, "The Forbes Fictional 15," *Forbes Magazine* (April 1, 2011), https://www.forbes.com/lists/fictional15/2011/forbes-fictional-15.html (Accessed March 21, 2020).
7. "We tried consciously to put some social meaning into one of our cartoons in the Silly Symphonies series (i.e., *The Golden Touch*), but it was a tremendous flop." Walt Disney cited in Mark Pinsky's *The Gospel According to Disney* (WJK, 2004); Walt argued that the important thing that he was doing was teaching "a child that good can always triumph over evil." Thus, *Time* magazine critic Richard Corliss suggested that Walt's credo seemed derived from the Jesuits' maxim, "Give me a child before he's seven, and he will be mine for life"(3).
8. Thomas, Frank and Ollie Johnston, *Too Funny for Words* (Abbeville Press, 1987).
9. Kinney, Jack, *Walt Disney and Other Assorted Characters* (Harmony, 1989).
10. Ditto, http://cinema4celbloc.blogspot.com/2006/04/greedy-humpty-dumpty-1936.html (Accessed January 22, 2020).
11. Lewis, *Screwtape Letters,* 96.
12. Chaucer's "The Pardoner's Tale" inspired J. K. Rowlings' "Tale of the Three Brothers" animated in the Harry Potter film.
13. Giesen, *Chinese Animation*, op. cit. 74.
14. Rollert, John Paul, "Greed Is Good: A 300 Year History of a Dangerous Idea," *The Atlantic* (April 7, 2014), https://www.theatlantic.com/business/archive/2014/04/greed-is-good-a-300-year-history-of-a-dangerous-idea/360265/ (Accessed February 8, 2020).
15. Schneider, Steve, *That's All Folks!: The Art of Warner Bros. Animation* (Henry Holt and Company, 1988), 11.
16. Beck, Jerry (ed.), *5o Greatest Cartoons as Selected by 1,000 Animation Professionals* (Turner Publishing, 1994), 49; In telling a fable, Jones pointed out how it "is easier to humanize animals than it is to humanize humans." *Chuck Amuck*, op. cit. 227.
17. Kenner, Hugh, *Chuck Jones: A Flurry of Drawings* (University of California Press, 1994), 73.
18. The revelation to use "Beep! Beep!" for their Roadrunner cartoons came when Jones and Maltese watched a delivery fellow walking down the hall with a load of backgrounds, and he couldn't see where he was going, but just shouted "Beep! Beep!" Maltese looked up and said, "O.K. God, we'll take it from here." Cited in Jeff Lenburg's *The Great Cartoon Directors* (McFarland, 1983), 32.

19. The deleterious impact on neighbors and lovers is brutally represented in Sylvain Chomet's *Carmen* (2015). An evil little Blue Bird of Happiness tempts its victim, an animated version of Euro-pop star musician Stromae, into a Twitter addiction and its consequences of a dystopian world.

20. Aquinas, Thomas, *Summa Theologica* (2, 118, ad 1).

21. Robinson, Chris, *Animators Unearthed* (Continuum, 2010), 204–205.

Chapter 9

Gluttony (*Gula* or the Swine)

Gluttony (*Gula* or *gastrimargia*) matches an unquenchably thirsty woman with her symbolic bestial counterpart, a hog. She sits on the gross porcine as she quaffs her pitcher of beer, becoming more and more like the men and pigs at the end of George Orwell's *Animal Farm*: indistinguishable. Everyone is guzzling, drinking, chewing, or vomiting, engrossed in filling their bellies and oblivious of the chaos about them. An amphibious creature eats a smaller fish (echoing one of Bruegel's favorite proverbs of "Big Fish Eat Little Fish"[1]), with its belly sliced open, pointing to the fact that its appetite will never be satisfied. A humanized building holds a giant man prisoner to his appetite, while a fat slob glugs and swigs his jug and an anthropomorphic windmill holds storehouses of food in an open mouth, but unable to chew all that he has. Historian Walter Gibson finds a comic fantasy in the images of the "legs and lower torso of a nude man that protrude from a hole smashed into the side of a wine or beer barrel." For Gibson, the man and his companion are in imminent danger of drowning even as the latter frantically addresses his prayers to heaven.[2] One of the extant paintings by Jacopo Ligozzi depicts Gluttony as a grossly haggard, nude old woman, with roundels of cheese and delectable fowl dangling from the ceiling, including plucked turkey and goose. She chomps on a greasy chicken leg. A naked youth voraciously sits astride a wine barrel, chugging a giant beaker of wine. The anthropomorphic emblem of a wild boar's carcass reflects the swinish appetite of the two figures. Gluttony is, if nothing else, extremely and grotesquely visual. One hears the parodic lyrics of Weird Al Yankovic singing, "If I have one more pie a la mode, I'm gonna need my own zip code; Because I'm fat, I'm fat, come on you know it." Yet, gluttony encompasses (and that's the most apt verb) more than obesity.

Gluttony started out quite innocently. The Latin *gluttire* meant simply to swallow. However, it soon devolved into swallowing or "gulping down" more than is needed. One gulp led to another. When the apostle Paul penned his letter to the Philippians, he warned against those "whose god is their belly" (3:19). An obsession with food can displace an appetite for the God who gave daily bread to His people. For those ruled by their natural appetites and minding earthly things, disaster waits, not to mention high blood pressure, heart disease, diabetes, arthritis, gout, or chronic indigestion. Dante's wages of gluttony in the Inferno offer death by feeding with grossness that approaches that of animals. Those who gorged themselves like swine end up wallowing in disgusting mire, shivering in damp, cold weather in a stinking bog swamp. Those who sought to worship the chicken and wine in their bellies now face eternal physical discomfort. In Purgatory, under a fruit tree, refreshments like those of Tantalus, are continually out of reach. Such frustrating desires purge the emaciated spirits. Their eyes have sunk deeply back into their sockets, as they starve and practice disciplines that aim to teach them to control their appetites.

One is reminded of the old German proverb that "gluttons dig their graves with their teeth." One of the earliest exemplary parables came out of the John Bray Studios, *The Artist's Dream or The Dachsund and the Sausage* (1913), in which a little dog smells a sausage and climbs a cabinet to retrieve it.[3] He eats so much that he explodes, digging his "grave with his teeth."

In Tomer Eshed's *Wonderful Nature: The Common Chameleon* (2016), a droll British documentary narrator praises the amazing reptile's peculiar design as "one of a kind It's equipped with double sighted vision, remarkably camouflage ability, and a tongue that can stretch out twice the length of its body. Despite all of its advantages, it has yet to develop appropriate countermeasures against it biggest weakness: its untamed sense of appetite." Gluttony is its inherent vice. As a small fly buzzes by, its tongue shoots out and captures the snack. Then a colorful butterfly floats by and it snatches it from the air, chomps and gobbles it down, slobbering with a huge belch and a turning of its belly's color. When a much larger round insect happens by, it salivates and licks its mouth, pulls it in, and stuffs the oversized beetle into its maw, pushing it in and down its gullet. The chameleon sighs, exhausted, laying down begins to digest its catch, when it espies another larger creature. However, it sticks its tongue on some larger distant organism, which pulls the rapacious lizard out of frame. Ruefully, the narrator informs us that it is "truly a wonder that this creature has managed to survive." We have seen that it does not. It digs its grave with its wonderful tongue.

The Desert Fathers pointed out that the first temptation that the Devil used to detour a fasting Jesus from His mission was the simple carnal offering of gluttony, challenging the Bread of Life to turn a stone into bread (so Satan moved on to appeals to covetousness and pride).[4] Almost ironically, the Gospel writer observed that the Son of Man came eating and drinking, and people said, "Here is a glutton and a drunkard, a friend of tax collectors and sinners." However, his deeds would vindicate the truth. (Matthew 11:19) To accuse God of being a glutton is an amusing attack by those whose legalism made them gluttons of another kind, of a snobbish particularity, only willing to eat certain foods and at certain times. A glutton can also be one who is pretentious and patronizing about diet. Gluttony involves not simply the quantity of what you consume, but also the overindulgence of one's fussy demands. The gluttony of Delicacy is as dangerous as the gluttony of Excess.

How disturbing is it that Dante discovers the punishment for this vice of an undue obsession with oral pleasure to be one where the glutton is force-fed rats, toads, and snakes, rarely part of anyone's chosen menu items? What we discover is not only are we punished for our sins; we are punished by our sins. Gluttons will even become the food of Satan in the maw of hell. The judgment in the Inferno is to lie in vile muck, slush, freezing rain, mud, black snow, and hail. Amid piles of human waste, Cerberus, the ravenous three-headed hellhound, with its three open maws, tortures gluttons (such as Ciacco, which was a popular nickname for hog), feasting on their souls and then defecating them so always to have an insatiable hunger for more in an unending cycle of digestion and excretion.

Serving in the Spenser's House of Pride, a deformed and loathsome Gluttony sits atop a nasty, filthy swine with a belly blown up with luxury, fat swollen eyes, a long crane-like neck for swallowing up excessive feasts (while the poor suffer through want), and then he often vomits up his gullet everything he dislikes. Clad in green vine leaves, (as he got too hot with other clothes), sweat trickles down a wanton garland on his head. Remarkably, even as he rode, he still ate, with a boozing can in his hand, so drunk he could scarcely sit up. He was unfit for any earthly thing and so consumed with thinking of meat and drink that he could not even discern between friend and foe. His carcass was full of diseases, such as a dry dropsy, and still he craved for something to quench his thirst,

Food is intimately and gloriously associated with spiritual realities: manna from heaven, the Passover Seder meal of flat dry matzah bread, *charoset* (nuts, apples, pears), bitter herbs, and four cups of wine, the Lord's supper of bread and wine, fish at the seashore, all invite one into gratitude to God and community with others. Heaven itself celebrates a wedding *feast* of the Lamb. However, while consumption of food and drink on earth can get out of control, eating is a primary good. Lewis noted that for humans,

> There is no good trying to be more spiritual than God. God never meant man to purely spiritual creature. That is why He uses material things like bread and

> wine to put the new life into us. We may think this rather crude and unspiritual. God does not: He invented eating. He likes matter. He invented it.[5]

Yet, eating can become an addiction, a substitution, or a rival for what really matters. St. Thomas Aquinas equated gluttons to children who are governed by their unchecked appetites. In a fascinating study on gluttony in children's literature, scholar Mary Stevens almost gleefully points out how food functions as the most basic temptation for child protagonists. Such works as *Hansel and Gretel*, *Alice in Wonderland*, *Charlie and the Chocolate Factory*, *Coraline*, and *The Lion, The Witch, and the Wardrobe* (all of which have been adapted, incidentally, to animated films) manipulate children with diverse foods.[6] The White Witch in Lewis' *Chronicles of Narnia* seduces Edmund through his unchecked appetite for Turkish delight. Food, Stevens argues, is "a tool to lure them to doing evil or mischief or disobedience." By succumbing, by not resisting, children do not learn to control their appetites now for future enticements. Teaching self-discipline to resist Reese's peanut butter cups or Snickers early in life provides moral equipment for living and provides a necessary lesson for children, preparing them for dealing with money, sex, or power in later life. Give in to chocolate now, and one will want wine and women later, or maybe just more chocolate.

The Grimm brothers weaved a story of hungry children whose parents (at least the stepmother) sought to dispose of them by sending them into the forest. Rooted in a time of famine, *Das Kindermärchen* of *Hansel and Gretel* suggests a link to both poverty and gluttony. Poverty is often the snare to both avarice and gluttony. The scarcer the food, the more likely one is to gobble it down when it becomes available. Disney takes the same tale in mouthwatering Technicolor with some of the most tantalizing treats ever offered to two skittish children in his *Babes in the Woods* (Burt Gillet, 1932), early during the Great Depression (figure 9.1). The two Dutch children—who, unlike Hansel and Gretel have no miserable background story—have wandered away on a bright sunny day, jumping at every imagined fright. They come upon a village of busy elves, washing and ironing their long white beards.

When a witch on her broom arrives and offers them a flight, they jump on and travel to a candy house dripping with icing. What almost destroys them, however, is their curiosity and appetite when they see the edible edifice. As Victor Hugo inserted in *Les Misérables*: "Curiosity is gluttony. To see is to devour." They turn into veritable gluttons, consuming candy canes, ice cream cones, and cherry pies, as the witch rubs her hands in cannibalistic glee. She throws them in with her snakes, rats, and bats (all of which Dante force-feeds gluttons in the *Inferno*), changing the boy into a spider. Just as she is about to curse the girl and make her into a rat, the elves come to the rescue, and the

Figure 9.1 ***Babes in the Woods*** **(Burt Gillet, 1932) Captures the Childhood Obsession with Candy, even a symbol for other temptations as one grows older.** *Source*: Screenshot taken by the author.

boy and girl then disenchant all the horrible animals back into children. The witch falls into a steaming cauldron of oil and turns to stone, witch rock. No punishment comes for the insatiable sweet-toothed mob, as they are content to delight in the petrification of the sorceress. Two romantic cats canoe on a lake on Moonlight Bay (crooning "by the light of the Silvery Moon"), when they debate about the foodstuff of the Moon. Not cheese, but sweets like candy, argues the girl.

In *Candy Town (*aka *Silvery Moon)* (Van Beuren, 1933), a stairway opens up for the couple to climb into the giant maw of the moon. A butterfly fairy admits them into a wacky land of strange creatures and chocolate cake, ice cream cones, and peppermint candy canes. They soft shoe and dance down the paths, until driven by craven hunger, they gobble and gulp up every dessert in sight. A panning smorgasbord of sundaes, bananas, cherries, and grapes. Lurking in the shadows are a sniggering spoon and a bottle of castor oil, awaiting their turn. Having eaten too much, the cat kids sit and hold their heads and their stomachs in a miserable state of indigestion. Pursued by the medicine across the surface of the moon, the pair escapes by falling back into the lake.

A much darker and more modern version of the Hansel and Gretel tale cautions against an undisciplined appetite for such sweet treats (figure 9.2). With the tinkling music (eerily *Turkey in the Straw* which harkens back to early

Figure 9.2 ***Who's Hungry*** **(David Ochs, 2009) Leads Children into Greater Danger through an Ordinary Appetite.** *Source*: Screenshot taken by the author.

Mickey Mouse) of an ice cream truck, a chubby boy eagerly accepts a cone while a thin little girl (looking like a gentle Helga Pataki from *Hey Arnold!*) reluctantly receives a Popsicle. They are both kidnapped by the Ice Cream Man of *Who's Hungry* (David Ochs, 2009). After abducting them, he puts the boy in a freezer and the girl on a hook. As the girl escapes, she sees eyeballs in an ice cream making machine. Sneaking up behind the kidnapper as he is watching TV and eating ice cream, she whacks him on the head with the meat hook. She rescues her tubby friend and leads him out of the house. However, when the boy sees a bowl of ice cream lying beside the fallen villain and goes to retrieve it, the Ice Cream Man awakens, takes the hook out of his head, and screams at the kids who scream back. Slipping on spilled ice cream, he falls into the giant blender, crushed into a bloody mess. Based on the Grimm fairy tale of Hansel and Gretel, the horrific cartoon works as a cautionary parable on gluttony.[7] It is a very scary lesson.

Gluttony may be the hardest vice to conceal. Social embarrassment over fatty tissue, the stigma of being overweight, supplanted the notion of spiritual sin. Gluttons, as Mary Stevens notes, are wrong in that they counter the "prevailing standards of beauty and health." Their deserved damnation is social rejection and having to buy two seats on a plane. Contemporary society, encouraging people to eat heartily and fast, seems to consider that gluttony "may well be the most widespread" vice, but also "the least harmful of sins."[8] Smorgasbords and buffets offer "all you can eat" and, greedily, we want such a good deal.

Our culture still offers diets, health remedies, and fat farms to free people of their failure to close their mouths. Gluttony may be the most immediately judged of all the sins. One cannot serve God and the belly, and the obsessively thin, ascetic-looking cadavers among us may judge others even more brutally. Prose suggests that gorging ourselves may be a little different from its other extreme, of fasting and starving ourselves so as not to appear fat. Yet, even the most emaciated woman may feel too fat. St. Francis of Assisi used to sprinkle ashes on his meals to abolish the temptation of taste and purge his appetite. Of course, the bulky St. Thomas Aquinas, the great Ox, was so large that the monastery cut a crescent shape into his dining table so he could eat more easily. For François Rabelais, only sex and defecation were as funny as overeating.

The glutton raids the pantry for help with spiritual malnutrition. It is most often associated with overeating, as when the chunky Augustus Gloop almost drowns in a river of chocolate in *Charlie and the Chocolate Factory* due to his undisciplined appetite. Ursula in *The Little Mermaid* suffers from two criteria set down by Pope Gregory the Great, namely the desire to seek "costly meats" or demand that "food be daintily cooked."[9] In the Broadway number, "I want the good times back," Ursula drools over gourmet meals served in King Triton's court, "trembling crowds of shellfish / Cracked and peeled for me to dine . . . Sipping bubbly . . . eating caviar before it hatches!" The desire for better (luxurious and costly, elaborately prepared) food is as sinful as eating greedily, consuming too much and chomping too hastily. Chesterton observed that no one despises the glutton as a glutton; it is only when the glutton imbibes the poison of pride and becomes a gourmet, that we see his sin of selfish indulgence. To deal with that qualitative excess of gluttony, Aquinas thought the best remedy was fasting, but his own girth (and that of Chesterton) suggests he did not practice that discipline. Actually, its corresponding virtue is temperance, moderation in what one eats or drinks.

The feature *Cloudy with a Chance of Meatballs* (Chris Miller and Phil Lord) quietly unveils a parable on conspicuous consumption. A nerdy inventor stumbles across a marvelous way that water can be changed into food, so that it rains hamburgers and hotdogs upon hungry citizens, "with a smorgasbord of epicurean delights descend from the sky like high-calorie manna from heaven."[10] People tilt their heads back, chew and swallow what falls into their mouths. The city's mayor exhibits greed and gluttony with gusto and has mammoth dreams for a profitable super-sized buffet. All is well until the unbridled consumption unleashes a culinary apocalypse, with pickles crashing into buildings, a humongous falling pancake, and a spaghetti tornado. The excess harkens back to the Proverbs (25:16) that asks, "Have you found honey? Eat only what you need. Lest you have it in excess and vomit it."

As one fat man discoursing on another, G. K. Chesterton explained that the bulk of St. Thomas Aquinas made it easy to regard him "humorously as a sort of walking wine-barrel, common in the comedies of so many nations; he joked about it himself."[11] But it was this large, very large, medieval theologian who identified the daughters of gluttony: "excessive and unseemly joy, loutishness, uncleanness, talkativeness, and an uncomprehending dullness of mind."[12] Aquinas pointed out that one could commit gluttony, "inordinate concupiscence in eating," in five ways. He connected the first three to the food itself: eating food that is too excessive in quantity (*nimis*, too much); eating food that is too luxurious or costly (*laute*); or eating food that is excessive in quality (*studiose*, too elaborately or delicately prepared). Such daughters dealt with the quantity and quality of food demanded.

In *Lady Fishbourne's Complete Guide to Better Table Manners* (Janet Perlman, 1976), the dainty and persnickety approach to eating fits gluttony as much as the amount swallowed (figure 9.3). Each guest is picky, even fussy and finicky, about what one eats, fastidiously sticking to one's diet or proper way of eating. The sly and wry *Lady Fishbourne's Guide* about proper eating etiquette might not strike one as an obvious choice for a parable on gluttony, but it points out how excessive obsessing over food is as dangerous as excessive consumption. In *The Screwtape Letters*, Lewis points out a finicky woman who is a "positive terror to hostesses and servants." She only wants something "smaller and less costly than what has been set before her; she never recognizes as gluttony her determination to get what she wants, however troublesome it may be to others." Gluttony demands its own way. It is a matter of arrogant consumption. A priggish person picking over her food is as sinful a glutton as the beer-guzzling oaf gobbling down double cheeseburgers is. Will Willimon includes those with bulimia, those who count carbs compulsively, those who demand organic servings, and Food Channel gourmands

Figure 9.3 Lady Fishbourne's *Complete Guide to Better Table Manners* (Janet Perlman, 1976) Reflects St. Thomas Aquinas' Other Kinds of Gluttony. *Source*: Screenshot taken by the author.

as classifiable under the rubric of gluttony. The qualities of eating "too soon, too much, too avidly, too richly, and too daintily" offer five branches of the Baobab tree of gluttony.[13] One finds hope in one of Lady Fishbourne's dinner guests who confesses the classic line, "A thousand pardons. I was most revolting."

Aquinas categorizes the latter two types of gluttony as related to the manner of eating. The first is eating too hastily, at the wrong time (*praepropere*); the second of eating too greedily, scarfing down one's meal (*ardenter*). One consumes when one should refrain or fast, when others are hungry and have nothing to eat.

Donald Duck in *Donald's Cousin Gus* (Jack King, 1939) sits down for a meal of spaghetti noodles, peas, corn on the cob, soup, and a frosted cake, but his cousin, the fat, waddling, and gluttonous Gus Goose, interrupts his daily repast (figure 9.4). Gus wears a bowtie and vest, carries an umbrella, and honks his tail feathers to make a point. Donald's Aunt Fanny sent him to visit him, and added a postscript that "He don't eat much." After being welcomed with a hearty handshake, Gus hears his alarm clock that ominously announces four times, Dinner, tea, supper, and lunch. Then, after one whiff of the food, Gus rushes to the table, takes Donald's chair and begins his feasting. He eats the corncob like a typewriter and shuffles the bread and meat like cards to make a Dagwood sandwich, popping it into his enlarged cheeks.

Donald, amused by his eating antics, laughs and claps; he takes the spaghetti with knitting needles and knits a sock that he slurps noodle by noodle.

Figure 9.4 ***Donald's Cousin Gus*** **(Jack King, 1939) Guzzles and Gulps with Gargantuan Hunger.** *Source*: Screenshot taken by the author.

However, when Gus grabs the bread roll from Donald and dips it into his coffee, steals the cake, swallows two bananas, and lures a line of peas into his mouth like a snake charmer, he proceeds to eat Donald out of house and home. Desperately, Donald serves a convenient supply of "Barking Hot Dogs: A Sure Way to Get Rid of Hungry Relatives." However, Gus tricks his way back into the refrigerator, indicating on his clock, that it is time for a cold lunch. Gus stands as a classic picture of an unending, voracious hunger. Cats are also notorious at wanting (and stealing) morsels not meant for them, as Garfield will gobble down lasagna anywhere or Sylvester, even in spite of taking a *Birds Anonymous* (Friz Freleng, 1957) pledge, will pursue Tweety Bird. Told by Clarence, a self-controlled cat, that such constant craving for birds only leads to self-destruction, Sylvester joins a support group without success to overcome his vices. At the end, Tweety opines on feline and human nature, saying, "Once a bad ol' puddy tat, ALWAYS a bad ol' puddy tat!"

One could not keep the porcine star of Warner Bros. animation out of this discussion. Porky Pig apotheosizes into *the* generic Piggy in his final Merrie Melodies cartoon, *Pigs is Pigs* (1937) (figure 9.5). In Friz Freleng's short cartoon, Piggy literally makes a pig out of himself; he translates the stereotypical metaphor into his own undisciplined behavior. He is always hungry, obsessed with eating hamburgers and watermelons and stealing food. Nothing sates his appetite. Sniffing the aroma of two cherry pies, he swipes them when his mother leaves them on a windowsill to cool. His mother catches him before he devours the second pie, spinning it around on his finger. At

Figure 9.5 In Friz Freleng's *Pigs is Pigs* (1937), Piggy remains oblivious of where his swinish cravings will lead him. *Source*: Screenshot taken by the author.

dinner, the Hamhock family says grace before sharing spaghetti. "And now children we can all say grace, all pray and please could we have lots of ice cream tonight." Before they say "Amen," Piggy deviously ties together all the strands of noodles on the table and slurps them down before his siblings take a bite. Mother Hamhock scolds her son, but Piggy has tied spaghetti strands together, so that he can devour all the spaghetti (enough to feed a family of eight) in a single slurp! His mother scolds him and warns that if he keeps eating like this, he will burst. Clearly, an annoyed Piggy does not care. That night, when all the other little piggies are fast asleep, he fantasizes about hot dogs, cake, and ice cream cones.

He dreams he is invited into the home of a seemingly kind, albeit hiccoughing, old bald man who offers Piggy a lavish feast of roasted turkey and various delicacies. "Hungry, my little man?" asks the stranger. Seated at a table, Piggy rubs his tummy in ravenous anticipation, as the man, now wearing red rubber gloves, imprisons him in a leather-bound chair that straps him to a robotic arm of a Feed-a-Matic machine that will force-feed him. In his laboratory with test tubes, beakers, and bottles of ulcer tablets and gastritis pills, this mad scientist fiendishly exclaims: "So, it's food you want! Ha, ha! (Hiccough) We'll give you plenty of it!"

A vat labeled super soup feeder unloads gallons of Oxtail, tomato, and pea soup down his throat; bananas shoot out of their skins into his mouth. In a scene inspired by Charlie Chaplin's *Modern Times*, Piggy is stuffed with Spanish olives from a gumball machine, overwhelmed with mustards, salt, and pepper on bread (only told to "hold the onions"), plied with an overstuffed Dagwood sandwich. For dessert, he is crammed with ice cream through a bellows contraption, and finally jammed with custard, cherry, lemon, and peach pies spinning out of a jukebox, dispensed from a Pie-a-tope!

Stuffed, Piggy swells to an immense, even huge, size, ready to burst, as his mother had warned. The maniacal scientist pokes his bulging belly and asks him if he has had enough. "Y-y-yes sir," he stutters. Releasing the obese pig, the scientist mocks him, "Why, you're not half full." Waddling toward the door, he espies a sumptuous roasted turkey and cannot resist. Tearing off a drumstick he bites, and explodes. Then he wakes up screaming in his bed. His mother calls him down to breakfast. Relieved, he rushes down, only to gorge himself on eggs and bacon. He has not learned his lesson.

The "Feed-A-Matic" is an apt Dantesque punishment, as those who committed the inordinate desires of gluttony on earth were to be force-fed rats, toads, and snakes in hell. The machine also occurs in Walter Lantz' *Apple Andy* (Dick Lundy, 1946). Strolling down a country lane, Andy Panda comes across an orchard of green apple trees, set off by barbed wire and signs declaring, "Keep out!" Tempted by a devil Andy to steal an apple, even as St. Augustine stole his pears, Andy ignores the warning of an angel Andy against the temptation to steal: "This foolhardy venture can only lead to your downfall." Andy, like Piggy, gives in far too easily, especially when the devil spray-paints the green apples red. Suffering from a stomach ache, and turning green himself, Andy falls out of the tree. However, in a nightmare, Andy finds apple cores dancing about him as in a pagan ritual, with a chorus line of bevy "Apple Core-us Girls" doing the can-can before him. (The musical score features an appropriate "Up Jumped the Devil, With the White Nightgown.") The devil tells him not to worry at all, because "sooner or later, we all have a fall." The boy ate the apples that were not quite ripe, eating them as Aquinas pointed out, at the wrong time. Falling into hell, Andy is strapped to the Feed-A-Matic machine, as the devil sticks green apples into his mouth, with a waiter-like worm shoveling gobs of applesauce down his throat, and a dead apple tree pouring pans of apple cider on the hapless bear. The song concludes that if he comes around to tempt you, "don't listen to the devil because he's not on the level, the devil in the white nightgown."

In *Butterscotch and Soda* (Seymour Kneitel, 1948), Famous Studio/Paramount's darling red pigtailed Little Audrey gobbles excessive amounts of candy and chocolate, which gives her a sugar high for a fantasy "trip" during her catnap (figure 9.6). With wide eyes and an eager appetite, she takes on a bag of chocolate, beginning with "Eeny, Meeny, Miney, Mo! I think that I will choose this one!" She repeatedly grabs a giant handful of chocolates and stuffs them all in her mouth. Her housekeeper, a surrogate mother, tries to persuade Audrey to eat a nutritious meal (steak, Brussel Sprouts, and potatoes): "I just can't understand a child eating candy 48 hours a day!" The

Figure 9.6 A Sweet Tooth in *Butterscotch and Soda* (Seymour Kneitel, 1948) Leads Little Audrey into an Uncontrollable Addiction. *Source*: Screenshot taken by the author.

willful child forks the steak under the table to feed the dog. She is confined to her room for a whole weekend until she is ready to eat a healthy meal. Following her to her room, the housekeeper finds bags of candy for everyday of the week, alluding to Frank Sinatra's hit "Sunday, Monday, or Always."

Audrey is an addict, and panicking to find her stash, looking in clothes drawers, in the ceiling lamp (where a fat resident mouse has eaten it), and even hoping for a candy cane in an umbrella case. Even the bird in a cage looks like a chocolate bar and as she attempts to grab it, it flies away. Suddenly, as in *The Lost Weekend* (Billy Wilder, 1945), she hallucinates, thinking the mouse has turned into a carnivorous vampire bat that covers the room with darkness. Out of the black screen, we enter Audrey's open mouth, with the camera pulling away to reveal the little girl clutching the wall and screaming (as if in Hitchcock's 1945 *Spellbound*). Her sugar high "trip" throws her into a spinning Candyland of chocolate roads, lollipop flowers, marshmallow clouds, Boston baked jelly beans, and licorice coal unloaded from a dump truck. Behind her, a billboard parodies an advertisement of the era, declaring, "I'd walk a mile for a Caramel," (a subtle dig at another addictive substance). She eats and eats, with her cheeks puffing and expanding until she finally turns nauseously green, then red-and-white candy cane striped, holding her stomach.

A large intimidating ghost accosts her with a jeremiad against her gluttony, joined by some flying black gumdrops and a chocolate candy bar ghost:

"You've got the Tummy Ache Blues!
The Tummy Ache Blues!
The Tummy Ache Blues!
You've got the Tummy Ache Blues
From eating all the candy you did!"
Chocolate Bar Ghost:
"You bit off more choc-o-late than you can chew!
You went and made a big, big pig of little you!"
All:
"You've got the Tummy Ache Blues!
From eating all the candy you did!"[14]

Anthropomorphic candies pursue her in truly nightmarish chase, leading to rock candy and candy canes chasing her through a fresh fudge road and through a miry slough of chocolate. Finally, a candy steamroller threatens to squash her. The bag and his fellow saccharine fiends sit her in a chair, wag fingers at her, reprise their *Tummy Ache Blues* ditty, and pour a cornucopia of candy into her mouth.

The housekeeper wakes up from her treacly delirium, patting her head with a cool washcloth, and offers her "all the candy you want!" An unnerved Little

Audrey freaks out and runs to the dining room table, taking the place of her dog, who now feeds her those healthy Brussels sprouts. The phantasmagoria of the traumatic nightmare works to sway the impish little glutton to amend her ways.

Other animated characters suffer from gluttony. Winnie the Pooh's obsession with honey also leads to a tummy ache. The sweet, slow-witted bear's addiction leads him into all kinds of trouble. On the other hand, J. Wellington Wimpy, with a compulsively insatiable appetite, will "gladly pay you on Tuesday for a hamburger today." Popeye held to his healthy diet of a can of spinach every seven minutes. In *Spree Lunch* (Seymour Kneitel, 1957) at Popeye's Diner, the sailor sweeps his sidewalks and sings his riffing mumbles. When Bluto pulls his giant diner into the neighborhood for a little chow wagon competition, the battle for dominance is only the stage backdrop for mooching customer Wimpy's descent into an epicurean fantasy. Between their battling, Popeye and Bluto throw, catapult, and waste all manner of food that Wimpy salvages: sausages, chicken, pancakes, frosted cake, cheese, and ham, and as food flies over him, Wimpy pulls down ketchup to make his meal tastier. However, he never nibbles spinach. Popeye invariably mumbles and grumbles while Wimpy chomps and swallows his hamburger, even into a crisis. In the earlier, greater adventure of *Popeye the Sailor Meets Ali Baba's Forty Thieves* (Dave Fleischer, 1937), Wimpy imagines a mirage of ham, pineapple, chicken, wines, grapes, and bananas, under a palm tree. Alas, the food becomes sand. Finding a café in the desert, Olive Oyl exclaims in hope, "Boy, am I starved!" Drawn into the kitchen by aromas, Wimpy finds hot dogs that the thieves abduct from his fork each time he tries to feed himself.

Abu Hassan Bluto eats his feast, chewing a whole side of meat and guzzling his spirits. Wimpy, in chains, sneaks in a whole chicken for his meal, and mumbles, "if I had some bread, I'd make a sandwich if I had a witch." Popeye speaks to a can of Spinach, "Open, Says Me," and within his giant forearms, tanks form in his biceps. Throughout the adventure, with Popeye fighting lions and giants, Wimpy simply chases a duck with a meat grinder. Stunned, Popeye wonders how Wimpy got into the cave, with the ever-ready glutton explaining his motive instead: "There's nothing in the world that can compare with a hamburger, juicy and fair" as there is nothing in the world "so divine, as a hamburger, tender and *mine.*" Wimpy's love song remains "I adore you hamburger mine." Lust cannot compete with Gluttony.

Capitalizing on the diet fads of the suburban 1950s, Walt Disney's short, *Tomorrow We Diet!* Goofy (Jack Kinney, 1951), plays with the modern aphorism (given by a mirror): "Eat, drink, and be merry; for tomorrow we diet" (figure 9.7). The cartoon comically proposes that eating became a habit from the early man who was hungry and thus developed a taste for food. Goofy inherits that habit and inhales a mass of food. However, when he looks into

Figure 9.7 ***Tomorrow We Diet!*** **(Jack Kinney, 1951) Attacks Goofy's Gluttony of Slide.**
Source: Screenshot taken by the author.

the mirror, it greets him: "Hello Fat." Arguing that he is as fit as a fiddle, he converts into a cello. From being all-round athlete to just being all round, the mirror fat shames Goofy for being too big for his britches. When he sits around the house, he sits around the house, perched on two pedestal seats at a diner. He rationalizes that he is just a jolly, genial, and lovable guy, but he is so fat that he can't even see his toes. Trying to push away from the table, he parodies a biblical admonition, "Get thee behind me, Salami!" But a refrigerator full of tender ham, delicious apple pie, mashed potatoes, candied yams, fried chicken, whipped cream, macaroni, cake, ice cream, luscious grapes, cold cuts, bananas, trout, French pastries, ham and eggs calls him to EAT! EAT! In the mirror, neon signs advertise all manner of food and abet his addiction to "Eat, drink, and be merry; for tomorrow we diet." Ironically, this mirror conscience is the one who eats all the food, suggesting not only is the flesh weak, but the willing spirit is also a slave to appetite.

The consequences of such gluttony are all too evident. Joe Harris' animated Trix Rabbit, over seventy years old, craves his sugar-coated, fruit-flavored General Mills cereals. Garfield the cat obsesses over lasagna and Homer Simpson indulges in beer and donuts. In the animated mockumentary, *Where Are They Now?* (2014), Steve Cutts traces the current-day miserable lives of 1980s cartoon characters, such as He-Man, Skeletor, the Carebears, the Smurfs, and Super Mario (figure 9.8). "Facing reality long after they hey-day prime," a character like Garfield has ended up as a fat, lazy slob, sitting on a mattress in a litter box. Too large to move, he barely has any strength to ring his bell. Roger Rabbit lounges with his girlfriend, Jessica Rabbit, who

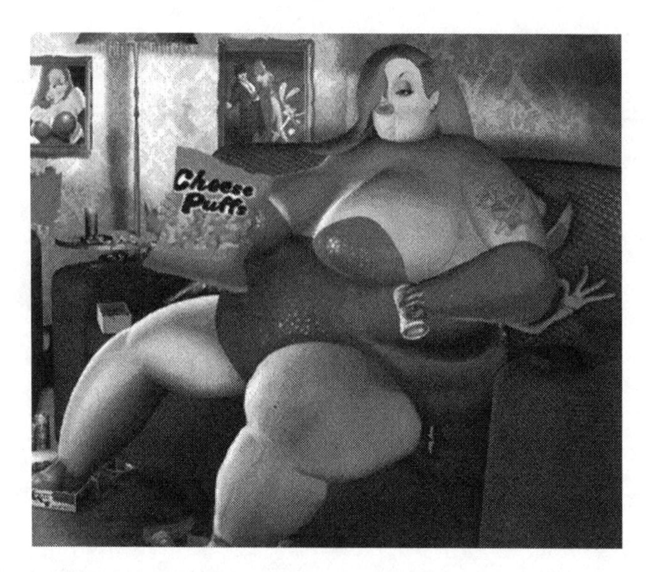

Figure 9.8 In *Where Are They Now?* (2014), Steve Cutts prophesies the old age of classic cartoon characters, such as Jessica Rabbit who snacked too much. *Source*: Screenshot taken by the author.

is larger than life ("I'm just drawn that way") with a KFC tattoo. She is most thankful for donuts.

Meanwhile, in *South Park,* Cartman devours Cheesy Poofs with gusto and abandon. When he offers himself as the spokesperson for his snack, he claims, "I could sing the Cheesy Poof song with both hands tied behind my back!" His sarcastic peer, Kyle responds: "You couldn't get both hands behind your back, fatty!" Stoned Shaggy Scooby and his inarticulate dog Scooby would slouch on a couch with their Scooby Snacks. Sesame Street would garner laughs from their gluttonous "Me eat cookie!" Cookie Monster.

Gluttony inevitably becomes the sin of selfishness, of satisfying oneself and thinking only of oneself. One does not expect a parable of judgment on such self-absorption, a spiritual gluttony, when a cartoon bursts out in effervescent colors and the unexpected galloping music of duck calls, whistles, bagpipes, xylophone, ukulele, and a slide flute. Something of the contagious bubbly music of the 1930s Fleischer Bros. cartoons bounces through the score by Bob Armstrong and Al Dodge's Cheap Suit Serenaders, but the rhythms and beats do not mask the consequences of selfishness. Tapped for inclusion in the Library of Congress' National Film Registry in 2009, Sally Cruikshank's vibrant and quirky *Quasi at the Quackadero* became a cult sensation at its release in 1975. Starring the slothful and rude protagonist, Quasi, whose sins are manifold, is a fowl creature right out of a Bosch painting. A sort of walking eggshell wearing a beach cap, he sits up in bed, watches his television, and Yuks it up with a perverse glee. "I love to look at pictures of people working," he mockingly laughs in undisguised *Schadenfreude*. His girlfriend Anita appears and reproves him for not being ready for their holiday, as they are going to the Quackadero. Throughout this prologue, animator Cruikshank reveals her wacky debt to such influences as Carl Barks' duck comics (e.g., Uncle Scrooge and Donald Duck), a fluid cartoon tradition of such animators as Winsor McCay, Otto Messmer, Max Fleischer, and Bob Clampett, and the underground comics of Robert Crumb and George Dunning's *Yellow Submarine*.

As Quasi acts like author Jerzy Kosinski's classic "videot," Anita tells him that Rollo, her pet robot (and a prototype version of a BB8 Droid), is already in the car, Quasi spouts, "That no-good set of training wheels," revealing a streak of meanness. Like her cartoon precursor Betty Boop, Anita shoots out literal daggers from her eyes at such a slight. Already we see the seeds of pride, arrogance, and cruelty encapsulated in Quasi.

Quasi, wearing a red cape and blue short pants languidly rises and rolls out of bed onto his rocking horse dinosaur. As a portent of her strained relationship with her boorish boyfriend, Anita confides to her Rollo that she cannot wait to see "the last of him." As Quasi jumps into Anita's Jetson's saucer, an anthropomorphic roof face says goodbye to him. They arrive at the Quackadero, a surreal amusement park, where hordes of creatures stream in through Dantesque gates into a 1970s San Francisco universe, eating, drinking, and amusing themselves to death. A character with an ice-cream curly top points out all the weirdos that inhabit the park and points to our friends.

The sensory overload of the thrill-seeking trio shows a world crackling with grotesque energy. Passing by the Tunnel of Youth, the first game show attraction Quasi and his friends enter is "Your Shining Moment," an interactive, embodied "humbling game." A garbled Ed Sullivan sideshow barker promises to probe a customer's past and show a shining moment, which for one character, a Winky Orlando, is being at a National Vegetable convention where illicit behaviors occur. He protests vainly: "that never happened to me," as his sins become shameful public presentations. The exposure of human perversity even in a cartoony universe brings a guilty conviction.

Our trio enters the Hall of Time Mirrors where they see themselves at every age. In a Praxinoscope mirror circling round and round, Rollo's reflection is still short, but with a flat tire, Anita is squat and fat and Quasi, in 100 years, is a skeleton. In childhood, Anita has pigtails and a lollipop while Quasi is in diapers wearing a dunce cap. A cutaway gag shows a woman in a fur coat, feathered hat, and purse looking and discovering birds, mammals, and an alligator, respectively. An anthropomorphic cow, pig, and chicken are horrified to discover themselves as a hamburger, hot dog, and chicken leg.

Prophetically, the "Think Blink Paints Pictures of Thoughts" offers technology itself invading the minds of its customers, sort of like Google knowing the tastes and predilections of present consumers, providing exposes of their patrons. A picture of Rollo's thoughts reveals his obsession with everything about Anita, as the house, the car, and the flowers plastered with the face of Anita. Anita, of course, finds such worship very "sweet." When Anita encourages Quasi to experience the carnival ride, he pushes her roughly and demands she go first. The painter captures her egoist image as a dancing Egyptian priestess.

Quasi sits for his portrait and the painter reels back in shock. Quasi's repressed hostile thoughts show Anita and Rollo sliding down his tongue into his mouth. He is ready to gobble up his friends with his gluttony and ambition for control. Anita yells out his name and he mutters, "Let's get out of here." They got to Madame Xano and Her Fabulous Dream Reader where one is summoned to "See Last Night's Dreams Today!" an unending kaleidoscope of psychedelic images (e.g., an Escher-like world circling back on itself; vegetables at a table about to eat an Adam and Eve character; a globe in a rocking chair falling off the side into oblivion). We come out of the trippy dream only to find the trio at Porky's Diner stuffing their mouths, chewing loudly, and belching.

In the ultimate Coney-Island sideshow attraction of Time Holes, Quasi asks Anita "Is that really a hole in time?" Anita warns him, there is, but he must be careful not to fall into one of the historical exhibits or he would be stuck there forever. Situated before a museum exhibit of 3,000,000 years BC, Quasi marvels at the beauty of dinosaurs. A sign warns, "DANGER! DO ***NOT*** LEAN OVER RAILING!" Anita whispers to Rollo, "When I give you the sign, you know what to do." He winks.

Their conspiracy puts a chocolate cake just over the rail and while Quasi's uncontrolled appetite takes over, Rollo shoves him into a black hole of time back to the Jurassic period. Two guards notice his presence in the prehistoric exhibition, where Quasi with his two-buck front teeth once again sits eating. As he spits out the seeds of his melon, a large horned pig rises up to devour him. Cruikshank has taken a simple sin of gluttony and expanded it with its cousins of selfishness, rudeness, and malice, to extend the theme of warped consumption from old Donald Duck cartoons to a logical conclusion, of the excessive epicure becoming the feast himself.

Cruikshank worked on Sesame Street cartoons, commercials for The Gap, and animated Joe Dante's horror comedy segment "It's a Good Life" in John Landis' anthology film *Twilight Zone: the Movie* (1983). In the latter episode, an angry young boy Anthony sends a surrogate older sister (played by Nancy Cartwright who would ironically garner fame voicing Bart Simpson) off to her doom into a hallucinogenic television cartoon. She ends up in animated hell with a leering wolf/monster belching fire out of his nostrils, chasing her with his hatchet, and devouring her; Quasi would find a similar fate. Her little brother delivers her parodic eulogy like Porky Pig at the end of his WB cartoons: "that's all, Ethel." In one of her YouTube chats, Cruikshank confesses that one does not "need to take acid to have weird thoughts and imagine weird things." While things get weird in this colorfully offbeat cult film, they underlie a truth of the consequences of selfishness.

In one of early animator Winsor McCay's lesser-known films, *Dreams of a Rarebit Fiend: Bug Vaudeville* (1921), a hobo gorges himself on a hand out of cheesecake and falls asleep, under a tree only to enter a nightmare vaudeville show performed by insects. A grasshopper and some ants toss each other in acrobatic stunts, a daddy longlegs imitates a drum with his six boots, Professor Cockroach rides a trick bicycle (falling off and being run over), tumble bugs tumble, while potato bugs box. The Beautiful Mademoiselle Butterfly and her Equestrian marvel, Black Beetle. The last show is the spider and the fly and when attacked by the giant arachnid pouncing on the man to devour him; the man cries out "oh Mama!" Donald Crafton observes that the "dream of the catastrophic demise of the protagonist provides a suitably autophagous moral: He who gorges may dream of being gorged upon."[15] Animator Ruth Hayes captured the notion in a very succinct way in her *Gluttony* (1985) in which one of two slobbering and licking characters ultimately devours the other.

Francine Prose paints a picture of the Land of Cockaigne, in which the construction of a glutton's paradise consists of "house walls made of sausages, doors and windows of salmon, table tops are pancakes, the roof rafters constructed of grilled eels."[16] Animals seek their purpose in life, as offerings consumed by humans. Geese roast themselves and fish prepare their own flesh for lunch. Excessive eating invites the grotesque and carnivalesque. For example, Rabelais' Gargantua is farcically born after his mother eats so much tripe that she blunders into labor. People mutate into beasts. In Japan's premiere anime storyteller, Hayao Miyazaki's *Spirited Away*, gluttonous parents gorge themselves at a lavish buffet and morph into swine, a reverse evolution of *Animal Farm*'s finale.

One of the first computer-generated animated films borrows the creative technique of metamorphosis from the early Emile Cohl films, but instead of a playful incoherent smorgasbord of changing images, Peter Foldes' experimental, computer-generated *Hunger/La Faim* (1974) unnerves the viewer with a haunting and disturbing parable of gluttony, greed, and consumption (figure 9.9). Beginning normally enough with a man who enjoys his wine,

Figure 9.9 Peter Foldes' Early Computer-generated *Hunger/La Faim* (1974) Echoes John Cassian's Connection of Gluttony and Lust, ending in a most gruesome contrapasso. *Source*: Screenshot taken by the author.

woman, and food, it flows into a horrific parable of overindulgence. A lean man pops a candy cube into his mouth, as one hears electronic metronomic beats and telephones ringing. Overworked, he summons his secretary who takes dictation while her face transforms into a clock, hands on the number 5, to indicate closing time. She disappears.

Tall and thin, he leaves the office, becomes his large symbolic automobile, and drives past a delicatessen. He peers in its window and snakes his body into the store to buy several banana-like items. He wanders the restaurant where the menu becomes a scantily clad waitress who serves him pig-headed pork, fish, and chicken, each of which he eats whole. He then points to more items, stuffing them into his sharp teeth and gargantuan mouth, then pulling in the tablecloth as he grows to an obese size. The waitress returns, and he imagines love, as she morphs into a naked woman, then transmogrifies into an ice cream cone, which he licks and takes home. They stop at a supermarket, where his hand buys everything. In his bedroom with his waitress, he serves her pork and pours her wine. Then, he leans down to stuff more potatoes, pork, chicken, and fish, into his growing corpus; soon he has three mouths and four arms scarfing up the food, grabbing becoming a gargantuan monstrosity. Then seven mouths and multiple arms continue the feasting, until it becomes a digger excavation truck, dumping piles of food into his obscene body.

Sitting contently with his belly obtruding, he watches a shadowy woman dance in silhouette sort of erotic dance; she dissolves into pots and pans, which he kicks away. He moves from the kitchen into the bathroom, exposing lards of overlapping fat. His stomach begins to ache, with digestive problems; his naked body heads to the medicine cabinet when he takes tums; suddenly he is falling from his bed into a dark abyss. Turning over-and-over, and landing with a thud, his head turns around to see eyes looking at him, with dozens of thin razor-sharp pupils gazing at him. As the light comes on, he finds himself a huge mass of adipose tissue, surrounded by hundreds of starved children from around the world. They look at him with wide innocent eyes, until one and then another open up starved mouths that all consume and attack him.[17] One thinks of the *contrapasso* of Dante's Canto 25, where a thief transmogrifies into a reptilian monstrosity, in which he loses his identity as he had exploited others. Such a bizarre morphology horrifies us as we see another serpentine sinner steal into the soul of another thief, through his belly button.

In a similar vein, the appetite of *The Ogre* (Laurene Braibant, 2016) surveys plates of bright yellow lemons, fresh watery oysters (figure 9.10). The gargantuan man in black pushes through a cocktail party, shoving others out of the way to sit at his table, a tiny napkin tucked under his chin. A parade of lean and lithe waiters serve pig's head on a platter, whole chickens, lobster, and all the fixings of French cuisine. The ogre smells the aroma of his feast, delicately picks at his prawns and pate, fish and foods disappear with an increasing alacrity, as he and other gourmets slurp and devour whatever is set in front of him, sexually swallowing strawberries. His obese girth expands across the room, but a Japanese-decorated waiter smiles secretly and calls

Figure 9.10 ***The Ogre*** **(Laurene Braibant, 2016) Cannot Resist Consuming and Polluting.** *Source*: Screenshot taken by the author.

for more. The miniature waiters haul deserts and fruit and pour them into his mouth. Suddenly, an oblivious diner is sucked into his unsatisfied maw. His wife screams and the ogre sweats and then vomits his meal, barely squeezing out of the front door, shedding his outgrown clothes. His immense size dwarfs the city and he rests his obscenely large butt upon an airplane. He continues to belch feathers, fart, and vomit excessive food substances, even defecating a whale. His vomit pollutes the earth. As he sits astride the planet, like the cat and mouse in *King Sized Canary*, he stretches toward the heavens, floating out into space with all his waste flotsam and jetsam of the skies, disappearing into the cosmos. Braibant quietly connects the grotesque vice of gluttony to the self-destructive waste of human consumption and pollution. We have met the ogre and the ogre is us.

Novelist Francine Prose looks at overeating in an age of obesity in her *Gluttony*, marking how what was a medieval sin has become a health crisis, where one counts calories, eschews red meat, and flees cholesterol. The modern sin of the body is worse than that of the soul. The vice of excessive food consumption (an early form of capitalism's desire for more?) is condemned as binging self-indulgence and appetites gone wild while it ironically ignores the luxury of the gastronomic connoisseur who voraciously demanding his or her palate be served.[18]

The fruit of gluttony is ripe, perhaps too ripe. Not only obesity but also all manner of foul excess. Church father Tertullian denounced the mass belching that soured the air at lavish Roman feasts.[19] The more ascetic John Chrysostom delivered a stinging diatribe against gluttony for its end results: "discharge, phlegm, mucus running from the nose, hiccups, vomiting and violent belching. The increase in luxury is nothing more but the increase in excrement."[20]

The Rabelaisian Bill Plympton, one of animation history's most hilariously vulgar and bizarre artists, easily mixes the digestive, excretory, and sexual aspects of human existence. Gluttony receives its orthodox wages in *EAT* (2001) (figure 9.11). As the Chez D Mange restaurant opens, an old, stubby, bald diner arrives and sits at his table where he magically conjures up a voluptuous and sumptuous female out of an ordinary plate of spaghetti. A married couple comes in and she proceeds to gab on unceasingly (her mouth metamorphoses into a goose, a frog, a balloon leaking air, a vacuum, bagpipes, and finally giant lips with a piece of lettuce stuck on the teeth). Her husband grabs all the food he can, from his own plate, his wife's, and from the lonely bachelor's plate. A family arrives with two undisciplined boys whose food fight escalates. When a server presents a check to the husband, he argues and she dives into his stomach to retrieve the food he has eaten. Suddenly, with digestive juices running wildly, he upchucks a vast array of food dishes. The waitress stuffs his mouth with vomit emitting from his ear. The

Figure 9.11 Bill Plympton, *EAT* (2001) Allows Digestion and Retching to Go Wildly Rabelaisian. *Source*: Screenshot taken by the author.

boys' father tries to hold down his own puke, but hurls it forth to his sons' frolicking delight. As the spaghetti woman tickles the old bachelor, he sucks the strands of her pasta into his mouth, devouring first the woman and then the table. Finally, he gorges on himself. The glutton is gorged.

These parables of gluttony connect us back to the medieval iconography. One recalls Taddeo di Bartolo's *The Last Judgment*, (1394), in which a party of fat, naked gluttons gathers around a table in hell, but with hands held behind their backs and their faces stuck down looking at the treats, unable to partake.

Perhaps the pinnacle of judgment on gluttony comes with Zofia Oraczewska's *Bankiet/Banquet* (1976) in which a diligent staff of green, cadaverous-looking waiters busily bring plates of various delicacies and culinary delights into a dining hall (figure 9.12). Looking out a window, he sees a train of limousines letting out passengers wearing expensive fashionable coats. The waiters bring in giant plates of meats, roasted pig, fowl, fish, clams, mussels, and lobsters, along with bottles of expensive wines. The eager and wide-eyed guests gossip and primp waiting for the doors of the banquet to open while the waiters prep a few finishing touches and light the candles.

Rushing to the table, one woman sits and grabs a clam, which violently bites off two of her fingers, blood spurting on the tablecloth and the mollusk spitting out a jeweled ring. In front of a bottle of Walker's Bourbon, a pheasant suddenly stands and starts pecking at the writs of a wealthy matron trying to slice one of its legs. The bird cuts the wrist off the arm and tosses it aside,

Figure 9.12 In Zofia Oraczewska's Harrowing *Bankiet/Banquet* (1976), the guests become the feast. *Source*: Screenshot taken by the author.

with a bracelet falling to the table. A mussel attacks and severs the second hand. A large bird alights on another woman's head and pecks out her eye, while a large red lobster follows the suit of the mussels and chops off other hands, blood spurting everywhere. A sharp-toothed pig bites into the large bosom of a grimacing woman. Even the lettuce cleans up on human body parts left on the table. Empty wine bottles fill up with blood. Noses, eyeballs, lips, hands, and bits of hair plus jewelry are scattered throughout the table, with all humans having been eaten. The food then returns to its plates, the waiters come in to clean up and one looks out the window to see the next parade of guests/victims arriving for a banquet, and claps his hands in glee. On the table, an oyster burps and a fish menacingly opens one eye, just before the next meal arrives. The glutton shall be gorged.[21]

In Dominican monk Fra Angelico's painting of *The Last Judgment* (1431), Christ does sit on his white throne, awaiting the judgment of the living and the dead (figure 9.13). Below him is an image of Hell, where the demons with pitchforks drive the Damned into the mouth of a mountainous Inferno. As the demons torture the naked sinners with ghastly torments, Satan sits in his crock pot of hell, squeezing two souls in his muscular hands and chews on a few of the choicest ones. Even with such a horrific image, Florence can advertise, "To eat well in San Gimignano is not a sin." Even the devil *mangia bene*. (In Rome, concierges advise tourists looking for restaurants to follow where the Jesuits and Dominicans head out for lunch, as they will eat and drink well and cheaply.) In Bosch's painting of *The Last Judgment*, gluttons have become food, doomed by one of hell's heavy-handed ironies: the eaters are being eaten.[22]

Figure 9.13 In Fra Angelico's Painting of *The Last Judgment* (1431), Satan chews on unrepentant sinners, even while clutching a few more tasty treats. *Source*: Screenshot taken by the author.

In a corner of the *Allegory of Gluttony*, a frog-like creature swallows a fish down its throat (*gula*) while its previous foods spill out of its belly upon the ground. It warns viewers to "shun drunkenness and gluttony, because excess makes man forget God and himself."[23] Gluttony stares at its plate and forgets the Giver of all good gifts. It does not sit alone in its obsession.

In his *Imitation of Christ*, the saintly Thomas à Kempis warned, "When the belly is full to bursting with food and drink, debauchery knocks at the door."[24] Chaucer's Pardoner waxes grossly on these dangers, first decrying, however hypocritically, "O womb, o belly, o stinking bag, filled with dung and corruption. At either end of thee, foul is the sound (belching and farting)." However, he takes another step and connects gluttony to our next sin, lechery. "For the holy Scriptures I take as my witness that lust is in wine and drunkenness." See how Lot drank so much that he slept with his daughters. As these two sins are visibly carnal, the Pardoner, speaking apparently from experience, confesses that anyone who gives in to gluttony becomes a sucker for lust.[25] When Fielding's Tom Jones, the lusty bastard, ate sumptuous, juicy meals with the sumptuous Mrs. Waters, chomping, sucking, gnawing on chicken bones, everyone knew what was to follow. In contrast, a child who learns the discipline of not eating an extra cookie may also learn the discipline of abstaining from sexual sins. Alas, some of us ate too many cookies. Let Gregory the Great have the last word to preview the next chapter: "But is it plain to all that lust springs from gluttony, when in the very distribution of the members, the genitals appear placed beneath the belly. And hence when the one if inordinately pampered, the other is doubles excited to wantonness."[26]

NOTES

1. A Zagreb mini-mini-cartoon entitled *The Fish* (Milan Blazekovich, 1970) follows a little fish eaten by a bigger fish, which in turn becomes food for a larger fish, a process in which each fish increases in size. Finally, a very large fish filling the frame sees this little fish that he swallows only to find that it was a fishing lure that has caught him on a hook.
2. Gibson, op. cit. 35.
3. The 1920s would introduce the Jazz Age glutton and drunkard, Felix the Cat, whose felicitous career, John Canemaker noted, was "underscored by human folly on a grand scale." In *Felix Doubles for Darwin* (1924), a starving Felix reveals his obsession for food declaring, "I'd give eight of my lives for a square meal." In a Prohibition-defying speakeasy, Felix whoops it up drinking, as in *Felix the Cat Woos Whoopee* (1928). In *Flim Flam Films* (1927), after his children film a philandering Felix flirting with a bathing beauty, his wife sees the amateur movie and pounds her wayward husband. *Felix, the Twisted Tale of the World's Most Famous Cat* (Pantheon, 1991), 9.
4. Cassian, *Institutes* 5: 10.
5. Lewis, C. S., *Screwtape Letters,* op. cit. 41.
6. Stevens, Mary, *Nothing More Delicious: Food as Temptation in Children's Literature* (MA Thesis) (Georgia Southern University, 2013), https://digitalcommons.georgiasouthern.edu/cgi/viewcontent.cgi?article=1050&context=etd (Accessed August 28, 2020).
7. German Wilhelm Busch, one of the originators of the modern comic strip, drew cruel verse/picture tales of his "paper theater" such as *Max and Moritz- Eine Bubengeschichte in sieben Streichen* (1865) (what he called *Bilderbogen* or picture sheets) as scrolls of consecutive pictures like Hogarth and Struwwelpeter's illustrated stories. See Annan, Gabriele *The Genius of Wilhelm Busch: Comedy of Frustration* (edited and trans. Walter Arndt) (University of California Press, 1981). A grisly and darkly comic 1951 stop action cartoon by Ferdinand Diehl shows the boys strangling geese with their sadistic pranks.
8. Ibid., 41.
9. Gregory, Saint Thaumaturgus, *Fathers of the Church: Life and Works* 98 (trans Michael Slusser) (Catholic University of America Press, 1998).
10. https://www.wired.com/2009/08/geekdad-talks-cloudy-with-a-chance-of-meatballs-with-directors-chris-miller-phil-lord/ (Accessed July 21, 2020).
11. Chesterton, G. K., *The Dumb Ox: St. Thomas Aquinas* (Image Classics, 1974), 97. Chesterton continued, "It may be that he, and not some irritated partisan of the Augustinian or Arabian parties, was responsible for the sublime exaggeration that a crescent was cut out of the dinner table to allow him to sit down."

12. Aquinas, Thomas, *Summa Theologia* 2:2 Question 148, article 4 (trans. Timothy McDermott) (Christian Classics, 1991).

13. Fisher, MFK, *An Alphabet for Gourmets* G is for Gluttony "Great Moments in Gluttony" (North Point Press, 1989).

14. I am indebted to Rik Tod Johnson of *Cinema 4 Cel Block* for his February 13, 2006 posting on this film: http://cinema4celbloc.blogspot.com/search/label/gluttony (Accessed January 22, 2020).

15. Crafton, Donald, *The Shadow of the Mouse* (University of California Press, 2012), 283. The University of Notre Dame scholar points to the parabolic nature of such cartoons to comment on changes between traditional and digital technological and on the relationships between animator and his/her creations.

16. Prose, Francie, *Gluttony* (Oxford University Press, 2006), 88.

17. Canemaker John, "What's New in Animated Films? Sex, Gluttony and Computers" (*New York Times*, October 19, 1975), https://www.nytimes.com/1975/10/19/archives/whats-new-in-animated-films-sex-gluttony-and-computerswhats-new-in.html.

18. Prose, op. cit.

19. See Roberts, Alexander and James Donaldson (eds.), *The Ante-Nicene Christian Library: Translation of the Fathers Down to AD 325* XVIII (trans. Rev. S. Thelwall) (T&T Clark, 1866–72), 123–153.

20. Shaw, Teresa, *The Burden of the Flesh: Fasting and Sexuality in Early Christianity* (Fortress Press, 1998), 133.

21. https://www.youtube.com/watch?v=ZSEZCTi3D1w (Accessed March 19, 2020).

22. A fifteenth-century manual on vice and virtue, *Book of God's Providence*, likely shaped the imagination of Bosch himself. Gluttons gather around a burning hot table, starved and parched where they beg for straws to eat, urine to drink, excrement to devour, makes us stop thinking of nibbling a donut. Even the dozens caught the spirit of gluttony as when "Your mama is so fat that when she goes to a restaurant and looks at the menu, she says 'okay.'"

23. Smith, David (ed.), *Parody and Festivity in Early Modern Art: Essays on Comedy as Social Vision* (Taylor & Francis, 2017), 99.

24. Kempis, Thomas à, *The Imitation of Christ* (Dover, 2003), 11.

25. Okholm, Dennis, *Dangerous Passions, Deadly Sins: Learning from the Psychology of Ancient Monks* (Brazos, 2014), 37–38.

26. Gregory the Great cited in Shawn Tucker *The Virtues and Vices in the Arts* (Cascade, 2015), 105.

Chapter 10

Lust (*Luxuria* or the Goat)

Father Robert Barron once spoke about a friend who confessed that he suffered from the sin of Glust, a combination of Glutton and Lust. It is only one small step from Gluttony to Lust. The belly is not too far above from what lies below. Of Evagrius' eight thoughts (*logismoi*), the thought of fornication (*porneia*) assails one when least expected, but frequently accompanied by an undisciplined appetite, pops up uninvited. One cannot ever repress the irrepressible wit of Dorothy Parker who reflected that "if all the girls who attended the Yale prom were laid end to end, I wouldn't be a bit surprised." Wherever one loiters in laziness, a stray thought of *luxuria* joins in a double entendre or in simply observing the Grand Tetons. No doubt, one can experiment in isolation to find that "an idle mind is the devil's workshop."

Luxuria, as a religious painting, seems odd at times. Reminding one of an inspiration for R. Crumb's cartoons, Bruegel's central character in *Luxuria* (Lust), a nude female, kisses a beak-faced demon that fondles her breast. A rooster, or cock, stands above them, while all about copulating couples and beasts spread their legs or find themselves literally devoured by their own carnal appetites. Aphrodisiacs, such as a mussel shell, offer aids to unnatural or excessive erotic couplings. In a parade of madness, a legion of demons and bizarre frog-like characters, including a nude man whose hands are tied and adorned with a fool's cap of judgment riding a blanketed skeletal horse, follow a musician with his bagpipes, the symbolic instrument of folly, an "instrument allied with unbridled oafs."[1] A hooded demon nonchalantly "slices off his *membrum virile* with a large carving knife," hinting that Freud was centuries behind the time.[2]

In Spenser's parade, riding on a bearded goat with rugged hair and white eyes, sat the lustful Lechery, who looked just like the goat he was riding.[3] He was rough and wore a green gown which hid his filthiness and was very unseemly to appeal to a lady's eye, but these same women loved him dearly ("O, who does know the bent of women's fantasy?" asks Spenser). In his hand, a "burning hart" he carried full of vain follies and new "fangleness" (fashionableness). For he was false and fraught with fickleness, and had learned to love with secret looks and could dance and sing with ruefulness, and tell fortunes and read in loving books to "bait his fleshly hooks." Inconstant, he loved all he saw and lusted after all, enjoying weak women, tempting their hearts, if from their loyal loves he might move them; lewdness filled him with a reproachful pain of that fowl evil, which all men reprove, namely syphilis, that rots the marrow and consumes the brain.

Some of the earliest lustful cartoons (other than the pornographic Eveready Horton in *Buried Treasure* (1928) likely erected by the Fleischer Brothers and friends for a stag party), featured various vices. Animation historian Mark Langer listed a naughty assortment of sins exhibited in the early *Out of the Inkwell* series. In contrast to the Protestant sense of morality in the West Coast studios like Disney's that espoused middle-class moral values, the gritty New York environment encouraged such vices as gluttony in *Reunion* (1923), sloth in *Bedtime* (1923), homosexuality in *KoKo the Convict* (1926), hallucinating cigars in *KoKo Smokes* (1928), and vengeance in *KoKo's Hot Ink* (1929).[4] However, the Fleischers delighted in forbidden behaviors of lust, that erupted in *KoKo's Magic* (1928) and *No Eyes Today* (1929). In the latter cartoon, KoKo ogles a curvaceous bathing beauty and so his live-action producer Dave Fleischer erases his eyes, an unintended allusion to Matthew 5:29. Such immoral antics peaked in Fleischer's hottest star of the early 1930s, a Jewish princess "made of pen and ink, she will wink you with a wink. Ain't she cute?"

Betty Boop cartoons fulfilled dark sexual fantasies in *Boop Oop a Doop* (1932) and *The Old Man of the Mountain* (1933) (figure 10.1). In both films, loutish lechers paw, fondle, and molest what they can of Grim Natwick's curvy Jazz Age flapper. In the first, a lewd ringmaster threatens Betty's job as a circus bareback rider if she will not give in to his libidinous desires, stroking her legs, bottom, and "mature bosom."[5] Having escaped his horny clutches, Betty's friend KoKo whispers to her: "No," she sings back alluding to her virginity, "he couldn't take my boop-oop-a-doop away!" The sizzling hot jazz and swing of Cab Calloway ignite an atmosphere of sexually suggestive bits (three babies in a carriage look suspiciously like The Old Man) and a lascivious pursuit in which the randy old predator chases Betty. Asking him "Whatcha gonna do now?" he quips, he "gonna do the best I can," ripping off her dress to leave her in her underwear (yes, before the Production Code, and possibly contributing to its existence). Some animals (symbolizing a good and decent natural sexuality as with the fauns and satyrs of the *Faerie Queene*) tie his limbs into a knot. The New York studio's rubber hose style

Figure 10.1 ***The Old Man of the Mountain*** **(Fleischer, 1933) Chases Betty Boop Like a Hollywood Producer**. *Source*: Screenshot taken by the author.

of animation enhances Betty's sexuality, as she and inanimate objects around her bounce and gyrate in undulating ways. Boop swivels with eroticism. Within the year, with the enforcement of the Production Code, the Fleischer Brothers domesticated Betty and such scenes tamed dramatically.[6] Critic Erwin Panofsky observed about these early pre-Code cartoons, that they contained such "folklorist" elements as "sadism, pornography, the humor engendered by both, *and* moral justice" (italics added).[7] One titillated and judged simultaneously.

In a 1943 Columbia Color Rhapsody Cartoon, a degenerate, roly-poly Hollywood producer turns into a perverse wolf, slobbering over an under-aged doll. Combining transvestitism with pedophilia, all under the title of *Imagination* (Bob Wickersham), the film unleashes the creepiest onslaught of lust in a children's cartoon (figure 10.2). Molesting what he thinks is the Raggedy-Ann type poppet (which is actually Raggedy-Andy in pig-tailed disguise), the producer strokes his moustache, briefly transforms into the salivating Hollywood wolf, and leeringly asks if she would "like to be in pictures? You look like Garbo's twin. If you play your cards right, I can get you in!" In an ensuing battle and chase, the little girl crashes into a car and loses sawdust fast, with the end as "almost here." The boy doll sheds a tear and tells her not to cry because she will be "up above, where it's very nice, they say." However, the boy doll sacrificially gives off his sawdust in an emergency transfusion and saves his friend. The cartoon's theme song, "Try imagination, just like the little kiddies do" returns at the end, suggesting that, "perhaps the things we make believe are all really true." The disquieting cartoon, nominated for

Figure 10.2 A Disturbed *Imagination* (Bob Wickersham, 1943) Previews the Impending Crisis of Sexual Harassment. *Source*: Screenshot taken by the author.

an Academy Award, actually alarms one to the disturbing world of power and lust that awaits the little kiddies.

A wittily optimistic and condescending Simon Blackburn circumscribes a definition of lust that sounds more like conflating it with natural sexual desire. He argues that it is "not merely useful, but essential," with lust as merely a keen desire for sex and its pleasures for their own sake, rather than seeing it as thoughts and acts of sexual desire gone wrong.[8] Blackburn champions Thomas Hobbes, who reduces lust to sensual pleasure and delight of the mind that leads to intimate personal communion. That is not lust, as the church fathers understood it. That is just good old natural sexual desire. In actuality, lust is a twisted desire for sex with the wrong people or in the wrong way.

For some ascetics, fundamentalists, and Gnostics, carnal desire, itself, is evil. Not so the Western Hebraic and Christian traditions. Sexual desire in the sacred canopy of marriage is most welcome and sometimes wonderfully fecund and procreative. The Bridegroom ravishes the Bride, a blessedly erotic and playful set of imagery that John Donne caught in his poems as well. The vice appears as a twisted sister of desire gone astray in *Luxuria*.

Aquinas defined lust as "a special kind of deformity, whereby the venereal act is rendered unbecoming; there is a determinate species of lust. This may occur in two ways: First, through being contrary to right reason and this is common to all lustful vices; secondly, because, in addition, it is contrary to the natural order of the venereal act as becoming to the human race: and this is called the unnatural vice." Lust involves more than craving venereal pleasures. Aquinas points out that we may succumb to lust for power, lust for status, lust for gold, desire for wanton pleasures of excess, or even lust for Twinkies (which I fear are still around on some shelf). Blackburn happy with his cynics and skeptics, reduced the judgment on Sodom and Gomorrah to a lack of hospitality to strangers rather than some forced sexual demands. A reasonable reading of the text shows unruly neighbors demanding to have sex with Lot's angelic guests. Blackburn's hermeneutic elicits laughter at such a deconstruction of the story into a community's distorted welcome wagon policies.

Jewish perspectives offer a healthy celebration of *yetzer hatov* (as opposed to *yetzer hara*) of an innate sexual desire applicable for good pleasure or for perversion. Lust corrupts the gift. The passionate and descriptive *Song of Solomon* wildly throws out blazons of playful imagery. Judaism and Christianity—each of which sees matter as good—are almost the only great religions that thoroughly approve of the body. For the latter, the belief is that God himself once took on a human body; that some kind of body is going to be given to His people in heaven and is going to be an essential part of their happiness, beauty, and energy. Even the hoary old St. Paul was surprisingly approving of God-given sexual desire.[9] Even to the decadent citizens of Corinth, who were too fond of sex (the ancient Greek word "κοριντηιασεζτηαι"—to "do the Corinthian thing"—meant "to fornicate"), Paul described the church as the *body* of Christ. He gave honor to the "unseemly members," not just muscles and sinews. He also wrote perceptively of erotic realities, that the woman has sexual power over the man's body and that the man, if he learns the "art of woo," has power over the woman's body. He concludes by warning married couples not to deny themselves such sexual pleasure lest they fall away into *luxuria*. Eros is good.[10]

The striptease short cartoons not only show how culture objectifies and fetishizes the female body, but they satirize what it says about human nature. Suppose, suggested one British satirist, that we found a country where you could fill a theater by simply bringing a covered plate onto the stage and then slowly lifting the cover, so as to let everyone see, just before the lights went out, that it contained a mutton chop or bit of bacon. Would you not think that in that country something had gone wrong with the appetite for food?[11]

Italian animators Guido Manuli and Bruno Bozzetto's spoof of *Striptease* (1977) as well as the Zagreb Studio's *Strip-tiz* (Nedeljko Dragic, 1971) take on the lust of the wayward eye. In the former, a legion of little cartoon men run amok over a live-action woman doing a striptease. They buy binoculars; eyes pop out Tex Avery style; when one Swiss climber scrambles up her leg, she swats it and another is squashed by her boot; as she undresses, each climaxes by melting, turning into a werewolf, or shooting his own groin. In the latter, what appears to be a naked female body gyrating turns out to be a cow chewing its cud as the camera moves further away from the action. Both films mock the male lust instinct, completely void of reason and self-control.

A revelatory parable on censorship, *None of That!* (Isabela Littger, Anna Hinds, and Kriti Kaur, 2015) playfully matches a happy but officious Italian security guard of an art museum against an unrelenting and mischievous nun with her stash of censor fig leaf stickers (figure 10.3). As the guard strolls among the statues on his night patrol, he suddenly comes upon a nude Greek figure with a black rectangular board pasted onto its private parts. Outdone, the cop calls for backup. The little, lightning-quick Carmelite sister in her brown habit races about the museum like the infamous Cardinal Carafa (even though a patron of the arts, he ordered that Michelangelo's nudes in The Last Judgment be covered, instituting the Vatican's "fig leaf" campaign), covering up breasts and genitalia with alacrity. The contest to protect the art and to cover it up heightens as the nun is about to mask the naughty bits of Michelangelo's statue of David. However, as a decoy, the guard does a striptease, removing all clothing so that he is naked from his jolly belly to his toes. As the nun throws sheaths at him like Ninja dragon star coverings, he dodges every screen. At the last moment, two guards appear and look shocked at the naked man and the nun. They arrest the guard and drag him out, as the nun slaps another veil over his delicate parts; then looking at the camera directly, she slaps a black mask over the viewer. The hilariously enjoyable battle points to a battle to liberate and expose or to cover and censor. Dealing with sexual matters often divides humans into these two camps. The human seems

Figure 10.3 In the Tradition of the Fig-Leaf Campaign, an undeterred nun seeks to quash visual titillations in None of That! (Isabela Littger, Anna Hinds, and Kriti Kaur, 2015). *Source*: Screenshot taken by the author.

stuck between being prudish and Puritanical or profligate and prurient, and sometimes we fall to both sides, like Luther's proverbial drunk man on the horse, falling first this way and then that.

Psalm 101:3 promises that the poet would set no unclean or vile thing before his eyes. *If Your Eye Offendz Thee* (David Wilcox, 1988) takes on the lust of the eye with a literal rendering of Jesus' admonition that "if your eye offends you, pluck it out." A country revivalist preacher takes on the passage with gusto, admonishing those in his congregation (including caricatures of actual cultural celebrities), who struggle with such carnal temptations to pluck out their eyes if necessary. Suddenly, the congregation throws one, then dozens of eyeballs at the preacher, who tries to hide behind his pulpit. A pile of disembodied eyes buries him. He emerges and muses, "Maybe I better reconsider next week's sermon on Abraham's circumcision." His crowd goes screaming out of the church. The clever student film nominated for a Student Academy Award hinted at the sin in the congregation.

During World War II, various animators enlisted and taught GIs about safety regulations, the dangers of loose lips, and sexual predators who were also spies. Artists like Ted Geisel and Chuck Jones created an instructional series that ridiculed the foolish antics of a foolish *Private SNAFU* (yes, Situation Normal All Fouled/Fucked Up) (figure 10.4).[12] With *Cat in the Hat* rhythms, the writers would catch their audience's attention, but with crude sexual inserts, they could communicate with the most stupid soldiers. For example, in directors Chuck Jones, Robert Clampett's and Frank Tashlin's series, in films like *Booby Traps* (1944) and *Censored* (1944), Private Snafu succumbs to the temptations of the flesh. In the latter, he sends his girlfriend Sally Lou a letter betraying his location. Enemy spies listen and watch from every corner and telephone booth. When Snafu comes upon any female enemy agent, he does not realize that her

Figure 10.4 Produced for the *Army/Navy Screen Magazine*, Frank Tashlin's Pvt. Snafu series, *Booby Traps* (Robert Clampett, 1944) warned GIs of stupid behaviors, with many leading to Snafu's demise. *Source*: Screenshot taken by the author.

Figure 10.5 In his *Red Hot Riding Hood* (1943), Tex Avery unleashed the libido through his Wolfie character, chased by an oversexed grandmother figure. *Source*: Screenshot taken by the author.

boobs are recording his careless speech and her rear-end buns are bombs. The dangers of following one's sexual instincts were clearly set forth.

Lust rears its rampant libidinal head in Tex Avery's wartime Wolfie films. Known for "shattering cartoon shibboleths," Avery's hilariously exaggerated images of lust have become iconic.[13] Legendary sketches of Red by Preston Blair stop the hirsute protagonist in *Red Hot Riding Hood* (1943) and the other burlesque striptease films (figure 10.5). In this inaugural cartoon, Avery cracks open the sentimental fairy tale template: "Once upon a time, Little Red Riding Hood was skipping through the forest," begins a banal humdrum narrator.

The wolf interrupts with contempt: "Ah, stop it! I'm fed up with that sissy stuff. It's the same old story, over and over. If you can't do this a new way bud, I quit!" A Brooklyn-accented Little Red throws down her basket and agrees, as does old Granny.

Thus begins the new fairy tale of the war years (as Tex Avery noted in an interview with Joe Adamson, it was made for the military—with a Colonel demanding the uncensored version of the cartoon). The gyrating Red sings and dances provocatively at a nightclub where the playboy Wolf arrives. Her movements drive him crazy. He throws diamonds pearls, ermine, war-rationed sidewall tires, and everything he can put his hands on to entice her into his arms. She escapes to "Grandma's Joint" where the neon sign invites in Mae West style, "Come up and see me sometime."

Granny is as sex-starved as the eye-popping Wolf and pursues him with an unbridled libido. Ultimately, he throws himself out a window onto Hollywood and Vine, exclaiming that he would kill himself before looking at "another babe." Red reappears and he blows his brains out, only to return as a ghost whistling and stamping his feet. Animation legend Avery shared his view of animation gags in an interview with animation historian Jim Korkis in 1980: "I never thought of kids when I was making my films. I made them for me. I tested them out on my friends. I always aimed at adults. I think this whole thing of aiming at children is very destructive. When I directed cartoons if an idea got laughs that was fine with me. I got stung once-in-a-while, but a greater percentage of the time it would go over."[14]

Avery followed up his classic with *Little Rural Riding Hood* (Tex Avery, 1949), a take-off spoof of satirist Horace's old country mouse and city mouse fable, but like a Preston Sturges' screenplay, with a "little bit of sex" thrown in (figure 10.6). This time, Red is a lanky country girl taking refreshment (a little brown jug of whiskey) to her grandmother. Disguised as her grandma, The Country Wolf tells us (confidentially) that he is not the real one, but the wolf, but he is not going to eat Red, but chase her and catch her and love her and hug her and kiss her. He gets all gushy and eager as he wraps the bed covers around himself. When she appears at the door, he asks, "How about a kiss for your dear old grandma?" and shutting his eyes, he runs to her puckered up. She opens the door and he ends up kissing a cow. After numerous hounding, dashing and hurtling around the house (in and out of doors like a French farce), the couple crash together,

Figure 10.6 ***Little Rural Riding Hood*** **(Tex Avery, 1949) Plays with the City/Country Mouse Trope, except focusing on sexual attraction.** *Source*: Screenshot taken by the author.

she puts on red lipstick and puckers up for him. Interrupted by a Western Union telegram from his cousin who tells him to quit wasting his time on the country girl, he decides to go to the city where he will meet a "*real* Red Riding Hood!"

Looking at an enclosed photo, his body splits into pieces; his eyes dilate and pop out into a gigantic Laura Mulvey male gaze; and his feet dance on his head, all the while with a long tongue hanging out and stretching across the floor. He joins his cousin, wearing a purple smoking jacket, smoking a long cheroot, and sitting sangfroid. Alas, most men can identify the moment. The sophisticated cousin tells him that here in the city one does not whistle or shout at females. Taken to a nightclub in a tuxedo and tails, he giddily waits for them to bring on the girl. Red, with her big blue eyes, appears, bops, shimmies, and sways, singing how all the girls are crazy for a certain burly wolf, and teases with "oh Wolfie, ain't you the one?" The male fantasy is "incartoonated" with an unchecked cheery, carnal chauvinism. Country Wolf goes wacky, with madcap eye-popping, hooting, and hollering catcalls, all undeniably symbolic actions of lust performed through his body. He was the screwball poster child of every horny GI of World War II.

The sophisticated City Wolf tries to control his cousin's libido in assorted ways, often with a baseball bat. Putting his finger to silence his cousin's hooting, the whistle is so robust that it amplifies through the self-controlled canine's lips. Country Wolf smokes a cigarette that burns his face to ash. Throwing off his tuxedo jacket and trying to rush the stage, the Country Wolf is thwarted by his cousin, inserting a giant mallet into his suspenders, after which he wheelbarrows him out to take him back to the country. In a smug British accent, the City Wolf decides city life is too much for his cousin and must motor him back home. When they arrive, the hillbilly Red Riding Hood breathes, "howdy boys!" and suddenly the tables are reversed, with the city slicker succumbing to his libidinal antics of his cousin, eyes popping, body fractured into Picasso parts, and tongue hanging out. This time, the Country Wolf uses the mallet strung in the suspenders and the head wheelbarrow trick, to send his cousin back home as the "country life is too much for him." The hyperbolic comedy would be repeated in various versions such as *Swing Shift Cinderella* (1945), not only reducing the male to his most basic primitive animal nature, but allowing the sexual desire of a fairy godmother grandma ("Miss Repulsive 1898," who can chase the wolf around the room, literally on the walls) to take center stage. The whirling reminds one of the punishment for the carnal sin (e.g. Cleopatra, Queen of Carthage Dido, Helen of Troy) in Dante's *Inferno*: namely to be blown about by every gust of wind of desire and driven by restless fury.

The cure for lust in Dante's *Purgatorio* is to walk through flames. The refining fire sounds worse, but the "P" on one's forehead is as ephemeral as

Figure 10.7 Johanna Quinn's *Girls' Night Out* (1986) Allows Beryl, a humdrum housewife, to explore a seedy male strip joint and expose a little secret. *Source*: Screenshot taken by the author.

the sexual act itself. It will burn off. However, there is no rest from the unending winds, eye-popping explosions, and body deconstructions of lust.

Female lust goes haywire in Johanna Quinn's *Girls' Night Out* (1986), in which a wonderfully ordinary and dumpy housewife, Beryl, escapes the doldrums of her daily routine by going to a seedy male striptease theater (figure 10.7).[15] Quinn's graduation film follows several female cupcake factory workers out for the evening to celebrate Beryl's birthday. Beryl's is out to have a good time with her friends, and express repressed, or suppressed, passions. Hearing of what they plan to do, Beryl laughs hysterically, full of hearty and happy humor, even fantasizing that some Tarzan in a loincloth will offer to take her "away from all this." "Okay," she thinks. She leaves her dull husband watching television (he and the lazy cat fit too comfortably in sloth) and goes off to the Bull pub strip joint, where drinks are ordered and the girls let loose.

A muscular and haughty male stripper, looking like a mustached porno star, seeks to tease and titillate his female spectators with his daring machoism. With a large overbite and flexed muscles, he gyrates to arouse the women. The women hoot and holler, acting like female Wolfies from a Tex Avery cartoon and inverting gender stereotypes. As he unzips his shirt to reveal a hairy chest, a bespectacled Beryl grins, gulps, and grows little devil's horns. Standing akimbo over the little woman, he vaunts his potency. Then

Beryl, with the comic audacity of someone with nothing to lose, strips off his jockstrap to expose his tiny penis and twirls the clothing with triumph. The women go wild! Returning home, Beryl tells her torpid husband, "just had quiet drink with the girls, Hon" and hangs her trophy with a guffaw. The sexuality of what critic Chris Robinson calls "normal" middle-aged women, flabby, unruly hair, and wearing too much makeup, is unharnessed with playful passions. Sex here is fun and funny as much as the Greeks recognized that Venus is a comic spirit.[16] Quinn acknowledged that Beryl was an alter ego, even using her mother, a single parent, as her model, "someone struggling but uncomplaining, battling against adversity to provide stability and security."[17] Here is one who burlesques the carnal temptation with gusto.

Pointing to the *animal* in our nature, where being in heat incites one to follow what comes next, a dog indiscriminately humps a stump or a guest's leg. The Protestant author Edmund Spenser anthropomorphizes such uncontrolled instinct in a lustful bearded goat. The image in its melancholy form haunts Claude Debussy's *Prélude à l'après-midi d'un faune* segment of Bozzetto's *Allegro Non Troppo* with an aging satyr (figure 10.8). The old creature sits by his birthday cake of scores of candles in the shape of nude women. Two bumblebees pop drunkenly out of a Bacchanalian cup and then indulge in what bees and birds do. Watching one comely maiden collecting flowers, the satyr throws away his cane, puffs up his chest, and seeks the conquest. His pathetic antics scare her away. He desperately and futilely tries to attract the dancing dryads and naiads, even dying his gray beard. As younger fauns

Figure 10.8 In the *Prélude à l'après-midi d'un faune* Segment of Bozzetto's *Allegro Non Troppo* (1976), an aging satyr discovers a pathetic end to his life of unrepressed sexual pursuits. *Source*: Screenshot taken by the author.

fondle the lovely creatures, he vainly seeks to rejuvenate his shrinking virility. His fetishes grow more desperate, as he envisions cloud balloons of floating breasts. This one afternoon, he wearily picks up his cane and grows smaller and smaller, wandering across hills and dales, which all turn out to be the nude body of a voluptuous woman.

Lust does not have to lose its luster with age, particularly in British animator Bob Godfrey's short films, The British hold a reputation of being quite prim and prudish, due in part to opinions on sex like that expressed by Englishman Lord Chesterfield, who explained that "the pleasure is momentary, the position ridiculous, and the expense damnable."[18] Perhaps the best chronicler of creative marital desire, erotic fantasies, and the frustrating inability of anyone to be a good lover is this director of wonderfully randy cartoons about lust. Godfrey exposes lust as more than carnal desire. As Jesus said that even if a man thinks lustful thoughts, he is guilty of adultery, so, the irrepressible Godfrey portrays the average, office-working man, who goes to work and fantasizes about women all day as equally guilty as the man who visits a prostitute (figure 10.9). In *Henry from 9 to 5* (1970), the first animated British film to earn an X rating, the titular star of the film is a bald, dull, bowler-hatted, corporate commuter, who dryly confesses: "I don't like my job very much." He continues, "I have discovered a way of defeating boredom and all its vicissitudes." He spends excessive time and energy "thinking about sex all day," daydreaming about "nice buxom girls" walking about nude. He mentally undresses them and imagines chasing them through fields of daisies. His sexual fantasies consume his workplace. At five o'clock, he finds the day

Figure 10.9 Bob Godfrey Satirizes the Suppressed Erotic Fantasies of *Henry from 9 to 5* (1970). *Source*: Screenshot taken by the author.

has passed quickly "when your mind is fully occupied." When he returns home and his happy wife inquires whether he wants to make love, he excuses himself: "Not tonight dear, I'm exhausted," ultimately denying the opportunity of true intimacy at home. His mental perambulations have worn him out for genuine erotic contact and Godfrey spoofs the libido of a man avoiding intercourse with an actual erotic woman. The wild ribald cartoon obliquely underscores the moral injunction against adultery, even in its mental forms.

Godfrey's work on the seven deadly sins extends back to his interstitial segments in an otherwise forgettable British feature, *The Magnificent 7 Deadly Sins* (Graham Stark, 1971). It begins with the disrobing of a comely live-action blonde and a cartoon director guiding her actions. As she nakedly faces the camera, the little animated director confides to us that this scene has nothing to do with the forthcoming film, unless being a Peeping Tom is one of the deadly vices. Godfrey goes on to spoof the psychology of the sexual revolution and its privileging of technique separated from human intimacy in his "sexual punch-up" cartoon nominated for an Oscar, *Kama Sutra Rides Again* (1971). A middle-class, suburban couple, Stanley and Ethel, experiments with a riotous variety of odd sexual techniques, positions, and locations to explore *eros*. Basing the character of Stanley on his friend and screenwriter, Stan Hayward, Godfrey allows his very droll and stodgy characters to try every acrobatic position they can try, while satirizing the fantasies of every man and every woman, exposing not only full frontal nudity, but also the silliness and folly of the quest for the orgasm.

In dealing with indecent or bawdy humor, Lewis's devil divided humans into two classes in *The Screwtape Letters*. He pointed out that there are some for whom "no passion is as serious as lust" and "for whom an indecent story ceases to produce lasciviousness precisely in so far as it becomes funny: there are others in whom laughter and lust are excited at the same moment and by the same things. The first sort joke about sex because it gives rise to many incongruities: the second cultivate incongruities because they afford a pretext for talking about sex. If your man is of the first type, bawdy humor will not help you—I shall never forget the hours which I wasted (hours to me of unbearable tedium) with one of my early patients in bars and smoking rooms before I learned this rule."[19]

The judgment for lust is to be covered or even smothered in fire and brimstone, hinting that St. Paul's admonition that it is better to marry than burn carries an apocalyptic judgment. As was mentioned, Dante sees the lustful punished in the second circle of the *Inferno* unceasingly twirled around in a whirlwind. Two representative characters are the adulterous lovers Paolo and Francesca, who will never find rest or consummation for eternity. In contrast, the lustful in Purgatory must walk through flames in order that they may be "purged" for their iniquities. The symbol of continuously being gusted about one's own winds of passion, with no hope of rest, fits too well with an ancient legend about obsessive female lust and unrequited love in *Dojoji Temple* (Kihachiro Kawamoto, 1976). Based on a famous Noh play adapted for Kabuki Theater, the story tells of a pilgrimage that an older priest and his young acolyte Anchin take to the shrine of Kumano. Stopping on their annual trek to rest at a steward's house, they would bring gifts for the daughter, Kiyohime. Smitten, she expresses a crush on the young priest who once teased her that when she grew up, he would marry her. However, for the maiden, it was no joke and she now demands that he marry her. She sneaks into his room at night and embraces him while he sleeps. Rebuffing her advances because of his religious vows, he prays to Buddha, but she snuggles up to him, caressing him and seeking to seduce him. Even as cherry blossoms fall and purple butterflies flit about, he flees to the Temple.

Spurned, she follows him fanatically, chasing him across a raging Hidakagawa river. Faster and faster, she pursues, losing her slippers and her hair blowing fiercely in the wild wind. Anchin looks fearfully at this woman and sees a heavily breathing demon. Offering her silk kimono to a boatman to take her across, but he says no. With her white porcelain skin and flowing dark hair, she leaps wildly into the waters, daring to swim across, with flames of fire emanating from her strokes. She turns into a serpentine dragon. The novice runs to the Temple, and begs with his beads and folded hands for protection against the dragon lady. An old priest points to a prayer canister, a bell that covers the young man, hiding him. He seems safe within this sacred cell as two guards with spears vainly protect the gate.

Having seen her own diabolical reflection in the waters, she transforms herself into a slithering dragon. When this monstrous and malevolent serpent arrives, she coils herself around the bell. With her intense passion, breathes fire and melts the iron-hiding place with white-hot flames. Dropping tears of blood, the green-maned serpent leaves and turns back into the maiden, who with unrequited love throws herself back into the waters and vanishes. When the men come to open the burned bell, they find the boy in prayerful pose, as a skeleton. All pray for him as cherry blossoms again fall, with the wind turning everything to dust.[20]

The worst of sexual sins seems to be adultery, which, considering Israel's infidelity to God, invites the most excoriating denunciations by Hebrew prophets. Russian animator Ladislas Starewicz's *The Cameraman's Revenge* (1911) satirized the seemingly private nature of adultery, suggesting that the camera could reveal sin and put it on display for a public audience by a jilted filmmaker. It was a disconcerting thought to think that movies could expose one's vices. Like the later shocking tale of casual but lethal infidelity, *Fatal Attraction* (Adrian Lynne, 1987), the little stop-motion film with a grasshopper filming a beetle businessman's indiscretions with a dragonfly lady could be projected onto a big screen. The animated film vividly conveyed a parable of lust and its consequences, as the unerring eye of the movie camera functions as an evidentiary tool. Starewicz's story of infidelity exposes the dull bourgeois home of Mr. and Mrs. Beetle. In search of spontaneity and change, each one cheats on the other. Mr. Beetle meets the beautiful Dragonfly, and heartlessly steals her away from her lover Mr. Grasshopper. The Grasshopper, being a cameraman, begins his plot of revenge by filming Mr. Beetle's affair with the Dragonfly. Before this revenge unfolds, however, Mr. Beetle happens to catch his wife at home with another insect, the artist.

The irascible hypocrite that he is, Mr. Beetle throws a fit, smashes things in the house and gets rough with Mrs. Beetle. Eventually, he forgives her and takes her to a movie. Unbeknownst to him, the projectionist at the theater is Mr. Grasshopper, who runs the footage he shot of Mr. Beetle and Miss Dragonfly having their fling. The cheering, insect audience loves this spontaneous slice of life, but Mrs. Beetle has other thoughts and chases her husband straight through the movie screen and out of the theater.[21] Curiously, the film functions as an instrument to expose the vice. The well-placed eye of the camera hints at the central eye of Bosch's tabletop painting and one almost expects to read the Latin: *Cave cave d[omi]n[u]s videt* ("Beware, Beware, The Lord Sees"). What is done in secret will be shouted from the housetops or perhaps just exhibited on a very large screen.

The consequences of lust may involve more ice than fire, but it still carries its own frustration. Lust does not satisfy. In *Knick Knack* (John Lasseter, 1989), a character literally falls into an unfulfilled desire (figure 10.10). In this cartoon "shot entirely on location," a motley assortment of curios, souvenirs, and knick-knacks lounge on a bookshelf. One expects a festive pool party with the various characters: a sunny Florida pink flamingo, a beach boy skeleton having surfed Death Valley, a Jewish cactus, a sunny Egyptian pyramid, a Palm Springs palm tree with springs, and a sunny Jamaica tree with dreads. Finally, one spies a buxom, blue-bikinied, Miami blonde, wearing sunglasses, clearly inspired by Tex Avery's exaggerated women, with the digitally enhanced breasts of the bric-a-bracs (allegedly due to the technical director with a Gil Elvgren pin-up fixation).

The computer/camera slowly pans over to a "Nome, Sweet Nome, Alaska" snow globe, inhabited by a snowman wearing a top hat and green tie, with coal buttons and eyes, and a carrot nose. Checking out all the sunny people, he notices the blonde. She waves at him and gives a "come hither" gesture. It is then that he realizes he is stuck in his glass prison. He uses a plastic igloo to break the glass, but it does not work. Then, in true Chuck Jones Wiley Coyote ACME fashion, he employs a variety of useless items: a hammer pounds his carrot nose, only to bend it; a jackhammer only shakes up his face. The girl is getting bored. He puts on a gas flamethrower and detonates TNT explosives, but the cartoonish violence only vibrates up the snowstorm

Figure 10.10 In the Original Version of *Knick Knack* (John Lasseter, 1989), a globe snowman encounters voluptuous temptations. *Source*: Screenshot taken by the author.

in the globe. Finding himself on edge of the bookcase, he tips it over and it falls down, with everyone watching. On his free-fall descent, he notices an Emergency Exit and escapes! He is free to pursue his desires, yet he frustratingly finds himself falling into a fishbowl. He realizes that all is not lost; for he sees a lovely, well-endowed Sunny Atlantis mermaid. Stars barely cover her breasts. (On a subsequent release of the cartoon, the Pixar staff reduced the breast size and covered the mermaid with a seashell bra, because, as Lasseter felt it was crossing the line for him as a father.)

The Snowman's fantasy was about to be realized. While racing over to her, the falling globe finally landed on him, closing him doubly in the globe and in the fishbowl, with no access to any woman. Musician Bobby McFerrin improvised just the most appropriate *a cappella* vocal jazz with his final lines of "Blah, blah, blah, blah, blah." Lasseter's brief parable captures that tantalizing appeal that Dorothy Parker so succinctly summarizes: "Brevity is the soul of lingerie."

Perhaps no vice makes such willing fools of men and women as lust. While animated films, as well as Hollywood feature films, display the consequences of unbridled passion, hormones still drive reason and self-control away. The parables, employing everyone from Hollywood producers to homemakers, from satyrs to snowmen, continue to preach.

In an incisive address on "The Other Six Deadly Sins," given to the Public Morality Council in 1941, Dorothy Sayers puts these sins into a modern perspective. From her translation of Dante, she perceptively categorized the classic seven deadly sins. Lust, gluttony, and wrath gather into those characterized as "warm-hearted and disreputable." The other four, pride, envy, avarice, and sloth, she identifies as "cold-hearted and respectable." She notes "that Christ rebuked the three disreputable sins only in mild or general terms, but uttered the most violent vituperations against the respectable ones." In contrast, the powers of the church and state, "Caesar and the Pharisees," castigate the warm-hearted sinners, while practicing cold-hearted vices, even so much as to be "in conspiracy to call virtues."[22] Alas, it is a tendency that endures today.

NOTES

1. Frantis, Wayne E., *Dutch Seventeenth-century Genre painting: Its Stylistic and Thematic Evolution* (Yale University Press, 2004), 212; Generally played by troubadours and minnesingers, it was the rascally Miller of Chaucer's *Canterbury Tales* who is described with "a baggepipe wel koude he blowe and sowne,/And therwithal he broghte us out of towne." It would symbolize tony, folly, and lasciviouness. Block, Edward A. "Chaucer's Millers and Their Bagpipes" *Speculum* 29: 2 part 1 (April 1954), 239–243.

2. Gibson, *Pieter Bruegel and the Art of Laughter*, 36.

3. Regarding the image of the goat for lust, the hilarious but sobering documentary *"Nuts!"* by Penny Lane introduces the tale of Dr. John Brinkley who offered a specious cure for impotence through goat testicle transplants with crudely but effectively animated scenes of goats copulating. The inventive film establishes the goat as the hope for sexually deprived and feebly equipped men. Surgically transferred goat gonads seem the best cure for those incapable of fulfilling lust.

4. Langer, Mark, "Polyphony and Heterogeneity in Early Fleischer Films," in *Funny Pictures: Animation and Comedy in Studio-Era Hollywood*, ed. Daniel Goldmark and Charlie Keil (University of California Press, 2011), 32.

5. Cabarga, Leslie, *The Fleischer Story* (Da Capo Press, 1976), 80.

6. Betty devolved from being a provocative mini-sexpot to a schoolmarm: "First, her garter was taken away; next the hemline on her very short skirt was lowered; finally, her neckline was raised." Fleischer, Richard, *Out of the Inkwell: Max Fleischer and the Animation Revolution* (University Press of Kentucky, 2003), 104.

7. Panofsky, Erwin, "Style and Medium in Motion Pictures," in *Film Theory and Criticism* eds. Gerald Mast and Marshall Cohen (Oxford University Press, 1974), 160.

8. Blackburn, Simon, *Lust* (Oxford University Press, 2004).

9. For St. Paul and Augustine and church tradition, sexual desire can screw itself into fornication (sex without intimacy), adultery (sex without the covenantal spouse), masturbation (sex without anybody), homosexuality (sex with no diversity), and other alternative modes, even bestiality that some shepherds might be tempted to try (one

tries to get Gene Wilder and his sheep out of the imagination). All these are sin in that they fall short of the ideal, a wife and a husband enjoying connubial pleasures.

10. Even when he was still an old celibate bachelor, C. S. Lewis saw the divine gift of *eros* (and even conjectured on the aphrodisiac power of some foods). Lewis, *The Four Loves.* While in an apocryphal tale, Alexander the Great's courtesan, Phyllis, ensnared the conqueror's rational teacher, Aristotle, through his libido, Lewis suggested that professors were more likely to be seduced by their vanity, as when a female student praises his teachings or writings. 10.

11. Lewis, C. S., *Mere Christianity* (HarperOne, 2015), 96, 98.

12. PES's first animated film *Roof Sex* (2002), which allowed furniture to get it on with hilarious audio soundtrack, doesn't quite work as a parable as much as a bawdy pleasure. Animated feature films have tackled the world of lust, from Osamu Tezuka's adult anime *A Thousand and One Nights* (1969) and Ralph Bakshi's *Fritz the Cat* through the erotic sci-fi *Heavy Metal* (Gerald Potterton, 1981) and *Sausage Party* (Conrad Vernon, Greg Tiernan, 2016). Even Disney alluded to sexual obsession with the hypocritical Claude Frollo's desire for the Gypsy girl Esmeralda n *The Hunchback of Notre Dame* (Gary Trousdale, Kirk Wise, 1996).

13. See Joe Adamson's *Tex Avery* (Da Capo, 1985).

14. Korkis, Jim, "Animation Anecdotes" (November 21, 2014), https://cartoonresearch.com/index.php/animation-anecdotes-188/ (Accessed February 4, 2020).

15. Quinn also animated Chaucer's great sexual *Canterbury Tale* of *The Wife of Bath* (1996), where a knight who assaulted a woman has a year to find out "what women want" or face execution. Animator Susan Pitts directed a wild erotically charged film, *Asparagus* (1979), that I find fascinating and bold, but have yet to understand. Primarily about the pleasures of her own creative process, it suggests a Jungian daydream with unfathomed meanings (for my little mind).

16. Lewis, *The Four Loves*, 141–142.

17. Robinson, *Animators Unearthed*, 232.

18. Blackburn, op. cit. 8.

19. Lewis, *Screwtape Letters* "Chapter 11," 49–52.

20. Klein, Susan Blakeley, "When the Moon Strikes the Bell: Desire and Enlightenment in the Noh Play Dojoji," *Journal of Japanese Studies* 17: 2 (1991), 291–322.

21. After a fateful bumper car collision at a fairground, the paths of stud Jake and bombshell Ella intersect to bring them into an idyllic romance in Bill Plympton's *Cheatin'* (2013). They frolic and rollick about until a devious *femme fatale*, who like Spencer's deceiving Duessa, conjures up a false scenario of adultery. She frames Ella and a broken-hearted Jake decides to become a serial adulterer out of revenge.

22. Sayers, "The Other Six Deadly Sins."

Conclusion

Virtues and Redemption

> Art may tell a truth
> Obliquely, do the thing shall breed the thought
> Nor wrong the thought, missing the mediate word.
> So may you paint your picture, twice show truth,
> Beyond mere imagery on the wall.
>
> —Robert Browning

Hieronymus Bosch's painting in the Prado Museum in Madrid showcases the seven cardinal sins as spokes of a wheel or the rays of the sun emanating from the center of his tabletop. At the core of the work, right in the middle of the chaos of sin, is a large eye, a pupil of God that sees all secrets. The presence of Christ, even circumscribed by the Four Last Things, remains a reminder of grace in the heart of the painting. In the wide and wild universe of vices, holiness whispers its presence.

Swiss theologian Karl Barth once quipped that we must take care not to take sin too seriously. As former Duke University Chaplain William Willimon points out, sin is "*Das Nichtige*—nothingness, pointlessness. It would be theologically perverse to remain more fascinated and impressed with human sin than we are with divine redemption of our sin."[1] Luther went so far as to jest that we should sin boldly, so that we might taste grace more abundantly. Even in dealing with lust, Willimon points to the great sinner St. Augustine, who in his reflective *City of God*, pointed to how ineffectual our wills are in handling the most natural and congenial of body responses. The Bishop of Hippo mockingly noted that the male sexual organ is limp when it ought to be firm and firm at the most inopportune times when it should be limp. "If we cannot even control such an inferior organ of the body through our determination, decision, and will, what makes us think that we can control our souls?"[2]

The addiction to evil deadens the soul with dull substitutes. Goodness, as especially seen in Spenser's *Faerie Queen*, is thrilling, enchanting, and ultimately more fecund and energetic than vice.[3] Vice wilts into lackluster memories. Virtue, even attempted virtue, brings light; indulgence brings fog.[4] However, few animated films teach virtue without sounding like schoolmarms.

This study highlights the consequences of vice, as shown through brief, but provocative, short animated films. Visually arresting, they chronicle wrong choices of life's journey, illustrating Cassian's stairway to heaven or Chaucer's pilgrimage to Canterbury. Short animated "spiritual journey" films include such wonderfully odd travelogues as Alison de Vere's *The Black Dog* (1987), Nedeljko Dragic's *Diogenes, Perhaps* (1967), Bruno Bozzetto's *Life in a Tin* (1967), Claude Cloutier's *Overdose* (1994), Signe Baumane's poignant and funny history of *Rocks in my Pockets* (2014), and Don Hertzfeldt's melancholic, existential works like *The Meaning of Life* (2005) and *World of Tomorrow* (2015).[5] These spiritual pilgrimages do not always progress, and sometimes regress, but they show struggles over temptation. Director Norman Stone and Bob Godfrey traced such journeys in their shorts like *The Key* for the Anglican Church's *Screen Tests* (figure C.1).

Jesus' parables tend to be baffling, even to his own disciples. As Father Robert Capon put it, "they set forth comparisons that tend to make mincemeat of people's religious expectations. Bad people are rewarded (the Publican, the

Figure C.1 Director Norman Stone Employed Bob Godfrey's Ribald Humor to Preach a Gospel in *The Key* (1976). *Source*: Screenshot taken by the author.

Prodigal, the Unjust Steward); good people are scolded (the Pharisee, Elder Brother, the Diligent Workers) and everybody's idea of who ought to be first and last is liberally doused with cold water (the Wedding Feast, the Great Judgment, Lazarus and Dives, the Narrow Door)."[6]

One remarkably clever animated parable is an unheralded version of *The Sower and Seeds* (Rod March, Max7, 2010), adapted from the Gospel of Luke (8:4–9) (figure C.2). Infused with pulsating indigenous music, an African farmer throws out his seed upon four kinds of soil, the hard ground of the road, among the rocks, the thorns, and then upon good soil. The round, happy cartoony seeds have no idea what kind of life awaits them. The first set of goofy-looking kernels go flying onto the hard surfaces of a path, their wide mouths grinning in foolish glee. As they sit basking up the sun, suddenly a foot tramples a few of them; then a blue-beaked red bird alights beside them, staring at their futile attempts to bury themselves in the ground until it decides to snatch them up. A second batch falls on stony places, springing up and boasting with yellow glory. However, without any earth to establish their roots, and a scorching sun beating down upon them, they dry up, wilt, and wither, coming to an ignominious end. The third round of sown seeds land in good earth, but among spiked villainous thorns, whom they weakly try to resist, but are to be choked. Finally, the blessed silly seeds fall on good ground, find the nutrients they need, and grow into a golden field of a magnificent crop.[7] What is most remarkable about the story is that even Jesus' closest disciples could not comprehend what it meant. The parable works that some seeing do not see and hearing they do not understand.

Figure C.2 ***The Sower and Seeds*** **(Rod March, 2010) Comically Chronicles Luke's Parable of the Lives of Seeds Thrown on Four Kinds of Ground.** *Source*: Screenshot taken by the author.

Parables hide in the land of left-handed mystery—they are not theological propositions calling for analysis or requiring extensive dissection. They are pictures, riddles, poetry, and images, showing the backside of God rather than telling about Him, communication addressed to the imagination, where the meanings of faith, repentance, grace, and joy come to life. Chesterton writes of the doctrine of unconditional joy, which comes with acts of obedience. Obey (which literally means to put yourself under the hearing of) this law and joy will be yours. Disobey and you suffer the consequences. Open the box and all sorts of mischief will escape. Get home before the clock strikes twelve or your coach will turn back into a pumpkin. Do not look at the face of a god or you will be cursed. The condition of joy depends upon keeping one little rule. Do not eat of the fruit and you will live in Paradise forever. The stories we learn in the nursery or in cartoons remind us of this doctrine of unconditional joy.

The marriage of animated film and parable etches an idea in our minds, implanting a mental image that lingers and perseveres. David Morgan argues that such a material "picture, a photograph, a sculpture" "endures." It hibernates and then springs forth in fresh and lively ways, awakening us to its moral or spiritual example.

The Reverend William Dalglish speaking for the United Methodist Church General Board of Education indicted those denominations that ignored the media. In particular, he pointed to the resources (many short films and Academy Award–winning animations). Such as *Neighbours* (Norman McLaren, 1952), *Munro* (Gene Deitch, 1960), *The Hat* (Faith and John Hubley, 1964), *Hangman* (Les Goldman, Paul Julian, 1964) that instructed one in Christian Formation.[8] One of the most entertaining humorists of the 1960s was radio comedian Stan Freberg who innovated advertising parodies (e.g., his subversive attack on the over-commercialization of Christmas in *Green Chritma*, with cash register bells). In addition to his satires, the United Presbyterian Church hired him to create hip radio spot parables.[9] Several audio parables were adapted into clever animated films. In *The Good Western Samaritan*, a bucking cowboy goes riding through the west. A gang of bandits attack and rob him, and leave him for dead. A minister, Parsons Jones, passes by, sees him, and mutters, "Drunk again." He whips his buggy off into the distance. A righteous-looking undertaker comes upon the body by the side of the road, and says, "Whoa" to his horse; then adds, "Better not get involved." Finally, Paco Diaz, a Mexican, comes upon him, stops and puts the poor cowboy on his burro to take off and get him help.

Freberg and the Presbyterians followed it up with *It Will Teach Him a Lesson*. Once upon a time, there was a cattle baron that had a million-dollar ranch that he stole from the Indians. He called it the Promised Land. He had a mess of men working for him and would ride into town and take his men

Figure C.3 Art Clokey's Classic *Davey and Goliath* Offered Moral Instruction in His Short Stop-Action Stories. *Source*: Screenshot taken by the author.

to church because "it's good for them; it'll teach them a lesson." Next to his Promised Land lived a poor man with a wife and kid who were starving and stole a calf, but he did not quite make it. They "brung" him up to the baron and he said, "string him up; it'll teach him a lesson." That old man, with a huge cigar in his mouth, kept right on going to church and thinking himself a proper Christian. He'd sit in the front row with one of his steers and look mighty pious. However, that night, he fell asleep and in his dream, he was standing before his Maker. God looked down at him and said, "Forgive him; it'll teach him a lesson." And the baron took off his hat and bowed.

One can trace the history of didactic religious and moral communication through animated films in three distinct series. First, one finds the international appeal of Art Clokey's *Davey and Goliath*, a series of sixty-four 15-minute clay-animated episodes conceived in 1961 by the Lutheran Church Department of Telecommunications (figure C.3).[10] Director of the children's programming, Roy Lee explained how each related to the Christian faith and values for children. "The church has always had a strong concern for family life and Christian values, and it was decided that that TV would be an excellent way to reach families across the nation, as well as the general public."[11] For example, one episode entitled "The Runaway" paralleled the biblical story of the Prodigal Son, but it remained moralistic and didactic, even with the charm of Goliath the dog.

Like the very first animated series of short films for Christians, the Southern Baptist Radio and Television Commission produced *Jot the Dot* from 1965 through the early 1970s. Conceived by Ruth Bayers, one of the first women to guide an animated series, episodes sought to teach moral themes about loving one's neighbors and forgiveness. JOT, a bouncy circular character with a smiley face, would change colors according to his emotional temperament. In the "Dirty Hands" episode, JOT would show his frustration when his mother told him to stay in the house and not to get dirty as they are going to Sunday school. The temptation of playing with a ball outside gets him into the mud and he sneaks into class with stained hands. However, his teacher reminds him that he should obey his parents because they love him. As he resolves to obey them from then on, the moral homily explicitly makes its point. In George Woolery's study on early television programming for children, he opined that JOT's "abstract messages captivated and inspired children far beyond anticipation" and sparked a tremendous outpouring of support and interest.[12]

In Darragh O'Connell and Cathal Gaffney's unconventional retelling of religious stories, *Give Up Yer Aul Sins* (2002), Irish students in Dublin are invited to share their version of John the Baptist or Saint Patrick with a television reporter (figure C.4). The Oscar-nominated short animated "documentary" from Brown Bag Films humorously illustrates original 1960s recordings of little school girls spontaneously (and quite impressively) chatting away on the story of the Angel Gabriel and the Annunciation to the Virgin Mary. Clever animated images depict God the Father sitting in an easy chair wearing sunglasses, the angel descending an escalator stairway to earth, and a plumb-looking Mary taking a three-day walk to see her sister Elizabeth (because there were "no bicycles."). A second film about John the Baptist, King Herod, and Salome (a "terrible wicked woman" who would not do penance and "give up me aul sins") focuses on John in prison, sending a

Figure C.4 Darragh O'Connell and Cathal Gaffney Regale with Unconventional Retelling of Religious Stories, *Give Up Yer Aul Sins* (2002). *Source*: Screenshot taken by the author.

messenger to Jesus asking if He is "really God or is he a shickin' Holy Saint?" The messenger wades into a river and asks Jesus the question. Jesus, standing on the water with a fishing pole, tells him to report to John what you are seeing: "the leapords (*sic*) are cured, people that are blind can see and the people that are on crutches can walk—and leapords means that they were all full with sores all over them." Hearing the news, John rejoices, "Oh, they're all miracles, that's God." The perky storyteller celebrates how God gives John faith; even though at a party Herod throws, Salome is offered anything she wants and asks for his head. A catechism of grace, hope, and faith has rarely been so enchanting.

Short comic sketches inspired by Disney, Dr. Seuss, and Monty Python (with such characters as the French peas Jean Claude and Philippe along with professorial Archibald Asparagus, a John Cleese parody) erupted out of the cheerfully twisted imaginations of Mike Nawrocki and Phil Vischer in their *Veggie Tales* series. Featuring Larry the Cucumber who would sing silly songs like "O Where is My Hairbursh?" (even though he didn't really need one as he is bald) and Bob the Tomato, the Big Idea Productions used humor to sneak past the watchful dragons of perfunctory religious education and inculcate children into biblical teachings and ethical lessons. In 1993, they released a classic episode of "Where's God When I'm S-Scared?" that dealt with children's fears, connecting faith and the cardinal virtue of courage. The CGI animated series starred Vischer as the hopping, squat host, introverted Bob the Tomato and Nawrocki as his lanky, goofy, scatterbrained extraverted Larry the Cucumber, a vegetable comedy duo akin to Abbott and Costello. Limited in resources, Vischer's technological pragmatism led to characters that were "limbless, naked, and bald." At the end of each short, Bob and Larry would sum up the lesson for the day. Vischer created a quirky computerized character, Qwerty, that would offer specific Bible wisdom to correspond to the short bits. As Vischer confessed,

> If we can't teach anything, we might as well just sell all the computers and stop. There's no point in making people laugh for five seconds and then sending them back to their miserable lives without God. It's pointless. I want to put smiles on kids' faces, and then also put enough content that they grow up to be better people or relate better to their parents. The same simple message is for everybody, whether it's about relationships or honesty.[13]

The creativity of Vischer's work transcended the moral simplicity of both Davey and JOT, mostly because of the cultural satire and self-reflexive wit of the writers and of the catchy musical numbers. Big Ideas illumined not only courage and wisdom but also tackled the other cardinal and theological virtues.

Hope, faith, and charity do inhabit less didactic cartoons. A compelling image of hope as virtuous expectation wedded with hints of Divine Providence appears in two romantic nonverbal delights, *The Box* (Murakami/Wolf, 1967) (figure C.5) and *Paperman* (John Kahrs, 2012). In the former, a grizzly old bearded coot wearing a yellow raincoat walks into a bar during a rainy and stormy evening. Beside him is an ordinary box, yet one full of mystery. A rhino-faced man tries to find out what is in the box, asking if it is a bird or a reptile. He buys the old man drinks and offers him money to peek into the box. After persistent petitions, the old man lets him look, but after a quick glance, the rhino-man quakes in fear. A shapely elephantine woman in a red dress orders a cocktail and tries to cajole and seduce him into seeing. When he relents, she sees nothing at first, but soon reacts in outrage, shaking her fist at him. Left alone, the man puts out some food, opens the box's lid, and a quick little brown critter runs to get the food, retreats back into his container, and spits out one bit.

Finally, a redheaded woman wearing a raincoat and carrying her own little black box sits beside him. Now, he is curious to see what she has. She puts out some food, opens her lid, and a quick little green critter runs out and eats it all. They smile at each other and then push their boxes near each other, open their side lids, and suddenly two creatures chase and ravish each other. The old man and the woman look at each other, nod, smile, put on their raincoats, and depart into the rain, walking to an ark. A comic sense of Providence, of hope, the little thing with feathers, or at least fur, teases us throughout the little romantic comedy.

Figure C.5 On a Dark and Stormy Night, a Man with *The Box* (Murakami/Wolf, 1967) Awakens Fear, Anger, and Joyous Providence in His Mystery Package. *Source*: Screenshot taken by the author.

In the Disney Academy Award winner *Paperman* (John Kahrs, 2012), a young accountant named George (based on the main character George Bailey in Frank Capra's *It's a Wonderful Life* (1946)) waits for his commuter train at a Grand Central Station elevated platform in this urban fairytale about how a wind-blown paper can bring two strangers together (figure C.6). A gust of wind blows a piece of paper against his shoulder, and as it flutters by, a young woman, Meg, chases it. Retrieving it, she looks coyly at George and he smiles bashfully. Another puff of air blasts a sheet from his binder smack into her face, imprinting it with a bright red lipstick-smudged kiss in this black-and-white world. As he pulls the paper from her face, she coquettishly sees the smudge and chuckles. He stares at the mark and laughs, only to look up and see she has gotten on the train and he has missed it. As the train pulls out of the station, he holds the paper fluttering in the breeze as she demurely looks back out of her window.

Sitting at his desk forlornly, musing on the lip-smacked paper and the moment that seemed lost, his boss dumps a pile of ledgers for him to complete. Another piece of paper flies off his desk toward the window. He recovers it only to see Meg in the skyscraper across the street, sitting down for an interview. Excitedly, he desperately tries to get her attention, waving his arms. Then, taking the stack of forms, he folds scores of paper airplanes, launching them repeatedly to reach her. Yet, vanity of vanities, circumstances foil his every effort. Some fall to the street stories below; one travels into another office where a man crumples it up and throws it away; one is interrupted by a flying bird; most just falling short on a ledge. Left with only the love-marked sheet of paper, he carefully prepares to send it off, but another

Figure C.6 The Mysterious Gift of Love *Paperman* (John Kahrs, 2012) Comes to Him Who Seeks. *Source*: Screenshot taken by the author.

draft of wind blows it serendipitously away. His boss approaches him sternly, with another stack of work papers. Suddenly, like his paper airplanes, he has flown away, leaving work to frantically chase after love. Yet this pursuit is chasing after wind as well, having lost her in the traffic of the city. He finds his lip-smacked plane resting on a mailbox. Frustrated he heaves it away and it glides to a dark alley, where it falls among many of the other lost missives.

Unbeknownst to George, hope arises in a breeze that tilts the plane and lifts it gently back into the air. It leads a squadron of paper airplanes in a whirlwind that soars out of their urban grave and attach themselves to a frustrated George. Covered with a cloud of planes, he watches the divinely appointed flight leader lead him away from his desperation. The plane descends to a street florist booth, where Meg stands and then is stunned by its planting among the flowers. She twists and turns in trying to catch it herself as the plane guides her back onto a train. George, completely clothed in paper, sits on a train traveling in the opposite direction, until both come to the original station. Meg gets out and weighs the plane, reflecting, when suddenly, a host of angelic planes breeze by her. She looks up and sees her puzzled Paperman. While she serenely brushes back her hair, they move toward one another. As the credits roll, the destined couple sit at a street café, chatting and smiling.

While the book of *Proverbs* marvels at the way a man has with a maiden, *Paperman* celebrates how providence works with a clumsy and befuddled suitor to find his woman. Again, Emily Dickinson's hope, that thing with feathers, flies about and is dizzyingly dependent upon the wind, *ruach*, *spiritus*, breath, that blows wherever it pleases. The Gospel of John (3:8) continues with its wildness, "You hear its sound, but you cannot tell where it comes from or where it is going." As the prophet, Koheleth, observed, "As you do not know the path of the wind, or how the bones are formed in a mother's womb, so you cannot understand the work of God, the Maker of all things."[14]

Following faith and hope is the greatest of these, charity. The various modes of love in animated films do include *agape*, that pure and selfless love that God demonstrates to humanity and humanity to God and fellow creatures. A playful parable of such love within a community inhabits what is ironically an advertisement for Spain's national lottery, *Anuncio Lotería de Navidad* (aka *The Lottery* or *Justino*, 2015) (figure C.7). An introverted night watchman faithfully goes to his mannequin factory every evening, never meeting the people who work there in the day. The drudgery of waking up at 10:00 p.m. and taking a lonely bus to work sets his isolation in contrast to the convivial day workers. Walking his rounds in the graveyard shift, the solitary guard uses his whimsical creativity to set up the mannequins in humorous poses for his coworkers. He situates the life-like figure in amusing and moving ways to encourage and uplift those whom he never sees. On Christmas Eve, riding the bus to work, he sees a photograph in the newspaper of all the factory's day

Figure C.7 Those Who Give to Others Will Receive in Turn in *Anuncio Lotería de Navidad* (aka *The Lottery or Justino,* 2015). *Source*: Screenshot taken by the author.

workers who had just won the grand lottery. Sensing the bittersweet victory, he yet faithfully enters the factory late at night to find a mannequin greeting him, holding a winning ticket stub with his name on it. Suddenly, all the day workers appear with champagne and confetti to celebrate his year of quiet, generous, and hilarious service to them, welcoming him with a gift of more than money, but of family and community.

The virtue of charity or love is covered in a multitude of cartoons. Using Claymation, Will Vinton captured various strands of love, with Noel Paul Stookey singing his ballad of "Christmas Dinner" in *A Christmas Gift* (1980). A young hungry boy, cold and shivering in the night, peeks into windows where opulent dinners lay on holiday tables decked with turkey, geese, and cherry pie. He shuffles upon a hovel lit by candlelight, where he sees an old, gray-haired lady sitting at a bare table, with tears in her eyes. He knocks on her door and enters, taking out his small bit of cheese and bread as they share wine and kindness on this "happiest Christmas," with a "toast to everyone's Christmas, especially yours and mine."

Demonstrating how service and kindness to the least of God's children was a gift to God, the Vinton Studio also produced *Martin the Cobbler*, a 1977 adaptation of Leo Tolstoy's short story "Where Love Is" (figure C.8). Taken from the Gospel of Matthew in which Jesus tells his disciples that whatever kindness they have done to the least of these, they have done unto Him. Narrated by Alexandra Tolstoy, daughter of Leo, the clay animation creates an air of expectancy for the lonely, widowed shoemaker. A visiting angel announces that the Lord Himself will visit him the next day. Throughout the

Figure C.8 Vinton Studio Also Produced *Martin the Cobbler* (1977), a Claymation Retelling of Tolstoy's Short Story "Where Love Is." *Source*: Screenshot taken by the author.

day, he whistles, accompanied by his resident mouse, waiting for the Lord. Answering a knock on the door, he finds a young woman with a baby, shivering. He invites her in and gives her his wife's shawl. Another knock opens up an elderly woman who needs help with her groceries and the cobbler sets her up with a mischievous boy. Finally, an old friend comes out and they go out to show the young men how to howl. At the end of the day, he wonders why the Lord did not show up, and the angel reappears. He reveals to the expectant saint how the Lord did appear in the guises of the young woman, the old lady, and the rascally boy.

The sacrifice of love comes joyously in the Academy Award–winning *Hair Love* (Matthew A Cherry, 2019) (figure C.9). Zuri, a young girl wakes leisurely to her purring, hungry cat and sees on her wall calendar that this day is marked with a heart. As she dresses and rushes to meet the day, she pulls up a stool in front of the bathroom sink. She takes off her bedtime bonnet and puff, her tight locks exploding into a shock of giant hair. She scans her computer to gander at various styles, her cat disapproving of many that she considers. She arrives at one that sparks memories of her mother Angela braiding and fixing her hair with a bow. Her mother says, "It just took a little bit of work and a whole lot of love."

Spectators realize her mother is absent as Zuri vainly tries to fix her hair herself. Her dad appears at the bathroom door with some laundry, looks at the hair disaster, and drops his load. He picks her up and delivers her to her mother's dressing table, overwhelmed with the bottles, brushes, and clips that he sees. Zuri hands him a comb as he parts her hair like Moses at the Red

Figure C.9 In *Hair Love* (Matthew A Cherry, 2019), a Father Triumphs over Obstacles of Life with a Poignant Trope of Untamable Hair. *Source*: Screenshot taken by the author.

Sea. He begins the comic challenge of combing her thickly textured hair for what seems like the first time. The hair fights back, whacking his wrist with a comb. A surreal battle of wrestling with the hair unwinds in a boxing arena, with a muscular cloud of follicles egging him on. About to be overwhelmed, he grabs a cord and begins to tie up the loose ends. The beast of hair breaks free and he runs away, with his daughter looking askance at this defeated parent. He surrenders by sticking a cap on her unwieldy locks, but she runs away sniffling and sad. She opens her door with a vlog from her mother, indicating how easy this would be: "And remember the road ahead might look rough, but you can make the journey with a little bit of work . . . and a whole lot of love."

At the end of the recorded scene, the absent mother kisses her daughter, "Muah." The father, with tears in his eyes, determines to overcome the challenge. He follows the instructional video and moisturizes those beautiful thick curls and detangles the kinks. He parts her hair into sections and clips it away, braids it, and finally, he completes it. "That was so much fun," says the mother's encouraging voice. Zuri jumps on her father's neck and hugs him happily.

They get dressed and head out to a hospital, where a woman sits in a wheelchair, a yellow turban covering her head. Her door opens and Zuri comes running in to her mother. Her husband enters with daisies, violets and sunflowers, and kisses his wife tenderly. Zuri tells her mother that her dad fixed her hair, and then she hands her mother a drawing of a bald woman wearing a golden crown. Angela is touched and takes off her bandana to reveal herself as a cancer patient. Zuri rubs her head and all three embrace, with Zuri's eyes bright and joyous.

The profoundly heartwarming story adds comic touches throughout the end credits, with a sleeping dad having his dreads tied up with a bow, as well as an unhappy gray cat's fur all tied up in blue bows. A bonus appears when one discovers Angela's hair growing back. What struck so many viewers was that the short film did not kill off the mother, unlike several Disney features. The triumph of hope ends with new life. The tackling of tending a young girl's untamed hair works as a spiritual journey film as well, as father and daughter persist to overcome their limitations to present hair love to a suffering mother. This intimate ode of a father, daughter, and the challenge of her hair celebrates the perseverance and love that bring joy.

Parables of death and resurrection are rare, but two delicately drawn films that suggest the immortality of the soul, and perhaps the body, stem the sweet death of the self.[15] Animation scholar Paul Wells perceptively noted the "symbolic, parable-like quality" of the Grand Prix winner at the 1979 Annecy Animation Film Festival, Alison de Vere's *Mr. Pascal* (figure C.10).[16] The redemptive film spins its tale with unobtrusive and gentle compassion. An aged and exhausted Jewish cobbler widower sits on a bench outside a Roman Catholic cathedral, in poignant solitude. Pigeons peck at his feet. A mother and child pass by while a romantic couple kisses. As the church bell rings, he takes off his hat, pulls a photo of his wife out of his wallet, and slips into a reverie. She is naked on their honeymoon, laughing

Figure C.10 Alison de Vere's *Mr. Pascal* (1979) Depicts Loss, Labor, and Hope in the Quiet Story of a Lonely Widower. *Source*: Screenshot taken by the author.

as he approaches her in the nude, and sweet memories of *eros* and affection float by. He reminisces how his wife chats away and their baby cries. He smiles, but now he is alone.

Mr. Pascal holds his hands on his face and looks up to notice a crucifix. He studies Jesus hanging on the cross and then runs back to his shoe shop. He returns with pliers and pulls the nails out of the feet and hands of Jesus. As the statue creaks, lightning strikes, and he hauls the body down from its cross. As the rain begins, Mr. Pascal covers the dead body of Jesus with his cloak, as the wooden cross falls down and shatters. He covers Jesus with a shawl, binds his wounds with bandages, and uses the crown of thorns as kindling for a fire. He places socks and sandals on his feet. He then shares a bottle of wine with Jesus, who drinks it and smiles.

A congregation of hippies and street people gather and celebrate with him. Miracles of healing happen, as well as Jesus multiplying the bread and wine. Wine keeps pouring out, and the bottle, like Elisha's miracle with the widow's jar. Pascal looks at Jesus, who raises his eyebrow and grins. Flower children dance and St. Francis heals a leper. Finally, as the old man falls asleep, a smiling Christ covers him and departs into the stars. The next morning two angels appear to sweep up the ashes, plant a tree, and as Mr. Pascal awakens, it blossoms with new life. Amid these miracles of community, healing, and Eucharistic celebration, her luminous film joyously celebrates the sacrificial paschal Lamb of God.

So, too, a shabby old soul, a homeless artist, salvages an old box from the teeth of a garbage truck, a symbol of modern civilization devouring and dismissing what appears useless and unnecessary in *An Old Box* or *Une vieille boite* (Paul Driessen, 1975) (figure C.11).[17] Set against a gray backdrop and with minimalist lines, the box rests among discarded trash through which the long-faced scavenger picks. The approach of a gluttonous garbage truck speeds up his sense of urgency when he sees the box, claps his hands in glee, and rescues it. He takes it to his hovel, and tinkers with it, painting it and then drawing a six-pointed blue star. A simple coin inserted into the box brings it to life, with plain and unpretentious messages "*joyeux* noël" and "*merry christmas*" appearing with enchanting music. Switching to the town square, loud and raucous music blares, as Santa carries his bag of toys and people hawk candy and sausages, lining up to sell the world their commercial holiday specials. An accordion plays as the village people dance or watch a brutal Punch and Judy entertainment, evoking cruel laughter as a puppet man whacks the woman with a frying pan.

The camera dollies through the streets to find the homeless man sitting quietly in a desolate corner. While the festivities continue, he sits still in the cold wind as the sun sets; all others set up their decorated trees and then close their curtains to the world. The shivering old man gets into his box, submitting

Figure C.11 One of the Most Subtle and Transcendent Parables of Resurrection Unravels in *An Old Box* or *Une vieille boite* (Paul Driessen, 1975). *Source*: Screenshot taken by the author.

himself to death; unobtrusively a Divine star descends and enters the box with him. With a tinkling, and then a crescendo of exquisite Norman Roger music, an exuberant Christmas joy appears. The film inaugurates a brilliantly hued celebration of reds, yellows, and blues. Wise men look for the star; shepherds in their field follow it; and all arrive at the manger, where rainbows, sunshine, angels, animals, and a trio of "Can-Can" dancing Santa Claus characters burst out of the ordinary box. Then the music fades as the star takes the soul of the old man from his earthen treasure to the heavens. The old box, the old body, is discarded and eaten by the trash dumpster. The revelatory parable hints at the transformation of the least and the lost by One who enters his life and transforms it with glory.

In a 1963 panel debate about violence in American cartoons, British legend John Halas described the American civilization as the "most violent in the world." Academy Award–winning director Peter Burness responded that one must not forget one important thing: "In the American cartoon, death, human defeat, is never presented without being followed by resurrection, transfiguration." No matter how crushed, fragmented, or pulverized a character like Wiley E. Coyote might be, one finds a "permanent illustration of the theme of rebirth."[18]

The transformation of the ordinary into the supernatural also occurs as vices convert to virtues. Both *The Big Snit* and *Pies* originate in the vice of anger, with all its frustrations and resentments, and end with grace and forgiveness. The ordinary moments in their narrative lead to a disparity and then into that stasis of decision that has marked transcendental style. They become sublime parables through their depiction of this tension in the everyday aspects of life.

The Big Snit (Richard Condie, 1985) offers a very funny moral tale on forgiveness through an altercation between a goofy-looking husband and his tall, busy wife (figure C.12). Animator Condie's big-nosed married couple are hilariously quirky and ordinary. Sitting down to play scrabble, she leads the competition while he is stuck with a letter holder of EEEEEEE. During their game, they begin to squabble and he accuses her of "shaking your eyes, shaking your eyes here; shaking your eyes there." She cries and leaves the room. His own habit, endearing when they first romanced, is that he likes to saw (anything from his armchair to the cat) just as her cute idiosyncrasy was "shaking her eyes." But now, old affections become old snits.

After she leaves the room, he begins to watch his favorite television show, *Sawing for Teens*, during which he falls asleep. While asleep, an announcer appears to warn of a universal nuclear catastrophe. The world is ending. As the cat chews the cable wire, the television goes off and he wanders to find his wife vacuuming the bathtub and other odd places. He tries to apologize by performing another of his gifts to the marriage, playing the accordion. As they reminisce of their courtship, the magic returns and they embrace. They move to the front door while outside chaos and pandemonium have overwhelmed the world. An ark floats by. Santa Claus speeds by. Suddenly they have encountered what seems to be a larger snit, but the way Condie frames

Figure C.12 ***The Big Snit*** **(Richard Condie, 1985) Juxtaposes a Cosmic Apocalypse with the Bigger Snit of a Marital Argument.** *Source*: Screenshot taken by the author.

it, the simple argument of husband and wife has more eternal significance than the whole world's existence. As they open the door, they are transfigured into spiritual bodies, a Second Coming and a new birth. Their love transcends the disasters around them and they decide to go back and finish their scrabble game. Reconciliation through grace dominates this silly story; in fact, the word silly, coming from the Russian "Sali" means blessed. The couple forgive each other for their big snit even as the universe has its little apocalyptic snit. The cartoon ends in what British author J. R. R. Tolkien called a "eucatastrophe," a good ending to a major cataclysmic upheaval. Michael Scott, Condie's executive producer, explained, the film "reflects the difficulties of marriage and relationships and that love conquers all."[19]

In *PIES* (1984), Canadian Sheldon Cohen contrasts a meticulous, immaculate German Lutheran hausfrau with her sloppy, easy-going, Polish Catholic neighbor (figure C.13). The Polish woman owns a cow that makes manure "pies" which disgusts her finicky neighbor and leads to an angry snit between the two. The meticulous and immaculate German, Mrs. Meuser, steps in the poor Polish Mrs. Cherak's cow dung. A fight ensues between the two, as they challenge each other with a tit-for-tat, "who is dirty now?" mentality. Seeking revenge upon the cow woman, the German bakes a mincemeat pie with a "special" ingredient, borrowed from her neighbor's pasture yard, and serves it to her neighbor. Over coffee and the poop-filled mincemeat pie, ("What is it?" "It is a special way I make it."), they begin to discuss their children and how they have trouble with them, just like "the Holy Mother"

Figure C.13 In *PIES* (1984), Canadian Sheldon Cohen Reconciles a Persnickety Immaculate Woman with Her Slovenly Neighbor in an Act of Humility and Grace. *Source*: Screenshot taken by the author.

had trouble with her child. As they share and laugh, the vindictive Meuser discovers her righteousness is like, as St. Paul wrote, dung. She prays to the Holy Mother, the Virgin Mary, confessing that she had hated her neighbor. She asks for strength to swallow what she had done and then chooses to eat her own shit. "No neighbor should eat by themselves," she prays. Turning the other cheek and forgiving, she learns to love her neighbor, her cow, and the two women bond. Rarely has G. K. Chesterton's observation that God told us to love our neighbors *and* to love enemies—probably because they are the same people—ever been so accurately captured on film. Yet the "pie," an instrument of vengeance becomes a means of grace and reconciliation in this remarkably effective cartoon.

Just as Cain envied his brother Abel, envy underlies the sibling relationship in *Anna and Bella* (Borge Ring, 1984), in which a prettier sister seduces her sister's boyfriend, only to lead to jealousy, rage, and death (figure C.14). Fortunately, however, confession and many glasses of wine lead to forgiveness and laughter, and then more wine in the hereafter. Such parables contain the fruit of the Gospel in a carafe, promising drink, nourishment, and blessed conviviality to any who will recognize the invitation to the merry feast. The parable offers a new wineskin for a new gospel, defamiliarizing a prosaic approach to understanding our lives.[20]

Both *The Big Snit* and *Anna and Bella* confirm sociologist Lewis Coser's notion that the more intimate the relationship, the more intense the conflict (or the bigger the snit). Yet the two films accentuate the grace that follows forgiveness, with humor and joy. Such emotions in animated parables, most of which are nonverbal, speak through an international language. Silent films, proclaimed early filmmaker D. W. Griffith, augur the new millennium, as they speak this universal tongue. They are global moving hieroglyphics for those who look and seek to understand the Kingdom of God. Yet, the parable,

Figure C.14 ***Anna and Bella*** **(Borge Ring, 1984) Portrays the Need and Joy of Familial Forgiveness (and a Little Wine) in the End of Life.** *Source*: Screenshot taken by the author.

as Mark Kermode suggests, "may proclaim a truth as a herald does and at the same time conceal truth like an oracle."[21]

An animated adaptation of Oscar Wilde's fairy tale, *The Selfish Giant* (Peter Sander, 1971) quietly envelopes the spectator in the parable of grace, encasing the Gospel of Christ in a lovely nutshell. A giant has built a stall around his lovely garden to keep out children from playing. He experiences a change of heart after enduring the cold winter winds, snow, hail, and consequences of the hardness. One little child in particular has enchanted and softened the callous giant, but he disappears as the ogre grows older. Then one winter day, the giant looks out of his window and sees the boy's favorite tree in bloom. He rushes down and finds the little child. Then in a rage, lifts his cane and shouts, "Who dared do this to you?" For on the child's hands and on his feet were the scars of nails. The Christ child looks up at the giant and takes him by the hand, saying, "You once let me play in your garden; now, let me take you to mine, which is called paradise." The film gently preaches a *sermo* on both the inherent selfishness of all giants (all humanity) and a need for repentance and reform, which allegorically, arrives as a gift through the wounds of love on the palms and feet of a small child.

One thing that the biblical parables consistently pointed back to was the identity of God, the identification of Jesus to the Father, and the doctrine that humans are *imago Dei*, people are made in the image of God. This last doctrine underlies a sub-genre of animated films from the earliest days of their history, from Winsor McCay interacting with his creature Gertie to the Fleischer brothers trying to control Koko the Clown and Otto Messmer helping out Felix the Cat. Such self-reflexive animated films frequently point back to their Maker, to the Cartoonist author behind the design and story of the cartoon. Chesterton said that if life is a story, then there must be a storyteller. The meta-cartoon tells us that such an entity exists, although the author may not be whom we imagine.

The most celebrated film of this group is Chuck Jones' classic *Duck Amuck* (1953) where the animator constructs a Job-like story for the hapless Daffy Duck (figure C.15). So many catastrophic things happen to his character that one almost wonders, "Why do bad things happen to good people?" With Daffy, one realizes the character is not that good. Yet one asks, what is the justice for seemingly worse things happening to ordinarily bad people? Discovering that the Author of Daffy's misadventures is Bugs Bunny, who impishly confesses at the end of the cartoon, "Ain't I a stinker?" confirms those who think of God as either an underachiever (Woody Allen) or a sadistic brute (C. S. Lewis). The unveiling of Bugs as the Author behind Daffy's pilgrimage underlies a suspicion that God does not play ethically. He seemingly commands His people to kill other people. He rains judgment down upon His people through the Egyptians, the Assyrians, and the Babylonians.

Figure C.15 Chuck Jones' Classic *Duck Amuck* (1953) Hints at the Presence of a Very Mischievous "author" behind the Vicissitudes of an Ordinary Duck. *Source*: Screenshot taken by the author.

Daffy, as a preposterous, you might say, cartoon Job, is seemingly stuck in an arbitrary and absurd existential universe. The settings change willy-nilly from old MacDonald's farm to an Artic setting with an igloo to the Old West, and Daffy pleads, "Would it be too much to ask if we could make up our minds? Hummm?" Throughout his Kafkaesque travails, of playing the musketeer or a scuffling dandelion, Daffy appeals to the normal grammar of cartoon syntax to assert some order for this world gone askew. "This *is* an animated cartoon," he tells whoever may be listening, "and in animated cartoons they have scenery."[22] He will not go gently into that dark The End credit, but fights the covering blackness with a stick to prop up his existence. Adapting to the chaotic environment, including the bizarre metamorphoses of his own image, he yells, "Who is responsible for this? I demand that you show yourself? Who are you?" The mysterious and sovereign creator, whose malevolent whimsy makes sport with him, frustrates Daffy at every turn. Finally, the camera pulls back to show the unseen artist as Bugs Bunny. "He is his own auteur," observed Richard Corliss, "the cartoon director's alter-ego. He knows what's going to happen in the next frame or three scenes away, and he knows how to control it."[23]

The final unveiling of Bugs Bunny as the tormenting "stinker" behind the whole mess elicits one last laugh, but also leads to an awareness of the supernatural or super-celluloid Artist, who does exist and seems to "play" with his creatures. The joke expands and culminates in the realization that the impish rabbit exists only as the imaginative expression of another—more genuine—cartoon director, Chuck Jones. In the chaotic world of the simulacra, one finds not a referent, but an author. Despite Roland Barthes' assertion that the "birth of the reader must be at the cost of the death of the Author,"[24] this cartoon parable brings the presence of an Author into dialogue.

Cartoon authorship may involve a screwy coterie of animators on Termite Terrace or just one auteur like the incomparable Norman McLaren, but the cartoon is a genre that highlights the name below the title; the authors leave their signatures or thumbprints on their work. Chesterton observed that "as God made a pigmy-image of Himself and called it Man, so man made a pigmy-image of creation and called it art."[25] Women and men, as *imago Dei*, imitate their Creator, becoming what J. R. R. Tolkien called "sub-creators." Their cartoons carry what Peter Berger has called "signals of transcendence," clues and hints to a reality beyond their two-dimensional existence.

Such self-reflexive parables point back to creation and ultimately a Creator. Filmmaker Terry Gilliam puts it succinctly when he suggests that as an animator, "You get to be an impish God. You get to reform the world. . . . You turn it upside down, inside out."[26] Animation historian Donald Crafton illumines this process of sub-creation in the silent animated film, where the "tendency of the filmmaker to interject himself into his film . . . can take several forms: it can be direct or indirect, and more or less camouflaged." Crafton calls this technique of invading the cartoon with one's identity as a "self-figuration."[27] The grand incarnation of animator into animation can be found in films like the Fleischer Bros.' series of *Koko* cartoons where the Clown interacts and tricks producer Max or with the hand of Otto Messmer's showering gifts upon Felix and even help in his romance in *Comicalities*. Messmer's *Trials of a Movie Cartoonist* (1916) even allows the cartoon character to rebel and claim the Cartoonist "has no right to make slaves of them even if he is their creator."[28] Self-figuration occurs in a wide variety of animated parables suggesting the Storyteller behind the stories, as in Osvaldo Cavandoli's comic *La Linea*, Guy Jacques' poignant *L'invite* (1984) and Daniel Greaves' theological *Manipulation* (1991). Such films point back to their authors/auteurs and may show a benevolent creator or a mean-spirited one. In the latter one, the Academy Award–winning animated short film *Manipulation* places the creature in conflict with his creator, a not unlikely scenario, asserting his independence. Here, however, the artist's hand manipulates and hoodwinks his creature. Greaves' sought to persuade the audience that the vulnerable "paper character was as alive as the hand of the Creator" and to imagine such a relationship between the two protagonists, with the character growing from 2-D to 3-D. The attempt to escape is futile, however, and for its disobedience, the rebellious little hand-drawn paper character is tossed into the hell of paper cartoon characters, a wastepaper basket.[29]

Most remarkably, the self-reflexive cartoon parable can suggest such an orthodox doctrine of the incarnation, but perhaps as an "incartoonation." "If you want to make a good cartoon, you have to be in one first," one of the characters in Kathy Rose's *Pencil Bookings* (1978) tells the artist (figure C.16). In one sense, Rose emulates Chaucer, who impishly inserted himself as one of the characters in *The Canterbury Tales* whose verse is so tedious that the Host, Harry Bailey, abruptly shuts him up with "thy drasty rymyng is nat worth a toord!"

Rose has directed a dreamy and fluid cartoon in which she appears in two cartoon forms: in her own rotoscoped cartoon incarnation and in the redrawn image of her by her cartoon characters. As the film begins, she is sitting at her drawing table and her tiny cast of bubbling characters emerge from a bottle (like Fleischer's inkwell) and complaining about their voices. One whines that its voice is too squeaky. Others chime in: "I don't like my voice either." "We don't want to be in your film." The characters incessantly give advice to their creator, often ordering her where and when to insert a "nice cycle."

Eventually Rose reproves them: "I can't make a film if everyone here is fighting." She makes a brief exit, and when she is gone, the characters decide to remake their own world. "Hello, I'm Kathy's pencil," one says and joins the other to "make our own film just like Kathy." Exhilarated by freedom from Kathy's control, they reconstruct their universe with a goofier, cartoonier image of the maker. They want to make their distorted image of Kathy

Figure C.16 Kathy Rose Incarnates Herself into the Sub-created World of Her Rebellious Cartoon Characters in *Pencil Bookings* (1978). *Source*: Screenshot taken by the author.

talk like they talk. However, no one will participate unless each can have her own way; so they float without direction until communication with their creator is re-established and life begins anew. Through identification with her doodled characters as a doodle herself, Kathy is able to communicate with them and gain their obedience. The author recognizes how her text can take on a life of its own and add to the original text. Fellow animator and scholar John Canemaker praised Rose's ability to draw us into this original, fascinating world, and make us "believe in its special reality . . . . In one breathtaking scene, Ms. Rose 'becomes' one of her characters. Later, Ms. Rose oozes and bleeds her cartoon cast from her body, as strong a visual statement of an artist's identification with her art as you liable to find in animation."[30]

Both Tolkien's recognition of a human artist being a sub-creator and Canemaker's insight on the identification of Artist with her art are caught cleverly in *God Film* (Gil Beach, 1975). The simple two-minute cartoon opens with the pronouncement that "In the beginning, God created the heavens and the earth." A white-bearded old man stands and waves His hand at the camera, and one realizes He is communicating with His creation, pleased and joyous. Then the film intones in a whimsical voice: "Since then, he has been doing self-portraits." The man starts tugging and pulling at His own face. He pulls off a replica of His image and places it on the camera, with two openings. Suddenly we realize these are two eyes looking back at Him. He waves and smiles at His image and the image blinks back. Beach's parable of the Kingdom suggests not only that God creates and communicates with His art, but that He has re-created each person in His own image, *imago Dei*.

In 1991, international award-winning Canadian animator, Richard Condie, released the perplexing and comic short animated film, *The Apprentice/ L'Apprenti* (figure C.17). The hilarious cartoon about a medieval master jester and his young foolish apprentice evoked laughter at festivals for its slapstick humor and its computer-generated dialogue of gargling voices and gong noises. However, what was missed in the comedy of a frustrated fool trying to find his own way to a royal Kingdom, with many other idiots going to their destruction by stubbornly hurling off a cliff, was its parabolic source. According to Condie, there are "talking parts, but stuff and strange sounds come out of people's mouths. We can understand it, but it is not a definable language." He explains that he and composer Patrick Godfrey "would lay on the floor with towels under our heads and necks, all padded up. Then we kept filling our mouths with water; and we lay there and talked, gargling, water running down the sides of our faces."[31]

In the Gospel of Matthew, Jesus warns his disciples to "Enter through the narrow gate; for the gate is wide and the way is broad that leads to destruction, and there are many who enter through it; for the gate is small and the way is narrow that leads to life, and there are few who find it" (17:13–14).

Figure C.17 The Apotheosis of Animated Parables, Richard Condie's Hilarious *The Apprentice* (1991), Points to Jesus' Parable of the Broad and Narrow Ways. *Source*: Screenshot taken by the author.

For many viewers, the silly short is only a cartoon, a drollery with a dragon coughing up the head of a princess or marginal *grillos* of mocking flowers. For those who have eyes to see and ears to hear, the pithy little film offers a profound moral lesson about choosing the right road of life. Emblematically, the obstacle that continually stops the buffoon from toppling over the cliff himself is a tree in the middle of a bare field. The tree, a symbolic cross, preserves the apprentice fool while many others rush headlong to their perdition. Only the fool, once he returns to his Master Fool, who holds the key to the castle, finds the narrow path to the Kingdom. The visual primacy of this cartoon with its universal language offers what Paul Wells called the "iconic status" of the animated film. It also augurs global parabolic possibilities of disseminating moral and theological ideas through visual media.[32]

The question this animated film poses and answers: "Can the short animated film function as a religious parable?" Might we even dare to say that cartoons could be scripted by Jesus? He did have to explain certain parabolic storyboards to his disciples. However, we find similar characteristics connecting his Gospel parables and the short animated films. First, their mutual brevity precludes one from falling asleep. Second, they frequently interrupt expectations with surprise. Third, various recognizable tropes are used, of sheep or pigs or foolish men or the need to suffer. Just as the zoomorphic images of the vices riding suitable beasts, each according to their nature, pop up in Bosch, Bruegel, and especially Spencer's *Faerie Queene*, where one sees fabulous animals or wayward creatures with whom one could identify, however uncomfortably. New and unfamiliar themes occupied these ordinary forms, which are, at first, camouflaged. Fourth, they begin with a familiar opening scenario, such as "A man had two sons". An apprentice set out for the kingdom of God. Fifth, they both contain latent truth that require active thought, teased out through indirect communication. They incite the hearer or spectator to explore and discover the meaning of the story, to wrestle, think, and participate in understanding it. Sixth, and this item requires a whole other book, they frequently offer comic perspectives. If one can see the joke of the log in one's eye, one can see the truth of the tale. To adapt Rebecca DeYoung's observation about the importance of studying vices, these animated parables work to prick our consciences and invite us to draw closer to God and other people. They work to awaken us to see our habits in the morning light and to seek a more abundant life in practical daily matters.

Scholar Shawn Tucker argues that medieval art employed vivid imagery of virtues and vices to instruct church members. The figures in the church of Saint Pierre in Aulney, Giotto's paintings in Padua, and Hildegard of Bingen's theatrical presentation dramatize an ongoing *Psychomachia.* Visual parables of the battles between the virtues and vices taught viewers about right and wrong. Where the church once taught of the soul's struggle, now mere and seemingly insignificant cartoons take up the mantle, comically and profoundly posing moral and spiritual questions. Animated parables show the consequences of sin, and suggest those ironic moments of *contrapasso.*

One last word, a palinode, a retraction of all that has gone before, may be apt. Interpretations, and even descriptions, of these animated parables are indubitably subjective and I could be obliviously facile, superficial, askew, or downright wrong in my assessments. However, in one of his Snoopy cartoons, Charles Schulz drew Charlie Brown chatting with Snoopy sitting on his doghouse. "I hear you're writing a book on theology," Charlie noted, "I hope you have a good title."

Confidently Snoopy replied, "I have the perfect title . . . *Has It Ever Occurred to You That You Might Be Wrong*?" Thus, it is in this often ambiguous and liquid world of animated parables, I confess that I may have missed the boat altogether. On the other hand, I enjoyed it thoroughly. I feel like that old man watching an experimental cartoon in a crowded movie theater in Mel Brooks' Academy Award–winning *The Critic* (1963). Other customers tell him to shut up. He yells back, "I'm 72 years old, lady, and I'm going to die soon." There is freedom in being old. I also feel like Condie's *Apprentice*, not always quite sure where I am headed or what obstacles are thwarting me. However, I see the Master ahead, with the key to unlock the kingdom of understanding. Perhaps I only need to echo the Duchess in Alice: "Tut, tut, child!" said the Duchess. "Everything's got a moral, if only you can find it."[33] My task has been to describe these curious kinetic artifacts and spark the imaginations of readers to go back and see what parables they might uncover in the most unlikely of texts, the short animated cartoon.

NOTES

1. Willimon, *Sinning Like a Christian,* 13.
2. Ibid., 136.
3. See C. S. Lewis' *Spenser's Images of Life* (Cambridge University Press, 1967).
4. Lewis, *Mere Christianity,* op. cit. 102.
5. Along with spiritual journeys are parables of memory that point to more than the mundane, as in *Uncle Thomas Accounting the Days* (Regina Pessoa, 2020), *Tale of Tales* (Yuri Norstein, 1979), and in *Coco* (Adrian Molina and Lee Unkrich, 2017). *Coco*'s visit to the Dead offers a haunting award-winning song "Remember me," performed in three unique renditions (egotistical, familial, and Eucharistic).
6. Capon, *Parables of Grace,* op. cit. 10.
7. See also *The Wise and Foolish Builders,* https://www.max7.org/en/resource/WiseFoolishBuilders.
8. Dalglish, Reverend William A. (ed.), *Media for Christian Formation: A Guide to AV Resources* (Dayton: Pflaum, 1969).
9. Freberg's work was distributed through the Broadcasting and Film Commission of the National Council of Church to counter the death of God movement. In Warner Bros. cartoons, Freberg voiced such characters as the mild-mannered gopher Tosh and a bumbling Junyer Bear, and was dubbed the "the Stradivarius" of comic voices by the *Washington Post,* https://www.washingtonpost.com/news/morning-mix/wp/2015/04/08/stan-freberg-beloved-genius-of-radio-comedy-and-advertising-dies-at-88/ (Accessed January 13, 2020); See also Bevilacqua, Joe, "This Here is Your Life, Stan Freberg" Interview *Cartoon Carnival* Program #20 (Feb 22, 2010), https://beta.prx.org/stories/47380 (Accessed January 13, 2020).
10. Stross, R. M., "Davey and Goliath Meet the Philistines," *WACC Journal* 26 (April 1978), 34.
11. Woolston, Suzanne, "*Davey and Goliath*: One Church's Response to the Media" Interview with Mr. Roy Lee, Regent University (March 31, 1986). See Klos, Frank William, Jr. "A Study of the Origin, Development, and Impact of the Davey and Goliath Television Series, 1959–1977 and Its Present Effectiveness in Teaching Religious Values to Children." Diss. Temple University, 1978.
12. Woolery, George W., *Children's Television: The First Thirty-Five Years, 1946–1981* (Scarecrow Press, 1983), 156–157.
13. Smith, Sarah, "Veggie Tales," *National Religious Broadcasting* (May 1998), 15 Edwards, Catherine, "Values on Video" *Insight on the News* (July 5, 1999), 47; Vischer, Phil, "Address for Hollywood Connection" Transcript Regent University (October 27, 1997), 71–72; See Valkenburg, Patti and Sabine Janssen, "What do Children Value in Entertainment Programs? A Cross-Cultural Study," *Journal of Communication* 49:2 (1999), 3; Kloehn, Steve, "One Cool Cucumber," *Chicago*

Tribune (October 2, 1998), C1; Brunner, Lincoln, "Watch Your Vegetables, Johnny," *Christianity Today* (May 19, 1997), 58.

14. Ecclesiastes 11:5.

15. In Bruno Bozzetto's *Dancing* (1991), the Grim reaper comes to a man stuck on an island, dancing with joy, what Chesterton called the secret of the Christian life, and death cannot take it away. Death dies, and the man dances. Joy of the Resurrection defeats death.

16. Wells, Paul, *Animation: Genre and Authorship* (Wallflower, 2002), 131.

17. Paul Driessen's *Cat's Cradle* (1976) also offers a thrilling Christmas story adventure of the rescue of the holy family by a spider giving its all to hide them from Herod's soldiers. R. O. Blechman's *Simple Gifts: No Room at the Inn* (animated by Ed Smith with Tissa David) sketches a straight animation satire of the commercialization of the Christmas story. *R. O. Blechman: Behind the Lines* (Hudson Hills, Press, 1980), 105.

18. Thompson, Richard "Meep Meep!" *Film Comment* (May-June 1976), 211 Thompson ends his article wryly, suggesting that what such cartoon characters are denied is "the solace of eternal rest." (215)

19. Crider, Alisa, "Interview with Michael Scott" (2009) cited in *Condie's World* xii.

20. Angela Carter mischievously opts for "putting new wine in old bottles, especially if the pressure of the new wine makes the old bottles explode." "Notes from the Front Line," in *Critical Essays on Angela Carter*, ed. Lindsey Tucker (G. K. Hall, 1983), 24.

21. Kermode, Frank, "Hoti's Business: Why are Narratives Obscure?" in *The Genesis of Secrecy: On the Interpretation of Narrative* (Harvard University Press, 1980).

22. Much of this section is owed to an earlier article Matthew Melton and I published. "Toward a Postmodern Animated Discourse," *Animation Journal* (Fall 1984), 44–63, but it is so long ago that even my wife did not remember it. For it, I still thank Maureen Furniss.

23. Corliss, Richard, "Warnervana," *Film Comment* 21:6 (Nov/Dec 1985), 18.

24. Barthes, Roland, "The Death of the Author," in *Image-Music-Text* (trans. Stephen Heath) (Hill and Wang, 1977), 148.

25. Chesterton, G. K., *As I Was Saying . . .* (Eerdmans, 1985), 264.

26. The Monty Python animator explained that for a brief moment, the artist has a bit control over this constructed world "At least you get to humiliate it for a moment and that's what all the cartoonists get their kicks from." Gilliam, Terry in "Interview with the Author" Paul Wells *Understanding animation*, 127.

27. Quoted in Wells, Paul, *An Animated Bestiary: Animals, Cartoons, and Culture* (Rutgers University Press, 2000), 157.

28. Crafton, Donald , *Before Mickey* (MIT Press, 1982), 11, 187.

29. Cotte, op. cit. 143.

30. Canemaker, John, "Animation for Adults" *Take One* (November 1978), 37, 40–41. One of the most exhilarating moments for my graduate students was when we placed Mike Jittlov's pixilated *Wizard of Speed and Time* (1980) on a Steenbeck to ascertain whether we were "seeing" something subliminal tucked away in the frame.

His secret signatures were unveiled clearly in the frame-by-frame analysis. In his frames, Jittlov spelled his name out in lights, hid messages against the Hollywood industry, and even listed his home phone number on a clapboard, inviting any amateur detective who discovered this message to call him. We immediately dialed the number and had a live, direct line back to a very live and friendly author.

31. Walz "Masters and Apprentices" 4 Mr. Lee Rother used the film in his Alternative Career Education program as a pedagogical tool to teach students with learning problems how to read a visual text. "Coming up ACEs: Using Media to Develop Students' Literate Behavior," *English Quarterly,* 25:2–3 (1990), 39–40. Students concluded that "The teacher knows that the apprentice needs a nose because he's been there before." "Thank God this apprentice had a teacher and a tree to get him out of trouble." Wilson Linda "Some Things Dick Said and Did, phone calls, August 1997," *ASIFA Canada: The Life and Work of Richard Condie* 25: 3 (November 1997), 20; Condie was reluctantly known for his "trademark" howling screams and a bishop hearing the confession of a pig in "The Confession of Saint Vinny," "Clips from Films I have Yet to Do." Cited in Crider xvi and 90, 96. Alisa Crider's greatest contribution in her personal interview was his response to a question of whether his "former wife really used to shake her eyes" and "Do you saw things or scream when you are angry?" He responded "you must be joking . . . this is a perfect time toad to all the myths about me and my films, but I'll pass. The answer to the question is 'no, no, and no.'" 127.

32. Wells, *The Animated Bestiary*, op. cit. Among his many stellar analyses, Wells celebrates the "parable-like quality" of Hans Fischerkoesen's humanitarian works (e.g., *The Silly Goose*, 1944) to be not only indirect but also subversive to the status quo of Nazi Germany. Parables as such challenge the Zeitgeist of the era (189–191).

33. Carroll, Lewis, *Alice's Adventures in Wonderland* (1865) (A& C Black Ltd., 1949), 120.

Bibliography

Abraham, Adam. *When Magoo Flew: The Rise and Fall of Animation Studio*. Wesleyan University Press, 2012.

Adamson, Joe. *Tex Avery*. Da Capo, 1985.

Alciati, Andrea. *A Book of Emblems: The Emblematum Liber* [1531] *in Latin and English: 1492–1550* (trans. and ed. John F. Moffitt). McFarland, 2004.

Annan, Gabriele. *The Genius of Wilhelm Busch: Comedy of Frustration* (trans. Walter Arndt). University of California Press, 1981.

Aquinas, Thomas. *Summa Theologiae*. Coyote Canyon, 2018.

Attardo, Salvatore, ed. *Encyclopedia of Humor Studies*. Sage, 2014.

Augustine. *On Christian Doctrine*. Beloved Publishing, 2014.

Augustine. *On Lying* (ed. Philip Schaff). Createspace, 2015.

Barthes, Roland. *Image-Music-Text* (trans. Stephen Heath). Hill and Wang, 1977.

Bax, Dirk. *Hieronymus Bosch: His Picture-Writing Deciphered*. CRC Press, 1978.

Baxandall, Michael. *Painting and Experience in Fifteenth-Century Italy: A Primer in the Social History of Pictorial Style*. Oxford University Press, 1972.

Beck, Jerry. *50 Greatest Cartoons*. Turner, 1994.

Benjamin, Walter. *The Storyteller, Tales out of Loneliness* (ed. Sam Dolbear). Verso, 2016.

Benedek, András, and Kristóf Nyíri, eds. *Beyond Words: Pictures, Parables, Paradoxes*. Peter Lang, 2015.

Blackburn, Simon. *Lust*. Oxford University Press, 2004.

Boccaccio, Giovanni. *Decameron* (trans. John Payne). Independent, 2020.

Boccaccio, Giovanni. *Life of Dante* (trans. J. G. Nichols). Hesperus Press, 2002.

Buechner, Frederick. *Wishful Thinking*. Harper and Row, 1973.

Brandt, Sebastian. *Ship of Fools* (trans Alexander Barkley). Project Guttenberg, 2006.

Brubaker, Leslie. *Vision and Meaning in Ninth-Century Byzantium: Image as Exegesis in the Homilies of Gregory of Nazianzus*. Cambridge University Press, 1999.

Byrne, Eleanor, and Martin McQuillan. *Deconstructing Disney*. Pluto Press, 1999.

Cabarga, Leslie. *The Fleischer Story*. Da Capo Press, 1976.

Campbell, Joseph. *Myths to Live By*. Bantam, 1981.

Camille, Michael. *Image on the Edge: the Margins of Medieval Art*. Harvard University Press, 1992.

Canemaker, John. *Felix, the Twisted Tale of the World's Most Famous Cat*. Pantheon, 1991.

Capon, Robert Farrar. *The Parables of Grace*. Eerdmans, 1988.

Carey, Frances, ed. *The Apocalypse and the Shape of Things to Come*. University of Toronto Press, 1999.

Case, Steven. *Toons that Teach: 75 Cartoon Moments to Get Teenagers Talking*. Zondervan, 2005.

Cassian, John. *The Institutes* (trans. Boniface Ramsey). Newman Press, 2000.

Chesterton, G. K. *As I Was Saying . . .* Eerdmans, 1985.

Chesterton, G. K. *The Dumb Ox: St. Thomas Aquinas*. Image Classics, 1974.

Cohen, Karl F. *Forbidden Animation*. McFarland, 1997.

Cotte, Olivier. *Secrets of Oscar-Winning Animation*. Focal Press, 2013.

Crafton, Donald. *The Shadow of the Mouse*. University of California Press, 2012.

Crafts, Wilbur F. *National Perils and Hopes*. O. F. M. Barton, 1910.

Curley, Michael J. *Physiologus: A Medieval Book of Nature Lore*. University of Chicago Press, 2009.

Czeslaw, Milosz. *The History of Polish Literature*, 2nd ed. Berkeley: University of California Press, 1983.

Daily, Eileen M. *Beyond the Written Word: Exploring Faith through Christian Art*. St. Mary's Press, 2005.

Dante, Alighieri. *The Divine Comedy: Purgatory* (trans Mark Musa). Penguin Classics, 1983.

Danto, Arthur C. *Mark Tansey: Visions and Revisions*. New York: Harry N. Abrams, 1992.

De Lille, Alan. *Holy Dogs and Asses: Animals in the Christian Tradition* (trans. Laura Hobgood-Oster). University of Illinois Press, 2008.

DeYoung, Rebecca Konyndyk. *Vainglory: The Forgotten Vice*. Eerdmans, 2014.

Dodd, C. H. *The Parables of the Kingdom*. Scribner's, 1958.

Dolbear, Same, ed. *The Storyteller, Tales out of Loneliness*. Verso, 2016.

Dyson, Michael Eric. *Pride*. Oxford University Press, 2006.

Eco, Umberto. *The Name of the Rose* (trans. William Weaver). Warner Books, 1984.

Eklund, Rebekah, and John E. Phelan Jr., eds. *Doing Theology for the Church: Essays in Honor of Klyne Snodgrass*. Wipf and Stock, 2014.

Elsaesser, Thomas, and Adam Barker, eds. *Early Cinema: Space, Frame Narrative*. British Film Institute, 1990.

Epstein, Joseph. *Envy*. Oxford University Press, 2003.

Evagrius of Pontus. *Praktikos* VI.12 (trans. R Sinkewicz). Oxford Early Christian Studies, 2003.

Fisher, Stefan. *Hieronymus Bosch: The Complete Works*. Cologne, 2013.

Fleischer, Richard. *Out of the Inkwell: Max Fleischer and the Animation Revolution*. University Press of Kentucky, 2003.

Frantis, Wayne E. *Dutch Seventeenth-century Genre Painting: Its Stylistic and Thematic Evolution.* Yale University Press, 2004.

Fraser, Ben Fraser. *Hide and Seek, The Sacred Art of Indirect Communication.* Wipf and Stock, 2020.

Freedberg, David. *The Power of Images: Studies in the History and Theory of Response.* University of Chicago Press, 1989.

Furniss, Maureen. *A New History of Animation.* Thames and Hudson, 2016.

Gibson, Walter S. *Pieter Bruegel and the Art of Laughter.* University of California Press, 2006.

Giesen, Rolf. *Chinese Animation.* McFarland, 2015.

Gilliam, Terry. *Animations of Mortality.* Methuen, 1978.

Giroux, Henry A., and Grace Pollock. *The Mouse that Roared: Disney and the End of Innocence.* Rowman and Littlefield, 1999.

Glum, Peter. *The Key to Bosch's "Garden of earthly delights" Found in Allegorical Bible Interpretation.* Chuo-koron Bijutsu Shuppan, 2007.

Godwin, Joscelyn. *Athanasius Kircher: A Renaissance Man and the Quest for Knowledge.* Thames and Hudson, 1979.

Goldmark, Daniel, and Charlie Keil, eds. *Funny Pictures: Animation and Comedy in Studio-Era Hollywood.* University of California Press, 2011.

Gombrich, E. H. *The Story of Art.* Phaidon Press Ltd., 1972.

Gowler, David B. *The Parables after Jesus: Their Imaginative Receptions across Two Millennia.* Baker Academic, 2017.

Grant, R. M. *The Letter and the Spirit.* London, SPCK, 1957.

Greene, Maxine. *Releasing the Imagination: Essays on Education, the Arts, and Social Change.* Jossey-Bass, 2000.

Gregory, Saint. *Fathers of the Church: Life and Works* 98 (trans. Michael Slusser). Catholic University of America Press, 1998.

Gregory the Great. *Morals on the Book of Job* (trans. John Henry Parker and J. Rivington). Patristic Publishing, 2018.

Hagen, Rose-Marie. *Pieter Bruegel the Elder c. 1525–1569: Peasants, Fools and Demons.* Taschen, 2007.

Harris, Maria. *Teaching and the Religious Imagination.* HarperSanFrancisco, 1987.

Holloway, Ronald. *Z is for Zagreb.* Tantivy Press, 1972.

Jensen, Robin M., and Mark D. Ellison. *The Routledge Handbook of Early Christian Art.* Routledge, 2018.

Jeremias, J. *The Parables of Jesus.* Scribner's Sons, 1972.

John of Damascus. *On the Divine Images* (trans. David Anderson). St. Vladimir's Seminary Press, 1994.

Jones, Chuck. *Chuck Amuck.* Farrar Straus Giroux, 1989.

Kaplan, Aryeh. *Rabbi Nachman's Stories.* Breslov Research Institute, 1983.

Kaplan, Rabbi Aryeh, trans. *Rabbi Nachman's Wisdom.* Breslov Research Institute, 1973.

Kavaler, Ethan Matt. *Parables of Order and Enterprise.* Cambridge University Press, 1999.

Keizer, Garret. *The Enigma of Anger*. Jossey-Bass, 2002.
Kempis, Thomas à. *The Imitation of Christ*. Dover, 2003.
Kenner, Hugh. *Chuck Jones: A Flurry of Drawings*. University of California Press, 1994.
Kermode, Frank. *The Genesis of Secrecy: On the Interpretation of Narrative*. Harvard University Press, 1980.
Kern, Adam. *Manga from the Floating World*. Harvard UP, 2006.
Kierkegaard, Soren. *Either/Or* (trans. and ed. Victor Eremita). Penguin Classics, 1992.
Kierkegaard, Soren. *Point of View* (trans. Walter Lowrie). Oxford University Press, 1939.
Kierkegaard, Soren. *The Present Age and of the Difference between a Genius and an Apostle* (trans. Alexander Dru). Harper Torchbooks, 1962.
Kinney, Jack. *Walt Disney and Other Assorted Characters*. Harmony, 1989.
Kline, Daniel T., ed. *Medieval Literature for Children*. Routledge, 2003.
Koerner, Joseph Leo. *Bosch and Bruegel: From Enemy Painting to Everyday Life*. Princeton University Press, 2016.
Kottler, Jeffrey. *Stories We've Heard, Stories We've Told: Life-Changing Narratives in Therapy*. Oxford University Press, 2015.
Krasicki, Ignacy. *Bajki: wybór Fables and Parables* (1779) (trans. Christopher Kasparek). Warsaw: Państwowy Instytut Wydawniczy, 1974.
Krysmanski, Bernd W. *Hogarth's Hidden Parts: Satiric Allusion, Erotic Wit, Blasphemous Bawdiness and Dark Humour in Eighteenth-Century English Art*. Georg Olms, 2010.
Kuttna, Mari. *Hungarian Animation: A Survey of the Work of the Pannonia Studio*. Budapest, 1970.
La Fontaine, Jean. *The Complete Fables of Jean de la Fontaine* (trans. Norman R. Shapiro). University of Illinois Press, 2007.
Lehman, Christopher P. *The Colored Cartoon: Black Presentation in American*. University of Massachusetts Press, 2007.
Lehmann, Helmut T., and Eric W. Gritsch, eds. *Luther's Works*. Fortress Press, 1966.
Lenburg, Jeff. *The Great Cartoon Directors*. McFarland, 1983.
Levy, Sandra M. *Imagination and the Journey of Faith*. Eerdmans, 2008.
Lewis, C. S. *Abolition of Man*. HarperCollins, 1974.
Lewis, C. S. *The Four Loves*. Harcourt Brace Jovanovich, 1960.
Lewis, C. S. *God in the Dock*. Eerdmans, 1970.
Lewis, C. S. *Mere Christianity*. HarperOne, 2015.
Lewis, C. S. *The Screwtape Letters*. Macmillan, 1961.
Lewis, C. S. *Spenser's Images of Life*. Cambridge University Press, 1967.
Lindvall, Terry, Dennis Bounds, and Chris Lindvall. *Divine Film Comedies*. Routledge, 2016.
Lindvall, Terry. *Sanctuary Cinema: The Origins of the Christian Film Industry*. New York University Press, 2011.
Lindvall, Terry. *The Silents of God*. Scarecrow Press, 2001.

Lowrie, Walter. *A Short Life of Kierkegaard*. Princeton University Press, 1970.
Lubbock, John. *Storytelling in Christian Art from Giotto to Donatello*. Yale University Press, 2006.
Lyman, Stanford M. *The Seven Deadly Sins: Society and Evil.* Rowman and Littlefield, 1989.
Macrobius Ambrosius. *Dream of Scipio* (trans. William Harris Stahl). Columbia University, 1952.
Maniura, Robert, ed. *Presence: The Inherence of the Prototype within Images and Other Objects*. Ashgate Publishing, 2006.
Manson, T. W. *The Teaching of Jesus*. Cambridge University Press, 1935.
Mazur, Eric. *Encyclopedia of Religion and Film.* ABC-CLIO, 2011.
McCabe, Bob. *Dark Knights and Holy Fools: The Art and Films of Terry Gilliam.* Orion, 1999.
McGowan, David. *Animated Personalities*. University of Texas Press, 2019.
McGrath, Alistar. *Christian Literature: An Anthology*. Blackwell, 2001.
Mendez-Flohr, Paul, ed. *Martin Buber: A Contemporary Perspective.* Syracuse University Press, 2002.
Metz, John. *The Fables of La Fontaine, A Critical Edition of the 18th Century Settings*. Pendragon Press, 1986.
Morgan, David. *The Embodied Eye: Religious Visual Culture and the Social Life of Feeling*. University of California Press, 2012.
Morgan, David. *The Lure of Images: A History of Religion and Visual Media in America*. Routledge, 2007.
Morgan, David. *Protestants and Pictures*. Oxford University Press, 1999.
Morgan, David. *Visual Piety: A History and Theory of Popular Religious Images*. University of California Press, 1997.
Nachman of Breslov, Rebbe (trans. Rabbi Aryeh Kaplan). *The Seven Beggars and Other Kabbalistic Tales.* Jewish Lights, 2005.
Nelson, Robert, S., and Kristen, M. Collins. *Holy Image and Hallowed Ground: Icons from Sinai*. J. Paul Getty Museum, 2006.
Newhauser, Richard. *The Early History of Greed: The Sin of Avarice in Early Medieval Thought and Literature*. Cambridge University Press, 2000.
Oden, Thomas, ed. *Parables of Kierkegaard*. Princeton University Press, 1978.
Okholm, Dennis. *Dangerous Passions, Deadly Sins: Learning from the Psychology of Ancient Monks*. Brazos, 2014.
Ousepensky, Leonid. *Theology of the Icon: Volumes I and II* (trans. Anthony Gythiel). St. Vladimir's Seminary Press, 1992.
Ozment, Steven. *The Serpent & the Lamb: Cranach, Luther, and the Making of the Reformation*. Yale University Press, 2011.
Peet, Bill. *Bill Peet: An Autobiography*. Houghlin Mifflin, 1989.
Pelikan, Jaroslav. *Imago Dei*. Princeton University Press, 1990.
Philostratus. *The Life of Apollonius of Tyana,* Book V: 14 (trans. Christopher P. Jones). Harvard University Press, Loeb Library, 2005.
Pilling, Jayne, ed. *A Reader in Animation Studies*. John Libbey, 1997.
Pinsky, Mark. *The Gospel According to Disney*. WJK, 2004.

Plate, Brent, S. *Religion, Art, & Visual Culture: A Cross Cultural Reader*. Palgrave, 2002.

Postman, Neil. *Amusing Ourselves to Death: Public Discourse in the Age of Show Business*. Viking Penguin, 1985.

Prose, Francie. *Gluttony*. Oxford University Press, 2006.

Prudentius, Aurelius Clemens. *Prudentius* (ed. and trans. H. J. Thomson). Loeb Classical Library, 1961.

Quintilian. *Insitutio Oratoria* I ix.1 (trans. Walter Russell). Harvard University Press, 2012.

Rackham, H. J. *The Fable as Literature*. Athlone Press, 1985.

Ramsaye, Terry. *A Million and One Nights*. Simon and Schuster, 1926.

Randall, Lilian M. G. *Images of Gothic Manuscripts*. University of California Press, 1966.

Ricoeur, Paul. *Figuring the Sacred: Religion, Narrative, and Imagination*. Minneapolis: Fortress, 1995.

Rindge, Matthew S. *Profane Parables: Film and the American Dream*. Baylor University Press, 2017.

Robinson, Chris. *Animators Unearthed*. Continuum, 2010.

Russell, Daniel. *The Emblem and Device in France*. French Forum, 1985.

Sammond, Nicholas. *Birth of an Industry*. Duke University Press, 2015.

Schimmel, Solomon. *The Seven Deadly Sins: Jewish, Christian, and Classical Reflections on Human Psychology*. Oxford University Press, 1997.

Schneider, Steve. *That's All Folks!: The Art of Warner Bros. Animation*. Henry Holt and Company, 1988.

Shaw, Teresa. *The Burden of the Flesh: Fasting and Sexuality in Early Christianity*. Fortress Press, 1998.

Silver, Larry. *Pieter Bruegel*. Abbeville, 2011.

Smith, David, ed. *Parody and Festivity in Early Modern Art: Essays on Comedy as Social Vision*. Taylor & Francis, 2017.

Smoodin, Eric. *Animating Culture: Hollywood Cartoons from the Studio Era*. Rutgers University Press, 1993.

Snodgrass, Klyne. *Stories with Intent: A Comprehensive Guide to the Parables of Jesus*. Grand Rapids: Eerdmans, 2008.

Spenser, Edmund. *Faerie Queen Book I Canto IV* (ed. Carol Kaske). Hackett, 2006.

Spitz, Ellen. *Inside Picture Books*. Yale University Press, 2000.

Sullivan, Margaret A. *Bruegel's Peasants: Art and Audience in the Northern Renaissance and Bruegel and the Creative Process, 1559–1563*. Cambridge University Press, 1994.

Taylor, Mark C. *The Picture in Question: Mark Tansey and the Ends of Representation*. University of Chicago, 1999.

Taylor, Richard. *The Encyclopedia of Animation Techniques*. Focal Press, 1996.

TeSelle (McFague), Sallie. *Speaking in Parables: A Study in Metaphor and Theology*. Fortress Press, 1975.

Thiselton, Anthony C. *The Power of Pictures in Christian Thought: The Use and Abuse of Images in the Bible and Theology*. SPCK, 2018.

Thomas, Frank, and Ollie Johnston. *Too Funny for Words*. Abbeville Press, 1987.
Thurman, Robert A. F. *Anger*. Oxford University Press, 2005.
Tickle, Phyllis A. *Greed*. Oxford University Press, 2004.
Tonelli, Tonelli. *Approaches to the Visual in Religion*. Vandenhoeck & Ruprecht, 2011.
Tucker, Shawn. *The Virtues and Vices in the Arts: A Sourcebook*. Cascade Books, 2015.
Tummers, Anna, Elmer Kolfin, and Jasper Hillegers. *The Art of Laughter: Humour in Dutch Painting of the Golden Age*. Frans Hals Museum, 2018.
van der Zee, T, and T. J. Lovat, eds. *New Perspectives on Religious and Spiritual Education*. Waxmann, 2012.
Via, Dan. *The Parables: Their Literary and Existential Dimension*. Wipf and Stock, 1967.
Ward, Annalee. *Mouse Morality: The Rhetoric of Disney Animated Films*. University of Texas Press, 2002.
Wasserstein, Wendy. *Sloth (and How to Get It*). Oxford University Press, 2005.
Weinreich, Beatrice. *Yiddish Folktales*. Schocken, 1997.
Wells, Paul. *An Animated Bestiary: Animals, Cartoons, and Culture*. Rutgers University Press, 2000.
Wells, Paul. *Animation and America*. Rutgers University Press, 2002.
Wells, Paul. *Animation: Genre and Authorship*. Wallflower, 2002.
Wells, Paul. *Understanding Animation*. Routledge, 1998.
White, Cynthia. *From the Ark to the Pulpit*. Publications de L'Institut D'Études Médiévales, 2009.
Wilder, Amos. *Early Christian Rhetoric: The Language of the Gospel*. Harvard University Press, 1964.
Williams, Anne L. *Satire, Veneration, and St. Joseph in Art*. Amsterdam University Press, 2019.
Willimon, William H. *Sinning Like a Christian*. Abingdon Press, 2005.
Woolery, George W. *Children's Television: The First Thirty-Five Years, 1946–1981*. Scarecrow Press, 1983.
Zeri, Federico. *Bosch: The Garden of Earthly Delights*. Bologna: Poligrafici Calderara, 2000.

FILMOGRAPHY

Afternoon Class (Seoro Oh, 2015)
Afterwork (Luis Usón and Andrés Aguilar, 2017)
Ali Baba Bunny (Chuck Jones, 1957)
Allegro non Troppo (Bruno Bozzetto, 1976)
Animal Farm (John Halas and Joy Bachelor, 1954)
Anna and Bella (Borge Ring, 1984)
Anuncio Lotería de Navidad (aka *The Lottery* or *Justino*, 2015)
Apprentice, The (Richard Condie, 1991)

Are You Lost in the World like Me? (Steve Cutts, 2016)
Are You My Neighbor (Phil Vischer and Mike Nawrocki, 1995)
Artist's Dream, The or The Dachsund and the Sausage (John Bray, 1913)
Asparagus (Susan Pitts, 1979)
Augusta Makes Herself Beautiful (Csaba Varga, 1985)
Babes in the Woods (Burt Gillet, 1932)
Balance (Wolfgang and Christoph Lauenstein, 1989)
Bambi Meets Godzilla (Marv Newland, 1969)
Bankiet / Banquet (Zofia Oraczewska, 1976)
Bedtime (Fleischer Bros., 1923)
Beard, The (Ian Eames, 1978)
Big Snit, The (Richard Condie, 1985)
Birds Anonymous (Friz Freleng, 1957)
Black Dog, The (Alison de Vere, 1987)
Blind Vaysha (Theodore Ushev, 2016)
Booby Traps (Robert Clampett, 1944)
Book of Ecclesiastes (Jon Collins and Tim Mackie, 2016)
Book of Job (Jon Collins and Tim Mackie, 2016)
Boop Oop a Doop (Max Fleischer, 1932)
Bosch & Bruegel (SMK, National Gallery of Denmark, 2012)
Boundary Lines (Philip Stapp, 1946)
Box, The (Murakami, Fred Wolf, 1967)
Brave Little Tailor (Bill Roberts, 1938)
Brotherhood of Man, The (Robert Cannon and John Hubley, 1945)
A Bug's Life (John Lasseter and Andrew Stanton, 1998)
Buried Treasure (possibly Fleischer Bros, 1928)
Butterscotch and Soda (Seymour Kneitel, 1948)
Caliph Stork, The (Valeriy Ugarov, 1981)
Cameraman's Revenge, The (Ladislaw Starewicz, 1911)
Candy Town (aka *Silvery Moon*) (Van Beuren, 1933)
Canterbury Tale of The Wife of Bath (Johanna Quinn, 1996)
Cat Came Back, The (Richard Condie, 1988)
Cat's Cradle (Paul Driessen, 1976)
Cavallette (*Grasshoppers*) (Bruno Bozzetto, 1990)
Censored (Frank Tashlin, 1944)
Cheatin' (Bill Plympton, 2013)
Christmas Gift, A (Will Vinton, 1980)
Clayride: A Gallop through Methodist History (UMC, n.d.)
Coco (Adrian Molina and Lee Unkrich, 2017)
Conceited General, The or *The Proud General* (Te Wei, 1956)
Confidence (Walter Lantz, 1933)
The Creation (Will Vinton, 1981)
The Critic (Mel Brooks, 1963)
Cured Duck, A (Jack King, 1945)
Dancing (Bruno Bozzetto, 1991)

Danny Boy (Marek Skrobecki, 2010)
Davey and Goliath (Art Clokey, 1961)
Death Fairy (Kajetan Obarski, 2017)
Dji Death Fails (Dmitri Voloshin, 2012)
Dinosaure d'Aveugle (Gaëtan Borde, 2014)
Diogenes, Perhaps (Nedelijko Dragic, 1967)
Dojoji Temple (Kihachiro Kawamoto, 1976)
Donald's Double Trouble (Jack King, 1946)
Donald's Cousin Gus (Jack King, 1939)
Dragonfly and the Ant (Ladislas Starewicz, 1913)
Dreams of a Rarebit Fiend: Bug Vaudeville (Winsor McCay, 1921)
Duck Amuck (Chuck Jones, 1953)
EAT (Bill Plympton, 2001)
Educated Fish (Fleischer Bros., 1937)
Ersatz (Dusan Vukotic, 1961)
L'Étranger or *The Wanderer* (George Ungar, 1988)
Fallen Art (Tomek Beginski, 2006)
Fantasia (Walt Disney, 1940)
Felix Doubles for Darwin (Otto Messmer, 1924)
Fish, The (Milan Blazekovich, 1970)
Flim Flam Films (Otto Messmer, 1927)
For the Birds (Ralph Eggleston, 2000)
Fox and the Grapes (Frank Tashlin, 1941)
Free (Robert Mitchell and John Kimball, 1972)
Frog's Day Out, The (Arena Dilsukhnagar, 2012)
Frogs Who Wanted a King or *Frogland* (Starewicz, 1922)
Garden of Earthly Delights: Hieronimus Bosch, An Homage (Robert Morris University, 2016)
Gerald McBoing Boing (Robert Cannon, 1950)
Getting Started (Richard Condie, 1979)
Girls' Night Out (Johanna Quinn, 1986)
Give Up Yer Aul Sins (Darragh O'Connell and Cathal Gaffney, 2002)
God Film (Gil Beach, 1975)
Golden Touch (Walt Disney, 1935)
Good Time for a Dime (Dick Lundy, 1941)
Good Western Samaritan, The (Stan Freberg, n.d.)
Grasshopper and the Ant, The (Ladislaw Starewicz, 1911)
Grasshopper and the Ants, The (Wilfred Jackson, 1934)
Gravity (Ferenc Rofusz, 1984)
Greed (Alli Sadegiani, 2011)
Greedy Humpty Dumpty (Dave Fleischer, 1936)
Grim Tale of Ananias and Sapphira (Stevers, 2015)
Hair Love (Matthew A. Cherry, 2019)
Hand, The (Jiri Trnka, 1965)
Hangman (Les Goldman and Paul Julian, 1964)

Happiness (Steve Cutts, 2017)
Harvest Time (Connie Rasinski, 1940)
Hasty Hare, The (Chuck Jones, 1952)
Hat, The (Faith and John Hubley, 1964)
Heavenly Appeals (David Lisbe, 2009)
Helping Hand (WCC, n.d.)
Henry from 9 to 5 (Bob Godfrey, 1970)
History of the World in 3 Minutes Flat (Michael Mills, 1980)
How to Cope with Death (Ignacio Ferreras, 2006)
Hunger / La Faim (Peter Foldes, 1974)
Icarus (Paul Bochner, 1974)
Icarus and Daedalus (Peter Bollinger, 1998)
L'Idee (Bartolt Bartosch, 1933)
If I Was God: a true story (Cordell Barker, 2015)
If Your Eye Offendz Thee (David Wilcox, 1988)
Imagination (Bob Wickersham, 1943)
Inside Out (Pete Docter, 2015)
It Will Teach Him a Lesson (Stan Freberg, 1960s)
JOT (Ruth Bayers, 1965)
Jungle Book, The (Wolfgang Reitherman, 1967)
Kama Sutra Rides Again (Bob Godfrey, 1971)
Killing of an Egg, The (Paul Driessen, 1977)
Kinematograph, The (Tomasz Bagiński, 2009)
King Sized Canary (Tex Avery, 1947)
Knick Knack (John Lasseter, 1989)
Lady and the Reaper La dama y la muerte (Javier Gracia, 2009)
Lady Fishbourne's Complete Guide to Better Table Manners (Janet Perlman, 1976)
L'invite (Guy Jacques, 1984)
La Linea (Osvaldo Cavandoli, 1971–1986)
Letter, The (Marie Hyon and Marco Spier, 2015)
Life in a Tin (Bruno Bozzetto, 1967)
Lion and the Bull, The (Fyodor Khitruk, 1983)
Lion King, The (Rob Minkoff and Roger Allers, 1994)
Little Mermaid, The (John Musker and Ron Clements, 1989)
Little Rural Riding Hood (Tex Avery, 1949)
Maestro (Geza Toth and A. Kedd Bemutatja, 2005)
Magnificent 7 Deadly Sins, The (Graham Stark, 1971)
Man Who Had to Sing (Milan Blažeković, 1971)
Manipulation (Daniel Greaves, 1991)
Mantis Stalks Cicada (Hu Jinqing, 1988)
Martin the Cobbler (Will Vinton, 1977)
Mascot, The (Ladislav Starewicz, 1933)
Mickey's Christmas Carol (Burny Mattinson, 1983)
Midnight Parasites, The (Yoji Kuii, 1972)
Mind the Steps! (István Orosz, 1989)

The Miracle Maker (Derek W. Hayes and Stanislav Sokolov, 2000)
Monkeys Fish the Moon (Zhou Keqin, 1981)
Most Precise and Nuanced Look into the Life of the Man, Legend, and Visionary, Martin Luther, A (Magnus I. Moller, 2017)
Munro (Gene Deitch, 1960)
Mr. Pascal (Alison deVere, 1979)
Myth of Icarus and Daedalus (Jeremiah Dickey, 2017)
Neighbours (Norman McLaren, 1952)
Netherlandish Proverbs, The (Martin Missfeldt, 1998)
Night on Bald Mountain in *Fantasia* (Walt Disney, 1941)
No Eyes Today (Fleischer Bros., 1929)
None of That! (Isabela Littger, Anna Hinds, and Kriti Kaur, 2015)
Northwest Hounded Police (Tex Avery, 1946)
Nosehair (Bill Plympton, 1994)
Note from Above (Anonymous, 1972)
Of Holes and Corks (Ante Zaninovic, 1967)
Ogre, The (Laurene Braibant, 2016)
An Old Box or *Une vieille boite* (Paul Driessen, 1975)
Old Man of the Mountain (Fleischer Bros., 1933)
One Froggy Evening (Chuck Jones, 1955)
Overdose (Claude Cloutier, 1994)
Paintings in Motion: Netherlandish Proverbs (Martin Missfeldt, 1998)
"*Pardoner's Tale*" *Canterbury Tales* (BBC, 1998)
Paradise (Ishu Patel, 1984)
Paperman (John Kahrs, 2012)
Peace on Earth (Hugh Harman, 1939)
Pencil Bookings (Kathy Rose, 1978)
PIES (Sheldon Cohen, 1984)
Pigs is Pigs (Friz Freleng, 1937)
Playful Pluto (Burt Gillet, 1934)
Players (John Halas, 1982)
Popeye the Sailor Meets Ali Baba's Forty Thieves (Dave Fleischer, 1937)
Porky in Wackyland (Bob Clampett, 1938)
Porky's Hare (Hunt, Ben "Bugs" Hardaway, 1938)
Preacher (Pavel and Stania Prochazka, 1970)
Prince of Egypt (Brenda Chapman, Simon Wells, and Steve Hickner, 1988)
Quasi at the Quackadero (Sally Cruikshank, 1975)
Rabbit (Run Wrake, 2005)
Red Hot Riding Hood (Tex Avery, 1943)
Reformation Polka, The (Sam Mulberry, 2014)
Rocks in my Pockets (Signe Baumane, 2014)
Roof Sex (PES, 2002)
Sandman (Paul Berry, 1991)
Scabies (Pavao Statler and Zlatko Grgic, 1969)
Screentest (Norman Stone and Bob Godfrey, 1976)

Scrub Me Mama with a Boogie Beat (Walter Lantz, 1940)
Secret of Kells (Tomm Moore and Nora Twomey, 2009)
The Selfish Giant (Peter Sander, 1971)
Sept péchés capitaux, Les (*The Seven Deadly Sins*, Antoine Roegiers, 2011)
Show Biz Bugs (Friz Freleng, 1957)
Silly Goose, The (Hans Fischerkoesen, 1944)
Single Life (Job, Joris, & Marieke, 2014)
Sisyphus (Marcell Jankovics, 1974)
Skeleton Dance, The (Ub Iwerks, 1929)
Sloth (Ruth Hayes, 1988)
Sower and Seeds, The (Rod March, 2010)
Spree Lunch (Seymour Kneitel, 1957)
Spring (or *Fountain*) *of Life* (Borislav Sajtinac and Nikola Majdak, 1969)
St. Patrick's Bad Analogies (Hans Fiene, 2013)
Stop Driving Us Crazy (UMC, 1961)
Striptease (Guido Manuli and Bruno Bozzetto, 1977)
Strip-tiz (Nedeljko Dragic, 1971)
Sunbeam (Paul Vester, 1980)
Sun Flight (Gerald McDermott, 1966)
Swing Shift Cinderella (Tex Avery, 1945)
Symphony in Slang (Tex Avery, 1951)
Tale of Tales (Yuri Norstein, 1979)
Tale of the Three Brothers (Alexandre Desplat, 2010)
Tell-Tale Heart, The (Ted Parmelee, 1953)
Temptation of St. Anthony, The (Antoine Roegiers, 2010)
This Land is Mine (Nina Paley, 2012)
Three Little Pigs (Burt Gillet, 1933)
Tomorrow We Diet! (Goofy) (Jack Kinney, 1951)
Trials of a Movie Cartoonist (Otto Messmer, 1916)
trouble with facelifts, the (Bill Plympton, 1990)
Tulips Shall Grow (George Pal, 1942)
Unbalanced (Stan Prokopenko, 2013)
Uncle Thomas Accounting the Days (Regina Pessoa, 2020)
Unicorn in the Garden, A (William T. Hurtz, 1953)
UP (Pete Docter, 2009)
Uses of Envy (Lara Lee and Hannah Jacobs in *The School of Life*, 2019)
Village, The (Mark Baker, 1993)
WALL-E (Andrew Stanton, 2008)
The Way of Peace (Frank Tashlin, 1947)
Whazzat? (Arthur P. Pierson, 1975)
Where Are They Now? (Steve Cutts, 2014)
Who's Hungry (David Ochs, 2009)
Wildebeest (Birdbox Studio, 2012)
Wonderful Nature: The Common Chameleon (Tomer Eshed, 2016)
World of Tomorrow (Don Hertzfeld, 2015)
Zootopia (Byron Howard and Rich Moore, 2016)

Index

Aesop, 6, 15, 20, 24, 25
Amidi, Amid, 78
Ancrene Wisse, 22, 34n36
Angelico, Fra, 188–89
Aquinas, Thomas, 44, 63n19, 91, 110, 133, 136, 145, 168, 171, 196
Auden, W. H., 6, 104n2
Augustine, xiv, 51, 90, 210n9, 213
Avery, Tex, 119–20, 197, 199–203

Bagiński, Tomasz, 93–94
Baker, Mark, 99–100
Barker, Cordell, 101–2, 120–23
Barron, Robert, 193
Bayers, Ruth, 217–18
Beach, Gil, 236
Beavis, Mary Ann, 19, 21, 25
Beck, Jerry, 159, 163
Beginski, Tomek, 84–85
Benjamin, Walter, xv, xxn17
Berry, Paul, 57
Bettelheim, Bruno, 113, 137–38
Bezalel, 40, 62
Bierce, Ambrose, 117, 136
Blazekovic, Milan, xii, 214n1
Boccaccio, Giovanni, 24, 72
Bochner, Paul, 91
Bonventura, 41, 63
Bosch, Hieronymus, 48–50, 52–55, 57, 61, 65n44, 77, 96, 150, 157, 188, 191n22, 208, 213, 215n22, 236
Bozzetto, Bruno, 85, 127, 157–58, 197, 204–5, 214, 240n15
Bradbury, Ray, 158
Braibant, Laurene, 185–86
Brakhage, Stan, 61
Brandt, Sebastian, 46, 48, 105
Bray, John, 166
Brooks, Mel, 32n1, 238
Bruegel, Pieter, 49, 52, 54–58, 61, 66n63, 67, 73, 81, 91, 105, 117, 133, 149, 150, 155, 165, 193, 236
Buber, Martin, 32n2
Buddha, 19, 34n23, 73, 130n9
Buechner, Frederick, 106, 117

Canemaker, John, 190n3, 214n3, 236
Cannon, Robert, xv–xvi
Capon, Father Robert, 4, 214
Cassian, John, 79, 87n18, 214
Cavandoli, Osvaldo, 234
Chaplin, Charlie, 175
Chaucer, Geoffrey, 16, 157, 189, 210n1, 211n15, 214, 235
Chesterton, G. K., 77, 90, 135, 171, 172, 190n11, 216, 231, 234
Choju, Giga, 45

Clampett, Bob, 57, 199
Cleese, John, 76
Clokey, Art, 217
Cohen, Sheldon, 230–31
Cohl, Emile, 183
Coles, Robert, xiii
Condie, Richard, 49, 133–34, 147n7, 229–30, 236–37, 241
Crafton, Donald, xxiin15, 191, 234
Cranach, Lucas, 47, 48, 65n39
Cruikshank, Sally, 180–83
Crumb, R., 181, 193
Cutts, Steve, 142–44, 159–61, 179–80

Dante, Alighieri, 44, 52, 66n54, 72, 86n1, 91, 102–3, 107, 114–15, 136, 146, 150, 157, 167, 202–3, 206
Deacy, Christopher, 60–61
Deitch, Gene, 216
de Vere, Alison, 214, 226–27
Dickens, Charles, 151
Dickinson, Emily, xviii, xix, 222
Dilsukhnagar, Arena, 4–5
Disney, Walt, xii, xv, 24, 38, 57, 72, 86, 118, 137–38, 140, 151, 153–55, 157, 163, 178–79, 185, 219, 226
Docter, Pete, 114, 153
Dostoyevsky, Fyodor, 77, 156
Dragic, Nedelijko, 96, 197, 214
Driessen, Paul, 97–98, 227–28, 240n17
drolleries, 43, 45–46, 57
Durer, Albrecht, 28, 46, 47
Dyson, Michael Eric, 97

Eames, Ian, 77–79
Eggleston, Ralph, 114–15
Epstein, Joseph, 106–7, 116n12
Erasmus, Desiderius, 28, 55
Eshed, Tomer, 166
Evagrius of Pontius, 78–79, 124, 131–32

Ferreras, Ignacio, 84
Fleischer Bros., 155–56, 178, 180, 181, 194, 195, 210n6, 234
Foldes, Peter, 183–85
Freberg, Stan, 216, 239n9
Furniss, Maureen, xiii, 240n22

Geisel, Ted, 199, 219
Gibson, Walter, 72, 165
Gillet, Burt, 137, 168–69
Gilliam, Terry, xxin37, 1–2, 8n1, 46, 49, 234
Giotto, 37, 42, 238
Giroux, Henry, xi, xvi
Godfrey, Bob, 204–6, 214
Goodwin, Hannibal, 60
Greaves, Daniel, 234
Gregory I, Pope, 37, 71, 90, 189
Gregory III, Pope, 41
Grgic, Zlatko, 104n5
Grimm Brothers, 168, 170
Gunning, Tom, 60

Hadley, Henry, 60
Halas, John, 126–27, 228
Harmon, Hugh, 125
Hayes, Ruth, 135, 183
Hertzfeldt, Don, 214
Hitchcock, Alfred, 176
Hogarth, William, 58–59, 133
Hokusai, Katsushika, 45
Holbein, Hans, 82
Holloway, Ronald, 96
Horace, 27–28, 35n45, 73
Hubley, John and Faith, 121, 216
Hurtz, William T., 97
Huxley, Aldous, 87n15

Isaiah, 90

Jackson, Wilfred, 24, 138–39
Jacques, Guy, 234
Jankovics, Marcell, 92
Jesus, xv–xvi, xvii, 2, 3, 5, 20, 22, 42, 54, 56, 60, 63n22, 64n28, 65, 72, 124, 166, 198–99, 214–15, 237
Jinqing, Hu, 158
Jittlov, Mike, 240n30
Job, Joris, & Marieke, 102–3

John of Damascus, 40, 42, 62n10, 62n12
Jones, Chuck, 18, 25, 33n17, 86n5, 116n14, 120, 151–52, 158–60, 163n16, 232–34
Joyce, James, 86–87
Jump, Herbert Rev, 60

Kafka, Franz, 17, 82
Kahrs, John, 220–22
Kawamoto, Kihachiro, 207
Kempis, Thomas à, 189
Keqin, Zhou, 151
Khitruk, Fyodor, 125
Kierkegaard, Soren, 5, 7, 29–32, 35n54, 107
King, Jack, 118–19, 172–73
King, Stephen, 160
Kinney, Jack, 178–79
Kircher, Athanasius, 59–60
Kneitel, Seymour, 176–78
Krasicki, Ignacy, 27–28, 74
Kuri, Yoji, 50–51

La Fontaine, Jean, 6, 24, 26–27
Langland, William, 106
Lantz, Walter, 140–41
Lasseter, John, 86, 208–9
Lauenstein, Wolfgang and Christoph, 107–8
Lehman, Christopher P., 141
Lewis, C. S., xvi, xxn22, 1, 18, 68n84, 71, 107, 156, 167–68, 172, 206, 211, 232
Lisbe, David, 98–99
Littger, Isabela, 198
Lundy, Dick, 118, 175
Luther, Martin, 46–48, 82, 198, 213

Maltese, Michael, 159
McCay, Winsor, 183, 232
McGowan, David, xvi, 86
McLaren, Norman, 125–26, 216, 234
McLuhan, Marshall, 38
Méliès, George, 59
memento mori, 81, 162
Messmer, Otto, 181, 232, 234
Mills, Michael, 127, 158
Milne, A. A., 133–34
Mitchell, Robert, 97
Miyazaki, Hayao, 183
Morgan, David, 216
Mulvey, Laura, 201
Murakami, Takashi, 220

Nachman of Breslov, Rabbi, 14
Natwick, Grim, 194
Nawrocki, Mike, 145
Newland, Marv, 75
Niebuhr, Reinhold, 97
Norris, Kathleen, 144, 145
Norstein, Yuri, 239n5

Obarski, Kajetan, 82–83
Ochs, David, 169–70
O'Connell, Darragh, 218–19
Oh, Seoro, 131
Oraczewska, Zofia, 187–88
Orosz, Istvan, 21
Orwell, George, 17, 165

Paley, Nina, 127–29
Parker, Dorothy, 150, 193, 209
Parmelee, Ted, 77
Pascal, Blaise, 30
Patel, Ishu, 111–12
Perlman, Janet, 172–73
Physiologus, 22, 23
Pixar, xiv, 114, 117, 208–9
Plato, 72, 86n1
Plympton, Bill, 78, 90, 186–87, 211
Poe, Edgar Allen, 77
Prochazka, Pavel and Stania, 100
Prose, Francine, 84
Psychomachia, 80, 124

Quinn, Johanna, 203–4, 211n15

Rabelais, François, 28, 55, 171, 183
Rasinski, Connie, 139–40
Ring, Borge, 231

Robinson, Chris, 50, 204
Roegiers, Antoine, 57
Rofusz, Ferenc, 21, 92–93
Rose, Kathy, 234–36
Roussel, Gilles (Bouleau), 88n26

Sadegiani, Alli, 160–61
Sajtinac, Borislav, 96
Schrader, Paul, 60
Schulz, Charles, 238
Singer, Isaac Bashevis, 75
Snodgrass, Klyne, 5, 15, 33
Socrates, 29
Spenser, Edmund, 15, 80, 89, 106, 118, 133, 149, 150, 167, 193–94, 204, 214, 236
Spielberg, Steven, 150
Stanton, Andrew, xiii, 86
Starewicz, Ladislav, 58, 113, 140, 207–8
Stevers, Dan, 112–13
Stone, Norman, 214
Stookey, Noel Paul, 223
Strobecki, Marek, 76
Sturges, Preston, xv, xxn12
Swift, Jonathan, 17

Tashlin, Frank, 25, 26, 199
Taylor, John, 100
Terry, Paul, 140
Thurber, James, 97
Tickle, Phyllis A., 150
Tolkien, J. R. R., 230, 234, 236
Tolstoy, Leo, xxn15, 223–24
Twain, Mark, 27

Ugarov, Valeriy, 58–59
Ungar, George, 80
Ushev, Theodore, 75–76
Usón, Luis, 123–24

Van Beuren, Amedee, 169
Varga, Csaba, 90
Vester, Paul, 104n90
Vidal, Gore, 110
Vinton, Will, 223–24
Vischer, Phil, 145–46, 219–20
Vukotic, Dusan, 141–42

Ward, Annalee, 61
Wasserstein, Wendy, 136
Watts, Isaac, 135
Waugh, Evelyn, 133
Wei, Te, 95
Wells, Paul, xiv, xvi, xxn12, 23, 33n14, 226, 237
Wickersham, Bob, 195–96
Wilcox, David, 199
Wilde, Oscar, 42, 232
Wilder, Billy, 176
Willimon, Will, 79, 87, 172, 213
Wodehouse, P. G., 3
Wrake, Run, 161–62

Yankovic, Al, 165

Zagreb (Studio), xii–xiii, 95, 96, 100, 104, 141–42, 190n1, 197, 214n1
Zaninovic, Ante, 95–96

About the Author

Terry Lindvall is C. S. Lewis Chair of Communication and Christian Thought at Virginia Wesleyan University. His other books include *God on the Big Screen: A History of Prayers in Hollywood Films from the Silent Films to Today* (2019), *Divine Film Comedies: Biblical Narratives and Sub-Genres of Film Comedy* with Dennis Bounds and Chris Lindvall (2016), *God Mocks: A History of Religious Satire from the Hebrew Prophets to Stephen Colbert* (2015), and *Sanctuary Cinema: Origins of the Christian Film Industry* (2007). He also produced the documentary feature *Hollywood, Teach Us to Pray* (2022).